FIRST EDITION

A GENDERED GAZE: MEDIA IMPACTS ON PERCEPTIONS OF SELF AND SEXUALITY

EDITED BY SUZANNE REGAN

Bassim Hamadeh, CEO and Publisher
Kassie Graves, Director of Acquisitions
Jamie Giganti, Senior Managing Editor
Miguel Macias, Graphic Designer
Marissa Applegate, Acquisitions Editor
Gem Rabanera, Project Editor
Elizabeth Rowe, Licensing Coordinator
Joyce Lue, Interior Designer
Abbey Hastings, Associate Production Editor

Printed in the United States of America

ISBN: 978-1-5165-0588-3 (pbk) / 978-1-5165-0589-0 (br)

CONTENTS

CHAPTER 3: MEDIA AND THE REPRESENTATION OF GENDER AND SEXUAL DESIRE

CHAPTER 4: POLITICS OF REPRESENTATION AND IDENTITY

CHAPTER 5: NEW AND EMERGING INTERACTIVITY:
THE POLITICS OF SOCIAL MEDIA

INTRODUCTION

Understanding the world around us in all its complexity starts with a consideration of our own identity, our own sense of self. How do I identify myself and my place in society? How do we as individuals and community understand who we are and where we are heading? How can we better understand other people and the physical and social environment in which they live? How do we relate to others as we go about our day?

We perceive who we are and how we relate to others through a lifelong learning process that involves influences from multiple sources, including real life models and experiences as well as those provided by media models. Each individual develops a sense of self based on their interaction with those around them, family, classmates and teachers, religious leaders, and the many forms of media with which we interact.

Thinking of the development of personal identity is a way of looking at oneself through many lenses. While children very early on show unique characteristics and distinct personalities, life quickly offers challenges that require more sophisticated and socially acceptable responses than our basic instincts and predilections. As children we are likely to act and dress like the people around us; we see them as models of behavior and follow their lead. As we grow up and are increasingly exposed to information and references outside the family, school, and religious institutions, we start to go beyond the immediate models and explore the world thorough stories of favorite athletes, rock stars, authors, politicians, and fashion gurus. We find that our outside influencers start to reinforce and sometimes challenge the immediate role models in our lives.

GENDER AND SEXUALITY

The ability to love is a richly rewarding part of being human. The ability to accept love comes in part through early interactions with our family, friends, and eventually, and importantly, our interactions with our sexual partners. How we perceive ourselves as gendered, sexual beings is both a message of biology, personal development, and a complex integration of social, psychological, and communication messages we receive from our families, churches, politicians, magazines, advertisements, poetry, novels, films, social media, and television. The following chapters are designed to help you investigate media's contribution to this complexity.

CHAPTER 1
HISTORY OF MEDIATED COMMUNICATION

EDITOR'S INTRODUCTION

The invention of the printing press in the 15th century introduced a transformative period in human history. Previous to the introduction of mechanical printing, duplication of documents meant laborious copying by hand. Only the most significant of written documents were copied, and distribution was limited. Hand-copied papers and books were extremely valuable, and only a handful of the elite and the scholarly were able to read them. The invention of the printing press changed this. Being able to duplicate words quickly and economically meant that copies of materials of varying significance were available, and the ability to read became of increasing importance across all classes. The impact of the printing press was extraordinary. Printing diversified the categories of copied materials and increased literacy across economic classes. News and information circulated throughout society. Magazines and novels joined newspapers and traditional modes of storytelling, reaching diverse audiences. Educational institutions emerged to teach literacy and to train the literate across ethnic and class barriers. The new literacy and diversity of literature available had an enormous impact on social, political, and economic institutions and their evolution from the 16th century to today. The full impact of literacy worldwide has yet to be felt.

While the printing press offered the easy circulation of all manner of thought and interest, it took until the 19th century for new areas of mechanically captured and delivered materials to emerge. The invention of the still camera dates back to the mid-19th century. Photography added significant dimension to newspapers, magazines, and books. Documentary photographs supporting newspaper articles brought a sense of engagement with great events not possible through words alone. The ability to capture an image of a loved one, and maintain that image, even as distance or death removed the person photographed from our lives, offered a profound emotional connection beyond simple documentation. However, it was the development of the telegraph (1830–1840s) and telephone (1876) that brought many new possibilities for human communication, both for organizations and individuals. Innovation spurred by these inventions evolved at lightning speed, and propelled the communication revolution of the 20th century.

The invention of motion pictures can be traced to the invention of the still camera. As soon as stills of living objects could be captured, the next step was to put them into motion. Various inventions in multiple countries took up the task of bringing still images to life, and with the development of flexible film stock moving pictures were exhibited to an enthusiastic public by the end of the 19th century. The invention of radio allowed the sending of audible signals through the air. By 1906 it had been developed to broadcast the human voice. With the invention of the dictation machine by Thomas Edison in 1907, the essential prerequisites for radio, and eventually television, were established.

Downton Abbey is a television series that follows the lives of an aristocratic British family from 1912 and the sinking of the *Titanic* to the 1930s. In the opening minutes of the first episode, we witness the delivery of newspapers and a telegram to the family estate. As the wrinkles in the newspapers and ink are set through careful ironing by the butler, the telegram is laid beside Lord Grantham's breakfast plate. Both the newspapers and telegram deliver information of great importance to the household. The newspaper discusses the sinking of the passenger ship *Titanic* on its maiden voyage. The telegram informs Grantham that the heir to the family estate drowned when the ship sank. Incorporating the arrival of the telegram alludes to the receding role of traditional newsprint in our lives and the ascendence of personal communication. The information from rescue vessels about the fate of passengers was sent over radio waves to New York and then through cable and radio to Europe. The newspaper story and telegram arrive nearly simultaneously, using the same technology to transmit content that was then sent both personally by telegram and to the community at large through the newspaper. The prominent position of the telegram beside Lord Grantham's breakfast plate shows its immediate importance, as opposed to the leisurely preparation and reading of publicly available newspapers.

Radio was developed as the human voice replaced Morse code in communicating over the airwaves. Initially developed by independent inventors, the need of the military for audio communication during World War I brought government control and the standardization of radio sending and receiving equipment. When private enterprise gained control after the war, radio broadcasting of news, music, and story-based fiction sent the public to buy receiver sets as entrepreneurs built more and more transmission towers.

The media with which we all grew up was established by the first decades of the twentieth century. These inventions satisfied the evolving needs of international commerce and politics and post-war culture. The final piece in the story of the 20th century's revolutionizing of communication for us all came from the needs of governments to count their populations and to win wars. The computer, as with the 19th-century inventions we have identified, was based on the inventive genius of many people. With the need for crunching large amounts of data during World War II, and the competition to break the communication codes of the enemy, twentieth century governments provided the requisite funding for materials and personnel to bring the computer to productive fruition. The computer's reduction of information to a simple digital code allows not only for computation, but storage and transmission of large quantities of information. Digitization allows contemporary media to deliver sound, visuals, and print anywhere in the world nearly instantaneously. Also important is the interactivity that digitization provides. Video games and YouTube are just the beginning of your generation's integration into a world of direct interaction with characters as narratives unfold, and self-publishing goes far beyond text, image, and sound to multiuser interactivity.

But what will we have to say? And how will we get our message out as the rest of the world competes with us in our attempts to have our messages attended to?

The books, plays, films, and radio and television programming that come to us from those who preceded will undoubtedly offer examples of how to succeed. Novels, theatrical plays, and film and television scripts are written by people who have a talent for observing and describing human nature as well as the many challenges and foibles of everyday life. They understand how to transform their observations in a way that can be shared with others. They possess a working knowledge of how to construct stories using two very significant and powerful tools: 1) the construction of narrative, or storyline; and 2) the arc or personal story of each character who inhabits the constructed story. No matter the distribution method, story and character attract, engage and at times transform audiences.

NARRATIVE STRUCTURE

A story has a very simple and powerful characteristic, unlike the continuous ebb and flow of our lives, every story has a definable beginning, middle, and end. Hollywood films have traditionally structured their storylines using the following formula: the introductory thirty minutes presents all major characters and reveals their goals and intentions. Between the first twenty-five to thirty minutes, an impediment to the goals is introduced. The next hour is spent working through the issues that arise from the impediment to our main characters achieving their goals. The last fifteen to twenty minutes are spent resolving these issues. For example, a girl and boy meet, they like each other, and want to spend more time getting to know each other. Around twenty-five minutes into the evolving love story, a major obstacle is introduced; his girlfriend returns home from college, her mother is concerned about the relationship because he is of a different class, ethnicity, religion—or perhaps he is a she—and works to interfere. A traditional romantic narrative "resolution" requires that the couple will be united, and the story ends with a kiss. Examples of traditional romantic stories include *Cinderella*, *Pride and Prejudice*, *Clueless*, *Sleepless in Seattle*, and *He's Just Not That Into You*. The couple in these films presumably live happily ever after. Alternately, the resolution is tragic as in *Romeo and Juliet*, and true love does not win out over the impediments put in the couple's way. Though the "star crossed lovers" reunite, the drama ends in their deaths.

Narrative structure can be far more complex than outlined here, but it tends to be definable and relatively straightforward in order to ensure connection with a large and diverse audience. Narrative structure is the framework on which a story is built. The repetition of the structure offers us a familiar pathway to enter and exit a story. The narrative structuring of films and television programming has evolved through trial and error. Box office and television ratings have helped stabilize structures that resonate with audiences. Long-form stories, like dramatic television programs or situation comedies, also follow predictable structures that fit the mode of delivery and are familiar and comfortable to their audiences. Long-form television programs work from show "bibles" that project the development of the narrative over one to several seasons. Writers and directors work within these settled guidelines, and showrunners oversee story evolution.

STRUCTURALISM

Why is familiar structuring of programming successful with audiences? On grappling with this question theorists such as Claude Lévi-Strauss, in his books *Structural Anthropology* and *Myths and Meaning*, have identified certain tendencies that are worth considering. Structuralist theory identifies two parts to consider when thinking of how a story is put together in a way that resonates with its audience. The first part is the surface phenomena: objects, activities, and behaviors in the story that the audience members see every day. The second is the deep structure that underlies and organizes all of these phenomena so that we can make sense of them. When your friend asks you "how was your day?" your brain organizes all the happenings of the day and eliminates the bus ride, coffee line, and dropped books, and you quickly consider the essence of your friend's interest: your basketball game, your conversation with another friend, the text you did not expect to get, and that you finished your term paper at 3:00 a.m. and still made it to class on time. When another friend asks you the same question half an hour later, you might relate that another friend almost missed the bus, what you ate for lunch, and whom you asked to join the group forming to hear a favorite band this weekend. The multiple events of your day become edited and structured according to the interests of you individual friends.

The human mind is a structuring mechanism. We humans project structure onto an unpredictable and at times chaotic world. Narrative structure is a way of organizing and explaining our world through stories. Structuralism looks at relationships between and among concepts, characters, and events. Structuralist theory looks for the rules that underlie how the story is told, its use of time, space, objects, and characters to tell the story. One area to consider is the idea of "binary opposition." Structuralists believe that the human brain organizes the work in terms of defining opposites: day defines night, and vice versa. Hot defines cold, good defines evil. In media we see binary patterns such as "good guy vs bad guy, sympathetic vs unsympathertic characters, man or woman vs nature , humans vs aliens from outer space, or robots run amuck.

Our brains are geared to identifying and understanding information through structured messages. When we look to film or television we see a compression or elimination of information, a structuring that recognizes what the audience understands from previous life experiences and familiarity with previous mediated stories. The audience brings experience and expectations to the film, radio, or television program. The audience expects that mediated stories offer a unified, coherent theme and structured plot. Themes and plots differ according to story category, or genre. For instance action/adventure films offer variations on a good-conquers-evil theme. Themes of "good" versus "evil" also dominate early western and television crime stories. Romance novels, romantic comedies, and television sitcoms offer the theme of "love conquers all." Classic gangster films offer the concept that "crime does not pay," but contemporary dramatic programming in film and television often portrays a world far more complex.

Classic Hollywood cinema (CHC) provides a clear sense of direction and purpose, using preexisting stereotypes to shortcut complex characterization. CHC offers a logical resolution, with all outstanding problems solved by the end of the film. Television provides both capsulated and ongoing stories. Situation comedies, developed in the heyday of syndication, are series programs designed to be sold across the country and around the world. Each episode is complete in and of itself, and individual episodes can be played in any order. For instance, episodes of *I Love Lucy* play around the world, and the order of the episode is irrelevant to understanding each individual story unit. Long-form television evolves over a season; each episode is dependent on those that precede it and informs those that follow. *Game of Thrones* is an example of a long-form dramatic series where events unfold over a season and from season to season, requiring ongoing attention and memory from its audience.

REPRESENTATION

CHARACTER

If structure is predictable where does the excitement of a story come in? The details of the impediments to the main character's goals and efforts to overcome them offer a level of unpredictability to the narrative. The visual imagery and sound elements of the film or television program also offer a sensibility and excitement; the editing of a car chase or fight scene can enthrall, but the most significant element to the success of the narrative lies in the depiction of character.

Character is based on human characteristics that are familiar, but are written larger, and perhaps with more concentration and consistency than we usually see in our lives. James Bond has nonstop opportunity to act with courage, strength, and competence. Your friend may have had the opportunity to be a hero once in her life, but in fact most of her days consist of non-heroic actions and decisions. In film and television, heroes and villains are often identified by their actions, but also quite often we know who is the good guy and who the bad guy from the moment they are introduced. Meaning is often conveyed by a series of visual and aural signs that identify who is who and what part they will play in the film or program. Alternately, the story may introduce a character that we assume to be good, but who turns out to be evil, or vice versa. Again signs are used to lead us (or divert us) in a particular direction.

SEMIOTICS

Semiotics is the study of signs. Signs are made up of two parts, the signified and the signifier. The "signified" is what is being represented—for instance, you. The "signifier" is what represents you—for example, your name, your photograph, and your college ID number or e-mail address. None of these signifiers are actually you, but they are used to refer to you, to signify you for any number of purposes: to call you over, to remember you, to bring up your schedule for next term, to contact you.

There are three kinds of signifiers; each has a special relationship to the signified.

1. Iconic signifiers look like the signified. Your photograph, or a painting of you, is an iconic signifier of you.

2. Indexical signifiers have an associational bond with the signified. The jacket or ring you usually wear signifies you.

3. A symbolic signifier has an assigned meaning like a social security number or college ID number. It signifies meaning that is agreed upon by the community it serves. Symbolic signifiers often represent something conceptual that cannot be identified by similarity or association. A white dove represents peace in our culture, but does not look like or have direct association with peaceful behaviors or conditions any more than any other bird. It is an arbitrary sign whose meaning is agreed upon by frequent use in a specific culture.

Media uses all three kinds of signifiers to construct meaning, particularly in the development of character and the visual space in which a character operates.

The Hollywood "hero" is often constructed from a limited group of male actors who are repeatedly cast in the same heroic kinds of roles. These heroes are traditionally white, often blond, square-jawed, blue-eyed, and physically fit. Think a young, bleached-blond Brad Pitt or Leonardo DiCaprio. These heroes hark back to a young John Wayne or Alan Ladd. Darker-haired actors play lead characters with magical powers or the advantage of age such as Tobey Maguire in *Spiderman*, or Johnny Depp in *Pirates of the Caribbean*, or, in classical Hollywood cinema, Clark Gable and Humphrey Bogart played heroes whose maturity and worldliness added gravitas to their heroic portrayals. Female heroes are few and far between.

Villains (male and female) are often portrayed as racialized, politicized, or otherwise disenfranchised "others." Whether dressed in the dark cape of Snidely Whiplash, tribal clothing of Geronimo, or in the military uniform of a national power at odds with the politics of the United States at any given time, the villain is identified physically as the "other" to the Northern European hero. Thus the indexical converges with the symbolic in terms of the contextual information required to understand meaning.

What about the main female? She is also usually young, often blond, blue-eyed, and physically fit. Her clothing reveals her sexuality over her physical prowess. In traditional Hollywood films the female is often a symbolic signifier, the prize to be won by the hero; or the loyal enabler who supports the hero's efforts. Gradually this has shifted, and the female hero has developed more agency.

The indexical signifier of the hero can be seen in the white hat of early cowboy westerns or the famous costume into which Clark Kent changes when he chooses to reveal himself as Superman. Superman's costume is an interesting example of an associational bond between signifier and signified, which can also be read as symbolic. It is through cultural learning that we take the arbitrary sign and agree that it represents Superman, but also through that same learning process we have determined that the man, when wearing the suit, stands for "Truth, Justice, and the American Way."

Through costume and setting various genres offer differing sets of signifiers to flesh out a narrative's structure. Costumes, studio set, and location shoots are carefully chosen to support character construction and narrative development. We understand as much, or more, from the visual and aural signifiers that surround and identify characters as from the dialogue they speak. The western film genre employed creative geography to position its characters in the "old west." The Hollywood western used locations in California, Arizona, and New Mexico to position the European American quest to colonize and exploit lands long home to native tribes and previously claimed by Spanish colonizers. The symbolic signifiers of the wild, untamed territory contrasts with the promise of domestication and cultivation of the land, reinforcing the oft-repeated theme of the genre. Gangster films are usually situated in cities with dark interiors and shadowed landscapes that echo the dark natures of outsiders who challenge the laws of the dominant group and claim the resources of cities like New York and Chicago.

"Girl culture" provides the contemporary context for stories about young women navigating their way to adulthood in a modern-day United States. Chick flicks provide signifiers of "consumption capitalism" that include upper-middle-class, white-dominated neighborhoods containing girls trying to find themselves. In these stories young women compete for attention and acceptance. *Mean Girls* and *Clueless* show two sides of the "mean girl," one looking at the dominating type as vicious and reckless, the other showing the "queen bee" to be another hapless teen trying to figure things out. Cher in *Clueless* has the trendy clothes, new car, and the male attention of the mean girl; she also has the blond hair and blue eyes of Disney's Cinderella, the prototype female prize. How she evolves into a worthy reward for her Prince Charming is shown in her often-misguided, but sincere, interest in doing good for others. Slightly older versions of "girl culture" are seen in *Legally Blonde* and *Bridget Jones's Diary*. The character of Elle Woods in *Legally Blonde* provides a "Girls' Guide" to financial and domestic success. Reese Witherspoon, who portrays Elle, is visually similar in looks to Alicia Silverstone's Cher in *Clueless*. Both are slender, blue-eyed blonds whose fashion and makeup are spot on. While Cher attends Beverly Hills High School, Elle is a law student at Harvard. Bridget Jones is equally blond and blue-eyed. Bridget presents a version of Cher and Elle. Though technically older, she has not quite figured things out. She drinks too much, eats too much, smokes too much, and even at thirty-something, prefers "bad boys" to the strong and steady boy next door. As with Cher and Elle, Bridget's looks, her clothes, her weight are issues of concern to her character and the story line. In *The Devil Wears Prada*, the main character's transformation from poorly dressed neophyte deemed "desperately in need of Chanel" to a polished fashionista takes up a large portion of the film. Fashion is used to signify initial character in chick flicks and a girl's changing style indicates growth or decline in her development.

HOW WE PRESENT OURSELVES TO OTHERS

Representation is a two-way street. As in movies, we both read others and present ourselves for others to read. How we dress, act, and speak is a presentation to the world of who we are, or how we want others to see us. Young children make a decision very early when to stop letting others dress them and proceed to take on that task themselves. Children play dress-up trying on their parents' clothes. Halloween presents a ritual by which children try on both "good" and "evil" characters. Some insist on portraying the latest Disney princess or the traditional media villain Captain Hook; others choose even older representations of evil, dressing as witches and ghosts. All are rewarded with treats if they agree to move on and offer their inauthentic personas to the house down the block.

As we grow we continue to dress for reward, in part to fit in, as when we conform our clothing choices when we enter middle school or college to the looks presented by those around us. For a job interview our look changes to what is considered appropriate for the corporate, rock star, or fashion world we are trying to enter. We wear different clothing when attending a house of worship with parents than clubbing with friends. In "Men's Clothing and the Construction of Masculine Identities: Class, Lifestyle, and Popular Culture," Diana Crane explores the use of clothing to construct male (and female) identities and outlines the limited means twentieth century men had to express themselves through their clothing.

How people read us is influenced not only by how we portray ourselves visually, through our behavior, and what we have to say, but also through powerful images that stereotype how our culture defines us. Women and minorities are often defined inaccurately by the dominant group of upper-class white males who control much of the institutional apparatus in this country, including media. Female minorities are particularly vulnerable to the limited vision that society offers audiences through film, television, and other media institutions. The authors of *Chick Flicks and Chick Culture* discuss both the typing that occurs and the opportunities for media to break through stereotype and present fully developed representations.

READING 1

MEN'S CLOTHING AND THE CONSTRUCTION OF MASCULINE IDENTITIES: CLASS, LIFESTYLE AND POPULAR CULTURE

By Diana Crane

In the nineteenth and early twentieth centuries, identification with a social class was the primary factor affecting the way men perceived their identities and their relationships in their social environments. With the transition to a postindustrial society at the end of the 1960s, as Bell (1976) argued, people were less constrained than in the past by their occupational identities. According to this theory, the construction of personal identity outside the workplace became increasingly important. These changes are likely to affect certain types of men more than others, specifically those whose social statuses are marginal, ambiguous, or conflicted. Clothes are a major tool in the construction of identity, offering a wide range of choices for the expression of lifestyles or subcultural identities.

While theorists agree that the meanings of consumer goods are "open, flexible, and malleable" (Kotarba 1994:157; see also Hetzel 1995), exactly how new meanings are conferred on consumer goods is not clear. As Feath-erstone (1991:11) points out, part of the appeal of postmodernism is that "it ... purports to illumi-nate changes in the day-to-day experiences and cultural practices- of broader groups in society. It is here that the evidence is weakest ... we possess little systematic evidence about day-to-day practices." In contrast to Baudrillard's postmodernist interpretation of media images as "meaningless noise" and the public's response as "a flat, one-dimen'sional experience ... a passive absorption of images" (Kellner 1989:70), the public's responses are highly differentiated depending upon age and lifestyle. Meaning is not, as Baudrillard claims, disappearing from media texts and consumer goods such as fashion; instead they are interpreted in contradictory ways by increasingly fragmented publics.

During the twentieth century, two parallel developments have occurred: the public has become in-creasingly adept at "reading" culture, and culture itself has become increasingly complex. Popular culture constantly redefines social phenomena and social identities; artifacts continually acquire new meanings. In this chapter, I will show how the transition to postindustrial society has affected the meanings of items of masculine clothing in different contexts—business and leisure settings. I will argue that the meanings of clothes worn for economic activities have been relatively fixed, while the meanings of clothes worn for leisure activities have been subject to continual redefinition. In order to understand the ways in which new meanings are conferred on items of clothing and the role of popular culture in this process, I will draw on theories that argue that the meanings of some items of popular culture, including clothing, are "open," because they are frequently redefined by culture creators and consumers alike (Fiske 1984). Film and music media are important elements in this process. By associating salient images with specific types of garments, they alter the meanings of those garments and their symbolic power for the public. To be successful, leisure clothes for men have to be synchronized with media culture as it is expressed in television, film, and popular music.

Since men are more closely identified with the occupational sphere than women, who still remain to some extent "outsiders" whose presence is tolerated owing to economic necessity or government legislation, the postindustrial thesis is particularly pertinent to the nature of men's identities. My emphasis will be on men's use of workplace and leisure clothing, although ironically many of the types of clothing I will discuss are now also worn by women. As I will show in this chapter, meanings of clothing are perceived in various ways by different categories of men, some of whom merely consume clothing, while others both consume and create clothing styles. In general, those who belong to minorities, based on race, ethnicity, or sexual orientation, tend to use style as a means of expressing their identities and their resistance to the dominant culture (Janus, Kaiser, and Gray 1999). Members of youth subcultures produce styles that are eventually assimilated by "consumer" fashion, appropriating icons from media culture and engaging in various forms of fantasy, aesthetic expression, and bricolage. Another category consists of "sophisticated poachers," men who attempt to extend the normative boundaries of acceptable male attire. Although I will draw primarily upon American examples, the changes I am describing are taking place in other Western countries. The American case is particularly relevant, because much of the stylistic innovation in leisure apparel in recent years has come from American ethnic, minority, and sexual subcultures, in what a French observer has called the "hyperaméricanisation" of clothing (Valmont 1994:22).

WORK AND LEISURE: TWO CLOTHING CULTURES

In the late twentieth century, the business suit is the epitome of a style that expresses social class distinctions. Since it achieved its present form at the end of the nineteenth century, there have been strict rules about exactly how a business suit is to be made and worn.[1] Precise specifications still govern "the shape and proper proportions of ... details, such as lapels, collars, and trouser length and width" (Flusser 1989:7).[2] A very narrow range of colors is permissible for business suits (primarily navy blue and charcoal gray). These rules enhance the usefulness of the business suit as an indicator of social class. Knowledge of subtle changes in the basic style of the garment is more likely to be available to those who have access to the best tailors. According to Martin and Koda (1989:151): "The cut, fabrication, and accessories of the suit ... betray the social background ... of the wearer.... The suit is a nuanced and varied garment."

Observance of the rules about how suits are to be worn is thought to have a direct influence on success in business, politics, and the professions, as suggested by the slogan in an advertisement by Hart, Schaffner, and Marx (*New York Times* Magazine 1986): "The right suit might not get you to places of power. But the wrong suit might not get you anywhere at all." In conservative political circles, flouting this "uniform" can appear scandalous, as when the French minister of culture, Jack Lang, wore a suit with a mandarin collar and no tie to a meeting of the French National Assembly in 1985 (Déslandres and Müller 1986:327). A French menswear designer stated in 1999 (Middleton 1999): "There is still the situation that changing the number of buttons on a jacket can create a scandal."

Styles of clothing for middle-class men are described as tradition bound, stable, and oriented toward the past (Martin and Koda 1989:9). Not surprisingly, designers of men's business suits find inspiration in the prewar period, particularly the British suit of the early 1930s (Flusser 1989:3). Flusser quotes Yves Saint Laurent, the French fashion designer, as saying that a handful of basic shapes created in the early 1930s still prevail (6). Flusser states: "The thirties could really be considered the time when the American style of dress reached its pinnacle ... an era during which the foundations of good taste in men's wear were laid" (3).

In the 1980s and 1990s, role models for middle-class men's clothing were film stars of the 1930s and British royalty, most notably Fred Astaire and the Duke of Windsor. Armani, one of the most influential designers of men's wear, considers Fred Astaire to be "the supreme reference of elegance" (Fitoussi 1991). As a salesman at a leading New York men's store commented in 1988: "The past is what's happening" (Hochswender 1988:75).

Recently, the rising cost of the suit and changes in attitudes toward the expression of social class distinctions have restricted its use to a narrow range of upper-middle-class occupations, such as law, finance, and management. Sales of suits declined precipitously in the 1990s (Saporito 1993). Significantly, only 3 percent of American households purchase suits in a given year (American Demographics 1993). In the United States, the most conservative attitudes toward clothing are to be found in investment-banking houses on Wall Street, where the traditional suit is still required as an indication of a man's commitment to his profession (Hochswender 1989). The business suit is beginning to be perceived as a uniform which conceals a person's identity, rather than as a costume which reveals it (Barringer 1990). According to Joseph (1986:66-68), one of the distinguishing characteristics of a uniform is that it suppresses individuality. The tie, conservative or flashy, serves as a indication of the wearer's level of commitment to the message conveyed by the suit.

Until recently, constrained by the clothing norms set by the organizations that employed them, most men were unable to deviate very much from a standard masculine look during the day. The largest share of the clothing budget was likely to be reserved for clothes that were worn at work. While individuals in high status positions wore business suits, clothes for working-class or lower-middle-class occupations were frequently uniforms that indicated the wearer's status instantly, and unambiguously, as, for example, a policeman, a waiter, or an airline steward.

Although classic suit styles based on clothes worn by movie stars and trendsetters in the 1930s through the 1950s remain popular (*New York Times* 1995; Yardley 1996), changes in the types of clothing preferred by businessmen suggest that the values embodied in leisure activities and expressed in popular culture are beginning to take precedence over the values of the industrial workplace. The increasing tendency of the leisure sphere to encroach on the business sphere, signifying the growth in the symbolic significance of leisure, is suggested by the trend in the 1990s for businessmen in America and Europe to dress less formally, particularly on Fridays (Mathews 1993; Janus, Kaiser, and Gray 1999). This trend was most pronounced in computer and electronic companies on the West Coast but gradually spread to other regions and other occupations (Bondi 1995), producing a variety of costumes reflecting different social milieus within the upper and middle class (Nabers 1995:132): "What we have today are many types, often quite distinctive and varying by industry, profession, and region … business folk really do dress differently, even when dressing down, depending on whether they work in the Northeast or Northwest, Silicon Valley or the Motor City, not to mention whether they are proprietors, bankers, or lobbyists."

Men's costumes also change as their position in an organization changes or as their employers change. Men who deal with the public outside their companies alter their clothing styles depending upon the social characteristics of the individuals they expect to meet on a particular day. The director of a French banking firm reported: "I try to adopt the image that my associates or my clients expect. I wear a gray suit for a meeting of the board of directors, a more up-to-date get-up for a visit to a construction site, and a shabby old jacket to convince a communist mayor" (Villacampa 1989:98).

What differentiates middle-class men's clothing styles today from their counterparts in the second half of the nineteenth century is that styles worn in the workplace coexist with a completely different set of styles for masculine clothing.[3] Leisu reactivities tend to shape people's perceptions of themselves and are more meaningful than work for many people.[4] These changes are most noticeable in the clothing behavior of youth. Until the 1960s, college and high school students routinely wore suits to their classes (Lee Hall 1992). By the 1960s, these formal outfits had been replaced by the antithesis of the business suit, the blue jean, which became "the uniform of college youth" (O'Donnol 1982). The values expressed by the business suit no longer matched those of the typical college student. During the same period, artists and writers also deserted the values embodied in the business suit and adopted leisure clothing as their work attire. For example, in 1951, when America's leading avant-garde painters, the Abstract Expressionists, were photographed for *Life* magazine, all fourteen wore some version of the business suit (Sandler 1976:frontispiece). Forty-two years later, when art dealer Arnold Glimcher assembled a comparable group for a cover for the *New York Times* magazine, only one of the twelve artists wore a business suit (Schwartzman 1993). Diane Arbus's photographs (Arbus and Israel 1984) of young artists and writers in the 1960s suggest that the transformation in clothing choices was under way in these groups during that period.[5]

In contrast to the business suit, there are no set rules for how most leisure clothes should be worn. These clothes may be modified or even mutilated by the wearer in order to express his personal identity. The meanings of leisure clothes continually change, as can be seen with blue jeans, the most universally worn and widely accepted item of clothing ever made. In the nineteenth and early twentieth centuries, jeans signified physical labor and ruggedness; they were a uniform in which physical labor was performed. Between the 1930s and 1960s, they were adopted by the middle class for vacations on ranches in western states (Foote and Kidwell 1994:74), by working-class women for work and leisure (Olian 1992), and by members of various marginal groups such as motorcycle gangs, artists and painters, leftist activists, and hippies (Gordon 1991:32–34). In this period jeans signified leisure as well as work, but for different social groups. For the middle class, jeans became "an icon for American values of individualism and honesty" (Foote and Kidwell 1994:77). At the same time, jeans acquired connotations of revolt—freedom, equality, and classlessness—against the dominant cultural values. By the 1970s, jeans were widely accepted by both sexes and had become a fashion item whose characteristics changed slightly each year in order to increase sales. Designers altered their shape to highlight their erotic connotations and turned them into a luxury item by increasing their price.

The ease with which new meanings could be attributed to jeans eventually led to a decline in their significance as an icon. As Fiske (1989:2) shows, by the 1980s jeans had ceased to represent a particular class or sex or a particular location, city, or country, although they retained some of their connotations related to the American West (strength, physical labor, sports). There were indications that the myths from the 1950s that had endowed jeans with a special appeal to adolescents were fading. By the late 1980s, a new generation of teenagers was seeking new myths, new identities, and new types of clothing not identified with their parents (Friedmann 1987; Leroy 1994; Normand 1999). Sales of jeans dropped in the late 1990s in favor of other types of apparel, including khakis, chinos, cargo pants, and sweat pants (Tredre 1999).

Like the blue jean, the meanings of another leisure clothing item, the T-shirt, are open; it has been used to convey both rebellion and conformity, depending upon the context and the types of messages that may be inscribed on the front or back. Unlike the blue jean, the T-shirt decorated with lettering or a design appeared in the 1940s (Nelton 1991) and now epitomizes postmodern media culture. Printing on shirts as a means of identifying the wearer with an organization, such as a sports team, appeared in the middle of the nineteenth century and was being used by universities in the 1930s (Giovannini 1984:16–17). The use of a specific type of clothing—the T-shirt—to communicate other types of information began in the late 1940s, when faces and political slogans appeared on T-shirts and, in the 1960s, with commercial logos and other designs.[6] Technical developments in the 1950s and 1960s, such as plastic inks, plastic transfers, and spray paint, led to the use of colored designs and increased the possibilities of the T-shirt as a means of communication. Approximately one billion T-shirts are now purchased annually in the United States (McGraw 1996).[7]

The T-shirt performs a function formerly associated with the hat, that of identifying an individual's social location instantly. Unlike the hat in the nineteenth century, which signaled (or concealed) social class status, the T-shirt speaks to issues related to ideology, difference, and myth: politics, race, gender, and leisure. The variety of slogans and logos that appear on T-shirts is enormous (see fig. 46). Much of the time, people consent to being coopted for "unpaid advertising" for global corporations selling clothes, music, sports, and entertainment in exchange for the social cachet of being associated with certain products (McGraw 1996). Some of the time, people use T-shirts to indicate their support for social and political causes, groups, or organizations to which they have made a commitment. Occasionally, the T-shirt becomes a medium for grass-roots resistance. Bootlegged T-shirts representing characters on the television show *The Simpsons* appeared in response to T-shirts marketed by the network that produced the show (Parisi 1993). The bootlegged T-shirts represented the Simpson family as African Americans. Bart Simpson was shown as Rastabart, with dreadlocks and a red, green, and gold headband, as Rasta-dude Bart Marley, and as Black Bart, paired with Nelson Mandela. Using clothing behavior as a means of making a statement, the T-shirts appeared to be intended as an affirmation of African Americans as an ethnic group and as a commentary on the narrow range of roles for black characters in the show. Victims of gender-related violence, such as rape, incest, battering, and sexual harassment, have used T-shirts as venues for statements about their experiences that are exhibited in clotheslines in public plazas (Ostrowski 1996). By contrast, some young men use T-shirts to express hostile, aggressive, or obscene sentiments denigrating women or to display pictures of guns and pistols (Cose 1993; *Time* 1992). Teens of both sexes use them as a means of expressing their cynicism about the dominant culture, particularly global advertising (Sepulchre 1994b).

The significance of the T-shirt in Western culture, as a means of social and political expression, is seen by comparing its roles in Western countries with the response to it in a nondemocratic country, the People's Republic of China (Barmé 1993). In 1991, a young Chinese artist created T-shirts bearing humorous statements, some of which could be interpreted as having mild political implications. The T-shirts were enormously successful with the public but were perceived as "a serious political incident" by the Chinese authorities. The artist was arrested and interrogated, and the T-shirts were officially banned. Thousands of them were confiscated and destroyed, although many Chinese continued to wear them.

Despite recent changes in executive dress codes, two very different clothing cultures remain in effect, one representing the world of work and the other representing the world of leisure. Clothes worn in the workplace mark social class hierarchies very precisely. Leisure clothing, by contrast, tends to blur social class differences. Specific garments cannot be neatly ranked according to social class distinctions and have often been derived from working-class occupations, such as the farmer, the factory worker, and the cowboy (Martin and Koda 1989:45). Rich and poor participate in the same stylistic world, which is dominated by images from popular culture and the entertainment media. Leisure clothes are a means of expressing personal identity; they point to a wide variety of concerns, including race, ethnicity, sexual orientation, and gender. Many styles derive from popular music and are often highly androgynous. Leisure styles that originated in the 1950s and 1960s resonate with more traditional macho mythologies, generally American but sometimes with Latin influences, that are associated with male sports and leisure pursuits, such as riding, driving cars or motorcycles, and hunting. A French importer of clothes manufactured by companies such as Go West, Timberland, and Redskins, said: "We make our living from a myth" (Piganeau 1991:73). Still another set of styles, that appeal to the current generation of adolescents, are based on costumes for newer and more spectacular sports, such as surfing, snowboarding, and sky surfing (Valmont 1994). They are manufactured in new types of synthetic materials that are sometimes recycled or decorated with graphics created by computers.

Worn in conventional workplaces with steep status hierarchies, leisure clothes are anomalous; the absence of clear-cut norms in situations where statuses need to be clearly differentiated leads to confusion and engenders ad hoc solutions that, according to a corporate image consultant, vary "from industry to industry, company to company—even department to department" (Casey 1997; see also Janus, Kaiser, and Gray 1999).

NOTES

1. Comparable rules governing appropriate hemlines for women's clothes have disappeared.
2. According to experts, there is an appropriate size for each of these details—lapels: 3.5'; vents in jackets: 7'–9' (depending upon a mans height); and size of trouser cuffs: 1.63'–1.75' (Flusser 1989:32, 36, 51).
3. Leisure clothes for the upper class existed in the nineteenth and early twentieth centuries, but they were similar to the business suit in that their styles were dictated by precise rules.
4. Marx observed that leisure was more meaningful than work for members of the working class; this observation could be generalized to members of other classes today.
5. The photographic records of the Magnum photographers, a small organization of leading photographers from a number of countries, reveal the gradual shift in the nature of their attire at their annual meetings, from dark business suits in the 1930s through the 1950s to the adoption of leisure attire in the 1970s and 1980s (Manchester 1989).

6. The first short-sleeved T-shirts—white, crew-necked, and without lettering or designs—were marketed by Sears, Roebuck in 1938 (Giovannini 1984:14, 17). Green T-shirts without lettering were used by the American military during the Second World War; some soldiers added their own lettering. Long-sleeved cotton T-shirts were first manufactured in France at the beginning of the twentieth century and were used by the American military in the First World War.

7. Europeans consume fewer T-shirts than Americans. They buy an average of 1.5 T-shirts per person per year compared with 6.5 per person purchased annually by Americans (Germain 1997).

8. "Poaching" refers to the ways in which readers interpret material in texts to suit their own interests and needs (Jenkins 1992). It implies assimilating items without modifying them, as compared with "bricolage," which is more characteristic of subcultures that put existing items together in such a way that their original meanings are modified (Hebdige 1979).

9. The study was based on 2,800 interviews with men aged fifteen and over (Pujol 1992:39).

10. For a study of personal clothing that had special significance for women, see Kaiser, Freeman, and Chandler (1993).

11. These films include: *The Wild One* (with Marlon Brando), *Rebel without A Cause* (with James Dean), and *Jailhouse Rock* (with Elvis Presley).

12. In 1948, mainstream men's suit styles adopted a modified form of the zoot style (Chibnall 1985:61).

13. T-shirts and other types of clothes related to themes in the story lines of Hollywood "blockbuster" films in the 1980s and 1990s have sold very well, but these products have not produced a widespread transformation in popular styles.

14. Examples of this phenomenon include Michael Jackson and Prince, Bob Dylan and Jim Morrison (Jones 1987:99, 166).

15. Youth subcultures are generally defined as subgroups with identifiable social structures, distinctive sets of shared beliefs and values, and characteristic rituals and modes of symbolic expression.

16. The exhibition focused on specific outfits belonging to members of these subcultures, which were obtained through personal contacts and from specialty stores, secondhand clothing stores, and designers serving these markets. The objective of the exhibition was to present a broad overview of subcultural clothing styles. For a discussion of recent trends in styles worn by youth cultures in France, see Mopin (1997).

17. Polhemus (1994) lists forty-five street styles, ten of them not included in De la Haye and Dingwell (1996). When asked with what style they identified, a national sample of French boys and men aged twelve to twenty-four named thirty-five labels, although many were mentioned by a tiny percentage (Piganeau 1988; see also Obalk, Soral, and Pasche 1984).

18. These ads often rely on sartorial signs that gays use to identify themselves to other gays in public places, such as bootlaces or a bandanna of a certain color or the way a particular type of garment may be buttoned or unbuttoned (Freitas, Kaiser, and Hammidi 1996:96).

19. Byrde (1979:72): "Colour and decoration, so noticeably absent from twentieth century men's suits, were usual until the middle of the nineteenth century. Both silks and cloth in bright colors were worn by men in the seventeenth and eighteenth centuries and although black or dark-coloured cloth became

fashionable at the beginning of the nineteenth century, shades of blue, green, red and white were still worn for evening wear for the first few decades."

20. D'Orsay, a French dandy in the early nineteenth century, is described by Laver (1968: 55) as wearing "a sky-blue cravat, yards of gold chain, white French gloves, light drab greatcoat lined with velvet of the same colour, invisible inexpressibles (trousers), skin-coloured and fitting like a glove."

21. The market for experiments in the presentation of masculine gender identity is small, as suggested by sales of 3,000 men's skirts from Gaultier's collection in 1984 (Chenoune 1993:302). Worn with boots and over trousers in New York City, skirts on men were said to attract little attention in the mid-1980s (*New York Times* 1985).

22. What is missing in Herpins analysis is the role of uniforms in the wardrobes of employed working-class men and women.

23. See Brown (1984:287). Similar data for 1988 do not appear in Brown's book.

24. On the basis of a study of informants' interpretations of conventional and unconventional outfits, McCracken (1988:64–67) argues that clothing codes are extremely limited in what they can communicate. Alternatively, it can be argued that clothing codes are very diverse and that respondents' interpretations of specific combinations of clothing are inhibited by their inevitable lack of familiarity with codes used by social groups other than their own.

READING 2
CHICK FLICKS AND CHICK CULTURE

By Suzanne Ferriss and Mallory Young

In this [introduction], we consider chick flicks, a subject that inspires highly polarized and ambivalent responses. Chick flicks have been both championed and vilified by women and men, scholars and popular audiences. Like other forms of "chick culture," chick flicks have been accused of reinscribing traditional attitudes and reactionary roles for women. On the other hand, they have been embraced as pleasurable and potentially liberating entertainments, assisting women in negotiating the challenges of contemporary life.

We contend that the most valuable and productive consideration of chick flicks requires looking at them neither in isolation nor as simply one area of film studies. Rather, chick flicks are best addressed as one form of a prominent popular cultural phenomenon that can be termed *chick culture*.[1] In addressing chick flicks then, our book has a threefold purpose:

- To situate chick flicks in a larger context of chick cultural studies;
- To consider the place of chick flicks in film history and current film; and
- To consider various definitions, approaches, and responses to chick flicks without privileging any particular point of view.

Our collection seeks to examine the polarized responses and the range of positions in between, not advocating a single position but seeking to complicate and explore the questions chick forms, especially films, inevitably raise.

CHICK CULTURE

While we hesitate to pin it down to a single, possibly reductive definition, chick culture can be productively viewed as a group of mostly American and British popular culture media forms focused primarily on twenty- to thirtysomething middle-class women. Along with chick flicks, the most prominent chick cultural forms are chick lit and chick TV programming, although other pop culture manifestations such as magazines, blogs, music—even car designs and energy drinks[2]—can be included in the chick lineup. The dawn of chick lit, the wildly popular body of literature largely spawned by British author Helen Fielding's 1996 novel *Bridget Jones's Diary*, provides a fairly clear starting point for the chick cultural explosion.[3] The TV series *Sex and the City*, based on the book by Candace Bushnell, appearing at the same time, provides another clue to its origins. As a phenomenon dating from the mid-1990s, the chick culture boom both reflected and promoted the new visibility of women in popular culture. What links the products of chick culture is, above all, "the contemporary media's heightened address to women" (Ashby). This deliberate address to female audiences suggested a growing recognition of women's significance in contemporary culture. The media reflected and even shaped women's complex social positioning—with its continued restrictions and its new freedoms—and their aspirations. At the same time, however, the rise of chick culture provided evidence of newly concerted efforts to manipulate and influence the spending habits of young women, whom marketers had at last identified as a huge force in an economy based on consumption.

The moniker *chick flick* dates back considerably further than the mid-1990s. Although impossible to trace definitively, its original use was surely as a derisive term—most commonly applied by unwilling male theatergoers to their girlfriends' film choices. One problem in any consideration of such films is that unlike *chick lit* which has a precise historical meaning,[4] the *chick flick* has yet to be clearly defined—even though Merriam-Webster has at last included it in the eminent dictionary's most recent update. Once we move beyond the, perhaps original, derogatory meaning—a sappy movie for women that men don't like—which films are we referring to? What, precisely, is a chick flick? We might be tempted to answer that we know one when we see one. But it is helpful to make some effort at definition. In the simplest, broadest sense, chick flicks are commercial films that appeal to a female audience. Although we are focusing in this discussion on contemporary films, chick flicks can also be seen as a much more inclusive film category. We do not want to suggest that films from other periods cannot be included as chick flicks.

We are most interested, however, in how contemporary movies designated as chick flicks are enmeshed, for good and for ill, with the wide range of responses invoked by chick culture. The term *chick* itself—whether applied to film, literature, or other popular culture forms—invites immediate and conflicting reactions. The term and reactions to it point up some of the larger issues involved in responses to chick culture.[5]

At the height of the women's liberation movement in the 1970s, the word *chick*, along with the word *girl*, was considered an insult, a demeaning diminutive, casting women as childlike, delicate, fluffy creatures in need of protection and guidance or as appendages to hip young males. Rejecting such terms was a declaration of equality and independence. To the feminists harking from this period—those now known as second-wave feminists—the contemporary revival of these terms signals a return to the infantilizing of women and a failure of their efforts to create a society based on gender equality. For many second-wave feminists, the term invokes an immediate negative response.

For women of a younger generation, however, the word *chick*, like *girl* (and even *bitch*), has been wielded knowingly to convey solidarity and signal empowerment. This new generation made up of women who were born with feminism as their heritage—often referred to as a third-wave feminist or postfeminist generation—has rejected or at least questioned some of the central tenets of feminist thought. Part of third-wavers' response to feminism has been the deliberate re-appropriation and re-visioning of terms that make second-wave feminists cringe: *Girlpower*. "You go, *girl*." "*Chicks* rule!" Much as homosexual activists transformed the disparaging term *queer* into a slogan to proclaim solidarity and increase their cultural visibility—"We're here. We're queer. Get used to it"—so the women of the third wave seek to reclaim and refashion their identity through terms considered unacceptable by the previous generation.

Above all, as the term *chick* suggests, chick culture is vitally linked to postfeminism. The split between feminism and postfeminism has largely been viewed as a generational one.[6] That isn't an entirely valid distinction: certainly many women in their twenties and thirties consider themselves feminists while plenty of women over forty indulge in supposedly post-feminist interests and pursuits such as fashion. It's also possible—and perhaps more helpful—to see feminism and postfeminism in terms of a continuity rather than a conflict. While many definitions of postfeminism have been advanced and many types identified, the most pervasive form—which has appropriately been labeled "chick" postfeminism—is the one most relevant to the study of chick culture.[7]

The ideas associated with postfeminism—and the presumed conflict between feminism and postfeminism—are central to any consideration of chick flicks, which can be viewed as the prime postfeminist media texts.[8] At the risk of indulging in reductionism or oversimplification, we do think it's useful to note some of the major feminist/postfeminist distinctions:

FEMINISM

- Reliance on political action, political movements, and political solutions;
- The primacy of equality; resistance to and critique of the patriarchy;
- Choice is collective—it refers to women's right *not* to have children and to enter careers and professions formerly closed to them;
- A rejection—or at least questioning—of femininity;
- Suspicion of and resistance to media-driven popular culture and the consumerism it supports;
- Humor is based on the disjunction between traditional women's roles and women as powerful, independent people.

POSTFEMINISM

- The personal as political; agenda is replaced by attitude;
- A rejection of second-wave anger and blame against the patriarchy;
- Choice is individual—whether of family, career, cosmetic surgery, or nail color;
- A return to femininity and sexuality;
- Pleasure in media-driven popular culture and an embracing of the joys of consumerism;
- Humor is based on the discrepancy between the ideals put forward by both feminism and the media, and the reality of life in the modern world; as such, the humor of postfeminism is often ironically self-deprecating.

Not surprisingly, then, postfeminists might tend to view feminists as angry, humorless, self-proclaimed victims of patriarchy. Feminists might tend to view postfeminists as shallow, mindless, unconscious victims of media culture and consumerism.[9] Unquestionably film plays a significant role in framing and reflecting women's place in culture, particularly during moments of cultural shift. It is not surprising then that chick flicks raise questions about women's place—their prescribed social and sexual roles, the role of female friendship and camaraderie—and play out the difficulties of negotiating expectations and achieving independence. They do so, however, in complex and often contradictory ways. Chick flicks illustrate, reflect, and present all of the cultural characteristics associated with the chick postfeminist aesthetic: a return to femininity, the primacy of romantic attachments, girlpower, a focus on female pleasure and pleasures, and the value of consumer culture and girlie goods, including designer clothes, expensive and impractical footwear, and trendy accessories.

As a result, chick flicks are often accused of promoting a retreat into pre-feminist concerns and the unthinking embrace of consumerism, of endorsing not true freedom but "the freedom to shop (and to cook)" (Holmlund) through protagonists "whose preoccupations are likely to involve romance, career choices, and hair gels" (Mizejewski).

The women who identify with postfeminist films, however, welcome the inclusion of romance and femininity in their lives, and resist reducing femininity, as many critics do, to superficial markers such as high heels and frilly dresses. The admission of girliness, they argue, doesn't mean the loss of female independence and power.

By contrast, defenders of "girlie feminism" view femininity and sexuality as empowering. Many postfeminists seek to reclaim and refashion their sexuality, to unsettle traditional images of feminine virtue by substituting an image of themselves as "lusty feminists of the third-wave" (Stoller 84). This idea clearly applies to a number of women's films as well as to the popular TV series *Sex and the City*, *Bust* magazine, female pop singers, and more. The members of this "New Girl Order," as *Bust* editor Debbie Stoller styled the girlpower rebellion, defiantly embrace sexuality as its means: "Our mission is to seek out pleasure wherever we can find it. In other words, if it feels good, screw it" (79). The title of Stoller's essay, "Sex and the Thinking Girl," obviously plays on *Sex and the Single Girl*, the title of Helen Gurley Brown's 1962 bestseller. At once she embraces the message of sexual liberation first advanced by the creator of *Cosmopolitan*, and distances the "new girls" from the old, implying that young women are consciously seeking pleasure rather than using their bodies as tokens of exchange with men.[10] While second-wave feminists Andrea Dworkin and Catherine MacKinnon argued that pornographic films sexually objectified women, leading directly to sexual harassment, battery and even rape, some contemporary female erotic filmmakers have sought to revolutionize porn by representing women's sexual pleasure in particular. Winner of the first Emma Award for Feminist Porn (named in honor of feminist Emma Goldman) awarded recently at the "Vixens and Visionaries" event in Toronto, Canada, director Tristan Taormino said, "I consciously work to create images that contradict (and hopefully challenge) other porn that represents women only as objects and vehicles for male pleasure." While such films are by no means mainstream, they have been associated with a more pervasive "raunch culture"—from "Cardio Striptease" fitness workouts to Paris Hilton's sex tapes to *Girls Gone Wild!* to the sexually provocative music videos of Madonna, Britney Spears, and Christina Aguilera (Humphrey). Such manifestations can be seen either as allowing women the freedoms of sexual expression and pleasure previously denied them or as demeaning women by exploiting them once again as sex objects, leading them to overvalue appearance and embrace plastic surgery.[11]

Chick flicks do occupy this conflicted territory. While Drew Barrymore does indeed twirl around a pole in *Charlie's Angels: Full Throttle* (2003), she does so in a campy parody of a stripper and, in both films in the series, the Angels are kept far too busy chasing bad guys to engage in actual sex. As a sex worker, Julia Roberts in *Pretty Woman* (1990) spends more time lounging demurely in a tub than in bed. Cher (Alicia Silverstone) in *Clueless* (1995) is "hymenally challenged"—a virgin. Still, while it may not be overtly represented, many chick flick heroines—from Bridget Jones to *Legally Blonde*'s Elle—clearly do engage in sex outside of marriage and juggle multiple partners.

However, a substantial number of recent chick flicks, in adhering to older generic conventions of romance and comedy and responding to a more conservative political climate, have returned to the subtle promotion of chastity, allowing the heroine only one sexual partner or, in some cases—such as *Just Like Heaven* (2005), *The Family Stone* (2005), and *She's the Man* (2006)—offering the chaste kiss at the end as the only expression of sexuality.

It is equally important to note that many postfeminist chick flicks do continue to address issues and take stands originally considered feminist. To view chick flicks either from an entirely negative or an entirely positive perspective would be to oversimplify both the films and the issues involved.

We agree with Joanne Hollows and Rachel Moseley that "we need new ways of understanding the relationship between feminism and the popular" and "that such an approach need not imply that post-feminism is either a good or a bad thing" (8–9). Indeed recent films identified as chick flicks can be drawn on to provide clear examples of the claims of both attackers and defenders. On the one hand, some films do reinforce traditional gender roles, promoting a kind of ideological retrenchment similar to that promoted by many films of the late 1940s and early 1950s. As women returned to the home from the more challenging venues of wartime activities, Hollywood pointed them in the direction of the suburbs. Films like *Miracle on 34th Street* (1947) and *Funny Face* (1957) ridiculed or undercut women's efforts at intellectual and professional accomplishment. Similarly, some chick flicks from the 1990s and 2000s promote the choice of romance, family, and love over career and independence. Such films as *Kate and Leopold* (2001), *Thirteen Going on Thirty* (2004), *Raising Helen* (2004), and *The Family Stone* (2005) suggest that a career-oriented woman is a lonely and unhappy one.

On the other hand, just as some 1940s and even 1950s films showed women successfully navigating both career and romance, so do many of today's chick flicks. The idea that women can follow professions while wearing pink, have both successful careers and successful relationships—that femininity and feminism aren't mutually exclusive—appears prominently in both mainstream and independent films embraced by female viewers. *Legally Blonde* (2001), *Real Women Have Curves* (2002), *Bend It Like Beckham* (2002), *Mona Lisa Smile* (2003), *The Devil Wears Prada* (2006), and numerous others promote the idea that while it may not be possible to have it all, choosing education and career does not mean abandoning the possibility of happiness.[12] Many of these films also promote the value and benefits of female friendship.[13] Some contemporary chick flicks do focus on (often vicious) competition among women—seen most prominently in teen flicks such as *Mean Girls* (2004). But today's chick flicks far more often put forward a view of female solidarity and support. Even *Legally Blonde*'s Elle, who finds herself clashing with snobbish female students at Harvard, has the support of her former sorority sisters and the down-to-earth women at the local beauty salon.

The same diversity of perspectives appears with respect to the issue of marriage. Even some romantic comedies which, according to expected conventions, lead necessarily to wedding bells, actually question the desirability of marriage. The attraction between the married heroine (Claudette Colbert) and her bachelor rescuer (Clark Gable) in *It Happened One Night* (1934) suggests that romance and marriage are not necessarily linked. Similarly, the 1990s chick flick *Four Weddings and a Funeral* (1994) highlights the relationship between Charles (Hugh Grant) and Carrie (Andie MacDowell) who finally, after her failed marriage and his failed wedding, get together but agree to forgo wedding vows themselves. The primacy of beauty is another issue that chick flicks can be found simultaneously promoting and questioning. While the beauty makeover may be a chick-flick staple, a film like *The Truth about Cats and Dogs* (1996) is able to explore and finally reject the standard ideals of beauty while remaining solidly in chick-flick territory.

Still other films complicate the issues even further, taking an ambivalent position. Such films as *Bridget Jones's Diary* (2001), *The Princess Diaries* (2001), and *In Her Shoes* (2005) raise questions about the choices women confront, the possibility of having it all, and the effects of society's rigorous and capricious standards of beauty. Others combine pre-feminist and feminist ideas, refusing to choose between them. The 2005 film *Just Like Heaven* provides the ideal example of a postfeminist fairy tale. In this modern take on *Sleeping Beauty*, the film's protagonist lies in an accident-induced coma. As in the original pre-feminist tale, she will be awakened by a kiss. In both cases, the heroine will experience a sexual/spiritual awakening as well as a physical one. But in the postfeminist version, our sleeping heroine (played by Reese Witherspoon) will not simply lie around waiting for her prince to come. Rather, her spirit detaches itself and goes out to find him—and she must "wake" him so that he can appear just in time to wake her. As the movie's prince (played by Mark Ruffalo) pointedly claims, "when we first met, I kept saying that you were dead. But it was me that was dead, and you brought me back. You saved me. And now it's my turn to save you." At the film's end, Reese Witherspoon's character has found her prince but lost her chance to be an attending physician at the hospital where she obsessively worked before her accident. The film doesn't let us know whether her future will return her to a (perhaps more balanced) professional role—individual viewers are left to make that decision for themselves.

THE OTHER CHICK: RACE, SEXUALITY, AGE, CLASS

A charge frequently leveled against chick culture and chick flicks relates to their homogeneity. Feminist film scholars, in fact, frequently discuss chick flicks as part of "a white 'chick' backlash that denies class, avoids race, ignores (older) age, and 'straight'-jackets sexuality" (Holmlund). The nature of chick flicks' appeal and their potential value in illuminating women's lives are controversial issues partly because such films have featured protagonists who are overwhelmingly young, heterosexual, white, and middle-class. To at least some extent, this may be an issue of definition. Frequently the designation of *chick flick* has, for example, been automatically avoided in the case of films focused on women of color. Even such films as *The Color Purple* (1985) that clearly exhibit many of the most obvious characteristics and conventions of chick flicks, are rarely included. This may not be surprising. Krin Gabbard points out that many recent scholars in black media studies, while giving black performers credit for strides made in the film industry, are, nonetheless, "just as concerned with how the artists are appropriated by white culture" ("Cinema"). To identify films focused on women of color as chick flicks will strike some viewers and scholars as a move to de-legitimize them or assimilate them into a prevailing white culture.

Still, major elements of chick flicks appear in cinematic offerings focused on women of color and in films produced in other parts of the world. Accusing chick flicks of focusing entirely on "whiteness" risks oversimplifying the issues while ignoring or dismissing the contributions of other ethnicities. Instead, we should be asking how African-American, Latina, Asian, and other non-Anglo ethnic varieties have appropriated and transformed chick-flick conventions while also noting the features shared across ethnic, racial, and national lines. Issues of women's identity, sexuality, generational conflict (particularly between mothers and daughters), and romantic trials are indeed remarkably similar. Do these similarities reflect a similar experience for twenty-first-century women across ethnic boundaries? Or does the form itself—and the politics of production and reception controlling it—enforce artificial similarities? Could the answer be yes to both questions? If we simply dismiss chick flicks for failing to focus on various ethnic groups, we will neglect to ask these questions.

Unquestionably, woman-centered films from a variety of cultures are gaining mainstream recognition and attention. African-American chick flicks include, for example, those based on the novels of Terry McMillan—*Waiting to Exhale* and *How Stella Got Her Groove Back* (1998)—*Love Jones* (2004), and *Beauty Shop* (2005). *Girlfight* (2000), *Tortilla Soup* (2001) (based on the original Chinese *Eat, Drink, Man, Woman* [1994]), *Maid in Manhattan* (2002), and *Real Women Have Curves* qualify as Latina chick flicks.[14] Each film conforms to and significantly transforms what might be seen as prevailing chick conventions. These films and many others should, we believe, be considered in the context of chick culture.

Asian, Indian, and Pakistani cultures have also been prominent in the production of films that can be and have been labeled chick flicks. *Bride and Prejudice* (2004), the Bollywood version of Jane Austen's classic, suggests that the conventions of femininity and romance characteristic of the chick flick are present in Indian culture, despite the persistence of arranged marriages. Directed by Gurinder Chadha on the heels of her wildly successful paean to girlpower, *Bend It Like Beckham*, the film, it's worth noting, was intended not for Indian but Anglo-American audiences. We might suspect then that it makes Indian traditions conform to chick-flick formulas rather than creating a truly indigenous Indian chick flick that captures the complexity of women's position in the developing world. Still, the appearance of chick conventions beyond the borders of the Anglo-American world might suggest their adaptability to diverse cultures, as Mira Nair's film *Monsoon Wedding* (2001) more clearly demonstrates. Several Asian films including *Eat, Drink, Man, Woman* and the original Japanese version of *Shall We Dance?* (1996) also give evidence of the widespread appeal of chick-flick formulas. European filmmakers too, once distinguished by their reliance on dark, naturalistic themes, now participate in chick cultural trends, as evidenced by the enormously popular French film *Amélie* (2001) and the German/Italian *Bella Martha* (2002), among others.

Similar issues arise in considering sexuality in chick flicks. While Chris Holmlund has contended that the chick flick " 'straight'-jackets sexuality" by foregrounding heterosexual romance, others have pointed to possibilities for more complex, even resistant, viewing practices. Patricia White, for example, has argued that "cinema is a public fantasy that engages spectators' particular, private scripts of desire and identification" (xv). While some female viewers may identify with the attractive chick-flick heroine who is the object of male desire on screen, others may see her as an object of desire herself.[15] Lesbian viewers have also seen models of same-sex desire in secondary characters, as in Mrs Danver's worshipful devotion to the first Mrs De Winter in Alfred Hitchcock's classic *Rebecca* (1940).[16]

With the growing visibility of sexual minorities, a contemporary lesbian or "queer chick flick" has arguably emerged. In her study of lesbian representation in film, Shameem Kabir has identified a homoerotic subtext in *The Color Purple*, *Fried Green Tomatoes* (1991), and *Thelma and Louise* (1991). Such films certainly stress female friendship and solidarity. While they may only portray female bonding (or homosociality), it is entirely possible that they convey themes of lesbian desire. (In the case of *Fried Green Tomatoes*, the original novel indicates an underlying homoerotic theme far more strongly than the film, suggesting both its actual presence in the film and the tendency of mainstream films to suppress such elements.) Other recent films such as *Go Fish* (1993), *The Incredibly True Adventure of Two Girls in Love* (1995), *The Watermelon Woman* (1996), *Better than Chocolate* (1999), and *Saving Face* (2005) do address lesbian relationships openly. These explicitly lesbian films lead us to ask if the primacy of romance in the narrative offers a true "queer" alternative to the heterosexual romance or merely shapes lesbian desire to fit a heterosexual romantic model. Either way, it is important to note that the boundaries of the chick flick are being pushed.

In addition to a new lesbian heroine, recent films have offered a strange blend of hyperfemininity and hypermasculinity in the action heroines of films like *Lara Croft: Tomb Raider* (2001) and *Kill Bill, Vol. 1* and *Vol. 2* (2003, 2004). Whether these films offer women a pleasurable fantasy of postfeminist empowerment or rather cater to male fears and fantasies is an issue worth exploring in connection with postfeminist film. Once again, such films certainly stretch the generally perceived limits of chick flicks.

When it comes to the issue of age, woman-centered films have recently made significant strides in expanding their focus. Indeed a whole body of "older bird" films has gained prominence. Some of these—*Unconditional Love* (2002), *Calendar Girls* (2003), *Mrs Henderson Presents* (2005)—are independent or British films, intended for a small, select, non-mainstream audience. Others, however—*The Banger Sisters* (2002), *Something's Gotta Give* (2003), *Under the Tuscan Sun* (2003), and *Because I Said So* (2007)—are big-budget Hollywood star vehicles. In many of these films, women over forty discover—or rediscover—their independence, sexuality, or self-worth. Still, not all critics and viewers are pleased to see such an expansion of chick formulas. Like the films directed at younger women, many of these films, while allowing older women to display and explore sexuality, reinscribe that sexuality safely within the confines of the traditional family.

In *Unconditional Love*, for example, Kathy Bates' character is a fifty-something housewife whose husband walks out on her at the film's beginning. With the help of a handsome, much younger man and her feisty daughter-in-law, she tracks down a killer and finds self-respect. In the end, she is reunited with her repentant and reformed husband—on her terms.[17] In *Something's Gotta Give*, Diane Keaton's character has her confidence in her sexual desirability and desire restored. But, while the film offers the possibility of an older woman–younger man pairing, it doesn't follow through on that option. Keaton opts instead for a commitment-phobic but age-appropriate mate. The film thus manages to indulge middle-aged women's fantasies while allaying middle-aged male fears. Still, the supposedly narrow confines of the chick flick prove to be less narrow than might have been suspected.

Issues of class and consumerism are particularly controversial ones. The critique of the pursuit of status through purchase—and the role of women as the main symbols, if not the main suspects—goes back, of course, to Thorstein Veblen's 1899 *Theory of the Leisure Class*. The prevailing critique today suggests that women who, quite literally, "buy in" to post-feminist consumerist culture are the victims of a patriarchal order and a capitalistic media-driven system seeking to suppress and control them. It is certainly true that chick flicks, like chick culture in general, often uncritically embrace a supposedly feminine delight in consumer goods. The montage of the heroine joyously shopping—often as part of a physical and/or class-status makeover—is a staple of chick flicks including *Moonstruck* (1987), *Pretty Woman*, *Freaky Friday* (2003), and *The Devil Wears Prada*.

To assume that women are the unwilling and unknowing victims of manipulation, however, may be to demean and discredit them—and even to suggest that they are incapable of making choices for themselves. As Hollows and Moseley note, " 'consumption' in these debates frequently becomes reduced to the act of purchase and the reproduction of consumer capitalism, ignoring more extensive understandings of consumption" (11). Recent studies of film spectatorship and stardom complicate such readings, as do studies of women's uses of fashion to shape identity and even undermine gender conventions. The exaggerated presentation of femininity in *Legally Blonde*, for instance, is clearly part of the film's critique of the dumb-blonde stereotype. Elle (Reese Witherspoon) not only manages to graduate from Harvard law school, her success turns on her superior knowledge of perms. Obviously played for laughs, this plot twist does not imply that female viewers should devote more serious attention to hair care; rather, they take pleasure in the revelation that Elle's critics are more overinvested in appearance than she is.

In addition, the relationship between spectatorship and spending may be less clear than critics suggest. Rather than influencing women to spend more on consumer goods, such films—along with chick-lit novels— might just as likely satisfy or replace the desire to consume.[18] Viewers of chick flicks can spend $10 for a movie ticket to enjoy the vicarious screen experience of glamour instead of purchasing pricey Prada outfits or Manolo Blahniks. Chick flicks thus serve as a relatively guiltless pleasure.

While in the 1930s, Hollywood studios did blatantly attempt to forge fashion trends by joining forces with fashion houses, offering inexpensive knock-offs of designer dresses for middle-class consumers,[19] such tactics are relatively rare in today's chick flicks. Nonetheless, although the connection of present-day chick flicks to consumer desire is more complicated, the relationship between chick flicks and consumer culture cannot be denied. Luxury watchmaker Tissot did prominently feature its "Touch" watches on the wrists of Brad Pitt and Angelina Jolie in *Mr & Mrs Smith* (2005) and then featured the stars in print ads and jewelry store window displays. Chanel conscripted *Moulin Rouge!* director Baz Luhrmann to create a television ad for its classic fragrance No. 5 starring Nicole Kidman, a project then documented in the pages of *Vogue*. And the beauty supply chain Sephora launched a campaign based on *The Devil Wears Prada*—unimaginatively titled "The Devil Wears Sephora"—quite obviously trying to capitalize (literally) on the film's setting in the beauty industry.[20] The effects of such strategies are difficult to measure. Did these campaigns actually entice film viewers to buy the products by making glamour appear accessible through purchase? Or, given the campaigns' obvious emphasis on fantasy—particularly in the case of Chanel, which presented Kidman as a ball-gowned and bejeweled starlet—did the ads only reinforce the luxury brands as exclusive and out of reach of the average consumer/viewer? Either way the intent to promote consumerist desire is clear.

Certainly, chick flicks, like other commercial films, are enmeshed in a complex network created by mega corporations to reach a global consumer market.[21] The same corporation may produce and distribute the film featured on the morning programs and late-night talk shows on the network it owns, and reviewed in the pages of the magazine it publishes. And chick flicks, in particular, often intersect with other chick media, such as magazines. Celebrities such as Reese Witherspoon and Kate Hudson grace the covers of fashion magazines and others have been hired to advertise products, from Rachel Welch for hair extensions to Elizabeth Hurley for milk. However, similar strategies are used to reach male consumers, as well, suggesting that the indictment of popular women's media as consumerist may not only miss the complexities of contemporary media culture but unfairly single out female consumers for criticism.[22]

THE PLEASURE PRINCIPLE: CHICKS JUST WANNA HAVE FUN

Of course, most viewers of chick flicks never consider the political ramifications of postfeminism or the subtle subtexts of female friendship films. For most of the audience, watching chick flicks is a matter of pleasure. In *Chick Flicks: A Movie Lover's Guide to the Movies Women Love*, film critic Jami Bernard claims a chick flick is "any movie that makes a special connection with a female audience" (xii). In their almost identically titled *Chick Flicks: Movies Women Love*, Jo Berry and Angie Errigo define it as "a film made specifically to appeal to a female audience" (1). Rather than perceiving the term *chick* as a disparaging appellation that marginalizes women's films, they have instead embraced it to categorize films on the basis of the pleasure they bring women, emphasizing desire with their repeated use of the phrase "movies women love."

Until recently, most feminist film critics ignored the pleasures women have found in film stressing instead that Hollywood films have marginalized and objectified women, leading them to accept a position as victim. Molly Haskell claimed that the majority of the so-called "woman's films" of the 1930s and 1940s, often cited as precursors to chick flicks, presented the female protagonist as a victim. By identifying with her, the female viewer was led to wallow in self-pity rather than to rebel against unfairness and inequity. At its lowest level, she wrote, the woman's film "fills a masturbatory need, it is soft-core emotional porn for the frustrated housewife" (155). Like Haskell, Mary Ann Doane argued that the only pleasures offered by the woman's film were masochistic. She claimed that the films presented the female protagonist as an object of male desire, promoting the female audience's identification with her as passive objects, rather than active agents, of desire. Jeanine Basinger countered that the woman's film operated out of a paradox: "It both held women in social bondage and released them into a dream of potency and freedom. It drew women in with images of what was lacking in their own lives and sent them home reassured that their own lives were the right thing after all" (6).

More recent writing about the woman's film and its female audience has challenged such views. Pam Cook notes that such arguments "imply that the category of the woman's picture exists in order to dupe female spectators into believing that they are important, while subtly marginalizing and disempowering them" (229). Instead, she and others have suggested that cinema offers women (and men) more complex possibilities for identification. Judith Mayne, for example, has rejected the idea that spectators are seeking to identify with those most like them. Instead, "spectators may experience the thrill of reinventing themselves rather than simply having their social identities or positions bolstered" (Cook 234). It is unlikely, then, that chick-flick viewers presume they are or can become Julia Roberts or Renée Zellweger. In part, they take pleasure in the obvious difference between themselves and the women on the screen, just as women of earlier eras gravitated toward the glamour of Hollywood stars, who served as unreal, transcendent figures of desirability and femininity. In her study of British women's reactions to Hollywood films of the 1940s and 1950s, Jackie Stacey found that "the cinema … was remembered as offering spectators the chance to be part of another world and participate in its glamour in contrast to their own lives" (116).

Several recent chick flicks even take an ironic stance on overly simple theories of identification. *Down with Love* (2003), for example, a tongue-in-cheek homage to the films of Doris Day and Rock Hudson, consciously distanced itself from contemporary fashion with its retro 1960s art design, and even from contemporary sexual politics, with its campy send-up of a world of "playboys" and sexy stewardesses. Instead, viewers were invited to revel in the distance, credited perhaps with additional knowledge of Hudson's homosexuality which made any pretense to real romance between the film couple a joke.[23]

The pleasure women take in chick flicks is not, it should also be noted, a purely self-centered or solitary one. Like shopping, going to the movies is often an experience women share, rather than pursue individually. The chick flick *Sleepless in Seattle* (1993) self-reflexively stages a typical chick-flick viewing: Meg Ryan and Rosie O'Donnell cry together over *An Affair to Remember* (1957) while sitting next to each other on a sofa eating popcorn in their pajamas. (In a companion scene, Rita Wilson tells the plot to her male dining companions, who dismiss it as a "chick movie" and mock her own weepy response by claiming to have cried at the end of *The Dirty Dozen*.) The shared experience of chick flicks is surely a major contributor to their appeal.

The principle of pleasure clearly complicates some of the more censorious views of chick flicks. Reactions are polarized and reflect more general and entrenched divisions in response to popular culture. On one side are Marxists including members of the Frankfurt School, such as Theodor Adorno and Max Horkheimer, who criticized the "culture industry" for cranking out products for profit and inspiring passivity rather than resistance to capitalism. On the other are those such as John Fiske who stress the power of the audience to interpret media texts and create alternative or resistant readings. We would argue that positions in between such readings are not only possible but preferable, given the increased complexity of contemporary culture in a late capitalist society. If chick flicks are influencing female viewers to accept rather than resist the societal conventions that restrict them, then surely such films are open to censure. But given the complexities of spectatorship and psychology found in response to the woman's film, it is just as likely that chick flicks allow women to enjoy imaginative possibilities or to indulge in vicarious experience that assists them in returning to the challenges that face them. In fact, it's only fair to note that in this heyday of postfeminist chick flicks, the number and percentage of women attending college, graduate schools, and professional schools continues to climb.[24]

Women's complex negotiation with film may explain, in part, the range of films commonly designated as chick flicks. Some, such as *Bridget Jones's Diary*, stress the audience's identification with an ordinary working girl, seeking love and companionship in contemporary London while sidestepping the intrusions of her family and relying instead on her friends for support. Others, such as *Gone with the Wind* (1939), present female characters far removed from the daily grind, offering escapist fantasies of fulfillment.

Considering chick flicks as a group emphasizes the fluidity of generic classification. Chick flicks do not clearly align themselves with any particular genre. Certainly some contemporary chick flicks can be traced back to 1930s and 1940s woman's films. Although these films cannot be tied to a single genre themselves, those most often cited as "classic" woman's films—films such as *Dark Victory* (1939), *Rebecca* (1940), *Now, Voyager* (1942), and *Mildred Pierce* (1945)—are all melodramas. The origins, then, of at least one type of chick flick may be found here: the melodramatic woman's film may well be the source of chick-flick "weepies" such as *Terms of Endearment* (1983), *Beaches* (1988), *The Hours* (2002), and *The Notebook* (2004).

The woman's film cannot, on the other hand, be considered the source of chick-flick romantic comedies, such as *Four Weddings and a Funeral* or *French Kiss* (1995). Seeking the roots of these films, we need to look to another early film genre, the screwball comedy. Early romantic comedies such as *It Happened One Night* and *Bringing Up Baby* (1938) although not created for a specifically female audience, did, like the woman's film, feature a female protagonist. As James Harvey has noted, the "screwball comedy … was a special kind of woman's game nearly always favoring the heroine to win" (287); it was the "witty heroine who had the edge"

(409). These classic comedies also focused on the dynamics of heterosexual romance, treating obstacles and impediments not with sentimentality but as sources of humor. The prevalence of remarriage storylines allowed characters, particularly females, to acknowledge sexual experience.[25] Dialogue in classic remarriage comedies such as *His Girl Friday* (1940) and *The Philadelphia Story* (1940) featured witty banter between the sexes about sexual desire and performance that, while cloaked in innuendo, may prefigure the frankness of contemporary chick-flick comedies from *When Harry Met Sally* (1989) with its fake female orgasm scene to *How to Lose a Guy in 10 Days* (2003), in which Andie (Kate Hudson) deliberately causes an argument by nicknaming her boyfriend's member "Princess Sophia."

Even romantic comedy and melodrama together, however, do not account for the full range of chick flicks, which includes the gun-toting heroines in *Thelma and Louise*, the strange mix of cannibalism and humor in *Fried Green Tomatoes*, the Cinderella story of *Pretty Woman*, the old-world elegance of *Pride and Prejudice* (2005)—and possibly the leather-clad futuristic revenge fantasy of Lara Croft.

As the popular guides referenced earlier suggest, chick flicks can, in the broadest sense, be defined as films that give women pleasure. We would add, as we have above, that they are overtly commercial films tailored to appeal to a female audience. In our view, it is no shame that the films are successful and popular—that doesn't necessarily mean that the women who view them are mindless dupes of the patriarchal Hollywood machine. Instead, we suggest that they are legitimate consumers of film, desirous of entertainment that either speaks to them in ways that they can identify with or that offers them tried and true fantasies. Rather than mindlessly pining after a dream they've been fed to keep them down, they are exercising their imaginations and forging connections, however tenuously, with images of more glamorous femininity and purer, simpler visions of success and independence. Other definitions of chick flicks are put forward by other viewers and scholars. Each, we believe, enriches the discussion in some way. No single definition is finally possible—nor, we contend, is it necessary.

NOTES

We would like to thank Myra Mendible and Karen Hollinger for their insightful comments on earlier drafts of this essay. Our thanks also go to Gerald Duchovnay who included a version of this essay in the Fall 2007 issue of *Post Script: Essays in Film and the Humanities*.

1. Rochelle Mabry, in her essay "About a Girl: Female Subjectivity and Sexuality in Contemporary 'Chick' Culture," was, to our knowledge, the first to use this term in an academic context.

2. Coca-Cola, for instance, advertises its Tab Energy drink as "fuel to be fabulous." Commercials on screen and online describe it as "the deliciously pink 5 calorie energy drink created specifically for women with a sense of style and purpose." The product's interactive website offers music, desktop images, e-greetings and "daily thoughts" with a decidedly feminine appeal, boldly colored pink.

3. See the Introduction to Ferriss and Young, *Chick Lit: The New Woman's Fiction* for information on the genesis and development of chick lit.

4. See Ferriss and Young (Intro.), and Mazza.

5. See Ferriss and Young, "Chicks, Girls and Choice."

6. See Henry.

7. This term is put forward by Chris Holmlund in the October 2005 issue of *Cinema Journal*. Holmlund also identifies two other forms of postfeminism: "grrrl" postfeminism which can be identified with

third-wave feminism, and "academic" postfeminism which she uses to refer to academic theorists "steeped in French, British, and American postmodern, postcolonial, post-structural, queer, (etc.), theory." Cris Mazza, by contrast, presents a compelling view of postfeminism as the next phase of feminism, a phase in which women no longer see themselves as victims of patriarchy, blaming and harboring anger towards men. Rather, postfeminist women accept responsibility for their choices and their lives. For further discussion of postfeminism see Baumgardner and Richards, Dicker and Piepmeir, Henry, Modleski, Roiphe, Rowe-Finkbeiner, Walker, and Wolf.

8. For this reason, *Cinema Journal* devoted an "In Focus" section to the subject in Winter 2005. In it, one prominent film scholar defines chick postfeminism as a "backlash against or a dismissal of the desirability for equality between women and men, in the workforce and in the family" (Holmlund). That seems to us a reductive view. Instead, it is more legitimate to note, as Yvonne Tasker and Diane Negra do, that "the continuing contradiction between women's personal and professional lives is more likely to be foregrounded in post-feminist discourse than the failure to eliminate either the pay gap or the burden of care between men and women." Overall, the essays included do a fine job of presenting the issues from feminist film scholars' perspectives.

9. Joanne Hollows and Rachel Moseley argue that such resistance to popular culture on the part of feminists may be disingenuous. They contend that "apart from women actively involved in the second-wave of feminism in the 1960s and 1970s, most people's initial knowledge and understanding of feminism has been formed within the popular and through representation. Rather than coming to consciousness through involvement in feminist movements, most people become conscious of feminism through the way it is represented in popular culture" (2).

10. See Ferriss and Young, "Chicks, Girls and Choice."

11. Madonna's 1980s postfeminist discourse is clearly a precursor to and major influence on the 1990s movement we focus on here. Her later works, however, such as *Erotica* (1992), *Body of Evidence* (1993), and her book *Sex* (1992) provide ideal examples of the 1990s' postfeminist aesthetic. See, for example, Humphrey and Fricke for favorable accounts of Madonna's sexual power politics. On the other hand, both Ariel Levy and Pamela Paul have argued that participants in "raunch culture" mistake sexual power for power itself.

12. Nor does it necessarily mean eschewing domestic pleasures. Joanne Hollows argues that "the domestic can't be simply celebrated as a site of feminine virtue or as a site of pre-feminist subordination. Instead, the meanings of the domestic, and domestic femininities, are contextual and historical and what operates as a site of subordination for some women may operate as the object of fantasy for others" (114).

13. Karen Hollinger's book, *In the Company of Women: Contemporary Female Friendship Films*, explores this issue fully.

14. It is worth noting that the modern ethnic Cinderella story of *Maid in Manhattan*, unlike the other films mentioned here, was clearly aimed not at Latina but at white audiences.

15. Laura Mulvey argued that classic cinema positions the female protagonist as the object of a male gaze, that she embodies "to-be-looked-at ness," and that female spectators find pleasure in narcissistic identification with her, imagining themselves in her position. Recent film theory has criticized this theory for reifying gender stereotypes and presuming an exclusively heterosexual model of desire.

For a succinct overview of complications introduced by consideration of lesbian spectatorship, see Hollinger, "Theorizing."

16. See Berenstein.

17. *Unconditional Love*, however, was not successful at the box office.

18. On chick lit's relation to fashion and consumerism, see Van Slooten.

19. See Eckert and Gaines.

20. By contrast, television appears to have more successfully targeted viewers to sell products. The online shopping site SeenON! (www.seenon.com) allows consumers to search for the clothing, furniture, cars and even paint colors featured in their favorite shows, such as *Desperate Housewives* and *Grey's Anatomy*. The film category features only a handful of recent releases, while the TV section organizes dozens of shows by network.

21. See MediaChannel's chart for a compelling visual representation of the six major media corporations and their holdings.

22. It may also be worth observing that at least one recent film, *The Devil Wears Prada*, based on Lauren Weisberger's chick-lit *roman à clef* about her stint working for Anna Wintour at *Vogue*, holds fashionistas up to ridicule.

23. Still, it should be noted that the film was not a box office success, finding its primary audience through a cult appeal to gay men and academic women. The suggestion here may be that the distancing mainstream chick-flick audiences will embrace has a limit.

24. The National Center for Education Statistics in the US reports in *The Condition of Education 2006* that "At the graduate and professional level, as among undergraduates, women are outpacing men, in raw numbers and in particular fields. … Women now earn more degrees than do men in a range of fields once overwhelmingly male … and women earn as many degrees as men in such previously male-dominated disciplines as medicine and law, the report says. A generation ago, women earned only a quarter to a third of those degrees. And women have maintained their dominance in fields they have long flocked to, such as education" ("Enrollments Keep Rising").

25. The term "remarriage comedy" comes from Stanley Cavell.

WORKS CITED

Adorno, Theodor W. and Max Horkheimer. *Dialectic of Enlightenment*. 1947. Trans. John Cumming. New York: Verso, 1997.

Ashby, Justine. "Postfeminism in the British Frame." *Cinema Journal* 44.2 (2005): 127–33. <http://muse.jhu.edu/journals/cinema_journal/v044.2ashby.html>.

Basinger, Jeanine. *A Woman's View: How Hollywood Spoke to Women, 1930–1960*. New York: Knopf, 1993.

Baumgardner, Jennifer and Amy Richards. *Manifesta: Young Women, Feminism, and the Future*. New York: Farrar, 2000.

Berenstein, Rhona J. "Adaptation, Censorship, and Audiences of Questionable Type: Lesbian Sightings in *Rebecca* (1940) and *The Uninvited* (1944)." *Cinema Journal* 37.3 (Spring 1998): 16–37.

Bernard, Jami. *Chick Flicks: A Movie Lover's Guide to the Movies Women Love*. New York: Citadel, 1997.

Berry, Jo and Angie Errigo. *Chick Flicks: Movies Women Love*. London: Orion, 2004.

Cavell, Stanley. *Pursuits of Happiness: The Hollywood Comedy of Remarriage*. Cambridge, MA: Harvard University Press, 1981.

Cook, Pam. "No Fixed Address: The Woman's Picture from *Outrage* to *Blue Steel*." In *Contemporary Hollywood Cinema*. Ed. Steve Neale and Murray Smith. London and New York: Routledge, 1998: 229–46.

Dicker, Rory and Alison Piepmeier. *Catching a Wave: Reclaiming Feminism for the 21st Century*. Boston: Northeastern University Press, 2003.

Doane, Mary Ann. *The Desire to Desire: The Woman's Film of the 1940s*. Bloomington: Indiana University Press, 1987.

Eckert, Charles. "The Carole Lombard in Macy's Window." *Quarterly Review of Film and Video* 3 (1978): 1–21.

"Enrollments Keep Rising, and Most Are by Women, Says Annual Report on Condition of Education." *The Chronicle of Higher Education*, June 2, 2006. <http://chronicle.com/daily/2006/06/2006060205n.htm>.

Ferriss, Suzanne and Mallory Young. "Chicks, Girls and Choice: Redefining Feminism." *Junctures: The Journal for Thematic Dialogue* 6 (2006): 87–97.

_____"Introduction." In *Chick Lit: The New Woman's Fiction*. Ed. Suzanne Ferriss and Mallory Young. New York: Routledge, 2006: 1–13.

Fiske, John. *Understanding Popular Culture*. London: Unwin Hyman, 1998.

Fricke, Erika. "Material Girls: Behind the Seams of Beloved Pop Icons Dolly Parton and Madonna." *Bitch: Feminist Response to Pop Culture* 32 (Summer 2006): 62–67.

Gabbard, Krin. *Black Magic: White Hollywood and African American Culture*. New Brunswick, NJ: Rutgers University Press, 2004.

_____"Cinema and Media Studies: Snapshot of an Emerging Discipline." *The Chronicle of Higher Education*, Feb. 17, 2006. <http://chronicle.com/weekly/v52/i24/24b01401.htm>.

Gaines, Jane. "War, Women and Lipstick: Fan Mags in the Forties." *Heresies* 18 (1986): 42–47.

_____"The Queen Christina Tie-Ups: Convergence of Shop Windows and Screen." *Quarterly Review of Film and Video* 11 (1989): 35–60.

Harvey, James. *Romantic Comedy in Hollywood, from Lubitsch to Sturges*. 1987. New York: Da Capo, 1998.

Haskell, Molly. *From Reverence to Rape: The Treatment of Women in the Movies*. 1973. 2nd ed. Chicago: University of Chicago Press, 1987.

Henry, Astrid. *Not My Mother's Sister: Generational Conflict and Third-Wave Feminism*. Bloomington: Indiana University Press, 2004.

Hollinger, Karen. *In the Company of Women: Contemporary Female Friendship Films*. Minneapolis: University of Minnesota Press, 1998.

_____"Theorizing Mainstream Female Spectatorship: The Case of the Popular Lesbian Film." *Cinema Journal* 37.2 (Winter 1998): 3–17.

Hollows, Joanne and Rachel Moseley (eds). *Feminism in Popular Culture*. Oxford: Berg, 2006.

Hollows, Joanne. "Can I Go Home Yet? Feminism, Post-feminism and Domesticity." In *Feminism in Popular Culture*. Ed. Joanne Hollows and Rachel Moseley. Oxford: Berg, 2006: 97–118.

Holmlund, Chris. "Postfeminism from A to G." *Cinema Journal* 44.2 (2005). <http://muse.jhu.edu/journals/cinema_journal/v044.2holmlund.html>.

Humphrey, Michelle. "Bare Necessity: On Porn and Progress with Author Carly Milne." *Bitch: Feminist Response to Pop Culture* 32 (Summer 2006): 58–61.

Just Like Heaven Script—Dialogue Transcript. Drew's Script-O-Rama. <http://www.script-o-rama.com/movie_scripts/j/just-like-heaven-script-transcript. html>.

Kabir, Shameem. *Daughters of Desire: Lesbian Representations in Film.* London: Cassell, 1998.

Levy, Ariel. *Female Chauvinist Pigs: Women and the Rise of Raunch Culture.* New York: Free Press, 2005.

Mayne, Judith. *Cinema and Spectatorship.* New York and London: Routledge, 1993.

Mazza, Cris. "Who's Laughing Now? A Short History of Chick Lit and the Perversion of a Genre." In *Chick Lit: The New Woman's Fiction.* Ed. Suzanne Ferriss and Mallory Young. New York: Routledge, 2006: 17–28.

MediaChannel.org. "Ultra Concentrated Media: Top Selling Brands." <http://www.mediachannel.org/ownership/chart.shtml>.

Mizejewski, Linda. "Dressed to Kill: Postfeminist Noir." *Cinema Journal* 44.2 (2005). <http://muse.jhu.edu/journals/cinema_journal/v044.2mizejewski.html>.

Modleski, Tania. *Feminism without Women: Culture and Criticism in a Post-feminist Age.* New York: Routledge, 1991.

Mulvey, Laura. "Visual Pleasure and Narrative Cinema." In *Feminism and Film Theory.* Ed. Constance Penley. New York: Routledge, 1988: 57–68.

Paul, Pamela. *Pornified: How Pornography Is Transforming Our Lives, Our Relationships, and Our Families.* New York: Times Books, 2005.

Roiphe, Katie. *The Morning After: Sex, Fear, and Feminism on Campus.* Boston: Little, Brown, 1993.

Rowe-Finkbeiner, Kristin. *The F-Word: Feminism in Jeopardy: Women, Politics, and the Future.* Emeryville, CA: Seal, 2004.

Stacey, Jackie. *Star Gazing: Hollywood Cinema and Female Spectatorship.* London and New York: Routledge, 1994.

Stoller, Debbie. "Sex and the Thinking Girl." In *The Bust Guide to the New Girl Order.* Ed. Marcelle Karp and Debbie Stoller. New York: Penguin, 1999: 74–84.

Tasker, Yvonne and Diane Negra. "In Focus: Postfeminism and Contemporary Media Studies." *Cinema Journal* 44.2 (2005). <http://muse.jhu.edu/journals/cinema_journal/v044.2tasker.html>.

Taormino, Tristan. "Political Smut Makers: Feminist Porn Takes Center Stage at Historic Event." *The Village Voice,* June 8, 2006. <http://www.villagevoice.com/people/0624,taormino,73480,24.html>.

Van Slooten, Jessica Lyn. "Fashionably Indebted: Conspicuous Consumption, Fashion, and Romance in Sophie Kinsella's Shopaholic Trilogy." In *Chick Lit: The New Woman's Fiction.* Ed. Suzanne Ferriss and Mallory Young. New York: Routledge, 2006: 219–38.

Veblen, Thorstein. *Theory of the Leisure Class.* 1899. Introduction by Robert Lekachman. London: Penguin, 1994.

Walker, Natasha. *The New Feminism.* London: Little, Brown, 1998.

Wolf, Naomi. *Fire With Fire: The New Female Power and How it Will Change the 21st Century.* New York: Random, 1993.

White, Patricia. *unInvited: Classical Hollywood Cinema and Lesbian Representability.* Bloomington and Indianapolis: Indiana University Press, 1999.

CHAPTER 2
ETHNICITY AND REPRESENTATION IN US MEDIA

EDITOR'S INTRODUCTION

White patriarchal capitalism is a concept that identifies the major determination of influence and power in the United States. It is based on a long-standing acceptance that the descendants of Europeans who traveled across the Atlantic to colonize what is now called the Americas had the right to claim the land for their European sovereigns—despite the fact that the land was already populated. Indigenous peoples were forced into service to the foreign sovereigns, their wealth, lands, and freedoms confiscated. The term also refers to the economic system enforced by the colonizers. Finally the term recognized a system whereby males take precedence and hold control over women and children. White patriarchal capitalism continues to privilege white males of wealth and property. While white patriarchal capitalism prevails as the dominant system in the United States, it is frequently critiqued as an outmoded and prejudicial system.

Media institutions in the United States, like many other organizations, have been long dominated by white males, and this domination has privileged the values and ideologies of the group. Media critics evaluate the stories told in the media and work to balance the interests of media producers with the interests of the diverse audiences who participate in their storytelling.

MANIFEST DESTINY

In the 19th century, Manifest Destiny was a widely held belief in the United States that European American settlers were destined to expand throughout the continent. The justification for the colonization of the peoples and lands of the Americas was based on what were argued to be the superior religious beliefs and customs of Europe. The "right" of the colonizers to bring European-style "civilization" to the western wilderness was argued in terms of economics, education, and religion. The reality was that enforcement required violence, brutality, and the need to dehumanize those who had first rights to the land. The peoples who occupied the coveted territory were described as "savages" in newspaper stories and dime novels, and eventually in Hollywood movies and US radio and television programming.

Western films were a popular genre of the early Hollywood film industry. These films introduced the silent film narrative to audiences around the world. *The Great Train Robbery* (1903), directed by Edwin S.

Porter (and shot in New Jersey), helped establish the western territories of the United State as a place where those both inside and outside the law used guns to establish superiority. Robbers used guns and explosives to capture a passenger train and murder innocent passengers and railway employees at will. In the narrative of *The Great Train Robbery*, the basic binary shows those who are law abiding in competition with those who are not. A town posse tracks and surprises the robbers, shooting them as they recover the treasure that was being transported by rail.

Women and children play minor roles in the film; a young girl discovers the unconscious telegraph operator and runs to alert the peaceful townspeople, who are square dancing in the town hall. The European-American male townspeople are accustomed to civilized endeavors such as dancing, but are also capable of the manly and violent task of tracking and killing those who transgress.

The classic westerns directed by John Ford frequently featured John Wayne as the quintessential western hero. In Ford's westerns we see a complex querying of the relationship between what is identified as civilization and the violence that is required to maintain it. In *Stagecoach* (1939), John Wayne plays the role of the "Ringo Kid," a convicted murderer who has escaped from jail with the intention of killing the men who killed his brother. While conventional wisdom would indicate that "the Kid" is a villain, he proves to be just the opposite. He becomes instrumental in fighting the historic Apache chieftain Geronimo and proves his "civilized" status by deciding not to abandon the group when he sees smoke signals indicating an attack is imminent. Ringo's attachment to family, both through his loyalty to his brother and his affection for one of the coach passengers, Dallas (whom he asks to marry), proves him heroic. The combination of both violence and identification with and acceptance of social norms has identified the hero of American films from the beginning of film history.

In *The Searchers* (1956), John Ford and John Wayne portray a more expansive interpretation of the western hero. Ethan Edwards, played by Wayne, no longer young, is a jaded and weary soldier returning from the Civil War; his life has been defined by violence. Ethan finds that his home in Texas has been raided by native tribesmen and his niece kidnapped. His search for Debbie reveals evidence of the atrocities of the "savages" who stole her. His own violent behaviors are justified against the atrocities of the "others." The stereotypical and demeaning portrayal of Native and Latin American characters in *Stagecoach* and *The Searchers* are carefully juxtaposed with families who posit a white, European model of acceptable behavior traveling west.

DECONSTRUCTION

Film criticism looks at the narrative, or story, of a film and questions the certainty of produced meaning. In looking at the way the story is structured we ask how meaning is produced and whether its production reinforces certain values while deemphasizing others. Critics work to take apart the structure of the film to better understand the intended meaning of the story and make obvious that intention. In order to justify the extraordinary violence that was required against native peoples as European Americans forced their claims on the western land mass of North America, the natives who lost their lands, their ability to sustain their cultures and feed their children, were portrayed as savage beasts who needed to be conquered. Rather than portraying native people fairly as defending their homes, they are shown as destroying the homes of the colonizers. Rather than positioning the tribal warriors as defending their wives and children, they are shown as brutal rapists of European wives and mothers.

In *Stagecoach* we rarely see the face of an Apache brave; the great majority of screen time is dedicated to the faces of the European Americans on the coach. The Mexican American who operates the rest stop is heavily accented and negatively portrayed as a coward. The Comanche chief in *The Searchers* is named Scar and played by a brooding European American actor.

HEGEMONY

The concept of hegemony outlines the process by which the elite who generate a message use that message to persuade others to their way of thinking. This process describes how the media uses narrative to persuade the majority to support the ideologies of the privileged. Advertisers persuade audiences to buy products they do not need to achieve an advantage they are unlikely to attain. For instance a beautiful woman dressed in an expensive evening gown drapes herself around a man who is using a particular brand of breath mint/beer/car/deodorant as the unlikely prize for its use.

Hegemonic processes offer strategies that negatively lead to internalized discrimination and symbolic annihilation. In westerns, the impact of white domination of the west (and the film industry) teaches audiences negative attitudes toward Native and Mexican Americans. The stereotyping and negative portrayals foster discrimination toward our fellow citizens. Symbolic annihilation describes narratives that completely leave out groups from any portrayal at all. African and Asian Americans are barely mentioned in classic westerns, despite estimates that over 20 percent of western cowboys were African Americans. The railroad featured in *The Great Train Robbery* makes no reference to the Asian American laborers who helped build it.

TEXTUAL READING

We are all literate readers of the signs and understand well the intended meaning of the dominant cultural products of the United States. Having watched, listened to, and applauded thousands of hours of fairy tales, music videos, and Hollywood-produced television and films, we have earned the golden ticket that ensures full participation in the messages and meanings of the dominant culture they reinforce. Such literacy is powerful, but the power does not stop with understanding. Literacy allows us to question and review the proffered meaning and to disagree. Theorists have recognized three ways that we read the media messages to which we are exposed.

DOMINANT READINGS

A dominant reading is the reading of the media text as intended by the author. When we watch a film, read a novel, or listen to a political speech, we evaluate the meaning being signaled against our own value system, our own worldview. If the intended meaning coincides with how we see the world, and we agree with what is being offered, we accept the intended or dominant meaning of the author. So if you truly believe that someday your prince will come based on your good deeds and excellent cleaning skills, *Cinderella* is a film that you can accept wholeheartedly.

OPPOSITIONAL READINGS

When the text we are exposed to goes against our core values and we disagree with its premise and its arguments, we develop an oppositional reading of the text. A Native American watching a classic western like *Stagecoach* may find John Wayne's Ringo Kid an unacceptable depiction of an American hero, and instead see Geronimo as the hero. An oppositional reading can be formulated by positioning Geronimo as the hero of Stagecoach and the Ringo Kid as an unwanted invader of the territory of the Apache.

NEGOTIATED READINGS

Most texts offer ideas and positions, some of which we can agree with and some of which we find unacceptable or absurd. A fast paced-action film might offer a hero you may want around when being attacked by zombies or Martian invaders; however, you may not find such a person an acceptable partner with whom to raise a family. When mediated stories present us with the presentation of characters and story lines that go against our sense of self as gendered beings we often respond with oppositional or negotiated readings.

MEDIA IMPACTS HOW WE SEE THE WORLD AND HOW WE SEE OURSELVES

While family, friends, school, church, and community help shape who we are and how we see ourselves, media also has a strong impact on our worldview and how we see ourselves in relation to others.

"The Whiteness of of the Rings" by Sean Redmond and "Advertising Whiteness" by Entman and Rojecki, describe media's privileging of "whiteness" over ethnic "others" as a form of hegemony.

In "Hip Hop Is Not Responsible for Sexism," Tricia Rose queries the source of sexist images in the media and deconstructs assumptions about the roots of sexism in our culture. Blaming the lyrics and images of hip hop videos, rather than querying systemic sexism for sexist lyrics and images is analogous to blaming Native Americans for the violence colonizers perpetrated against them. While not condoning the sexism often found in music videos, Rose points to the hegemonic sexist culture that inundates us all on a daily basis and the lack of education afforded clearly talented and intelligent young rappers. She questions the value of blaming the victims for an excessive response to victimization.

In "Chica Flicks," Myra Mendible considers the tension created when romantic comedies, or "chick flicks," primarily featuring middle-class, college-educated, white female protagonists, are populated with working-class Latina heroes. In his essay "Boyz, Boyz, Boyz," Keith Harris takes the query further in examining what happens to the representation of "blackness" when approached by black writers and directors.

READING 3
THE WHITENESS OF THE RINGS

By Sean Redmond

In this essay on *The Lord of the Rings: The Fellowship of the Ring* I want to explore the way whiteness is metaphorically represented as a contradictory subjectivity that is as much about absence and negation as it is about racial power and idealization. On one level, *The Lord of the Rings: The Fellowship of the Ring* is saturated in racial metaphors and imagery that work to position whiteness as a universal ideal and Otherness as a horrifying and destructive force that comes into being through a monstrous form of reproduction. Idealized images of whiteness are found right across the film: in certain key forms of embodiment and costume; in the stylistic streams of bright light that bathe the good, the innocent, and the pure; in the Edenic, utopian natural settings; and in and through a number of the central characters, particularly Arwen and Galadriel, whose purity and innocence light up the screen in a well-choreographed form of heavenly white female beauty.

Evil, by contrast, is not only symbolically Other in the film, but racially encoded in the corporeality and actions of the Orcs and the Uruks. Created below ground in the smelting fires and liquid metal of an unnatural and polluted industrial hell, they are white stereotypes of the savage and dangerous Negro—all-body bucks who will fuck and fight their way through white communities if given the chance. The racial politics of the film, then, is also often played out in its spatial arrangements, with a high/low and rural/city binary opposition in place. Above ground, man, beast, water, earth and air are, or can be, in perfect, idyllic unison: below ground, chaos reigns, as hordes of barbaric "negroes" threaten to take flight. Frodo and Sam leave the shires—or their white rural Eden—and head off to the "city", where they are in constant danger from ghetto dwellers dead-set on ruining their quest.

However, *The Lord of the Rings: The Fellowship of the Ring* is also more contradictory in its representation of whiteness, and more critical of particular forms of whiteness as they are given representational definition. The film posits that too much whiteness—what Bonnett would call "hyper-whiteness"—is a dangerous, ultimately destructive subjectivity.[1] The two key figures in this respect are Saruman and Arwen. Saruman is excessively white (with white robes and long, flowing white hair) who has let the power that whiteness brings him *go to his head*. He is a death-like figure, a living corpse, so close is he to the absence effect at the centre of this type of cerebral-inflected whiteness. Saruman is a sorcerer whose alchemy and science has allowed him to reproduce, colonise, and reincarnate those slave negroes who will actually threaten the very survival of the white species. As such, he is doubly dangerous: he is incapable of his own reproduction (since he lives in/through his head) and he begets a species that threatens the annihilation of the white race.

Arwen is the personification of white female beauty: she is made up and out of light and is pure and innocent. However, such radiance is also imagined to be a type of death for her: a type of ephemeral spirituality that has little (sexed) flesh to it—something she so clearly yearns for. This will not do for Arwen: she desires Aragorn and will willingly sacrifice her immortality (here read idealized whiteness) for love, sex, and intimacy with him.

In more general terms, when whiteness is made symbolically visible it is essentially connected to the highest ideals of human civilization: to purity, innocence, rationalism, naturalism, and to the "higher" motifs of Christianity, such as ascending angels and the concept of "spirit." However, this purity in spirit and thought is also considered to be death-like because it necessarily brings white people closer to, or in touch with, the lack of life, corporeality, or sex drive that such higher ideals brings to bear on them as white subjects. When one reaches the highest ideals of whiteness, one literally disappears into the ether: in fact, one is already dead, since "the very things that makes us white endangers the reproduction of whiteness."[2] In *The Lord of the Rings: The Fellowship of the Ring* it is through the figures of Saruman and Arwen that this life-and-death struggle is principally played out and arguably to devastating consequences.

Nonetheless, it is the "one true ring" that seems to best represent the contradictory nature of whiteness in the film. On the one hand, the power of the ring to make those who wear it invisible and the vision it gives those who possess it to control past, present and future, speak of the racial power of whiteness itself; the power to be not seen as a racial category at all; the power to create a vision of the world in one's own image of whiteness.[3] The ring, in effect, comes to stand for, is a symbol of, the racial privilege that whiteness secures for (its) people. It reproduces the I/eye of whiteness or that master vision and metasubjectivity which holds the centre ground of identity formation. At the same time, the ring itself confirms how whiteness is itself a potentially terrifying and species-destructive subjectivity. Those who possess the ring, those who are enamoured by its power, become pathological: they suffer a form of white schizophrenia—desperate for the power that whiteness brings, and yet terrified by the death that will come with its possession.

In *Lord of the Rings: The Fellowship of the Ring* there is an absent/present paradox at the core of much of the representation of idealized whiteness, constantly threatening to tear it apart as a possible or ultimately desirable form of subjectivity. The more *present* or visible white people become in the film, the more culturally ideal they appear, the more *absent* or death-like/death producing they are.

IDEALIZED WHITENESS: TERRIFYING NEGROPHOBIA

A great many of what are supposedly the most prized of human qualities are symbolized through a visual aesthetic and a signification chain that encodes idealized white people with the highest attributes available to humankind. For example, one can find the extraordinary nature of whiteness in the stories of ephemeral, ascending angels; the hi-tech laboratories of scientific invention; in the embodiment of white-haired, white-coated inventors and scientists; and in the "make-up" of heavenly film stars who "light up" the silver screen—situating this iconic version of whiteness as the highest, brightest racial ideal available to humankind and one, therefore, it is culturally enunciated, that should be reached for.

In the main, whiteness is brought into the racially concrete through highly positive connotations, manifest in semiotically rich images that fill the cultural world with extraordinary visions of the power and the beauty of whiteness. Whiteness is located as a source of light: reflective, bright, shiny, and positive. This idea of light, of purity and "goodness" seems to be repeated, in a series of inter-textual relays, across a number of representations. For example, in terms of Western culture, especially in Western myth and fairy-tale, it is white skin, white body, blond hair, blue eyes which signifies radiant beauty, and in particular, it is idealized white femininity which resonates at the core of the beauty myth.[4] Idealized white women are bathed in and permeated by light: it streams through them and falls on to them from above. It is light that makes them glow, appear angelic, heavenly, and, ultimately, to be not-of-this-world, heavenly absences rather than fleshed beings.

In *Lord of the Rings: The Fellowship of the Ring* one can argue that both Arwen and Galadriel appear as heavenly creatures: as idealized white women who radiate light. They are narrativized in symbolically loaded white settings, with carefully selected iconography, that uses both the colour white to connote ideas of purity, innocence and radiance, and high key light to bathe them in an imaginary halo that marks them out as translucent, ephemeral, spiritual beings.

Arwen enters the film in a stream of bright, white light at the moment that Frodo is being taken over: he is soon to pass "into the shadowland" where he will become a spectre, a living corpse. Frodo's face is itself chalk-like: in fact the closer he gets to death the whiter he becomes, confirming the close proximity that exists between whiteness and the figure of the corpse. Arwen's entrance pours light onto Frodo's face and in his feverish state she appears as an apparition. Her "ideal" light momentarily brings him back into a state of near well-being. Initially there is no grounded corporeality to her: she is just an expanse of white light that floats towards Frodo. Chamber/choral music accompanies Arwen's arrival and in the Edenic setting of a hushed, lush green forest, she is enchanted and enchanting. As she moves further into view she is given greater physical definition: she has blue eyes, long, flowing black hair, wears a white satin dress and a white (gold) pendent that hangs from her neck. Nonetheless, a striking back light continues to illuminate her so that the very edges of her body, face and hair continue to glow, and this glow fills the scene with a not-of-this-world ethereality. Light is also central to this scene in the way it is used as a metaphor to keep Frodo away from the Shadowlands, and to differentiate between good and evil. Arwen softly calls to Frodo, "hear my voice: come back to the light", and in her "race against time" horse ride back to her kingdom, she is chased by the Black Riders/ringwraiths—diabolical henchmen for Lord Sauron. Arwen defeats the Riders at the river crossing, the boundary to Rivendell, her Elf home, by creating a tidal wave of white horses who take them down stream. *Lord of the Rings: The Fellowship of the Ring* is full of such light/ dark, day/night, white/black binary oppositions, with light/day/white the generally favoured ideological position—something I will briefly return to later in the essay. Galadriel enters *Lord of the Rings: The Fellowship of the Ring* in a strikingly similar way to Arwen: in an expanse of flooding white light and radiant white clothes before she is given corporeal characteristics. However, her physical introduction has been preceded by Gimli's description of her as an "elf witch of terrible power … all who look at her fall under her spell." When Galadriel emerges from the aura of her own being, she has long, blonde hair and blue eyes, and she is given a penetrating stare that sees through people—concretized through her telepathy which grants her direct access to people's subconscious. Galadriel, then, is also a white witch, in contrast to the black art of Lord Sauron.

Nonetheless, Galadriel's entrance occurs in a setting itself imbued with real spiritual meaning. She enters the film at the apex of a network of ornate, interconnecting bridges and passageways—all of them flooded with light—so that she stands at the head of what is a glowing cathedral. Frodo and the other Fellows of the Ring have had to move from the low to the high to meet her: rising up in what can be read as a mini-ascension scene. Galadriel's heavenly, spiritual appearance, then, is also confirmed because of the film's spatial positioning of her.

In summary, Arwen and Galadriel are idealized white women: an idealization that, by corporeal and symbolic definition, only thin white females can achieve. The film suggests that the glow that passes between them and through them is a natural essence that belongs to them, and to their made-of-nothing, or very little, white bodies. Suffused in this glow, caught up in all this innocence and tranquility, they appear to be able to float right off the screen. In fact, Galadriel seems to walk on air and travel through time because of the way she is enigmatically captured. In cultural terms, thin bodies do this *passing through* best because there is not "much to them" in the first place, their lines and shapes economical. But with glow, with haze and shimmer alongside, above, beyond, and flowing over the skin, the thinness makes it easier for the body borders to be seen to disappear, or float upwards.

But not only this: Arwen and Galadriel's thinness produces the sense that their bodies have been kept natural, unpolluted, and pure. The implied abstinence suggests containment and self-control. In this oscillating mix of fluidity and yet self-control, of translucence and yet fixity, the cultural significance/importance of the idealized, thin white woman is realized. She is body that is self-contained and controlled, and through such self-regulation marked by abstinence (nothing, or very little, enters her body) she is pure; by being pure she naturally glows, and in glowing the very minimal borders of her body are allowed to float away into a heavenly state of grace. Arwen is virginal, pure (although as I will go onto argue this is a death for her, since she loves and wants Aragorn), and Galadriel refuses Frodo's offer of possession of the ring—something that would have turned her inside out, white-to-black, innocent to sinful, according to the fantasy scene in which she plays out the scenario of having accepted the ring.

The star biographies of both Liv Tyler (Arwen) and Cate Blanchett (Galadriel) are important here. Liv Tyler is often found in films that foreground and problematize her purity and innocence. In *Stealing Beauty* (Bertolucci, 1996), for example, she plays the part of Lucy Harmon who visits Italy to lose her virginity. Liv Tyler, then, brings to the part of Arwen a character history of absent/present paradoxes that she is found resisting or transgressing. Similarly, Cate Blanchett often appears in films in which she is identified with the figure of the white corpse: alabaster white, cold and calculating, haunted, and engineered by her own death instinct. In *Elizabeth* (Kapur, 1998) this is brilliantly played out in the way that she paints herself white to appear as the Virginal Queen, only confirming her closeness to death in the process.

Versions of whiteness and idealized whiteness find their way into many of the core representations in the film. The Shires are rural, middle "England" and Frodo and Sam innocent white children who have no knowledge of the multiracial ghettos that exist outside their rolling hills and valleys, but who, nonetheless, have to travel there if the sanctity of "home" is to be protected and preserved. Frodo, in effect, is charged with securing for white people their continued privileged position at the centre of things—if (when) he throws the ring into the fires of Mount Doom, light will flood back into the world and the racial purity of the Shires will be ensured. Rivendell, the Enchanted Wood, the Aryan (blond, blue-eyed) Elves, Legolas, Gandalf, are places and people of (racial) purity and innocence, largely free of the shadows and darkness that stretches into the other lands and cities, and out of people/monsters who are less securely white and Other in the film.

Lord of the Rings: The Fellowship of the Ring produces its own racial hierarchy of whiteness. The whitest of white people are those who are the purest or who hold positions of power in the film—Gandalf, Saruman, Galadriel, Arwen—while those who are darker, more ruddy in complexion, more explicitly corporeal, are charged with undertaking the quest and/or threatening it. These white identities are also class-inflected. Spirit, purity and power become the markers of the refined upper class or nobility, while nature, earth/dirt, and primitive urges become the ideological indicator of the working class.

Bonnett writes about the "symbolic production of whiteness in nineteenth-century Britain," suggesting that white hue was pivotal in indicating the status and power differences between the gentlemanly bourgeoisie, who were located as hyper white and "almost superhuman," and the urban working class, who were located as "marginal" to this idealized paradigm.[5] The urban working class were in fact made to appear "dark", to have some of the colour of the primitive negro. The conflation between race and social class added symbolic weight to the idea that the working classes were themselves primitive, animalistic, and mindless.

There is a degree of this class and racial conflation in *The Lord of the Rings: The Fellowship of the Ring*. Gollum appears as a stereotype of the gentile Eastern European Jew: bony, sickly and sinewy, driven by a desire to possess or own the ring (here read the economic power that such jewellery, or gold, would bring him). Gimli, the "celtic" dwarf miner, is working-class embodied: mesamorphic, brutish, physically "dirty", crude, with traces of the simian in his movements. However, it is the unnatural and cannibalistic Orcs (fallen Elves) and Uruks who best demonstrate the film's racial hierarchy and suggested negrophobia. In particular, it is through the figure of Lurtz that *Lord of the Rings: The Fellowship of the Ring* reproduces the racist figure of the "bad buck" or the all-body negro brute, who is "over-sexed and savage, violent and frenzied as [he] lust[s] for white flesh".[6]

Lurtz, an Uruk-hai, is begot in a monstrous birthing scene. Industrial sounding music scores the *mise-en-scène* as a delicate white butterfly floats perilously over a large, burning gash in the earth. Under Gandalf's influence, the butterfly makes its way down into the semi-darkness: into the bowels of this flaming abyss, again confirming the contrast between light and dark, good and evil in the film. Tunnels, walkways, bridges, scaffolding, black holes and flame towers fill the underground landscape with the look and sound of large-scale industrial production. Steel is being forged: helmets and swords are being produced, and rivers of glowing, red hot metal pour forth. Orcs rush about, dirty, bruised, snarling, and unable to speak: revelling in the pain of their own tortuous subjugation, as far from the idealized perfection of the Aryan Elves as one could get. Nonetheless, at the same time, ancient trees are being cut up and thrown into the "engines" that fuel this inferno, and there is an organic, if oozing texture, to the landscape. A violent, ugly form of "nature" is found underground: one that when it is conjoined with the industrial seems to seed the violent births that are about to take place there.

At the very bottom of this underground pit, one finds a bubbling birthing pool of thick mud. At the exact moment Saruman appears to marvel at and direct proceedings, an Orc reaches into the mud to reveal a twisted face pressed beneath a soiled sac. In a terrifying reconstruction of the human birthing scenario, a brutish figure roars into existence, ripping open the sac it was contained within, killing the Orc who had moments earlier acted as his midwife. The sheer size, strength and ethnic identity of this man-beast are quickly established. Shot in close-up, his blazing nostrils, dreadlock hair and animalistic posturing directly recalls the stereotype of the all-body/no-brain black buck of racist imagination. This is confirmed later in the film when such "beasts" adorn themselves with tribal paint and leave the pit to scour the earth in search of white man-flesh.

At the core of *Lord of the Rings: The Fellowship of the Ring*, then, is a story of the fear of racial mixing and miscegenation: the black and bestial Uruk-hai uncontrollably reproduce themselves and leave their underground ghetto on a mission to destroy middle England and the white communities that live there. Frodo foresees such a destruction of the Shires in the mirror that Galadriel asks him to stare into. Frodo's journey into the heart of darkness is to protect white people from such species destruction. If he fails, whiteness fails.

Nonetheless, white people are under threat in the film in another sense, and the racial hierarchy constructed in the film is itself faulty and subject to internal contradictions. In *Lord of the Rings: The Fellowship of the Ring* whiteness is haunted by its own definition of perfection, by its own death instinct, and by those who are less securely white but have a vitality or corporeality that idealized white people crave.

THE DEATH OF WHITENESS

In terms of representation, the white body exists in a paradoxical state of being. On the one hand, the white body is represented as not-flesh and natural absence, or, as Dyer puts it, "what is absent from white is any *thing*; in other words, material reality".[7] On the other hand, the white body is subjected to and the object of a virulent construction process which attempts to make the white body ideal through identifying the absence quality of white flesh with the most prized attributes in dominant culture, such as purity, spirituality, and "light." In essence, this rather perverse form of white embodiment ensures that white bodies are seen and yet not seen as white bodies, and that this transparency *and* simultaneous corporeality has to be "manufactured" or put into representation to ensure its ideological meanings are rendered comprehensible, cohesive, and culturally dominant. However, this putting into representation of the contradictory nature of whiteness has the potential to not only draw attention to its inherently unstable and potentially unsatisfactory nature, but to reveal it to be as much a living tyranny of absence and negation for those who come to embody it, as an empowering and empowered subjectivity.

In *Lord of the Rings: The Fellowship of the Ring* Arwen seems to be suffering such a living tyranny: identified as an angelic, immortal creature, she yearns only for real and lasting intimacy with Aragorn. The spirit and purity that defines Arwen is one she wants to reject: her immortality—her idealized whiteness—is death-like since it forbids sexual relations and reproduction. As she laments to Aragorn, "I choose a mortal life," a life that is grounded, rooted, embodied, and therefore, in subtextual terms, not ideally white.

This desire is actually represented in corporeal terms: Arwen is the one who takes Frodo to his safety because she is the faster rider; and her sexualized body constantly threatens to sully or taint the very innocence that she is connected to—her body, her desire, is always there as a troubling presence in the film. In the courtship scene with Aragorn (set at night, under moonlight, on a bridge between two worlds) she is at her most physical and sexually charged: her body breathes, heaves, is full of curves, and it is as if her body (the heart-beat, the racing temperature, the first kiss) has more to offer her than the ultimately rather sterile spirit, absence, and grace of idealized white womanhood.

Asexual reproduction is central here, because it draws into the narrative one of the key signifiers, one of the key contradictions of what it means to be ideally white. To be ideally white is to be above and beyond those primitive, and impure, sexual and reproductive drives that "emerge" in and between heterosexual, sexed individuals. To be an ideally white male is to have resisted, denied, or negated the "dark drives" of sexuality.[8] To be a hyper-white female is not " … to have such drives in the first place … The model for white women is the Virgin Mary, a pure vessel for reproduction who is unsullied by the dark drives that reproduction entails."[9] Arwen is full of these "dark drives" and as such her idealized female whiteness is constantly under threat.

Galadriel is also important here in terms of the way her idealized whiteness also hangs on an unhealthy life/death paradox. However, in the film Galadriel remains a figure of spirit and light and as such is free of the corporeal desire that haunts Arwen. Nonetheless, her coldness, her relative detachment from emotion and empathy, empties her of life, so that she is closer to the figure of the corpse, to the relatives of the living dead, than she is to the Virgin Mary. Saruman can also be read in this way: in fact, one can argue that he is as close to the figure of the white corpse as one gets in the film. His hollow face, bony, extended figures, and the long white shroud that is wrapped around his frame, mark him out as a spectre or zombie—in fact he closely resembles the "inverted" figures of the Black Riders/ringwraiths that we get to see when Frodo puts on the ring.

Galadriel and Saruman exist within a tradition of representing white people as the epitome of the walking dead. As Dyer writes in relation to *Night of the Living Dead* (Romero, 1969): "There is no difference between whites, living or dead; all whites bring death and, by implication, all whites are dead (in terms of human feeling) … Whites are dead, bring death and cannot stand that others live."[10] Death is often visualized in paintings, horror and folk stories as ghostly white. One only has to think of the ash-white vampire as the archetype of this, "ghastly white, disgustingly cadaverous, without the blood of life that would give colour".[11] Connected to this is the theme where illness or ill health is often represented through pale skin, as if white embodiment is actually a form of corporeal disappearance or wasting away.[12] In short, death seems to be much in evidence when it comes to white people, and even more so when it comes to what might be termed "thinking" hyper-white men: men who are overly cerebral, scientific, and who simultaneously underinvest in the(ir) sex drive, and who, as a consequence, fail to reproduce.

Saruman is again central here since, on one level, he embodies the racial myth that "scientific" white men are cerebral entities, all brain and no body, that can and do wondrous things with science and nature, through their experiments and research. However, on another level, Saruman is a fantastical version of the hyper-white mad scientist/professor: one who has let the logic and power of science go to his head, and this at the expense of "normal" heterosexual relationships and sexual relations. Saruman craves more of the power that idealized whiteness brings him: he has let the power that he has a "hyper-white" scientist turn him into a pathological figure of destruction.

Saruman will destroy the white species if he gets his way because, first, he will fail to seed properly. Instead of monogamous intimacy between two committed lovers, Saruman opts for a monstrous form of reproduction since he is the "creator" of the Uruk-hai. He is there to witness and parent their arrival in the film's bloody primal scene. Second, these (his) man-children are sent forth to literally eat white civilization to death. Saruman, then, is by proxy a flesh eater in classic zombie tradition. Nonetheless, the presence of the Urukhai also confirm what it means to be hyper-white: they allow Saruman to reproduce asexually and thus to become truly hyper-white—free of the "dark drives" of normal, human sexual contact. In essence, Saruman gets to fuck in the film but it is an absent, non-human form of intercourse which for him is "ideal".[13]

Through the figures of Arwen, Galadriel and Saruman the cultural paradox of what it means to be ideally white is clear. Achieve and reach for the higher state of whiteness—spirit, rationalism, logic, and purity—and you move a step closer to absence, negation, pathology and, ultimately, death. But this is also a cultural curse since white people who fail to reach for the heavens are always haunted by their "dark drives." Haunted by their dark drives, white people often feel compelled to reach for perfection but in so doing risk death—and so the horror story of being white goes on ...

THE WHITENESS OF THE *RINGS*

The ring at the centre of the narrative trajectory of *Lord of the Rings: The Fellowship of the Ring* can be read as a metaphor of idealized whiteness. On the one hand, the ring is meant to have an unclouded purity about it and possession of it grants access to the eye that is all-seeing and all-powerful. When one puts on the ring it produces the invisibility that is itself the ideological and political marker of the white race—not to be seen as a race at all. The ring is wanted, desired by all who come close to it precisely because it is at the centre of things and has the power to grant one immortality. However, on the other hand, possession of the ring leads to madness and paranoia and the ring drains one of life and turns the wearer into a corpse, a blur in a shadowland where other deadly ghosts—mere skin and bone—roam. Frodo is nearly taken over by the ring and Boromir goes crazy with desire for it.

Lord of the Rings: The Fellowship of the Ring, then, allegorically "speaks" about whiteness in a contradictory way, precisely mirroring the life/death paradox at the core of this subjectivity. The film wants to throw the ring (idealized whiteness) into the fire of Mount Doom because it is death-inducing, and yet Frodo and Sam are the epitome of good white citizens, not only fearful of the ring but the bad bucks who have taken flight from their underground ghettos. In a sense, the film wants to have its racial cake and eat it: idealized whiteness is being rejected but whiteness per se is being re-centred, and the crude racial stereotypes used to fuel the fear of the Other mask the white trickery that sits in the belly of the film.

Finally, trickery or the alchemy of state-of-the-art digital effects is also central to the way *Lord of the Rings: The Fellowship of the Ring* situates the extraordinary power that whiteness has to shape the universe in its own image. The wonder of what can be done with digital technology is meant to be noticed: one is asked to gasp out loud at the most memorable of them, breaking the invisible wall that runs through much of mainstream fictional cinema.[14] These moments of technowonder are authored, the pioneering hands of Peter Jackson are symbolically witnessed, and revered. The film pays technophilic homage to this/his mastery, and in so doing situates itself within a wider discourse and history that connects science, technology and film innovation with white inventors. *Lord of the Rings: The Fellowship of the Ring* is part of a long line of spectacle-laden dramas that heralds the mastery of white auteurs to do incredible things with the moving image. Whiteness is this incredible; in cultural terms it remains a persistent representational and technological marker, shaping the way things are made and are seen.

NOTES

With thanks to Tim Groves and Lee-Jane Bennion-Nixon for their supportive comments.

1. Alistair Bonnett, *White Identities: Historical and International Perspectives* (Harlow: Prentice, 2000).
2. Richard Dyer, *White* (London: Routledge, 1997), p. 27.
3. John Gabriel, *Whitewash, Racialized Politics and the Media* (London: Routledge, 1998), p. 13.
4. Marina Warner, *From the Beast to the Blonde* (London: Chatto and Windus, 1994).
5. Alistair Bonnett, "How the British Working Class Became White: The Symbolic (Re)formation of Racialized Capitalism", *Journal of Historical Sociology*, 11, 3 (September 1998), pp. 316–40, p. 38.
6. Donald Bogle, *Toms, Coons, Mulattoes, Mammies and Bucks: An Interpretive History of Blacks in American Films* (New York: Viking Press, 1973), p. 10.
7. Dyer, *White*, p. 75.
8. Dyer, *White*, p. 28.
9. Dyer, *White*, pp. 28–9.
10. Dyer, *White*, p. 211.
11. Dyer, *White*, p. 210.
12. Judith Williamson, *Decoding Advertisements: Ideology and Meaning in Advertising* (London: Marion Boyars, 1978).
13. For an extended discussion of the pathological white scientist see Sean Redmond, "The Science Fiction of Whiteness", *Scope: An Online Journal of Film Studies*, 6 (October 2006).
14. Steve Neale, "'You've Got To Be Fucking Kidding!' Knowledge, Belief and Judgement in Science Fiction", in *Alien Zone: Cultural Theory and Contemporary Science Fiction Cinema*, Annette Kuhn (ed.) (London: Verso, 1990).

READING 4
ADVERTISING WHITENESS

By Robert M. Entman and Andrew Rojecki

Television commercials are leading cultural indicators. There are no people more expert in a society's cultural values and taboos than those who create television advertisements. And every year, most Americans see many thousands of their products: television commercials lasting from ten to sixty seconds. Although this experience would once have yielded almost no impressions of African Americans, Black persons now appear regularly in commercials playing a variety of roles. The quintessential manifestation of twentieth-century consumer culture once affirmed the racial inferiority of Blacks either through exclusion or demeaning stereotype. By century's end it presented a patina of inclusion and equality. More than news or primetime entertainment, a summary view of advertising offers seemingly compelling evidence that Blacks have attained cultural parity with Whites.

In our interviews, we found that interpersonal *contact* between members of the two racial groups is a vital force in shaping attitudes and feelings. Contacts of duration, depth, and equality can bring about racial understanding; contacts of the opposite sort have little potential beyond confirming existing fears and stereotypes. And commercials are all about human contact. They typically show people relating to each other in and through the consumption of products. The purpose of these scenarios is to create an emotional bond, a contact and then a connection between characters in the ad and its viewers/ consumers. This chapter explores the racial dimensions of contact images in commercials.[1]

As throughout the book, we are not claiming that viewing these images has a massive impact on Whites. But we do believe ads provide uniquely appropriate indicators of the culture's racial heartbeat. In pursuing public notice for its clients' wares, it is possible that advertising agencies, which are nothing if not creative, could be stretching cultural limits, exercising a potential to nudge Whites toward racial comity. Treating Blacks and Whites equivalently, showing them in comfortable contact across and within racial groups, could both reflect and spur such progress. On the other hand, a fear of controversy and a cleaving to the conventional could be leading the agencies to create messages that subtly reinforce the mainstream culture's racial divisions and apprehensions.

As Corner puts it, ads link products in varying degrees of directness with "established forms of goodness."[2] The goal of television advertisers is "value transfer," from the feeling tone of the ad to the product itself. To put a finer point on the concept of "goodness," we again invoke the work of anthropologist Mary Douglas[3] on the concepts of purity and pollution. This research provides theoretical purchase on the deeper cultural strands that may weave a constraining web upon the images of African Americans, even as Blacks attain increasing media prominence. As we have discussed, Blacks hold liminal status, moving in transition along the continuum from contaminated and contained to a more acceptable status. Since the delegitimization of overt racism during the 1950s and 1960s, Blacks seem neither fully rejected nor wholly accepted, neither categorized identically with Whites in a color-blind American community nor universally linked to a rigidly demarcated domain of pollution and danger.

Although the culture has progressed substantially, it still underscores racial categories in many ways, and the very act of categorization establishes an implicit hierarchy, according to Malkki: "Thus, species, type, race, and nation can all be seen in this context as forms of categorical thought which center upon the purity of the categories in question. They, all of them, tend to construct and essentialize difference. But more, such categorical types also operate to naturalize and legitimate inequality. In the most extreme case, the construction of one category may imply the denaturalization and even dehumanization of another."[4]

Does television advertising enact a symbolic spectrum between Whiteness and Blackness, situating Whites, the dominant group, closer to the region of the pure ideal and Blacks to a liminal realm that borders on the polluting and dangerous? Or are members of the two groups depicted equivalently? Do the many images of Blacks in commercials now hint that dividing people into racial categories is incorrect and morally wrong, spurring the groups toward acceptance, even closeness across a racial line finally receding in significance?

Images of contact undermine the validity and challenge the naturalness of racial classification, separation, and hierarchy. As suggested in our examination of prime-time entertainment in chapter 9, the absence of contact sends the opposite message. To measure contact, we look for images connoting closeness and trust among individuals on screen, or between them and the viewer. Thus closeness would be marked by direct physical contact between actors. Trust would be indicated by an investment of authority in a character who communicates with the audience; measures here would focus on the engagement of the actors with the audience, directly as in speaking and indirectly as indicated by the importance of their roles. Measuring the amount of interracial contact, and the degree to which contact *within* each group reaches equal levels for Blacks and Whites, also illuminates how far cultural change with respect to race has progressed. In addition, advertising should reflect any cultural idealization of Whiteness by drawing distinctions among African Americans, treating those of relatively lighter skin tone differently from those who are darker.[5]

SAMPLE AND CODING

We analyzed commercials from one week of prime-time programming on ABC and one on the Fox network, along with two weeks on NBC, yielding a total sample of 1,620 codeable ads.[6] No significant differences between these three networks appeared.[7] Eliminating 147 spots with East Asian actors and three where race of the actors could not be identified reduced the sample used in most analyses to 1,470.[8] The sample was designed to measure dominant cultural patterns and to reflect the viewing experience of an audience member tuned to prime-time programming. Thus we analyzed an *ad appearance* rather than an ad. In other words, if a particular spot for, say, Sears appeared five times during the sampled prime-time programming, its images were coded and added to the data set five times. The data do not include 1,470 distinct commercials, but 1,470 appearances of ads since many ran more than once.[9] This sampling method was checked extensively against the alternative of counting each different commercial just once, and the one chosen seemed best.[10]

We assume that prime time is the showcase of mainstream culture, but that advertising might alter as programmers head out toward the niches to address narrower audience tastes. The analysis therefore also encompasses samples of sports programming, MTV, and Black Entertainment Television (BET).[11] These supplements to the main sample allow us to explore exactly how flexible the culture is. To take an obvious example, if the taboo against interracial physical intimacy ever gets violated, we might expect to find the exceptions in cable programming for niche audiences like the youth-oriented MTV or Black-oriented BET rather than in the plain sight of broadcast prime time.

To be coded, a commercial had to depict at least one racially identifiable human character and promote a service or product other than a television program or theatrical feature.[12] Codes for contact among characters included intimate skin contact (a romantic, affectionate, or sexy caressing or nuzzling), as in razor commercials where a woman strokes a man's just-shaved face; speaking on screen to another character of the same race; hugging; or kissing. Contact between characters and the audience was measured by coding the race of characters appearing or speaking first or last on screen; in close-up or as a hand model; speaking to and/or instructing the audience in direct address; or in a manner emphasizing sexuality. A description of the coding protocol appears at <http://www.raceandmedia.com>.[13]

RISING NUMBERS AND DECLINING STEREOTYPES

Most previous research has focused on the relative paucity of Black actors in commercials and on stereotypes in the specific representations of African Americans. Our findings indicate a new era. Of the entire 1,620 prime-time ad sample, 952 or 58.8 percent featured only Whites while just fifty-three depicted Blacks alone (3.3 percent). But the full sample of 1,620 did include fully 465 ads featuring both Blacks and Whites (28.7 percent), and 147 more (9.1 percent) with actors of an East Asian facial cast (most of them also showing Whites and/or Blacks), so prime-time television advertisers could reasonably claim to represent a wide swath of America's ethnic diversity. Coding did not yield significant differences in such stereotyping images as performing to music or playing sports. It became apparent after coding the first week of prime-time programming that relatively few ads showing these actions appeared, and when they did, it was usually in integrated scenes. Thus we found overt conventional stereotyping diminished.

LUXURIES AND THE SINGLE-RACE COMMERCIAL

If advertisements provide unspoken indicators of genuine but obscured cultural truths, we might predict significant contrasts in the precise nature of Blacks' and Whites' appearances, actions and interactions. First, then, we compared all-Black with all-White commercials. We expected the former typically to tout necessities, rather than luxury or fantasy-arousing products. The latter usually allude to the realm of ideals and purity, and their texts tend to include more images of contact with the audience or between onscreen characters (such as in romantic perfume commercials). We suspected that Blacks rarely take center stage in commercials where

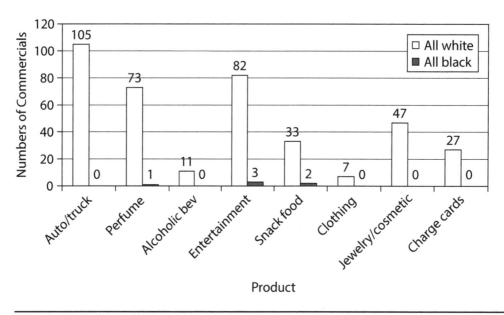

Figure 4.1 All-Black and All-White Luxury and Fantasy Product Ads

positive value transfer and ideal arousal is the primary pitch; when they star in ads, they usually hawk products with practical value in daily life. It is in ads for products that are luxurious, frivolous, or fantasy-related that positive value transfer may be especially important for advertisers, because they cannot hope to sell the goods simply by giving mundane information about how well it satisfies utilitarian needs. In the 545 commercials for luxury/fantasy products (including perfume, cars, and credit cards), only six featured an all-Black cast— whereas 385 were all-White. This ratio of 64:1 lends support to our suspicion that commercials tend to treat Blacks and Whites differently. The contrast is illustrated in Figure 4.1 below. Ads where Blacks' presence is unmistakable—because they are the only people visible—rarely appear when the product is designed to arouse fantasies of the ideal self, the ideal world.[14] Most of the all-Black ads promote items in the necessity category: groceries, household items, food, and drugs. Generally, these are the less-expensive products as well. Nacos and Hritzuk, in their study of print and television ads, found a parallel association between the nature of the product and the presence of all-Black or all-White casts: "Ads that promote expensive merchandise are likely to depict Whites only, while ads offering lower cost items are more likely to show models of both races or Blacks only."[15] The data may also be read as indicating that among the total of 952 all-White ads in the sample, 385 or about 40.4 percent touted luxury/fantasy products. This compares with just six ads touting such products among the fifty-three all-Black commercials in the sample, or 11.3 percent.

We discussed in chapter 9 the racial divide in television viewing habits. Networks know the demographic breakdown of their audiences from the ratings data and sell advertising time based on that information. Thus the production processes of programming and advertising are interlaced and driven by demographic informa-tion.[16] Most of the programs in our primetime sample are more or less consciously designed with Whites as the primary (though not exclusive) audience. It is therefore not surprising that we found these patterns in White-targeted programming. There were slight differences in the advertising on programs that featured Black stars, such as *Martin,* bolstering our belief that many advertisers do pay attention to racial representation in commercials and do employ racial targeting.[17] But the more useful data on the possible influence of audience demographics arise from comparing broadcast prime time with cable's BET, which is centrally targeted to African Americans (more on this shortly).

CONTACT

Next we assessed the images of interpersonal contact in the commercials. We expected the ads to display images of close contact far more frequently for White than Black characters. We predicted that advertisers choose dominant group members as the normal or prototypical representative of people using and extolling products, and use them disproportionately to enact scenes of close contact. This tendency would reflect market pressures and the assumption that the majority prefers seeing other Whites in commercials. Advertisers seem to believe

Table 4.1 Images of Contact among Blacks and Whites as Proportion of Opportunities in All Ads*

Race of character (s) Shown	Ads that Show Whites	% White of White opty. (n = 1,417)	Ads that show Blacks	% Black of Black opty. (n = 518)	W:B Ratio
Speaking to character of same race	209	14.8%	8	1.5%	9.6
Caressing skin	105	7.4	6	1.2	6.4
Hugging	148	10.4	15	2.9	3.6
Kissing	59	4.2	6	1.2	3.6
As hand model	669	47.2	51	9.8	4.8
First on screen	1274	89.9	118	22.8	4.0
Speaking last	723	51.2	78	15.1	3.4
Speaking first	718	50.7	88	17.0	3.0
Last on screen	1340	94.6	191	36.9	2.6
Speaking to audience	478	33.7	75	14.5	2.3
Receiving close-ups	753	53.1	127	24.5	2.2
Instructing audience	389	27.4	67	12.9	2.1
Sexualized	136	9.6	27	5.2	1.8
Total	6,865	Avg. 4.9/ad	830	Avg. 1.6/ad	3.0

Note: All differences between percent Black of Black opportunities and percent White of White opportunities (e.g., between 1.2 percent and 7.4 percent with respect to caressing) are statistically significant beyond p = 0.001, except for sexualization (p = 0.08).

*Opportunities in column 5 are calculated for Blacks as the total of all-Black plus Black-White integrated ads; for Whites in column 3 as the total of all-White plus Black-White integrated ads. Ads in which East Asians appear are omitted.

that Whites, at least unconsciously, identify with fellow Whites, and resonate to their on-screen relationships with each other and the touted products.[18]

The data in Table 4.1 illustrate how we measured contact through the content analysis. The table displays the total numbers of ads featuring each type of contact, and the percentage these represent as a proportion of all opportunities Blacks and Whites each had to appear in these situations. Whites had 1,417 opportunities: 465 in the integrated ads and 952 in all-White commercials. Blacks received 518 opportunities: 465 in those same integrated Black-White ads and 53 in all-Black ads. Overall, Whites had nearly three times more opportunities to be shown in contact with each other or with the audience than Blacks.

The first four rows of table 4.1 display the four measures of characters' contact with each other, within the scenario of the commercial; the rest show the measures we deem to tap closeness of contact with the audience. The bottom row of the table gives a kind of overview of what we'll call "contact images," while suggesting the relative peripherality of Blacks' roles. The 518 ads with Black actors featured an average of 1.6 contact images of African Americans. Yet the 1,417 ads in which Whites appeared included an average of nearly five (4.9) contact images. Thus White characters in commercials were about three times more likely to appear in contact with each other or with viewers than Blacks, even controlling for the larger number of appearances (opportunities) Whites had.

The table lists variables in descending order of the White to Black *appearance ratio*. For example, the first row in the table shows data for speaking to a same-race character. About 14.8 percent of all commercials in which Whites appeared showed one White talking to another; the comparable figure for Blacks conversing with another Black is 1.5 percent. This produces the ratio shown in the last column of the row of 9.6 (14.8/1.5), meaning Whites were 9.6 times more likely than Blacks to engage in this form of contact. After controlling for the many more opportunities Whites had, they still appeared almost ten times more often speaking to a same-race character than Blacks.

The appearance ratios shown in Table 4.1 indicate that television advertising conveys images suggesting racial separation and hierarchy, though the disparity was greater on some dimensions than others. Images of African Americans in contact with other characters on screen—speaking to other Blacks, caressing skin, kissing, or hugging—are nearly taboo in prime-time commercials judging by the substantial differences from Whites' contact images. Just one ad (for Robitussin) accounted for half of the six times Blacks kissed, and one other kiss appeared in a public service announcement (a subgenre presumably freer of market pressures). It almost goes without saying that commercials eschewed interracial physical contact. But the very fact that we expect this marks the continued power of racial hierarchy and pollution fear. By the end of the twentieth century, to our knowledge no broadcast network television commercial had ever shown a Black adult being caressed or kissed romantically by a White. Readers might think "of course not," but this expectation—alive almost a century and a half after slavery's demise—registers the profound barriers to acceptance of racial intimacy, and thus genuine equality, embedded within the culture.

Besides portraying characters involved with each other, conveying the existence of real connection between on-screen characters, commercials can also establish a kind of contact between the characters and the viewer. Shown in the rows below the bold line in the body of Table 4.1, the data here also reveal consistent racial disproportions, though not as great as for contact between characters.

The greatest disparity was in use of hand models. Nearly half of the ads (48.2 percent) featured a hand model, a shot where a hand was the main human feature on the screen. As a percentage of opportunities, White hand models appeared almost five times more than Black. The next rows of the table show that White characters were almost always among the characters shown first and last on the screen—positions likely to register strongly with viewers. Blacks were much less likely to appear in the all-important opening and closing shots, though the disproportion was greater for opening shots. Similarly, Whites had the opportunity to be the first and last characters speaking far more often than Blacks. The aspect of close contact with audiences that showed the least racial disparity was sexualization.[19] Perhaps surprisingly, Blacks were less comparatively disadvantaged on this dimension than on the others. Black actors' sexuality was highlighted in 27 showings, Whites in 136, for an appearance ratio of about 1.8:1.

So far we have emphasized the entire ensemble of 1,470 all-Black, all-White, or Black-White ads. But another revealing comparison might focus on images of Blacks and Whites in the 465 integrated ads, where Blacks' and Whites' opportunities for audience contact are equal.[20] The White:Black appearance ratios change when we isolate the integrated ads, but the outstanding impression is how consistent the disparities, and the limits on Black actors' contacts, appear. Thus, for example, for close-ups, the appearance ratio is 2.4; this compares with a ratio of 2.2 in the full prime-time sample.[21] In other words, to take an example, within integrated commercials where in theory there should be no difference in the frequency of Blacks and Whites receiving close-ups, Whites are more than twice as likely to be featured in this way—and thus to enjoy, we suggest, closer contact with audiences.

EXCEPTIONS: SPORTS, MTV, OR BET?

We did not expect the culture as inscribed upon the racial imagery of television commercials to be monolithic. Economic incentives drive advertisers to target increasingly narrow demographic segments,[22] and we expected images to differ accordingly. Thus, we also looked outside the mainstream of prime-time television, suspecting we might find exceptions to the patterns of symbolic separation and hierarchy. In particular, we looked at commercials on the Black-dominated BET cable network and expected them to contrast most markedly with those shown on mass-oriented shows by the major broadcast networks. We also examined ads in more narrowly targeted programs, specifically (male-oriented) football spectacles and (youth-targeted) music videos (MTV), believing they would come down somewhere in between.

With the caveat that the three samples of niche programming are too small to support definitive conclusions, we turn first to sports. African Americans provide a disproportionate share of the stars in the most highly rated broadcast sports, so it seemed possible that the commercials sandwiching the slices of athletic achievement would provide more equality of images. We found, however, that the commercials promoted virtually the same symbolic distinctions as revealed in the prime-time sample. Close contact between characters was slightly more prevalent than in prime time, though again not enough truly to breach the symbolic barriers. As to connection with audiences, Blacks were about 10 percent more likely to appear in the closer relationship positions with viewers than was true in prime time. The differences with prime time were slight, though consistently in the direction of more intimacy during sports programming. Rather than display all the data, we present in Table 4.2 (columns 2 and 3) the data on all-Black commercials promoting luxury or fantasy-linked

Table 4.2 Luxury/Fantasy Ads on Sports Programs, MTV, and BET

Product	Sports		MTV		BET	
	Total Luxury Ads	All-Black Luxury Ads	Total Luxury Ads	All-Black Luxury Ads	Total Luxury Ads	All-Black Luxury Ads
Auto/Truck	56	1	1	0	22	1
Perfume	0	0	19	0	5	0
Alcoholic beverage	23	0	9	0	20	11
Entertainment	4	0	29	2	16	4
Snack food	16	1	20	0	19	1
Clothing	3	1	23	0	2	1
Jewelry/Feminine products	0	0	11	0	21	9
Charge cards	13	0	1	0	1	0
Total	115	3	113	2	107	27

commodities during the sports broadcasts. Just three commercials out of 115 were all-Black. This is about the same as the proportion in the prime-time sample.

Turning to MTV, Gray[23] has suggested that advertisers targeting the White youth market deliberately employ symbols from the urban Black youth culture. Yet the MTV commercials did not differ radically from the main prime-time sample. Close contact among and between Whites and Blacks runs about the same as in prime time. As displayed in the fourth and fifth columns of Table 4.2, the dearth of African Americans in luxury/ fantasy product commercials appeared on MTV in about the same degree as on sports and prime time.

With BET we finally discovered significant differences. BET is largely controlled by Blacks and reaches an audience that is 89 percent African American.[24] If any television outlet transcends the boundaries and puts Blacks and Whites on more equal footing, it should be BET. This network establishes what is possible but apparently unachieved on the White-owned and White-targeted networks. On the sampled nights, at least, BET ran a substantially higher proportion of all-Black commercials than appeared in the prime-time sample: 44 of the 207 BET ads coded, around 21 percent were all-Black (compared with 3.6 percent of the prime-time sample). All-Black ads ran at a comparatively high rate for luxury or fantasy products also; as columns 6 and 7 of Table 4.2 show, around one-fourth of the 107 commercials for these products featured only African American actors. Recall that barely more than 1 percent of such ads in the other samples were all-Black.

Because we expected BET, being aimed at Black audiences, to show the most distinctive commercial images, we analyzed close contact images in the same way as for network prime time. Appendix table A. 14 displays the detailed data. On BET, *the rate of contact was about the same for Blacks and Whites*; on ABC, NBC, and Fox, it was, on average, three times greater for Whites. In some dimensions, such as sexualization and speaking to the audience, Blacks enjoyed higher contact on BET than Whites. The contrast with White-dominated, White-targeted broadcast prime time is dramatic.

INTERPRETING THE DATA

Arguably, the frequent appearance in prime time of images involving close contact among Whites connotes the existence of social trust within the dominant group, setting up an implicit comparison with Blacks, who received comparatively few such depictions with other Blacks (let alone across racial lines). The difference implies racial separation and hierarchy. Thus, for example, the stark disparity in appearances of caressing, kissing, and hugging among African Americans as compared with Whites suggests advertisers' belief that many in the White audience remain troubled by images of contact with Blacks. A similar indication arises from the relative paucity of Black hand models. Advertisers targeting majority audiences may prefer not to use clearly perceptible Black hands even where a commercial includes both Whites and Blacks using a product, because, consciously or not, they fear the White audience will make associations with pollution and danger. With respect to advertising outside prime time, the results indicate that those who produce and schedule television commercials believe at some level that cultural distinctions run very deep. They suggest that ad agencies assume that predominantly White audiences—even young ones or those simultaneously seeing Blacks in positive (albeit limited) roles, as athletes or musicians—must be served the standard fare of racial imagery. In accordance with their liminal status, African Americans are acceptable in some arenas, some strictly defined roles, but not in others: as exciting gladiators on sporting fields or entertainers on rock stages, yes; as symbolically attractive and thoroughly integrated product hawkers, relatively rarely.[25]

Beyond the data already discussed are both quantitative findings not displayed in the tables and limitations in this study that almost certainly led to an underestimate of the racial disparities. As an example of the first, consider the frequent depictions of White children being hugged (n = 59) and kissed (n = 14), symbolically embraced by the culture as precious. This compared with a paucity of Black children similarly celebrated (n = 4 hugged, none kissed). On the other hand, the considerable presence of sexualized images of Blacks in prime time is both intriguing and illustrative of this study's limitations. The very forbidden, threatening, or mysterious nature of Black sexuality in the White culture may make its use in some ads attractive to advertisers, as long as those images are carefully contained—as long as the portrayal is brief and does not show interracial intimacy. Exoticism is one result of this approach toward using Black models. Thus, where darker models are used in fashion magazines, they are likely to be treated as "exotics, tribal, ethnic, not just regular people," according to the dark-skinned supermodel Iman.[26]

The data suggest that advertisers who target predominantly White audiences find it more palatable to show Blacks being sexy than acting romantic (kissing, caressing) or simply talking with each other. Depicting Blacks kissing, hugging, or speaking to each other may be more humanizing, that is, it may promote more sense of commonality with Whites than highlighting their (allegedly exceptional and thus stereotyping) sexuality. Surprising at first blush, the controlled use of images from the liminal or polluted realms is predictable from Mary Douglas's research, and from the simultaneous exploitation and fear of Black sexuality that has long pervaded White culture.[27] As the impure and dangerous embody the forbidden, they sometimes represent allure and titillation. Group stereotypes often draw upon the temptation of illicit vices: immediate gratification, recklessness, unbridled sensuality. As Douglas points out, "order implies restriction; from all possible materials a limited selection has been made and from all possible relations a limited set had been used.... This is why, though we seek to create order, we do not simply condemn disorder. We recognize that it is destructive to existing patterns; also that it has potentiality. It symbolizes both danger and power."[28] These modes of thinking offer dominant and subordinate groups a symbiotic realm that defines forbidden pleasure for the former and a restricted arena for achievement by the latter.

The anxious self-consciousness of advertisers' practices in this area is suggested by the attention within the industry to a single commercial run in a few local markets by Ikea, a Swedish-owned furniture company. According to Bob Garfield, ad reviewer and columnist for *Advertising Age*, this "taboo-buster" of a spot was a "daring ... advertising breakthrough ... a departure...."[29] Garfield's year-end review of ads cited this one as the best of the year for its "understated daring...."[30] This enthusiasm arose merely because the ad showed a White man apparently married to a Black woman.

Beyond this, the count of sexual images in the sample is misleading. Our coding method made no distinction in degree of sexualization. The ad showing one shirtless Black weightlifter for half a second in a montage with several other (White) actors was coded, just as was the one displaying four or five White woman in revealing garb for several seconds each. Most sexualization of Black characters was, like the first example, fleeting, frequently accompanied by a depersonalizing or even dehumanizing of the actor. For example, a commercial for Hanes women's underwear failed to depict the face and head of a sexualized Black woman; viewers saw only the briefest partial glimpse of her torso and legs. Yet several White women's pelvic areas and faces appeared in lingering shots.

The BET sample reveals that advertisers can achieve more equal patterns of Black-White images when they target majority Black audiences. On the other hand, taboos on interracial intimacy remain as inviolate on BET as elsewhere, perhaps because they would be just as controversial among Black as White viewers. And the White-dominated culture prevailed even on a network designed for Black audiences; a high proportion of BET ads entirely omitted or gave only peripheral roles to African Americans. Whites predominated in some of the most intimate images on BET commercials, such as hugging, kissing, and hand modeling.

In part, this overrepresentation of Whites even on BET is traceable to the racial political economy of advertising. Because many corporations do not invest in filming separate commercials, they show the same ones on BET as on the White-oriented networks. If Blacks constituted a large enough market for their products, presumably more corporations would invest in all-Black or Black-dominated ads. Furthermore, the type of products BET promotes may help explain the divergence in images of Blacks. The most striking contrasts were the more numerous advertisements for alcoholic drinks and the lower proportion of commercials for financial and information services on BET than in the prime-time sample. The alcohol pitches also contributed most of the sexual images and other signs of same-race contact. There were actually more alcohol ads (twenty) in this two-night sample of BET than in the entire four-week prime-time sample (eighteen). This cultural artifact recapitulated the disproportionate presence of liquor stores and the paucity of banks in African American neighborhoods.[31]

The very fact that there *is* a racial political economy of advertising reflects the kind of implicit yet powerful hierarchical categorizing that Malkki writes about. The patterns of images hint at advertisers' belief that majority group audiences notice and respond to the racial makeup of commercials. In a world without racial hierarchies and boundaries, a truly race-blind world, we might see Blacks receiving as many close-up shots and hand modeling assignments as Whites. We might even see Black hand models in otherwise all-White ads, a phenomenon that did not occur in this sample. Similarly, White audiences might occasionally view an ad montage of ten different characters wandering the aisles of, say, K-Mart, eight of whom were Black and just two White. No such commercial appeared in the sample; the majority of characters in montage ads were always White.[32] In a raceconscious culture, depicting a Black majority would risk suggesting that if White people go to a K-Mart store, they would find most customers there African American and most products appealing mainly to that group. Even where Blacks are admitted into the world of an ad, then, it seems commercials still track the racial inequalities and anxieties of the larger culture.[33] The absence of scenarios featuring Whites and Blacks contacting each other and enjoying products, in which Whites are outnumbered by Blacks, captures the culture's racial disquiet.

It also reflects the advertising industry's own racial segmentation. The industry actually has openly identi-fied, separate ethnic "accounts." For example, *Advertising Age* reported on 7 May 1997, that K-Mart had named "an agency of record for its estimated $5 million African American account." The same story noted that a different agency handled K-Mart's "Hispanic account." Other reports appear throughout this trade magazine, the "bible" of the industry, registering the assignment of particular agencies to specifically labeled "African American" accounts. That the advertising industry routinely segregates advertising accounts indicates that racial segmenting—and thus racially conscious image production—are taken for granted in this field.[34] The racialized economy of advertising has been documented in radio, whose long-standing and stark racial seg-mentation may foreshadow the future of television. In that industry, there exist "no urban/Spanish dictates" and "minority discounts," meaning that many corporations instruct their ad agencies not to advertise on sta-tions formatted to appeal to Black ("urban") or Latino ("Spanish") audiences, and to demand steep discounts if they do. The rationales often arise from absurd stereotypes, such as that "Black people don't eat beef," or "Hispanics don't buy or lease cars."[35]

There are complexities in our own data that we can discuss here only briefly. For example, using population proportion as the standard for equal representation, one might argue that some of the findings reveal some-thing close to racial equivalency. Thus, in Table 4.1, we find 718 ads showing a White speaking first and 88 a Black, for a ratio of about 8:1, fairly close to population percentages. The dominant culture now clearly signals to unreconstructed White racists that, like it or not, African Americans are inescapable and at least on some levels acceptable members of U.S. society. Over time the mere presence of blacks in commercials may challenge and help further to reduce the traditionally racist component of the culture. On the other hand, the absolute numbers also can be read as showing how even in integrated ads Blacks play subordinated roles, appearing in intimate relationships less than Whites on every dimension coded. And we believe it is these implicit compari-sons, embedded in the appearance ratios, that crucially reflect and connote racial hierarchy and set boundaries to the inclusiveness of the commercial world. As an example, even controlling for numbers of appearances, a White is three times more likely than a Black to appear in the authoritative role of introductory spokesperson. Such implicit contrasts may naturalize unexamined assumptions of racial hierarchy.[36]

Equally important, our data underestimate the absolute disparities, because the *codes do not count numbers of characters.* In most instances, integrated ads had many more Whites than Blacks. Thus we coded an ad as including both Blacks and Whites first on screen when the first shot in that commercial showed a group of five Whites and one Black. A commercial that showed six Whites and a Black in close-ups was coded the same as one that depicted a single White and a single Black. Had we been able to count each separate actor in each separate scene (a totally impractical assignment), absolute and relative disparities would have been far greater. The figures given here, therefore, err markedly on the conservative side. In analyzing their data on Black images in print and television advertising, Nacos and Hritzuk discovered similar disparities: "[I]n the vast majority of ads showing members of both racial groups, Whites almost always outnumbered Blacks by far and were more prominently placed.... [I]n almost all ads and commercials we coded as depicting Blacks and Whites, only one or two Black and *several* White persons were shown. Had we counted each Black and White person in those ads, the dominance of White faces would be far greater...."[37]

SKIN COLOR

Finally, based on a prime-time subsample, we looked at skin shade among African Americans.[38] Darkness evokes danger and dirt, so that mental associations of the color black and the words *Black person* may be negative among most Whites; certainly the color evokes notions of difference. We therefore assumed that using dark-skinned actors would create real concerns among advertisers. Blacks themselves may have internalized dominant cultural ideals in ways that make their responses to cultural stimuli such as skin color more similar to Whites than might be expected.[39] These conditions would tend to produce an unstable, uneasy compromise: the frequent use of Blacks in advertising, but perhaps under tacit rules about the skin tone as well as numbers, roles, and product associations of Blacks. An implied preference for lightness would predictably follow from the hierarchy of ideal trait attainment as suggested in chapter 3. We therefore expected that in general advertisers would prefer lighter-skinned Black actors, even if unconsciously, particularly for products pitched to audiences' fantasy, luxury, and ideal self-images.

Since lighter skin is empirically associated with higher-status occupation,[40] and high status with attainment of U.S. cultural ideals, we expected Black actors playing characters of higher status or using higher-status or ideal/fantasy products to be lighter skinned than those playing low-status roles. Because women in ads are frequent carriers of symbolic associations to purity, safety, innocence, and beauty—and women's attainment and cultural value are more strictly tied to physical traits than men's—we expected advertisers' preference for light skin to be more pronounced for females than males.[41] Similar reasons led us to suspect a similar premium on lightness of skin for child models. Finally, all-Black ads in this subsample numbered 15 of the 122 ads shown. Given the hypothesized potency of skin color, we expected light-skinned Blacks to predominate in all-Black ads. Where advertisers go out on a cultural limb to employ all-Black casts, producing a commercial whose viewers cannot avoid noticing the Black actor(s), we felt they are especially likely to compensate by using those with lighter skin tones.

Reliability analysis confirmed that the best coding scheme would measure just two shades of definable Black skin color—light and dark.[42] For this study we randomly chose one of the weeks (27 November 1996 through 3 December 1996) of prime-time advertising on NBC. Of the 408 commercials shown, 122 (30 percent) included at least one identifiably Black actor; 107 were integrated, and fifteen had exclusively Black casts. We counted a total of 466 individual Black persons appearing in these 122 commercial showings.

Considering skin color for the sample at large, 44 percent were classed as dark skinned and 56 percent as light skinned. The difference was statistically significant.[43] This finding supports our expectation that a majority of Blacks employed by prime-time advertisers would be light skinned. The data also supported our suspicion that light skin shade would be more common among female actors: the vast majority (75 percent) of them were light skinned, and the preference for light-skinned females held among children too.[44] The expected link between lighter skin shade and luxury/fantasy product advertising did not appear consistently. One reason is that breaking a sample of just 122 commercials and 466 actors into fifteen categories yields small numbers. A larger sample might yield clearer results. Finally, we anticipated finding that commercials featuring only Black actors would include more light-than dark-skinned Blacks. Since light-skinned Blacks outnumbered darker ones overall (56 to 44 percent), the issue is whether this predominance is more pronounced in all-Black than in integrated commercials. This was indeed the case, as the light skinned outnumbered dark skinned by a 4:1 ratio in the all-Black ads, compared with about 1.3:1 in the integrated ones.[45] Though suggestive, we would not make too much of this finding, since there were only fifteen all-Black commercials; more generally, this sensitive but revealing area of skin tone is one that demands further research.

It is possible that the 56–44 percent split in light-skinned versus dark-skinned models parallels the actual distributions of skin tone in the general African American population. However, we suspect that a representative sampling of African Americans would yield a much higher proportion of individuals we would classify as dark skinned than of those falling into the light category.[46] In addition, previous research buttresses the assumption that advertisers are highly color or race conscious.[47] This reflects commercial considerations: in describing the preference for lighter skin shades—not just among Blacks but even among White models when casting the all-important cover—*Vogue* magazine editor Anna Wintour observed that, for fashion magazines, "it is a fact of life that the color of a model's skin (or hair for that matter) dramatically affects newsstand sales."[48]

Those Blacks with lighter skin—appearance closer to the White ideal—have greater opportunity than darker Blacks to earn money by appearing in commercials generally, and in specific types of commercials. This advantage of light skin accrues with particular strength to Black females. Black males (as males of all ethnicities) enjoy a wider latitude of variation in physical traits that can be considered attractive. In addition, the symbolic associations of darkness with exoticism, with strength and danger, can sometimes even be an advantage, depending on the image an advertiser seeks to convey. An obvious example is athletics; African American sports heroes can be dark skinned and still amass hefty advertising fees.[49] But in the main, the data indicate that advertising reproduces the racial hierarchy and liminal status of African Americans rather well. The culture awards Blacks provisional acceptability, with a preference for those whose physical features place them closer to the White end of the ideal trait spectrum. That cultural bias translates into greater upward mobility and easier social acceptance for African Americans with lighter skin. In this way advertising inscribes economic value as it ascribes cultural value to lightness of skin.

CONCLUSION

At one time the color hierarchy was so pronounced that even lightskinned Blacks were virtually absent from commercials. But the culture has been undergoing transition since the 1950s. As a sensitive barometer of cultural change, advertising indicates how far the transformation had progressed by the end of the century. Euro-Americans were seeing Afro-Americans in a high proportion of commercials. Good intentions, political pressure, and market forces have yielded real progress, making African Americans more visible in advertising. This reflects and bolsters a culture that disapproves of traditional racism, with its strict racial isolation and genetic inferiority. However, Blacks were not randomly distributed in commercials, as they would be if the transition to colorblindness had been achieved. No longer relegated to invisibility or exiled to a primitive realm of pollution and danger, Blacks' racial category nevertheless still matters. Black actors do not have the same opportunities as White actors in television commercials, and this both mirrors and reinforces the liminal status of Blacks in majority culture. The findings reveal the racial chasm still bisecting American culture, the distinctive messages about the two races still put forth by a genre exquisitely sensitive to the majority's anxieties. The results also support the validity of anthropological observations on the ways a society's dominant culture distinguishes between in-group and out-group members. And they closely track the underlying racial content of primetime television discussed in the previous chapter.[50]

The images we find do not arise from individuals deliberately setting out to sustain racism, but from normal institutional processes. Decisions on racial casting are rooted especially in the assumption that Whites react negatively to commercials that have "too many" Blacks. Advertisers usually choose actors with the goal of appealing to a predominantly White target audience. They frequently decide to represent Blacks on screen, but virtually always outnumbered by Whites, a pattern that reenacts racial categorization and preference. The inevitable by-product of these choices is to lower the frequency of images that show Blacks caressing skin, talking to audiences, talking to other African Americans, and so forth. The decision to include only one Black (or no Blacks) in a commercial is simultaneously a decision that ensures fewer images of Blacks in close contact with each other, with White characters, and with audiences.

When they want such concepts as "fantasy vacation," "luxurious," "cute baby," "warm family scene," or "sexy romantic couple" to animate an ad, most sponsors and their advertising agencies automatically think White. Those who craft commercials probably do not recognize the subtle but pervasive way their products may inadvertently perpetuate the traditional racial pecking order. Even if they did, advertisers may be correct to assume that consistently associating Blacks with luxury products, allowing African Americans to dominate Whites in numbers and roles, or showing Blacks as intimately as Whites could undermine the appeal of many products. If so, change may come slowly to this aspect of commercial culture, where Blacks' status may remain in the limbo of cultural liminality.

READING 5
HIP HOP IS NOT RESPONSIBLE FOR SEXISM

By Tricia Rose

I think the rap community always tells the truth. And I think that it's important that we listen to their voices so we can have a roadmap, because artists—almost every single artist in hip hop, they paint a picture that is overlooked. The misogyny, the racism, the violence, the homophobia, these are things that we try to avoid instead of dealing with. All of that, I see it so often.

—Russell Simmons on *The O'Reilly Factor*, April 26, 2007

Some people push the limits, you know, but that's in everything. Some people push the limits on daytime television. Some people push the limits in the movies.... We [rappers] push limits. I don't really think that anyone is really out to demean women.

—Nelly, rapper, on *The Tavis Smiley Show*, May 26, 2005

The truth is, misogyny is not a hip hop created problem. Misogyny is a deep-seated problem that is embedded in the historical evolution of the United States as a nation.

—Dr. Ben Chavis, president/CEO of the Russell Simmons Hip Hop
Summit Action Network, quoted in "Women's Media Center:
In Defense of Hip Hop," www.ThugLifeArmy.com, May 22, 2007

The Website for Power 106 FM in Los Angeles, a highly influential hip hop/contemporary R&B station in a major media market, listed the top-five songs on their May 13, 2008, playlist as follows:

1. "Lollipop," by rapper Lil' Wayne
2. "Love in This Club," by Usher and rapper Young Jeezy
3. "What You Got," by Colby O'Donis and rapper Akon

4. "The Boss," by rappers Rick Ross and T-Pain
5. "Hypnotized," by rapper Gemini

Nearly all of the lyrics for "Lollipop" detail sex acts between rapper Lil' Wayne and a woman he hooks up with at a club. Lines include "She licked me like a lollipop" and "Shawty wanna thug, bottles in the club, Shawty wanna hump." "Love in This Club" is about how much R&B singer Usher and rapper Young Jeezy want to have sex in a club with a young woman they think is very sexually desirable. "What You Got" is about a beautiful but self-centered and materialistic girl who constantly talks about what she possesses. Rapper Gemini raps about his sexual attraction to a beautiful female in stiletto shoes at a club. He can't take his eyes off of her (he's "so hypnotized" by her moves), and tries to figure out how to "get with" her. "The Boss" is a standard gangsta rap style boast about Rick Ross being "da biggest boss dat you've seen thus far" who has power, fancy cars, and stylish outfits. Women are not the direct subjects of this song, but when they appear, they are mere sex objects and symbols of Ross's control and prestige. One girl loves him so much she tattooed his name on her body; as for another, "she leak da backseat just to freak in da magnum."

This lineup reflects a distortion of youth music's long-standing and perfectly acceptable focus on sex and courtship into sexist and objectifying tales of male conquest. The lyrics for these catchy top-five songs do not distinguish between male sexual desire and the sexual objectification of women. In these songs and many others, women are valuable only because they are sexually desirable and willing. These five songs are just an example of the context in which women are frequently viewed. As noted by Gwendolyn Pough, a black feminist scholar who specializes in the topics of gender and hip hop, while hip hop has been a whipping boy, its images do affect women: "[M]essages in the music tell us what we should do to be desired and in some cases respected."[1]

When people criticize commercial hip hop's sexism, various explanations for its prevalence are offered. Six of the top defenses are that (1) society is sexist, (2) artists should be free to express themselves, (3) rappers are unfairly singled out, (4) we should be tackling the problem at the root, (5) listening to harsh realities gives us a road map, and (6) sexual insults are deleted from radio and video airplay. Each of these defenses evades the issue of sexism; none directly tackles the issue of sexist content.

SOCIETY IS SEXIST

The biggest claim made in attempting to explain hip hop's sexism is that society at its root is sexist, and that since it is a "deep-seated problem" in the United States it is well beyond hip hop's responsibility. This claim, that sexism is a larger, systemic problem, is entirely accurate. And it is also true that hip hop's sexism probably gets some unfair attention. But rap's stars and the corporations that distribute their songs get away with and have profited handsomely from highly vulgar and explicit forms of sexism specifically targeting black women—a fact that only encourages other up-and-coming artists to follow in their misogynist footsteps to get famous and rich. For all the recent and past outcry against the ways that hip hop generally depicts black women, this state of affairs has, for the most part (with just a few major challenges here and there), been allowed to expand and diversify mostly unchecked.

WHAT IS SEXISM?

> Sexism has been described as the practice of domination of women. It is a practice that is supported in many different ways that are critical to our socialization into our sex roles, and therefore makes this domination acceptable in society—through language, visual association, media representation, and stereotyping, especially on the basis of the mothering/caring role of women. Sexism is important also because all women experience it in different ways, depending upon their social and economic situation—within the family and in jobs—and it limits the ways in which women seek to actualize their potential. (*Oxford English Dictionary*)

The special reference to mothering in this definition reveals the extra scrutiny reserved for women's sexuality and the stigma attached to improper or socially unacceptable kinds of sexual expression and reproduction such as prostitution, lesbianism, stripping, and unwed motherhood. Sexist ideas often rely on labeling and controlling the value and expression of women's sexuality as a central vehicle for limiting women's potential.

Race is a critical aspect of this larger definition of sexism. Throughout the U.S. history of white men defining women's status and value, the systematic assumption that only white women would be able to reach the highest (but still subordinate-to-men) role of womanhood was a key element of women's oppression. Black women were not afforded the status of "womanhood" in mainstream society, and they were automatically less valued and more sexually stigmatized by society.

Sexism against black women took place in racially specific ways involving the labeling of their sexuality as automatically deviant and uncontrollable and the claim that they were unfit as mothers. Key sexual myths shape the three primary stereotypes about black women: "The Mammy, Jezebel, and Sapphire stereotypes are defined by their 'dysfunctional' sexuality and motherhood. The Mammy is generally an asexual, overweight, and middle-aged figure whose maternal qualities are expressed thorough her expert care for white women's children (at the expense of her own). The Jezebel is defined by her excessive, exotic, and unbridled sexuality. The Sapphire is the symbolic antithesis of the 'lady': loud, excessive, and irrepressible."[2] These racist and sexist evaluations continue to be powerfully and consistently reinforced in the legal system, in the cultural and social arenas, in imagery and language, and in popular media representations. Although revamped, these core, controlling stereotypes of black women remain powerful in society, and Jezebel and Sapphire, in particular, are constantly reproduced in commercial hip hop as well.

I've always been incredibly frustrated by the claim that hip hop isn't responsible for sexism because it's a long-standing problem and thus is "larger" than hip hop. It's worth showing the shell-game quality of this answer, since its inherent truth seems to silence legitimate challenges to commercial hip hop's role in amplifying sexism. The defense that hip hop didn't create sexism is valid, and thus often seems to silence and confuse fans who are critical of its sexism. How can we say that hip hop should be challenged for its sexism if sexism is everywhere and if its roots lie elsewhere? Is it unfair to target hip hop?

Sexism *is* everywhere; we know this. But should we simply accept it? Should we absorb as much of it as can be dished out just because it is around us? If we can't fight it everywhere, should we not fight it at all, anywhere? Should we not be concerned about how the sexism promoted by so many mainstream black youth celebrities affects black women and girls who are already facing oversized hurdles in our society? At what point are we responsible for our contributions to the state of the world? How can we hold others responsible—individually and collectively—for perpetuating ideas and perceptions that produce injustice and then decide we are never responsible for the impact of our words and images?

Clearly hip hop didn't create sexism, nor is it solely responsible for sexism. No one alive today created it, and there is nothing to which we can point that can be held responsible for all sexism. The power of gender inequality and sexual disrespect is its ability to be everywhere at once, to seem normal and inevitable. Thus, every fight against sexism (or against any systemic form of injustice, for that matter) is necessarily partial and incomplete; we cannot fight the entire system all at once. Telling people that they should fight on another front is evading the issue and thus our own responsibility. If we look for one culprit and at the same time say that it is "everywhere," no one is responsible for anything.

I don't expect many of the young black men who are being challenged about their use of sexism as a career-boosting identity to be on the front lines fighting sexism. Many rappers and their defenders are products (if they are lucky graduates) of terrible urban schools that, among other problems, rarely if ever discuss any kind of structural inequality, let alone sexism, in regular educational contexts. Discussions of how we support sexism and homophobia through accepted definitions of masculinity and manhood (as when weak men are called "bitches" or "faggots," for example) are rarely on the curriculum either, but they really should be in order to cultivate gender equality and consciousness.

Society itself is saturated with sexist ideas and images, and without much outcry. Major corporations in nearly every arena peddle a staggering array of products using sexist imagery and ideas. So, the current climate is not a fertile ground for informed, progressive, anti-sexist personal development. But since rappers are the ones who are writing sexist lyrics and who claim they are speaking their personal truth, they make themselves targets for direct attack. If they were to admit that their images and content are partly determined by the very same corporations, they would give us important ammunition against corporate investment in sexism, but they would also deflate their own and other rappers' street credibility and reveal that many rappers are really doing the dirty work for these corporations and empowering themselves by insulting and denigrating black women.

FREEDOM OF EXPRESSION

During their rare public statements and appearances, corporate executives such as Universal chairman Doug Morris, Warner chairman and chief executive Edgar Bronfman, Sony chairman Andrew Lack, and Viacom president and CEO Phillipe P. Dauman have defended their role as distributors of intensely sexist content by subsuming sexism under artists' right to express themselves freely. But quite to the contrary, artist freedoms are actually constrained and channeled by media corporations; claims about freedom of speech are made to defend the bottom line, not artists' rights to speak freely. We must pull back the veil on corporate media's ma-nipulation of black male and female artists and the impact this has on fans and the direction of black cultural expression. Mass media corporations profit extensively from promoting sexism and this is why they remain so quiet, letting rappers take the heat. In response to the outcry over BET's hyper-sexual brand of sexist videos that appeared on the now-defunct program "Uncut," BET spokesman Michael Lewellen said: "While we are sensitive to the concerns, let's not forget as well that we are running a business.... And somebody's watching

'Uncut.' Believe me, our ratings tell us that."[3] Because sexism and excessively sexist images of black women rappers sell, corporate executives are free to use rappers to promote sexism, but rappers are not nearly as free to express outrage at racism, challenge government policies, speak out against the war, or identify whiteness as an unfair advantage; these kinds of free expression are regularly discouraged or censored by the music industry so as not to offend white listeners, government officials, or mainstream institutions. As Lisa Fager Bediako from Industry Ears reminded the congressional subcommittee during the "From Imus to Industry" hearing of September 25, 2007:

> Freedom of speech has been spun by industry conglomerates to mean the b-word, n-word, and ho while censoring and eliminating hip hop music that discusses Hurricane Katrina, the Iraqi War, Jena 6, the dangers of gun violence and drugs, and songs that contain words like "George Bush" and "Free Mumia." In 2005, MTV and radio stations around the country self-regulated themselves to remove the words "white man" from the Kanye West hit single "All Fall Down." The lyrics demonstrated the far reach of capitalism by exclaiming: /*Drug dealers buy Jordans, crackheads buy crack*/*And a white man get paid off of all of that.*/When asked why they decided to dub "white man" from the lyrics the response from MTV was "we didn't want to offend anyone."[4]

RAPPERS ARE UNFAIRLY SINGLED OUT

Racism plays a role in the silencing of challenges to unequal racial power and it also contributes to the targeting of hip hop's sexism, but commercial hip hop artists make themselves massive bull's-eyes. Surely, many people attack hip hop to fulfill their own agendas; they want to restrict popular expression for reasons that are rarely progressive or democratic. Some also support policies that disproportionately hurt poor black people and help sustain disturbing stereotypes about black people. But this is not to sanction the ways that hip hop celebrates the disempowerment of black women as a means of pumping up black male egos and status. Sometimes one's enemies just might be right and still be wrong.

Civil rights leaders and anti–hip hop conservatives are not the only critics of sexism in hip hop. As I mentioned, many young black women who are a part of the hip hop generation and have supported hip hop and black men have also challenged the direction hip hop has taken. Many of these women have grown increasingly concerned about how black women are being represented and what this might mean for both the music and the young people who consume it and identify with it. Their concerns are valid and thoughtful. By responding to the few rabid commentators who suggest that hip hop is responsible for sexism, too many hip hop defenders evade the crucial issue that hip hop critics, especially black women in the hip hop generation, are raising.

It's not as though black women who are frustrated with hip hop's increasing dependence on degrading images have been looking for a needle in a haystack, trying just to "bring the black man down." To the contrary, many have stayed quiet too long, letting artists, black media executives, and the music industry off the hook. This has been the case primarily because attacking hip hop is read as attacking black men. And black women generally (despite the incredible emphasis in rap on gold diggers, bitches, hoes, chicken-heads, etc.) continue to be profoundly supportive of black men. As long as the equation between attacking sexism in hip hop and attacking black men remains in place, little critical commentary can occur within hip hop youth culture, and women and men will continue to be viewed as traitors for challenging it and for demanding less exploitative expression.

Instead of having a serious and sustained conversation about this issue, too many rappers and corporate music representatives interpret black women's concerns as an attack on all black men, a betrayal of hip hop. The "woe is me, I was attacked unfairly" argument (made by Nelly, for example, in the aftermath of the Spelman incident) turns the whole situation on its head. It turns an attempt to address sexist discrimination against black women into a moment about black male discrimination. It's as if the rappers are saying that *they* are the victims and should not be singled out, and thus one might guess that they should be given equal—even greater—rights to exploit black women! By this logic it is difficult to imagine that black male artists, magazine editors, and recording industry executives could themselves want to fight sexism and stand on behalf of the community as a whole when it comes to the treatment of black women.

The logic goes like this: Because sexism is all over society and media culture, and because somebody else—not you—created it, you can and should participate in it wholeheartedly, for great personal profit and prestige. Whatever happened to the adage "If you're not part of the solution, you're part of the problem"? All of this skirts the issue of what highly visible rap celebrities *are* responsible for—namely, what they do, say, and support. Without even asking them to fight sexism against black women, it seems fair to ask them to admit to the deep support of sexism that too many hip hop lyrics and images represent.

TACKLE SEXISM AT THE ROOT

While young black women are reduced to jiggling rumps and stripping, rappers can say that if we really want to get at this problem, we've got to tackle the big issue at its base, not focus on them. As rapper Nelly has said, "I just feel if you wanna get the roots out of your grass, don't cut it at the top. Dig down; you know what I'm saying? Dig down deep and pull it from the bottom if you really wanna get this situation resolved."[5] The fact is that although sexism is a systemic American problem, when it comes to the regular, sustained, celebrated misogynistic images of black women, hip hop stands center stage. It is the biggest black popular arena with the greatest number of highly sexually exploitative and dehumanizing images of black women. Sexism is everywhere, but not all forms of sexism exert an equal influence on black youth. Given its visible and influential role among young people and the often repeated claim that hip hop emerges from lived experiences in marginal and disregarded poor communities, its hostility toward black women is an amplifying mirror.

The idea that hip hop "represents" these communities gives an added stamp of approval to its sexism; it gives its sexism false black cultural legitimacy and authenticity. As T.I. said in October 2007 during BET's *Hip Hop vs. America* forum, "This music is supposed to be about what we open our door go outside of our houses and see on our streets."[6] Surely hip hop didn't create sexism, but far too much of it glorifies and encourages its growth and maintenance. Unlike the sexism that we find in Hollywood or on television or in politics, the sexism in hip hop resonates with even greater influence on this black youth constituency since it serves as a part of its homegrown identity. It is to hip hop that so many young black men look for models of black manhood that connect with their generation and their experiences. It is to hip hop that many young black women look to find a place in which to belong in their peer group, to figure out how to get attention from men. During the *Hip Hop vs. America* event, pioneer female rapper MC Lyte described this dynamic very well:

For the most part, hip hop has always presented itself as real and that's where the problem comes in because kids are looking at this and thinking that every aspect of it is real.... it goes through videos, with the men having these cars and homes and three girls waiting in the bed for them when they come in the house. Like all of that is *not* going on to a certain extent, but yet you have young boys who think these are women they need to go after, you have young women that are wanting to dress like these girls that are in videos because now that's what's defined as sexy.

If commercial hip hop has a special role as a "voice of the downtrodden," then shouldn't those who want to create justice for black communities be deeply disturbed by the constant peddling of ideas, images, and words that support such hostility toward the women of these communities? Isn't the point that hip hop has a special power—because of its credibility—to influence and reinforce a positive vision of community for black youth?

A ROAD MAP TO WHERE?

Russell Simmons's quote at the outset of this chapter says the truths about sexism told in hip hop give us a roadmap: "it's important that we listen to [rappers] voices so we can have a roadmap, because artists—almost every single artist in hip hop, they paint a picture that is overlooked. The misogyny, the racism, the violence the homophobia, these are things that we try to avoid instead of dealing with." There is a grain of truth in this passage, but ultimately the logic fails us. There is no doubt that exposing the depths of sexism, homophobia, racism, and violence is overlooked and exposure of oppression is a fundamental part of eradicating them. What does he mean by this? What kind of listening are we to do? And where is the road map taking us? In what way are the rappers who rely so heavily on glorifying sexism and reflecting homophobic beliefs helping to dismantle sexism, violence, and homophobia? Simmons wants us to consider the words of rappers as mere observers who should be celebrated for "bringing these problems to our attention." But he refuses to admit that these artists are not just mirrors of what is. Because of their status and influence, the content of their lyrics, and the lack of explicit progressive ideas from most of the most visible ones to serve as a counterweight, they reinforce the very ideas they express.

Lyrics that depend on expression of injustice without critique or challenge are reflecting them, not exposing them. Such use supports discriminatory beliefs while masquerading as truth telling. Some artists do a constructive form of truth-telling when it comes to the issue of violence, but when it comes to publicly standing against sexism and homophobia, and supporting this stance in their lyrics, the ranks are mighty thin. To tell the truth about just how much sexism and homophobia help create and support distorted and destructive forms of manhood and sustain injustice is not the kind of truth telling most of the commercially celebrated rap community to which Simmons refers is really interested in.

Hip hop is in desperate need of getting past this mapping impulse. "Representing" what is without critique, analysis, and vision of what should be is not a useful map. How can we figure out where to go if we are trapped in the act of representing, especially representing ideas that contaminate collective community action, mutual respect, and love for each other? Some have argued that you have to use recognizable language, attitude, and sentiment to reach otherwise unreachable youth. As T.I. put it during BET's *Hip Hop vs. America* forum, "If I have to throw some 'B's and 'H's in there to educate people, then so be it." But what kind of educating are we doing if we have to "throw some 'bitches' and 'hoes' in there"? When and how do we educate people—women included—about sexism? This kind of disjuncture, whereby women are asked to pay the price for destructive visions of community resistance, represents a tragic form of miseducation (to borrow a powerful term from Carter G. Woodson), which describes how oppression is maintained by keeping people miseducated about their condition. Former Fugee Lauryn Hill exposed the many facets of this miseducation on her brilliant album *The Miseducation of Lauryn Hill*.

This idea that we can successfully or meaningfully "educate" or "represent" poor black people while standing on the necks of black women is a fundamentally abusive form of community vision and education. It can create incredible levels of dissonance that lead men and women to think that one can promote the subordination and sexual exploitation of black women and still be politically radical. On Jay-Z's 2007 CD *American Gangster*, his song "Say Hello" boasts that he doesn't think Al Sharpton represents him—that when the public schools are fixed and when incidents like the Jena Six (a 2006 case in which people protested excessive criminal charges leveled at black male teenagers) stop happening, he'll stop using the word "bitch." When all structural and personal acts of racism end, *then* he'll stop promoting ideas that profoundly demean black women. This argument is blatantly illogical: Black women are not responsible for injustices in education and incidents like the Jena Six. If he's looking to punish those perpetrators, he ought to start talking and rapping about white racism and classism. Defending his "right" to call black women "bitches" because racial and class oppression exists represents a rage imploding on a community that pretends to be politically resistant. This is just the kind of sexism against black women that hip hop artists are responsible for, and it's the kind that we have to challenge and reject.

How do we transcend this madness if we must constantly represent it, reflect it, and reproduce it just to "get people's attention"? Russell Simmons's road map is a road map to nowhere. As Abiodun Oyewole, a founding member of the Last Poets (a political group of African-American poets and musicians many credit as a principal predecessor to hip hop), has said: "A lot of today's rappers have talent. But a lot of them are driving the car in the wrong direction."[7]

BLEEPING BITCHES AND HOES

Russell Simmons has made what is widely considered a courageous move in calling for record companies to voluntarily bleep out the words "bitch," "ho," and "nigga" from the songs distributed to mainstream radio and television, thus keeping these words out of mainstream consumption. According to Simmons, this recommendation preserves his twin concerns: artists' freedom of expression (they can write whatever lyrics they want, à la freedom of speech) and the protection of mainstream consumers (which might "bridge the gap between the activists who are so angry and the hip-hop community that is disconnected").[8]

This is surely a good and long-overdue idea. I, too, worry that the frenzy to "protect" the public would shut down dissent—political, social, and cultural. I have never supported government censorship and think that especially now—when fears about one crisis or another are being whipped into a frenzy and used to encourage broad infringements on all rights (the Patriot Act is a major example)—such potential for antidemocratic governmental intervention in creative expression is higher than at other times in U.S. history. But we must distinguish—and Simmons has done so—between governmental censorship and responsibility to a broader public. Furthermore, with freedom of speech comes a sense of responsibility to this same broader public. The idea of eliminating "bitch," "ho," and "nigga" from mainstream distribution appears to straddle this delicate balance: On the one had, they are deleted from the airways, but, on the other, artists can still use and record them.

But to what degree does this bleeping-bitches-and-hoes strategy undermine the overall logic and sentiment behind these words? If a song's lyrics send the message that black women are sexual objects, what real and lasting effect can we expect from replacing "bitch" with something else? In the music video for Lil' Wayne's song "Lollipop," words like "pussy" and "ass" are electronically twisted to make them unintelligible, but exactly how does this alter the sexist terms on which the song is based? Another strategy has been the replacement of offending words with less offensive ones. Nate Dogg's song "I Need a Bitch" was altered for radio play. The "clean" version substitutes "chick" in place of "bitch." Here's the gist of the lyrics: Each of several lines begins with "I need me a bitch/chick," and then describes what would make this woman desirable. The opening phrase is followed by phrases about her willingness to flirt, how she'll lift up her skirt in public places, how she's as important as his "crew," and finally how he intends to "pass on to my boys soon as I get through." How does changing the word "bitch" to "chick" really change the spirit and overall meaning behind these lyrics? It doesn't. Bleeping out or substituting words won't likely work against the driving force behind their use, nor will it fight the sexist intent of these stories. Furthermore, kids will spend endless time finding the "explicit" versions since these will be perceived as "authentic."[9] Snoop Dogg revealed this very dynamic in an *Esquire* magazine column, where he described his experience performing at a bar mitzvah: "They were singing my shit, they was cussin', they were singing the dirty version. I'm talking about twelve- and thirteen-year-old little white kids singin' this real gangsta shit. Man. I was shocked. I just gave them the mic and let them motherfuckers go."[10]

From a progressive social justice perspective, too, this strategy of deleting offensive words doesn't grapple with the bigger questions on the table—namely, fighting sexism in black communities, creating healthy and mutually respectful relationships between men and women, and enabling equal rights and social respect for everyone. If hip hop exposes widespread problems in society such as sexism, then we must actually address and support the development of anti-sexist, anti-homophobic ideas, not just make room for their increased expression.

The kinds of defenses that have been made regarding hip hop's explicit and constant sexism would be laughable and outrageous in this day and age if they were made in the context of racism. If, for example, racist images and lyrics were constantly repeated and celebrated in public and then defended with claims such as "this person or this film wasn't responsible for racism," "it's everywhere in society," "racism is a 'deep-seated' problem in America," "high-rotation songs that insult blacks on mainstream networks and radio stations are helping us deal with racism," nationwide marching and outrage would ensue. Yes, racism is a deep-seated problem, we know that; and this is a prime example of its pernicious effects. The issue would be: How are we going to fight it if we are making it seem normal and not exposing it with a purpose to end it? Unless the description of the condition "sexism is everywhere in society" is followed up with "and we are going to work on its eradication" or "we need to educate people about how to reduce it and here are some ideas for doing so," then what appears to be an honest confrontation becomes an evasion of the problem.

Couldn't we use some percentage of profits generated by hip hop to develop progressive anti-sexist programs in public schools or in after-school programs? What about working with Clear Channel, Radio One, BET, MTV, and all the hip hop magazines to *regularly* feature stories and shows that educate people on sexism, how it works, how racism relates to it, and why it is a problem? Maybe for every ten hours of music video, each station should air at least one hour of well-produced, prime-time media literacy programming. How do images work? What stories do they tell? Why are some images so popular, and how do images emerge from and feed back into everyday life and society?

Encouraging progressive young people to focus on and fight hip hop's sexism—rather than attempting to tackle the entire field of sexist culture—is logical for two central reasons: (1) Doing so would powerfully resist the amplification of sexism among the younger members of black communities for which hip hop is largely responsible. And (2) such activity would educate young people about what sexism is and how it works—thus perhaps reducing its power—rather than just reflecting and reinforcing the sexism that already exists. And this, in turn, would reduce the currency of the sexist ideas on which hip hop relies.

In short, the crisis in hip hop is also an opportunity. We can turn this moment into something powerful for all young people, especially those who most need to be empowered (not by degrading others), educated (not miseducated), enabled (not enraged), and encouraged to reflect the best (not the worst) of what surrounds them. Progressive voices in hip hop and beyond have an opportunity to make this a project of investment in social change and community building. Bleeping "bitch" and "ho" should not be simply a response to the expression of "black women's pain" or a strategic capitulation to mainstream pressure. It should be one small part of a larger and sustained commitment to creativity and justice and fairness for all. DJ Kool Herc, in reflecting on his years as a pioneering founder of hip hop street parties, said that kids who wanted to rhyme on the microphones at his parties had to find a way to be creative without cursing or promoting violence. These forms of negativity didn't support the community, and he wouldn't allow them at his parties. He felt that demanding that kids take a higher path when communicating with their peers was vital to creating the spaces that would support and nourish the community of which he was a part. There's no reason that we can't ask the same of the many creative minds that make up hip hop today.

NOTES

1. Quoted in Dana Williams, "Hip Hop's Bad Rap?" February 23, 2003, available online at www.tolerance.org.

2. Tricia Rose, *Longing to Tell: Black Women Talk About Sexuality and Intimacy* (Picador, 2003), pp. 390–391.

3. Quoted in Janell Ross, "It's Raw. It's Raunchy. Why Are Women Fed Up with Hip-Hop?" *The News and Observer*, January 1, 2006, available online at www.newsobserver.com.

4. Testimony of Lisa Fager Bediako of Industry Ears at congressional hearing titled "From Imus to Industry: The Business of Stereotyping and Degradation," September 25, 2007.

5. Nelly on *The Tavis Smiley Show*, May 26, 2005, available online at www.PBS.org.

6. "The Civil Rights vs. Hip Hop Generation," *Hip Hop vs. America*, BET, September 26, 2007.

7. Liz Funk, "Drop It Low: Sexist Rap Reconsidered," *The Nation*, May 22, 2007.

8. "Rap Music Mogul Russell Simmons," *The O'Reilly Factor*, April 26, 2007, transcript available online at www.foxnews.com.

9. Dana Williams, "Hip Hop's Bad Rap?," February 23, 2003, available online at www.Tolerance.org.

10. Quoted in Mike Sager, "What I've Learned: Cordozar Calvin Broadus Jr., aka Snoop Dogg, Rapper, 36, Los Angeles," *Esquire* magazine, July 2008, p. 104.

READING 6
CHICA FLICKS: POSTFEMINISM, CLASS, AND THE LATINA AMERICAN DREAM

By Myra Mendible

> *Through the pursuit of an ever-changing, homogenizing, elusive ideal of femininity ... female bodies become docile bodies—bodies whose forces and energies are habituated to external regulation, subjection, transformation, "improvement."*

Susan Bordo, *Unbearable Weight: Feminism,*
Western Culture, and the Body

The popularity of the chick-flick phenomenon poses new challenges for feminist criticism and politics. The genre's commercial success signals women's increasing clout as both consumers and producers of shared social meanings. The appeal of woman-as-spectacle is by now a film theory cliché, but the commercial success of the chick genre attests to women's influence as paying spectators. It suggests that female subjectivity and desire are marketable commodities, and that female audiences play a vital role in the cultural economy. But in a US media culture driven by the demands of the marketplace, can chick flicks muster the political commitment associated with earlier traditions of women's filmmaking? Critics debate whether chick flicks reflect women's increasing options and lifestyle choices or trivialize and de-politicize values associated with feminism. They note that chick heroines are often white middle-class women who embody consumer values and the mantra of individualism and self-gratification. Indeed, the genre is often identified with a "postfeminist" retreat from social activism and a "return to lifestyle choices and personal consumer pleasures."[1] Defenders counter that chick flicks revitalize feminism, positing more playful, ironic subjectivities and resisting claims to any "authentic" feminist agenda that can bind women across differentials of sexuality, race, and class.

This essay extends these debates to consider the cultural politics suggested by chick flicks in which the "chick" is neither white, middle-class, nor socially empowered. Part of the problem with the moniker *chick flick* is that critics seem to assume a clearly identifiable chick prototype and demographic. Yet neither of these presumptions has been adequately examined or contested. Since upwardly mobile, middle-class white chicks are often the subjects of romantic comedies, they frequently serve as the focus of these debates. This dissolves contradictions and differences under a universalizing "whiteness" and relegates variants of this model to the genre's periphery.[2] Thus the charge that chick heroines only aspire toward personal fulfillment, not social equality and community or that they unambiguously celebrate consumerist values is always already compromised by the chick's socially privileged position. The potential virtues and pitfalls of contemporary female-centered films are measured against this standard, skirting more nuanced critiques of the chick flick's multiply inflected relationship with both consumer values and feminist struggle. Just as significantly, the erasure of class from most of these discussions ignores the crucial economic relations and social hierarchies underlying the production and circulation of the genre.

In particular, I hope to comment on the ambivalent construction of working-class, female agency in recent films featuring Latina protagonists. *Maid in Manhattan* (2002), *I Like It Like That* (1994), and *Real Women Have Curves* (2002) incorporate prevailing social anxieties and contradictions, literally "resolving" them on the Latina body. The body is central in the articulation and naturalization of social differences, and the Latina's racially "hybrid" position in US culture (where she is historically represented as neither "black" nor "white") places her in ambivalent, often adversarial relation to dominant narratives of femininity and national identity. The films surveyed here offer a range of visions: *Maid* is directed by a man and qualifies as a Hollywood product; *I Like It Like That* and *Curves* are independent films directed by women. The latter two feature relatively unknown Latina actresses in lead roles, while *Maid* draws on Jennifer Lopez's box office appeal (and sexual allure). Yet all three focus on issues of particular concern to female audiences, emphasizing themes of empowerment in the context of work, family, and romance, in particular, marking domestic spaces identified with "Latino" culture in tense opposition with public spheres of production and consumption. Most notably, all invoke prototypes and settings of earlier "proletarian" films (i.e. maids, sweatshops, ethnic ghettos) thus foregrounding potentially volatile signs of resistance and struggle.

The Latina body has long been a troublesome presence in the US cultural imagination, alternately delighting, enticing, and instructing film audiences. Deployed as a sign of ethnic, gender, and class difference, Latina bodies have invoked a range of diverse and contradictory meanings.[3] Adrienne McLean argues that ethnic stars offer female spectators an opportunity to identify with a figure uniquely privileged to defy the social order of white, patriarchal capitalism. Culturally imbedded associations between ethnic femininity and disruption, unruliness, excess, and innovation, McLean notes, make it more likely that female spectators can enjoy such representations from a safe distance (11). But the status, popularity, and commercial success of ethnic stars often depends on their capacity to embody ideals of whiteness; as Richard Dyer has shown, the marketing of star bodies itself assumes a "white" audience and thus works to "deactivate" threatening racial elements that might impede crossover success (*Heavenly*). Hollywood films, Dyer explains, routinely use various forms of camera backlighting to emphasize female whiteness, while advertisements strive to "whiten" the female face because "to be a lady is to be as white as it gets" (*White* 57).

In today's transnational media markets, this ambivalent signifying role is syncopated to the rhythms of market forces. US Latino/as are a marketable, profitable target audience with a purchasing and spending power of over $500 billion a year; among US minorities, Latino moviegoers outnumber non-Hispanic blacks and represent the fastest growing admissions group in the US ("Loco"). As a result, Hispanic-themed media have emerged as a vehicle for shaping images of and for Latino/as, and for conveying normative ideals of cultural citizenship and "belonging" (Dávila).[4] An iconic Latina femininity, reconfigured to meet the demands of the marketplace, advertises products and lifestyles identified with US consumer society at home and abroad. In the film industry, the usual repertoire of spitfires, bombshells, cantina girls, and drug molls is undergoing revision, though Latina protagonists are still a rarity in Hollywood films. A crop of so-called "crossover" Latina stars—many born and raised in the US—today serve as enticing emblems of equal access and trans-cultural consumer pleasures. They also embody "Latinness" in the popular imagination, shaping not only external views of Latina/o identity but also enabling various forms of self-identification. Chica flicks participate in this broader socioeconomic process, alleviating underlying "tensions between the myth of American culture as all-incorporating and the reality of a fragmented, divided society" (Negra, *Off-white* 9). Operating through narratives of romance, the chica flick's harmonious matings can assuage racial and class anxieties, reflecting a reassuring vision of racial, gender, and class harmony. It can also, potentially, reveal cracks in the mirror.

This ambivalence and inconsistency exemplifies Hollywood's rocky romance with working-class protagonists generally, who are consistently marked as "ethnic."[5] The nation's self-image as a predominantly classless "free market" economy casts individual will as the measure of success or failure; thus it is no wonder that the "othering" of working-class characters (or the displacement of class on to "race") informs our cinematic tradition. Steven J. Ross reminds us of the interdependency between an incipient film industry and the labor class; working-class people, often immigrants, were not only the frequent subjects but also the main consumers and producers of movies. As a result, Ross points out, labor-friendly filmmakers set their features within the popular form of melodramas, love stories, and comedies, producing movies that were remarkably sympathetic to the working class. While black, Mexican, and Asian audiences were mostly excluded from white theaters, the appeal of movies was compelling enough that patrons of color endured uncomfortable seats in the balconies of segregated theaters or thronged to ethnic-owned movie houses in urban neighborhoods. This created a social space where workers and immigrants "often talked and fantasized about challenging the dominant political order and creating a very different kind of America" (24). The cinema's power to arouse desires and fuel political passion unnerved legal authorities and cultural conservatives, who felt threatened by the prospect of a highly politicized, predominantly foreign-born working-class populace. Thus the post-First World War studio system pushed the politics of American cinema in increasingly non-controversial directions. Studio moguls widened their appeal and increased profits by shifting attention away from class conflict and struggle toward "the pleasures of the new consumer society" (9).[6]

This is not to say that this relationship between mainstream cinema and the working class remained consistent throughout the twentieth century. The intersection where class struggle meets popular entertainment is never stable or predictable. John Bodnar contends that movies are subject to ideological "mood swings" and contradictions, producing ongoing tensions, for instance, between America's ideal of liberalism (with its emphasis on individual rights, freedom, and self-reliance) and participatory democracy (which works through collective action, affiliation, interdependence). While early "worker films" often set the individual in the context of collectivist social action (for example, labor unions), films focusing on working-class characters in the post-First World War period have tended to reconcile these tensions by personalizing social conflicts. Rather than endorsing collective activism or political organizing as a means to solve social problems, Hollywood films focus on individual experience—on the protagonist's personal hardships, longings, and triumphs. Films featuring working-class women as powerful leaders of collective action—such as *Norma Rae* (1979), *Silkwood* (1983), and *Places in the Heart* (1984)—emerged in the Seventies and Eighties, but Bodnar contends that even these set the broader issues in relation to the female protagonist's personal development or family concerns. In today's "post-Marxist" cultural climate, however, any references to "class-struggle" in current film discourse seems as passé as bra burning.[7]

This "mood swing" is also apparent in cinematic treatments of feminism as a socially transformative project. The ideological shift away from a collective gender politics corresponds, Barbara Ehrenreich points out, with an era in which feminism's earlier emphasis on social, cultural, and economic inequalities has been succeeded by a "mainstream feminism" that calls "unambiguously for [the] assimilation" of women into existing hierarchies (215–16). Thus women filmmakers in Hollywood today may not be transforming existing hierarchies as much as integrating into them. For example, Christina Lane has noted that in Hollywood women directors tend to become "pigeonholed" in less prestigious genres such as romantic comedy, melodrama, and teen film (37). As Lane points out, "most female directors are restricted to projects with middle range budgets that are 'dependent' upon the box office returns of current blockbusters" (37). These include romantic comedies and teen films—the staple of chick flick success.

In each of the chica flicks discussed here, the Latina body serves as iconic shorthand for the triptych of ethnicity, gender, and class. Given the political mood of the times, however, it is not surprising that Wayne Wang's rags-to-riches tale (specifically, maid's uniform to Dolce & Gabbana suit) starring "Jennie from de block" Lopez is the most commercially viable. The class conflicts and political undercurrents suggested by Kevin Wade's screenplay are mostly smothered in sugar and corn. (There is no spice in this Ralph Fiennes–J. Lo film mating.) Critics have understandably emphasized the film's ludicrous Cinderella plot, "pleasant" and predictable storyline, and of course, J. Lo's ubiquitous booty, the latter almost redeeming the film from the no-man's land of banal romantic comedies. But even as a romance, *Maid* was a miss: "don't look for this one on any future 'Greatest Chick Movies According to US!' list" quips one chick critic website.[8] My aim here is not to contradict these assessments, but to explore how the chica's literal and symbolic re-fashioning in this film reveals underlying political anxieties and social contradictions.

Single mom from the Bronx Marisa Ventura (Lopez) works as a maid in a luxury Manhattan hotel. One day she "borrows" a white Dolce & Gabana suit from a wealthy guest's closet and meets handsome (though stilted) Senate candidate Christopher Marshall (Fiennes), who mistakes her for a well-endowed socialite. The rest is history—film history, that is. *Maid* recycles earlier cross-class fantasy plots, which as Ross's study suggests, helped to shape the belief that participation in consumer society makes class differences irrelevant.[9] It is also worth noting echoes of nineteenth-century "imperial romances" in this post-NAFTA film product.[10] Just as the US's continental expansion produced border tales in which a "whitened" (i.e. "Castilian" looking) Mexican woman became a suitable marriage partner for the Anglo male, so this film allegorizes a happy mating between the growing Hispanic working class and the Republican party. Lopez's iconic body has been assimilated (i.e. "whitened") sufficiently in recent years to make her a privileged site for such mediations.[11] Critics have commented on Lopez's marketable "hybridity" (Valdivia); her "crossover" butt (Beltran; Negron Muntaner); and her visual transformation into a blonded, slimmed down version of pan-Latina femininity (Knadler). In this film, all of these resources come into play.

The opening scenes establish a series of binaries that structure this "border romance": uptown/downtown, rich/poor, white/others, public/private. Public transportation ferries Marisa between her working-class Bronx neighborhood and the ritzy Manhattan hotel where she works, traversing a space that is more than geographical. But there are signs that Marisa is socially redeemable: Marisa's bus reading is *The Drama of the Gifted Child*; her son Ty (Tyler Garcia Posey) is a precocious ten-year-old who happens to be fascinated with Nixon (Kissinger the year before), reminding us at one point that Nixon opened "the East" for "the West"; and Marisa is seen by her workmates as potential assistant manager material. Class differences throughout the film are racially inscribed—a black security guard, an Asian laundress, all-white hotel guests and management—but Christopher's description of Marisa as "Mediterraneanlooking" keeps her ethnicity vaguely, alluringly exotic. Even her name—Ventura—signals adventure. It also brings to my mind the commercial aims underlying this particular "venture."

As I noted earlier, most critics have underestimated the political undercurrents suggested here, particularly at a time when "compassionate conservatism" emerges as an appeal to the "working poor," the majority of whom are immigrants and ethnic minority women. A notable exception is Stephen Knadler's recent essay, "Blanca from the Block," which merits closer attention. In his incisive critique of the film, Knadler reminds us of recent attempts by the Republican and Democratic parties "to woo Latina/o voters." Increasing anxieties about the "crisis" posed to the GOP by Latino immigration has fueled nativist rhetoric—eerily familiar to anyone who has read nineteenth-century "sensational" papers and novels about unruly hoards of Mexicans scurrying across the border and undermining "American" culture. Knadler quotes a 1998 *National Review* article warning conservative readers that "without cultural and economic assimilation," Latinos are likely to push "the GOP toward minority status" early in this century.[12] This need to seduce "the Latino vote" (a phrase that assumes a nonexistent unitary Latino/a identity) was clear in the 2004 presidential elections, when both parties' conventions featured token "Latino" supporters on prominent display. But as Knadler aptly points out, wooing the Latino voter involves not just political strategy, but also subject formation: the constituting of a Latino citizenship disciplined into conformity with consumer values and behaviors. Knadler cites Lauren Berlant's argument that citizenship in the democratic nation increasingly translates into "consumerist identification with a set of privatized feelings" rather than a critical voice "that might effect collective action, protest, and social transformation."

Marisa's body is thus a contested site, a body marked by working-class "ethnic" ties (and as Knadler points out, politically neutralized "African" traces), yet potentially assimilable. The plot hinges on this ambivalence, hinting at resolving the social conflicts it poses. Marisa is situated somewhere between those inside the economic and social mainstream and those on the fringes of US society. While personally capable of transformation and improvement, she is also "representative" of her barrio community. For example, when Marshall mentions his upcoming speech on the deplorable conditions in Bronx housing projects Marisa decries his hypocrisy, asking him if he has ever actually been there. Marshall's well-intentioned but unschooled "compassionate conservatism" is set in contrast to Marisa's "authentic" ties to community and place. She is, as Marshall says, "no phony." At the same time, Marisa's link to Latino culture is tenuous and potentially stifling; her mother, who speaks with a heavy Spanish accent, appears in the film as the only real obstacle to Marisa's upward mobility. Not only does her mother's defeatism provide a negative role model, it also points to "culture" as the underlying problem to be overcome. But Marisa does "overcome" (even transcend) her place and community: in a white designer suit, she "passes" long enough to attract the white prince. This figurative cross (class) dressing magically transforms Marisa into a body that matters.

The plot twist hinges on Marisa's singular act of transgression, an act that reflects this ambivalent positioning and its underlying social anxieties. Wearing her maid's uniform, Marisa is docile, invisible, simply another dutiful "Maria." (Both Marshall's aide [Stanley Tucci] and the socialite [Natasha Richardson] repeatedly refer to Marisa as Maria.) But like other domestics, nannies, and workers who tend to the household needs of the affluent, Marisa holds a power rarely verbalized: she has access to the personal space of the elite she serves, cleaning their toilets, changing their bed sheets, literally and figuratively handling their dirty laundry. An element of fear and distrust underlies this social relationship, one that informs a variety of popular stereotypes about and attitudes towards the working class. If this were not a romantic comedy, Marisa's daring could help support such responses; instead, we are made privy to the transformative power of romantic love and designer suits. Marisa looks stunning strolling beside the Republican Senator-to-be in Central Park. In this contemporary "crossover" romance, the figurative mating of labor and capital ostensibly neutralizes the tensions between them.

After her masquerade is revealed, media headlines expose Marisa to the disciplinary gaze of society and employer: she is publicly admonished and shamed for her transgression and fired from her job. Marisa is fortified, however, by the encouraging words of the wise old butler (played with usual grace by Bob Hoskins), who speaks to the "dignity and intelligence" of those who serve and reminds her that, "what we do does not define who we are." Yet it is precisely through what she does—and more precisely, through what she wears—that Marisa assumes value. Marisa is only "seen" when she visually transforms herself from maid to socialite, when any meaningful sign of her difference is displaced and accommodated. More specifically, Chris's "love" casts a legitimating gaze that is gendered, classed, and raced. Marisa's self-affirmation and social "redemption" are intimately bound to Chris's authority: apologizing for her deceit, she humbles herself before him, confessing, "there was a part of me that wanted to see how it would feel to have someone like you look at me the way you did just once." Ironically, Marisa had earlier denounced such deference and deification. In a scene that confirms her mother's role as sign-bearer for a self-defeating and regressive group identity, Marisa accuses "people like her" of making "people like him some kind of God because he's rich, white, he's got things we don't have."

The final moments of the movie publicize Marisa and Christopher's wedding, his Senate win, and her move "up" in the hotel hospitality business through a series of magazine covers. The song "I'm Comin' Up" plays in the background. The final two covers are the most telling: Marisa's photo in *Hotel Management Magazine* proclaims her, "The New Breed of Manager," while Chris's *Newsweek* cover story bears the authoritative title, "Politics and the Working Class." Is this "new breed" signaling the emergence of an empowered Latina working class? Does Marisa's personal achievement "represent" a broader feminist social project? Knadler argues that Marisa's neutralized difference does not "signal an alternative sense of belonging, affiliation, or understanding" nor inspire "resistance to the economic and political status quo." Just as importantly, married to an "ex-maid," Marshall presumably gains direct access to knowledge about the working class. He is now "authorized" to speak on "their" behalf. But consider this: in the "new world order" imagined here, who is still doing the talking and who the cleaning up?

Perhaps, as one critic aptly remarks, "For movies like *Maid in Manhattan* to get much better, the economy may have to get much worse" (Scott). The economic prospects in Darnel Martin's *I Like It Like That* (1994) are much worse. The heroine lives in a cramped Bronx apartment with her man-child husband and three kids. Tight opening shots visualize a maddening sense of physical and emotional entrapment. Lisette (Lauren Velez) locks herself in the tiny bathroom twice throughout the film, blasting music on the radio and dancing away her frustration. The plot revolves around Lisette's efforts to support herself and her kids after her husband Chino (Jon Seda) is thrown in jail for stealing a stereo, a story sweetened by Lisette's undying love for her wayward hubby. Thus a basic romance ideology underscores the narrative, though it is certainly not a fairy tale *à la Maid*. Lisette's assertiveness (or desperation) lands her a job with a white record producer (Griffin Dunne) who needs help marketing Latino music artists. This sets up an uneasy threesome: Lisette is torn between her husband, who doesn't want her to work, a career that legitimizes her, and a relationship with the white boss.

The conflicts posed here are multiply inflected: Lisette's body is racially marked as "mulata," a physical and social status that relegates her "beneath" her lighter-skinned Latino husband, Chino (Jon Seda). Her body is sexualized in the opening frames of the film: her nude body is engaged in a marathon with Chino, who is testing his ability to maintain an erection for eighty-nine minutes. The children are pounding at the door and screaming throughout as Lisette "works" her husband, urging him to "hurry up and come." Chino's evil mother (Rita Moreno) despises the fact that her son married "down." Just as Marisa's mother expresses a regressive, "can't do" attitude that we can blame for her failures, Chino's mother embodies a Latino culture identified with racial and class bigotry. Given this domestic scene, it is no wonder that within the first few minutes of the film Lisette says, "I hate my life."

This sense of entrapment is also played out through the community itself, which is depicted as smothering in its "backwardness." The film is set entirely in a predominantly Puerto Rican ("Nuyorican") neighborhood in the Bronx, except on those occasions when Lisette is at work. It is a community where females fight openly over a man—where Chino's ex-girlfriend, Magdalena, publicly flirts with Chino and insults Lisette. Chino's "homeys" represent a repressive, disciplinary machismo that enforces a "Latino" masculine code by keeping an eye on Lisette while Chino is in jail. They spend most of their time hanging out on the street. When her boss, Stephen, drives her home at 4 a.m. in his red Lamborghini, the homeys tell Chino that his girl was "fucking a white guy" in his car. Later in the film Lisette defends herself against their accusation in another street spectacle, yelling at her nosy neighbors, "I got a job! What the fuck you people have?" Again "you people" suggests a Latino community that is poor, contentious, oppressive, racist, rigidly gendered, and self-defeating.

But Lisette's presumed "knowledge" of Latino style in its popularized, trendy manifestations marks her escape. As mediating body, she brings this knowledge to the world of popular culture, registered here through the music industry. Advising the young Mendez Brothers on how they should dress and pose for pictures, Lisette handles a precious commodity for her boss. This aspect of the film narrative offers a nod of recognition to the economics of popular culture; in particular, it reminds us that Latino music artists are a lucrative business. Lisette's boss woos the Mendez Brothers to sign with his label, telling them that "by some fluke of nature I wasn't born Latino … but I have an assistant." Yet the assistant that he originally had in mind was not Lisette, but the buxom senorita he points out in a bar. While Lisette's body doesn't measure up to his desired image, she can still serve as cultural translator; her genuine interaction with the Mendez Brothers and knowledge of a "hot Latino look" makes her hireable. In knowing how to package and market the Mendez Brothers into an image of Latino cool, she represents a behind-the-scenes figure in the booming business of Latino "crossover" success.

Martin's first feature film received positive reviews from critics who praised its "realistic" portrayal of "the concrete rhythm of downtown streets" and its "irresistible" heroine. She received the New York Film Critic's Award for Best New Director and the film earned four Independent Spirit nominations—with Velez winning

Best Cinematic Female Lead. An African-American screenwriter, actress, and producer who grew up in the Bronx and previously worked with Spike Lee, Martin does suggest a more complex view of her Latino protagonists than generally available. Despite Chino's stereotypically machista attitude (he wants her to go on welfare rather than work, and he responds to his homey's tale of Lisette's infidelity by moving in with Magdalena after his release from jail), he nevertheless has a gentleness and love for Lisette that hints at a redeemable Latino masculinity. Martin is uncompromising in her depiction of Lisette, whose resilience and spunk challenge the stereotype of Latinas as sexy but helpless victims of a macho culture. Not surprisingly, one critic hails the film's feminism, praising Lisette's "new-found self-confidence and economic independence" and effusing, "it's a joy to see how she changes" (McAlister).

Yet the film avoids broader cultural or economic critique, opting for "crossover" appeal by weaving strands of rebellion into a reassuring national self-image. The class and gender conflicts suggested here remain safely confined to the geographical and cultural borders of the urban barrio. Lisette's self-empowerment is defined in clear opposition to her Latino family and community, which serves as the Other to a more enlightened (though passionless) "American" society. Male domination and bravado have a foreign name, "machismo," deferring "blame" for male chauvinism away from "Anglo" males and masking broader regulatory regimes or mechanisms of control. Stephen's bland sexual performance is contrasted against Chino's virility, but only in Stephen's world does Lisette achieve self-determination and worth. And female friendships seem possible only where there is no competition, as between Lisette and her transvestite brother Alexis (Jesse Borrego). These strategic oppositions have a distancing effect that fosters a guiltless spectatorship; despite the maddening entrapment depicted in the film and the conflictive, volatile space it reveals, I Like It Like That is marketed as a comic romance.[13] The complex social conflicts the film poses are tidily displaced and disavowed, resolved through Lisette's personal triumph and potential assimilation into an American consumer society in which she can buy—not steal—her coveted stereo.

Only Patricia Cardoso's Real Women Have Curves manages to offer a positive example of feminist resistance fused with ethnic and class empowerment. The film features an eighteen-year-old chica protagonist who refuses to starve her body into compliance with prevailing beauty myths. Ana, warmly captured by newcomer America Ferrera, wants to revise these myths to include less docile bodies; she also rejects full-time work at her sister's garment factory, which Ana recognizes as a sweatshop. Estela (Ingrid Oliu) takes pride in owning her own business, though the gowns she makes and sells for $18 will later retail for $600. Ana defies this social order and refuses to join the ranks of the docile exploited. "You're all cheap labor for Bloomingdale's" she tells the women laboring at their sewing machines. Thus her personal challenge to dominant beauty ideals also hints at collective activism. Ana's right to be "fat" merges into a broader struggle for dignity and rights at the workplace: in the scenes where she rouses female workers at her sister's sweatshop, Ana recalls labor activist figures of early worker films. In this context, however, rebellion takes the form of a collective shedding of clothes; the oppressive heat sparks this defiant gesture, but it is fueled by the women's desire for self-affirmation. Comparing stretch marks and cellulite, the women momentarily forge an alliance that dares anyone, as Ana puts it, "to tell me what I should look like and what I should be."

A recent high school graduate, Ana is smart enough to be offered a scholarship to Columbia, but her "old world" Mexican parents want her to stay close to home. In this film, however, Latino culture is not stripped of complexity; as Desson Howe points out, no one in this film "is easily pegged." Ana's mother, played with dignity by veteran actress Lupe Ontiveros, is not just a "convenient villain." It is clear that she loves Ana and is struggling to reconcile her own life experience with her daughter's. The women workers are admirable without being mere victims of capitalist oppression; like many female laborers around the world, they are invisible cogs in the economic machinery, backroom producers never seen in those glossy fashion ads. But they are not simple props—they are humanized in their resilience, humor, and flaws. Finally, Ana's Anglo boyfriend, Jimmy, genuinely likes and appreciates her. He is neither her "savior" nor her "oppressor; in fact, as one grateful male critic points out, "this is a feminist motion picture where men are not demonized" (Berardinelli).

Most reviewers responded favorably to this female empowerment tale with an ethnic twist. "A solid chick flick" notes one (Berardinelli); "liberation cinema on multiple levels" proclaims another (Anderson); "a dyedin-the-womb female empowerment movie" writes yet another (Howe). The film also received several critical awards and nominations, including Sundance's 2002 Audience Award, Special Jury Prize (for America Ferrera and Lupe Ontiveros); the 2002 Humanitas Prize; the 2003 Independent Spirit Award (Best Debut Performance for Ferrera); and the San Sebastian International Film Festival's 2002 Youth Jury Award (for Cardoso). Unfortunately, reviewers share a need to label and categorize Cardoso's film; in numerous reviews, the film is repeatedly compared to *My Big Fat Greek Wedding* (both were distributed by Newmarket Films, which is targeting the "ethnic" niche market). This not only fuses differences between these films under a catch-all "ethnic" tag, but may also limit the film's broader appeal. Cardosa had tried to get the film made for ten years, and perhaps in an effort to reach mainstream audiences, she ultimately softened the political thrust that characterized Josephina Lopez's play (on which the film is based); Lopez's screenplay (with George LaVoo) tones down the labor angst that fueled the original script and individualizes the conflicts by focusing on Ana's personal development. It nevertheless manages, despite its familiar coming-of-age framework, to glean images of female solidarity and community.

In this brief sampling of contemporary chica flicks, I have tried to suggest some limits and challenges facing the genre. The ambivalent, uneasy political strains I have remarked on in these films no doubt reflect and negotiate existing structural and material conditions. While it is true that a Latina-centered Hollywood film like *Maid in Manhattan* can get wide distribution now, films that present Latina self-representations are still extremely limited in their ability to reach non-Latino audiences. As Chon Noriega points out, "Studios have yet to commit themselves to the grass-roots marketing strategies that ethnic and other specialty films require. And, more often than not, traditional saturation campaigns—especially the television trailers—have played into stereotypes that alienate the films' potential viewers" (147). Although writers, scholars, and filmmakers are making strides in promoting and showcasing Latina self-representations, power differentials affect access and resources. At this writing Latino/a centered films, like most independent films, do not have the wide distribution networks needed to reach mass audiences; many remain accessible primarily in cosmopolitan areas with "art house" theaters or to students in large urban universities with Latino/a or film studies programs.[14] It is notable, for example, that Cardoso's film opened in the US on October 20, 2002 on only 55 screens. Neither "newcomer" Ferrera nor veteran Ontiveros had mainstream name recognition. By contrast, Wang's *Maid in Manhattan* featuring "Latina" icon Lopez in the lead opened December 15, 2002 on over 2800 screens in the US alone; it was seen by almost nineteen million viewers during its opening weekend, and within six months had been seen by almost 60,000 Argentines, one and a half million Germans, and over a million Spaniards. There is also a gendered component to these equations: while the emergence of Latinos as a viable niche market has facilitated their entry into corporate mass media, it is still a male-dominated industry. Vicki Mayer's intriguing work, for instance, reveals the near invisibility of Latina writers for mass media and the scarcity of US Latinas in directorial positions and shooting crews.[15]

In closing, I would note that the foregrounding of career success and self-empowerment narratives for women accompanies an era of downsizing, outsourcing, budget cuts, and underemployment. Indeed, the much-heralded mobility of professional women in recent years obscures the enduring status of working-class women generally, whose real wages have actually declined.[16] Latinas' symbolic power in consumer tales also belies their embodied status as citizens: US Latinas are over-represented in high school dropout and teen pregnancy rates, and foreign-born Latinas comprise a majority share of low-wage factory or domestic jobs. For many women, the struggle for self-respect, dignity, and social justice is far from over. There is clearly a need for films that can challenge—not merely accommodate—our most comforting illusions and myths. This involves women at all levels of the film industry, from conception, to production, to distribution, and reception—the last marking one of the most contested, unpredictable, and yet accessible of "political" arenas. After all, female spectators help shape film tastes and values; let us begin by refusing to buy into self-help philosophies and better wardrobes as the panacea for what ails us.

NOTES

1. *Cinema Journal* recently devoted an In Focus section to examining the emergence of a "postfemi-nist" film and television culture in which "feminism is no longer relevant." See, in particular, Chris Holmlund's "Postfeminism from A to G" and Yvonne Tasker and Diane Negra's useful overview on the "postfeminizing" of cinema. Negra has also analyzed recent films featuring female leads that per-sistently stage "retreatist" fantasies in which a well-educated white female professional displays her "empowerment" by withdrawing from the workforce (and symbolically from the public sphere) in favor of domesticity. Here the rhetoric of "choice" works to mask and thus sustain structural inequali-ties ("Quality").

2. This tendency calls to mind Barbara Ehrenreich's remark that when Americans think about class, they "see the middle class as a universal class, a class which is everywhere represented as representing everyone" (4).

3. Extended analyses of this film and media history include Beltran, Lopez, Mendible, Noriega, Rios Bustamente, and Valdivia.

4. Dávila's use of the term "Hispanic" calls attention to its depoliticized and official status in the US, as opposed to "Latino," which stems from negotiations between an imposed and a self-generated identity grounded in activism and struggle. My practical application of the latter term in this essay refers generally to US inhabitants, both native and foreign-born, of Latin American and Hispanic Caribbean descent. Despite the homogeneity implied by such labels, however, "Latinos" in the US remain a diverse people whose histories, language usage, and circumstances may differ significantly and who may not speak Spanish or share other identifying criteria.

5. It's notable that the historical working class "ethnics" in film were so-called "white ethnics" (i.e. Irish, Italian, Jewish, Eastern as opposed to Western Europeans). The former have been generally

assimilated into the cultural mainstream, with echoes of this past heard only in names such as "Brockovitch."

6. Ross found that by 1926, film censorship boards, each employing different standards, all found films dealing with class struggle even more threatening than displays of sex and violence.

7. For recent texts that critique the dwindling interest in "class" as a subject of inquiry, particularly in cultural studies, see Cevasco, Ebert, McLaren and Farahmandpur, Milner, and Munt.

8. Interestingly, these "movie chicks" criticize the film for including "too much preachy stuff" and being "too much *Norma Rae* and not enough *Pretty Woman*." See <http://www.themoviechicks.com/dec2002/mcrmaidmanhattan.html>.

9. Following the decline of labor films in the 1930s, working-class characters no longer improved their lot through unionization or organized effort, but through miraculous strokes of luck, Ross found. For instance, in *The Millionaire* (1921), a bookkeeper inherits $80 million; in *A Daughter of Luxury* (1922), a homeless girl discovers she is really a wealthy heiress.

10. Amy Kaplan has shown that mid-nineteenth century "narratives of domesticity and female subjectivity" were "inseparable from narratives of empire and nation-building" (583). Shelly Streeby's investigation of popular fictions such as Charles Averill's *The Mexican Ranchero, or, The Maid of the Chapparal* (1847), Harry Hazel's *Inez, the Beautiful* (1846), Ned Buntline's *Magdalena, the Beautiful Mexican Maid* (1847) and *The Volunteer* (1847) suggests that these "border romances" shaped discourses of imperialist expansion in ways that would significantly influence early twentieth-century films.

11. Jennifer Lopez recognizes her place within this fluid racial category, commenting about her role in *Money Train*: "They wanted a Latina ... somebody who could be with Wesley, and with Woody. Apparently in Hollywood, brown is some kind of mediating color between black and white" (Murray 72).

12. Also see Morris.

13. The trailers and video blurbs emphasize Lisette's "marital problems" and the "amusing" interference of the nasty mother-in-law and Latino neighbors. I should also note that Martin's original title for the film was "Black Out," but according to the IMDB website, Columbia Pictures insisted on a name change. I leave it to my readers to speculate on their reasons.

14. There are several excellent volumes committed to showcasing Latino/a self-representation in a variety of independent and non-commercial venues. See de Alba, Flores, and Habell-Pallán and Romero.

15. The pinch is also felt by Latino/a actors, who are still underrepresented in mainstream films: a recent Screen Actor's Guild survey found that acting roles for Hispanics in Hollywood actually fell 10.5 percent in 2003 ("Screen").

16. Census analysis shows that only incomes for the top 5% of the population experienced real income gains in 2004, while incomes for the other 95% of households were flat or falling. Between 2001 and 2003, poverty levels in the US increased from 32.9 to 35.9 million. It rose again in 2004 by 1.1 million (Kerr). In the field with the highest proportion of female workers—kindergarten and preschool teachers (98% women), men had median earnings of $22,000, $5,000 more than women ("Census"). As for the dream of upward mobility: Jennifer Johnson's study suggests that women who

grew up middle-class tended to stay that way, while the majority of those who grew up working-class had difficulty overcoming the setbacks imposed by lack of education, low-wage jobs, and low self-esteem.

WORKS CITED

Anderson, John. "Real Women Have Curves." *Newsday*, 18 Oct. 2002. <http://www.newsday.com/entertainment/movies/ny-womenhavecurves,0,966395.story>.

Beltran, Mary C. "The Hollywood Latina Body as Site of Social Struggle: Media Constructions of Stardom and Jennifer Lopez's 'Cross-over Butt.'" *Quarterly Review of Film & Video* 19 (2002): 17–86.

Berardinelli, James. *Real Women Have Curves*. Online Review. <http://moviereviews.colossus.net/movies/r/real_women.html>.

Bodnar, John. *Blue-Collar Hollywood: Liberalism, Democracy, and Working People in American Films*. Baltimore: Johns Hopkins University Press, 2003.

"Census Study Finds That Men Earn the Most." *The New York Times* March 25, 2003: A13.

Cevasco, Maria Elisa. "Whatever Happened to Cultural Studies: Notes from the Periphery." *Textual Practice* 14 (3): 2000.

Dávila, Arlene. *Latinos Inc: The Marketing and Making of a People*. Berkeley: University of California Press, 2001.

de Alba, Alicia Gaspar (ed.). *Velvet Barrios: Popular Culture and Chicana/o Sexualities*. New York: Palgrave Macmillan, 2003.

Dyer, Richard. *Heavenly Bodies: Film Stars and Society*. Basingstoke, UK: Macmillan, 1986.

____. *White*. New York: Routledge, 1997.

Ebert, Teresa L. *Ludic Feminism and After*. Ann Arbor: University of Michigan Press, 1999.

Ehrenreich, Barbara. *Fear of Falling: The Inner Life of the Middle Class*. New York: Pantheon, 1989.

Flores, Juan. *From Bomba to Hip Hop: Puerto Rican Culture and Latino Identity*. New York: Columbia University Press, 2000.

Habell-Pallán, Michelle and Mary Romero (eds). *Latino/a Popular Culture*. New York: NYU Press, 2002.

Holmlund, Chris. "Postfeminism from A to G." *Cinema Journal* 44.2 (Winter 2005): 116–21.

Howe, Desson. "On 'Real Women' and Feisty Daughters." *Washington Post*,15 Nov. 2002: WE42.

Johnson, Jennifer. *Getting By on the Minimum*. New York: Routledge, 2002.

Kaplan, Amy. "Manifest Domesticity." *American Literature* 70.3 (September 1998): 581–606.

Kerr, Jennifer C. "Poverty Rate Rises to 12.7 Percent." *Washington Post* 31 August 2005.

Knadler, Stephen. "Blanca from the Block: Whiteness and the Transnational Latina Body." *Genders* 41 (2005). 30 Sept 2005. <http://www.genders.org/g41/g41_knadler.txt>.

Lane, Christina. *Feminist Hollywood From Born in Flames to Point Break*. Detroit, MI: Wayne State University Press, 2000.

"Loco for Hollywood." *Hispanic* 11.6 (June 1998): 16.

Lopez, Ana M. "Are all Latins from Manhattan? Hollywood, Ethnography, and Cultural Colonialism." In *Unspeakable Images: Ethnicity and American Cinema*. Ed. Lester Friedman. Chicago: University of Illinois Press, 1991: 404–23.

Mayer, Vicki. *Producing Dreams, Consuming Youth: Mexican Americans and Mass Media.* Piscataway, NJ: Rutgers University Press, 2003.

McAlister, Linda Lopez. "The Woman's Show." WMNF-FM Tampa, FL (88.5), 29 October 1994.

McLean, Adrienne. "I'm a Cancino: Transformation, Ethnicity, and Authenticity in the Construction of Rita Hayworth." *Journal of Film and Video* 44.3–4 (Fall/Winter 1993): 8–26.

Maltby, Richard and Ian Craven. *Hollywood Cinema.* Oxford: Blackwell, 1995.

McLaren, Peter and Ramin Farahmandpur. "Critical Pedagogy, Postmodernism, and the Retreat from Class: Towards a Contraband Pedagogy." In *Postmodernism in Educational Theory: Education and the Politics of Human Resistance.* Ed. D. Hill, P. Mclaren, M. Cole and G. Rikowski. London: Tufnell, 1999.

Mendible, Myra (ed.). *From Bananas to Buttocks: The Latina Body in Popular Culture.* Austin: University of Texas Press, 2006.

Milner, Andrew. *Class.* London: Sage, 1999.

Morris, Dick. "Hispanics: Key to GOP's Future." *New York Post,* 15 January 2004. Munt, Sally (ed.). *Cultural Studies and the Working Class: Subject to Change.* London: Cassell, 2000.

Murray, Y. "Jennifer Lopez." *Buzz* 69 (April 1997): 72.

Negra, Diane. *Off-White Hollywood: American Culture and Ethnic Female Stardom.* New York: Routledge, 2001.

___. "Quality Postfeminism? Sex and the Single Girl on HBO." *Genders* 39 (2004). <http://www. genders.org/g39/g39_negra.html>.

Negron Muntaner, Frances. "Jennifer's Butt." *Aztlán* 22.2 (1997): 181–94.

Noriega, Chon A. "Between a Weapon and a Formula: Chicano Cinema and Its Context." In *Chicanos and Film: Representation and Resistance.* Ed. Chon A. Noriega. Minneapolis: University of Minnesota Press, 1992.

Rios Bustamante, Antonio. "Latino Participation in the Hollywood Film Industry, 1911–1945." In *Chicanos and Film: Representation and Resistance.* Ed. Chon A. Noriega. Minneapolis: University of Minnesota Press, 1992: 18–28.

Ross, Steven J. *Working Class Hollywood: Silent Films and the Shaping of Class in America.* Princeton, NJ: Princeton University Press, 1999.

Scott, A. O. "Puttin' Down Mop, Puttin' On the Ritz." *New York Times,* December 13, 2002.

"Screen Actors Guild says Hispanics, Asians Losing Acting Roles." 8 October 2004. <http://www.tam-pabaylive .com/entertainment/stories/0410/041008guild.shtm>.

Streeby, Shelley. *American Sensations: Class, Empire, and the Production of Popular Culture.* Berkeley: University of California Press, 2002.

Tasker, Yvonne and Diane Negra (eds). "In Focus: Postfeminism and Contemporary Media Studies." *Cinema Journal* 44.2 (Winter 2005): 107–33.

Valdivia, Angharad. *A Latina in the Land of Hollywood.* Tucson: University of Arizona Press, 2000.

___. "Latinas as Radical Hybrid: Transnationally Gender Traces in Mainstream Media." *Global Media Journal* 2.4 (Spring 2004).

READING 7
BOYZ, BOYZ, BOYZ: NEW BLACK CINEMA AND BLACK MASCULINITY

By Keith M. Harris

In the Hollywood tradition of "mainstream film," the visual codes surrounding blacks and blackness on the screen have been stereotypical images, more contemporarily drug dealers, prostitutes, single mothers and complacent drag queens. These are the traditional encodings informed by popular discourse of race and gender, reflecting and sustaining popular convictions about blackness and black sexuality. Implicit in these encodings of blackness as deviancy is the encoding, the way of seeing whiteness as the social and sexual norm, as reason and rationality, as civility and tradition. In the realm of popular culture, these discursive images, as film transcodes them, dispense the "framework[s] of symbols, concepts and images through which we understand, interpret, and represent aspects of our 'racial' existence."[1] However, since the mid-1980s, Hollywood and independent American cinema have seen a rise in films by African American filmmakers. Often touted as being "by, for, and about African Americans," these films are social commentaries, indictments of racism and depictions of "everyday" African American lives. Afrocentrism and nationalistic pride often inform the aesthetic frameworks of these films, and they are replete with black cultural signifiers.

Juxtaposed against the traditional representations of blacks and blackness, New Black Cinema[2] takes on the project of cultural intervention and the recoding of blackness, "revising the visual codes surrounding black skin on the screen and in the public realm."[3] This is ultimately a political project within its relationship to the Hollywood tradition and the traditional racialist and, at times, racist codings of blackness and a project which is dialectical within the real/representation relationship of New Black Cinema. My interest is in the representational dialogic of racial difference within film and the real/representation dialectic of cultural, gender and sexual identity.

The number of films that I have viewed in preparation for discussion raises various complicated issues of race, class and gender and the representation of race, class and gender, ranging from sexual liberation in Spike Lee's successful independent film, *She's Gotta Have It*, to the coming of age story in John Singleton's *Boyz N the Hood*.[4] At the core of these films' complexities are the problematics and paradoxes of black masculinity and images of black men and black masculinity. The operation of recoding masculinity from established, now historic, Hollywood codings of black men and black masculinity visualizes a more ambiguous, more discursive image, producing the meanings of an intricately constructed masculinity, more complexly dimensional than the sub missive, docile Tom or the morally corrupt, conniving, sexually threatening drug dealer.[5]

However, these more aggressive, politically charged black masculinities, now turned difficult, involved, ideological metaphors, construct themselves, in the arena of meanings, from the existing, pop cultural and filmic representations of masculinity. By operating referentially to the popular cultural images of black men which are visibly recurring, or simply fixed, instructing homogeneous, monolithic, and culturally familiar (and therefore, quite culturally consumable) constructs, the critical attention that New Black Cinema markets as black men and masculinity then seemingly becomes reinforcement of singular, monologic meanings, only within different popular images. What is culturally familiar—hip-hop, rap music, commodified neo-national-ism and the cool, posed, "endangered black man"—becomes representationally and culturally totalized as the Black Experience of the young, heterosexual urban black man, the only experience possible.

I have chosen to examine three of the earliest New Black Cinema films: Spike Lee's musical, *School Daze*; Reginald and Warrington Hudlin's teenpic, *House Party*; and John Singleton's coming of age tale, *Boyz N the Hood*. I have chosen these three films for the purposes of critiquing the discursive visual recodings of black masculinity. I have selected these three particular films because the codings and recodings of masculinity and black masculinity are different across the genres of musical, teen comedy, and the more literary coming of age story. By examining these three films in a sequential order, I propose to interrogate patterns of formation of black masculinity as these patterns position (and reposition) women and female sexuality, male homosexual-ity, and the patriarchal construction of the family. These films, if unmediated, serve to construct a master narrative of black men and masculinity and sexuality that attempts to be seamless, unitary and phallic.

SCHOOL DAZE

> This film is … about our existence as a people in white America.[6]

School Daze is a musical, but not quite what one might expect. As Toni Cade Bambara notes: "Lee … chooses an enshrined genre of the dominant cinema … whose conventions were not designed to address an embattled community's concerns."[7] In the big MGM Hollywood tradition of elaborate sets, choreography, pageantry and spectacle, *School Daze* is a musical fused with the black cultural signifiers of jazz, Motown sound, and DC go-go. Using an all black, ensemble cast, the musical takes place during the homecoming events on the fictional campus of the historically black Mission College.

The focus of the film revolves around four gendered social groups: the Gammites, men; the Wannabees, women; Dap and da fellas, men; and the Jigaboos, women. The tension of the film lies in the shade/caste/class racial identity and community conflict that subdivides, and heterosexually aligns, the gendered groups into two binaries: the Jigaboos, the dark-skinned group, led by Dap and Rachel, made up of predominately working-class black folk, *versus* the Wannabees, led by Julien and Jane, made up of light-skinned, upwardly mobile, middle-class black folk. The women confront the shade complex and racial identity issue. What is at stake is who, culturally, is the "blackest," has internalized white aesthetics of beauty more, and is more naturally black. The men confront the class and community division as being one of who is going to lead black people and what political ideology will inform a people's cultural and economic mobility. The campus is divided along these lines, representing the political and cultural dilemma of black communities at large.

Thus in keeping with the popular, yet oppositional, cultural positionality of New Black Cinema, the musical takes place during the homecoming events on the Mission College campus, examining the politics of race in an embattled community. It is in this setting that Lee subverts the use of the musical. Richard Dyer analyzes entertainment, and particularly the Hollywood musical, as utopian fantasies inverting the signifiers of scarcity, exhaustion, dreariness, manipulation and fragmentation with the utopian sensibilities of abundance, energy, intensity, transparency, and community.[8] The entertaining inversions finally serve as temporal and spatial escapes from the "inadequacies of the society." With the musical, the result is a "utopian world" in which tension and conflict resolve in a burst into dance and song.

Dyer further notes that the "utopian world" of entertainment responds to real needs in society, but entertainment is also defining and delimiting what is a legitimate, real need in society. What are defined out of the category of "real need" within the utopian vision of entertainment are the social-cultural problems of race and gender, among other things. Spike Lee disrupts the musical form by placing the problem of race and racial identity into the field of vision, and by orienting this disruption in the utopian sensibility of community, the problem of race and racial disunity is then seen as an impediment and hindrance to community formation and function within an oppressive environment. Though Lee disrupts the utopianism inherent in the musical form, *School Daze* is not simply an alternative dystopian vision of the world in that it does not represent the imaginary as a wretched, fearful place. The disruption of the form allows for the representation of a black community as a thinking, self-critical body of people.

As the film is not a dystopian one, it is a masculinist one. The political question and possibility of unification seems to be the debate of the film, and by positioning the unification of black people and black communities within a narrative history of slavery, emancipation, reconstruction, migrations, segregation, civil rights, and economic plight (all of which are set in the photo montage as the film's credits appear on screen), *School Daze* and the question of unification then flow into a cultural current of self-determination and survival. With the Afrocentric vision, nationalist iconography, and urban, hip-hop cultural infusions, the fluent visuals, rhythms, and language of the film become messengers for the unification of a retrograde nation, a nation informed by the patriarchal demarcations of power and gender inherent in the nationalistic agenda.[9] As informed by the ideological and sexual paradigms of cultural nationalism, sexual difference becomes the discourse mediating intraracial relations, separating racial identity and community into heterosexual, gendered domains. Racial identity, the light/dark conflict, is feminine and signified by the female body; community and leadership are masculine. Unification then falls into the traditional construction of racial oppression and the recovery from racial oppression as a "man's problem," as racial emasculation, as the recovery of the phallus.

The women's color/shade problem is introduced in the first musical number, "Straight and Nappy." In the narrative, the two groups of women, the Jigaboos, the dark-skinned women, and the Wannabees, the light-skinned women, confront each other in the dormitory corridor. What ensues through the musical number is an argument over shade, weaves, naps, contact lenses, and men. In "Madame Ree Ree's Hair Salon," the Jigaboos and Wannabees are in a gang fight set to the sound of big band. The territory of dispute is the female body, the black female body. Rachel, Dap's girlfriend and head Jigaboo, and Jane, Julian's girlfriend and head

Wannabee, face off to the chorus: "Talkin' 'bout good and bad hair/whether you are dark or fair/go on and swear/see if I care good and bad hair." At one point in the number, the Jigaboos and the Wannabees don fans bearing images of Hattie McDaniel/Mammy and Vivian Leigh/Scarlet O'Hara, the perennial Hollywood images of the black woman *versus* the white woman. The fans of McDaniel and Leigh as they circulate within the spectacle serve as the choice for the women, neither one of which is a real choice for black women. The racialized masquerade, as indicated by the donning of fans, directs the spectator to the constructedness of women and racialized femininity and to the female body as the demarcation of the color difference and intraracial community problem. The female body is spectacle, objectified, scandalous, and contemptible. The spectacle of "Straight and Nappy" is cathartic in that it removes the skin color conflict of racial identity from the men and embodies it in the female body. Racial identity is then separated from the community of men, becoming an object for recovery.

Not surprisingly, in the narrative of the film, Rachel and Dap argue, in the course of which Rachel suggests that Dap only dates her because of the shade, the darkness, of her skin. Rachel argues that Dap's association with her, "the darkest thing on campus," is "good for [his] all-the-way-down pro-black image." The female body and the skin color/shade of the female body become commodities in exchange for power and control. As commodities, certain values are assigned. In this case there is the historic value of white over black, light over dark. The skin color/shade of the objectified woman, now the black body, determines the politic of the man in possession of the body.

A more explicit example than the demonstrated use of Rachel's body is the use of Jane's body in the Gammites' rite of passage. After the pledges go over, joining the fraternity and becoming Gamma men, Half-Pint (Spike Lee's character) is still a virgin. What follows is Julian's (the head Gamma) trickery and coercion of both Jane and Half-Pint: Jane is raped/what she bodily possesses—Half-Pint's manhood and racial identity—is exchanged for Half-Pint's virginity. Half-Pint, now a Gamma man, enters into the ranks of the future leaders of the race. The sexual act, his initiation into manhood, recuperates his authenticity, his blackness, and his political alignment with the Wannabees, as a class and as a community.

Even though Lee's disruption of the musical form allows for an interrogation and re-presentation of the representation of black masculinity, Lee does not subvert the male gaze (however, he does racialize it).[10] Operating in a classic narrative form, the images of the women remain static, eroticized and fragmented; the men are active agents, representing movement and resolution. Race and sexual difference are collapsed; the black woman then simultaneously represents the lack of blackness and the phallus. Consequently, race and sexual difference are fetishized. Sexual difference becomes containment in a conventional construction of masculinity.

HOUSE PARTY

I wanted to make a movie that had social messages, but was also entertaining, nonstop fun. ...[11]

In Warrington and Reginald Hudlin's House Party, coding of male homosexuality and the representation of the male homosexual both situate the recoding of black masculinity as racial and class responsibility. *House Party* is a teenpic as characterized by the simple plot, the narrative of the rebellious youth, sub merged in the urban, counter-cultural lifestyle of the day, the rhythms of hip-hop and rap. This is a very deliberate film, very much in dialogue with Hollywood, mainstream film and popular cultural images of black people, especially black men, and very conscious of its youthful black audience. Therefore, what is very formulaic and exploitative (of teenagers, music and adolescent angst) in a Hollywood convention is rendered critical and interventionist, foregrounding race and oppression.

What is so deliberate and intentional about this film is the inversion of the common, stereotypical representations of black men and black communities with opposing cultural codings that, in turn, bring into question the fabrication and falsity of the stereotype itself. These critical inversions lead Lisa Kennedy to comment: "[*House Party*] touches on many of the signs of the black familiar—the projects, police brutality, teen sex, teen drinking, … black on black crime. … "[12] By "touching" on these signs of the "black familiar," and inverting them, the Hudlins construct a cinematic portrait of a utopian, "imagined community," inventing the visual meaning of a nation of black people, in which the stereotypes are supplanted, in the case of this film, with revised, "positive" images: there is the single-parent family with a black man, Pop, who is the head of the household in contrast to the much-media-dogged single black mother; there is the absence of a drug-plagued, inner-city black ghetto, replaced by the sanitary, drug-free suburban community; class strife is submerged; the black middle class is attendant and responsible for the entire representational community; and there is the representation of sexually responsible black youth.

Kid, the protagonist, is introduced to the audience as the only child in a male-headed household, trustworthy, and obedient, a clean-cut young man. This introduction is determining of two things: first, it establishes the narrative of the teen film as one of disobedience; the acting out of disobedience and punishment becomes the narrative motivation and plot closure for the film. Second, the family setting with Pop, as the widower father, is in opposition to the abandoned, single black mother image that is so pervasive in the media and Hollywood representation of the black family (which leaves the image of the single black mother intact and unexamined, simply suggesting that a man is better). Placing Kid next to Pop and suspending them in idiomatic language and the hip-hop culture codings of the *mise-en-scène*, Kid and Pop become authentic community role models for black youth. The role model itself offers a unitary symbol of man, black man, and manhood, informing class, sexual, and aesthetic standards to which the nation is to aspire and maintain. Respectability, as in Kid's responsibility in sexual abstinence and respect to and for his father, defines the parameters of moral codes, what is acceptable and not acceptable, what is good or bad. The role model, then, becomes a form of social control delimiting the parameters and the permanence of the construct of the black man.

As a role model, Kid's disobedience must be a punishable and redeemable learning experience. In the cafeteria scene immediately following his introduction, Kid wrangles with thugs—Stab, Zilla, and Pee Wee. The premise: Kid accidentally spills milk, a sexual slur is directed at his mother, and finally the pheromonal battle cry, issued simultaneously from Stab, Zilla and Pee Wee: "I smell pussy!" Thus, Kid is effeminized. The "smell of pussy" leads to a fight, in which Kid is beaten and reprimanded and Stab is expelled. As the film continues, it becomes clear that the premise of the film, Kid's going to the party without his father's consent, is ultimately a test of his manhood.

Now I want to turn the discussion to a close reading of two of the film's discursive maneuvers: the manipulation of the presence of homosexuality and the absence of the homosexual in this film. Homosexuality is present and detached from the black man and the black community. This presence and detachment serves two purposes. First, there is the establishment of homosexuality as a deviation from and threat to heterosexual black masculinity. When Kid is arrested, the responsible heterosexual sex scene in which the use of the condom, the trope of safe sex, is solely contraceptive precedes the jail scene, which is ostensibly about safe sex and anti-rape. The fixed use of the condom as contraception without a hint of its prophylactic use reconfigures any configured safe sex message, as it re-inscribes heterosexuality. What is articulated in the homosocial jailhouse setting of leering, caged men is that homosexuality is solely a homosexual act of violence and rape—with AIDS as the signifier of a wrongful act of violence. (Not surprisingly, the discourse of AIDS is conducted in the confines of a jail cell as something arrested and criminal in the black community.[13]) The second use of homosexuality lies in the submerged text of class difference. If homosexuality is a metaphor for the conflict between black men and criminality, the metaphor of disavowal, then metaphor intersects with metonym at the point of class. Class is submerged in a discourse of heterosexual, masculine difference, and is defined, and subsequently undefined, by the removal of homosexuality and the differentiation of a good, straight black man from a bad, straight black man, a positive image from a negative image. The presence of homosexuality demonstrates a black masculinity that is fluid between the heterosexual poles of good and bad. The concealment of class difference behind the veil of a good/bad dualism and pervasive morality refigures class on a moral plane transcoding the accoutrement and the materiality of class into moral signs. In this refiguration "Jheri" curls, bulging muscles, tank tops, and dark skin, the working-class signifiers of black masculinity, become the signifiers of the morally corrupt. The narrative identification of Kid as the protagonist positions spectators to identify with middle-class righteousness, privileging the middle-class aesthetic of the film.

Curiously missing in the presence of homosexuality is its embodiment in the homosexual. The absence of the homosexual, the lack of the physical display or some textual disclosure of a character, is deceptive in that the physical absence itself gives presence to the homosexual. I mean that homosexuals, specifically gay men, are not in the film, but figuratively still there. The first three gay men appear on the body of Bilial, the dj for the evening's infamous party. Bilial is bedecked with Keith Haring "Free South Africa" buttons, the oversized Willi Smith clothing, and Patrick Kelly designer buttons and combs.[14] These three men, a pop artist and two designers, respectively, were all dying or had already died of AIDS by the release of House Party. All three of these men were gay; two of them, Willi Smith and Patrick Kelly, were black. During the jail scene, the last two gay men, Rock Hudson and Liberace, appear in reference to their deaths from AIDS.

The presence of the absent homosexual totalizes the coding of black men and masculinity as unitary and heterosexual. Gay black men, for example Willi Smith and Patrick Kelly, are commodified and erased, in the appropriated commodity form, from the representational black community, and gay white men, Rock Hudson and Liberace, signify the homosexual body. The cathexis of the homosexuality onto the absent, white, male homosexual body negates the possibility of a black gay man. Of course in view of the jail cell finale, the absent homosexual body, indeed the performative body, is doubly negated from the black community as it is contained within the film's insidious AIDS discourse, a discourse of criminality, confinement and race.

Again, as with School Daze, there is an oppositional aesthetic which foregrounds race and the construction of race, only to re-inscribe race in a discourse of patriarchy and heterosexuality. The reversal of denigrating stereotypes into the positive role model character of Kid is problematic in that the role model and role modeling are generative of another stereotype, perhaps more moral and corrective, but nonetheless a stereotype—a fixed and fixing conventional conception of black masculinity. The positive/negative image abstraction, as conceived, only serves to transpose one stereotype with another. The positive stereotype of black is exchanged with the negative stereotype of white. This limits the film's visual analysis of social messages to an us/them binary opposition, replacing "them" (white folk) with "us" (black folk), without interrogating the construct of us/them. The blind-sighted contradiction of this binary opposition is the re-inscription of the oppressor and the oppressed, or as in the film, heterosexual, masculine subject formation as determined by the negation of the homosexual.

BOYZ N THE HOOD

> My film has a lot of messages in it … but my main message is that African American men have to take responsibility for raising their children, especially their boys. Fathers have to teach their boys to be men. The audience will be able to see the direction that the characters take when there is an absence or a presence of fathers in their lives.[15]

In *Boyz N the Hood*, John Singleton employs some of the narrative conventions of the melodrama, as Jackie Bayars has outlined them, which provide a mode for constructing moral identity. As Bayars explains, the melodramatic form functions as a site of conflict over social values, is often situated in family struggle, and often serves to define and redefine gender and its relationship to the structure of the family.[16] Bayars also discusses the male-oriented melodramas in which men are coming of age and establishing identity and relationships with their fathers.[17] In a traditional reading, a masculine coming of age story follows a young man as he finds himself, establishes his masculinity, and masters his sexual awakening and sexual urges.[18] *Boyz N the Hood* does not break with this tradition; however, in an expansion of the notion of family to an inclusion of community, the film places the story in South Central Los Angeles, an urban black community. Again as with *School Daze* and *House Party* race is centered, central to the melodrama.

Unlike *School Daze* and *House Party*, *Boyz* does not use sexual difference and sexuality, women and homosexuality, to define and negotiate black masculinity and black men. In turn, in the absence of homosexuality and with the oppositional symbolism of father and mother, black men are defined against heterosexual, masculine differences, and, once defined, black men are presented in an Oedipal opposition to black women as mothers in a family structure. This distinction of the definition by differences in masculinity is crucial because it then is the cause for the filmic opposition of black men and women.

First I want to examine the men, Furious, Tre, Ricky, and Doughboy. There is a parental figure, Furious, from whom the codings of masculinity and the fraternal order of Tre, Ricky, and Doughboy are derived. The representation of black men and masculinity is in dialog with the representation of male heterosexuality. In this dialog the film gives an age and maturation continuum of black men. This allows the audience to see the men through childhood, adolescence and manhood. This also allows for the visualization of difference in black men, how this difference, supposedly, develops and how, finally, the singular image of black man is created. The difference in masculinity pivots on the representation of Doughboy. As a visual image, Doughboy is both narratively and aesthetically abject, the low point, the lost, the dispossessed, the visually banished, yet not disavowed, forcing, but not bursting, the seams of masculinity: Doughboy is very much a black man, not removed from the film's range of black masculinity, but nonetheless, not what a black man should be. Within the narrative Doughboy is the bad seed, the disfavored son of Ms Baker; he is unemployed and criminal. Aesthetically, and in contrast to the well-built, toned and well-groomed images of Tre and Ricky (Doughboy's brother), Doughboy is fat and physically sloppy, malt liquor totting and "Jheri" curled, all the trappings that have come to code the masculinity of the black underclass.

As the abject, Doughboy defines the possibility of black masculinity, indeed the nadir, which is descendent from Furious, the peak of black masculinity. This construction of masculinity, with its highs and lows, allows for the totalizing monolith of Furious as the father and re-claimer. For, once abject-ed, Doughboy challenges and narratively motivates the reconstruction of masculinity. Consequently, Furious must meet the challenge by raising his son, Tre, as only a man can, and since Furious is the only father, absent or present in the film, as only he can.

To Singleton's credit, the audience is not bombarded with heavy, and naively simplistic, good/bad moralism. Doughboy's abjection is not represented as bad in that he is not good, but Doughboy is an anti-hero, conscious of his abjection, knowing his environment and mastering it. As the rejected son and the ex-con, Doughboy creates his own community of men in which he is the leader and protector. On the fringes of black masculinity, beyond recovery, Doughboy defines black masculinity and, while avenging his brother's murder, redeems black masculinity.

At the core of the representation of masculine difference and the reconstruction and reclamation of black masculinity is the representation of women and the family, and family values. The singular father image of Furious is projected against that of three images of the mother: Ms Baker, the crack mother and Reva, Furious' ex-wife. While Furious is the instructive, politically aware, community-based entrepreneur, Ms Baker, Ricky and Doughboy's mother, is a single mother with no narrative means of income. Doughboy as the abject is the product of a female-headed, single-parent household. In contrast to Furious, who provides parental guidance and Afrocentric encouragements of self-determination, Ms Baker favors Ricky over Doughboy, giving some guidance and encouragement to Ricky and nothing but verbal abuse to Doughboy. The only other neighborhood mother whom we see is the crack mother across the street. This is the mother who allows her young child to wander, unattended, into traffic. This is the mother who offers fellatio to buy crack.

Reva, Tre's mother, who gives her son up to Furious because she feels she is unable to raise her man child, is depicted later in the film, surrounded by the professional, single-woman opulence of her plush apartment, as upwardly mobile and meddling, opportunistic in her request for Tre to return to her parental custody. In the café scene between Furious and Reva, what would otherwise be a pro-feminist stance is rendered feminist backlash as Reva asserts that by raising his son, Furious has done nothing special, has done nothing that black mothers have not been doing for years. This comes only after Reva has shown that she cannot raise Tre herself, nor can any other woman in the film rear a son.

These images of black mothers would not be so damning if they were not so pervasive. These three images are very calculated and positioned in a masculine coming of age narrative, in a community of men, in opposition to the only father in the film. This community of men is in struggle for salvation and survival. Consequently, Furious, as the father, is a messianic figure, bearing salvation, bringing control and order back to the community. With Tre as the son and protagonist growing up in the mire of South Central Los Angeles, the salvation of the community is through the resurrection and preservation of this masculinity. Again, as in

House Party, there is the instructional representation of the role model. In the case of *Boyz*, Tre is posited as the role model because he has a role model: his father, Furious Styles. As a consequence, Tre is invested with the future of the filmic community.

In 1991 there were some nineteen films by black directors scheduled for release. By the end of 1991, at least twelve of these films were released with the backing of big Hollywood studios.[19] Clearly these films were popular and profitable, but the content and subject matter of these films—black people, black people's lives and cultural space and identity—were seemingly in contrast to Hollywood's racial traditions. In terms of popular trends, New Black Cinema was preceded by rap and hip-hop music, the popular image of the "endangered black man" and the sociological interest in drugs, crime and the inner city, all of which are portrayed by the media as a black dilemma.[20] The strategy of New Black Cinema was to recode the existing codings of blackness, informing the symbolic with the social and cultural sensibilities of black culture, Afrocentrism, and the everyday experiences of black people.

On the one hand, the issues of blackness, nationalism, and masculinity present in these early New Black Cinema films, in my reading, raise critical questions about the representations themselves; on the other hand, as Guerrero notes, these filmmakers in their mainstream, independent, and insurgent forms and tendencies expose and negotiate discriminatory practices in Hollywood (around marketing, promotion, and development of "black-themed" films) and, in doing so, engage and often explicitly provide a reading, a hermeneutic investigation, of American culture: as problematic as *School Daze*, *House Party*, and *Boyz N the Hood* are, they do present blackness and black masculinity as a site of interpretation, critique, and ethical engagement, as ongoing projects and cultural formations.[21]

In the New Black Cinema films examined above, race as a discourse, especially as popular American discourse, functions in models of exceptionalism, talent and virtuosity, as these models are deployed for racial, social, and political uplift (not surprisingly, most of these films are often described as masculine narratives). Furthermore, the use of blackness is critical of the invisibility of whiteness as an organizing trope and discourse. In other words, the emphasis on blackness as a constructed visual representation, as generic and hermeneutic devices, directs viewers to the use of race, notions of black and white as organizing narrative and visual elements. This New Black Cinema moment is an example of the early self-positions in Cornel West's new cultural politics of difference, and exclusive "talented tenth" grouping, a grouping which opened market and audience doors. Yet, there has been a marked shift; the issues and questions of racial representation have markedly changed. One can, on the one hand, argue that New Black Cinema has integrated and been assimilated into the American film machine (older filmmakers who have benefited include Michael Schultz and Bill Duke, and, more recently, Forrest Whittiker); on the other hand, black filmmakers are now the interpreters of whiteness. By this I mean that black cinema has, through the efforts of New Black Cinema, developed a market and audience, which reflect not only its success as a popular form, but also its critical interrogations and interpretations of blackness and race. This latter aspect of black cinema as critical interrogation and interpretation is where New Black Cinema has shifted in emphasis.

Let me clarify: two high-profile national and media incidents reframed the discursivity of black masculinity in the 1990s: the Rodney King beating, the Simi Valley jury's acquittal of the police officers responsible and the subsequent protests and riots (1992); and the O.J. Simpson verdict (1995). With the Rodney King beating, verdict and riot, black masculinity is reiterated in notions of aggression, submission, and criminality, and simultaneously repositioned within notions of collective and historical victimhood and denied and delayed state justice. The black masculine is violently removed from a liberal discourse of race pathology and re-inscribed in a Foucaultian notion of the state. The simultaneity of iteration and inscription, on the one hand, serves to universalize the black man as victim (in that the Rodney King beating is an incident of state control, of which everyone is a victim); on the other hand, the simultaneity of iteration and inscription serves to particularize the state's relationship to the black body (in that the black male body is the demonstrative body).

In the O.J. Simpson case, there is a greater sense of cultural betrayal. As an actor and entrepreneur, Simpson was an exemplar of the democratic ethos of celebrity; a model of the athletic masculine ideal; and an exemplar of integration and racial harmony. However, the trial for the murder of Nicole Brown Simpson and Ronald Goldman re-blackened, so to speak, his celebrity and masculinity: the black man is re-criminalized as the brute, the rapist, and the threat to white femininity and civility. With his acquittal, O.J. Simpson became a figure of "black" justice (especially in light of the initial Rodney King verdict); at the same time, he became a figure of liberal white injustice. By this I mean that Simpson valorized the American justice system of fair trial, while he vilified the American dream and the American ideal of integration.

The question becomes, what is the impact of these ambiguous, discursive black masculinities in the realm of representation, mass media and entertainment? These two figures, Rodney King and O.J. Simpson—the quotidian and the celebrity, the everyday and the iconic—become a split image fused in the cultural imaginary as the limit and horizon of the representation of black masculinity.[22] It is the horizon of the representation of black masculinity because it is ambiguous, rendering the representation of black masculinity as inassimilable to stereotype and stereotypic representation; the split image is the limit of the representation of black masculinity because in its ambiguity the split image reveals the disavowed contradictions of American class and racial ideals, a productive and profitable disavowal, indeed the disavowal of entertainment itself.

The mediations of this split image have been subtle, partially through the co-optation and absorption of black-themed narratives and characters into popular culture as economically viable entertainment (films and especially hip-hop inflected films which use rap artists as actors) and partially through the movement of black filmmakers into more mainstream projects.[23] In the post-Rodney King/Simpson verdict era, the standardized hood film, unable to engage the conflicts and contradictions of the 1990s black masculine, fell into redundancy similar to Blaxploitation. At the same time, there were "applications" similar to those of Blaxploitation (the application of blackness to standard, tried and true narratives) in films like *Tales from the Hood* (1995) and *Vampire in Brooklyn* (1995), exploring race and horror. However, films that confronted race more historically, critically and confrontationally in the established masculine narrative mode of New Black Cinema failed at the box office.[24]

In partial recognition of the shifting significations of race and masculinity, Guerrero notes that the racial climate and popular audience mood immediately following the O.J. Simpson verdict contributed to the box office failure of two films; specifically, *Devil in a Blue Dress* (1995) and *Strange Days* (1995).[25] It is my contention that, yes, on that October weekend in 1995, the majority American audience was unwilling to confront a film like *Devil* or *Strange Days* because of their emphasis on race, but also I contend that black cinema, in its New Black Cinema permutation, can no longer support the masculine narratives of a film like *Devil* because of the conflicting split imagery of media black masculinity. In other words, the prototypical, recuperative images of black men in the early films of New Black Cinema are no longer viable representations because of their uncomplicated, simplistically redemptive discursivity.

Two things have happened. First, New Black Cinema has succeeded in changing the face of American cinema in that black-themed films, black male characters, and black male stars have multiplied and done so with economic and industrial success.[26] The aesthetic emphasis of these films has been on the representation and interpretation of filmic and pop cultural images of blackness as these images have been deployed to the service of representing whiteness as the norm, as normativity. Second, in the expansion of market and audience, there are greater demands on the black film. With the ambiguity of the black male and the black male narrative, there is necessarily a change in subject matter, different themes of racialized subject formations, different thematic contexts for the black male. This has entailed a move away from the masculine, urban-centered narrative of the initial outpouring of New Black Cinema[27] to the decidedly post-New Black Cinema focus on family (both urban and rural), the black middle class, and female-centered narrative, and to the post-New Black Cinema shift in the signifying practices of race and black cinema. With the second significatory component, I mean to suggest that blackness is inscribed in recent films in a more aesthetic manner as a way of looking, as a way of being, as opposed to the black character or *mise-en-scène* of blackness determining and defining the films of New Black Cinema. In the first instance and the broadening of narratives, I refer to films like *Soul Food*, *Down in the Delta*, *Eve's Bayou*, *Friday*, *The Brothers*, *Kingdom Come*, *Set It Off*, and *Waiting to Exhale*, to name a few. In the second instance, I refer to films like *Summer of Sam* and the more recent *From Hell* in which blackness is rendered as a transgeneric hermeneutic device which provides an interpretation of whiteness in narratives about white men.

NOTES

1. Michael Omi, "In Living Color: Race and American Culture," *Cultural Politics in Contemporary America*, eds Ian Angus and Sut Jhally (New York: Routledge, 1989), p. 114.

2. New Black Cinema refers to a period of black cinema, roughly between 1985 and 1995. This periodization follows Tommy Lott's demarcation of black cinema. See Tommy Lott, "A No-Theory Theory of Contemporary Black Cinema," *Black Literature Forum* (currently *African American Review*) 25.2 (Summer 1991): pp. 221–36.

3. James Snead, "Recoding Blackness: The Visual Rhetoric of Black Independent Film," *Whitney Museum of American Art: The New American Filmmakers Series*, Program 23, pp. 1–2.

4. These films include *Do the Right Thing*, *House Party*, *Def by Temptation*, *Juice*, *A Rage in Harlem*, *New Jack City*, *Five Heartbeats*, *Boyz N the Hood*, *Jungle Fever*, *Mo' Better Blues*, *Chameleon Street*, *School Daze*, *Straight Outta Brooklyn*, and *Harlem Nights*.

5. For example, see the three images, and their differences, among Nola Darling's suitors in Spike Lee's *She's Gotta Have It*.

6. Spike Lee, *Uplift the Race: The Construction of School Daze* (New York: Simon & Schuster, 1988), p. 179.

7. Toni Cade Bambara, "Programming with *School Daze*," *Five by Five: The Films of Spike Lee*, ed. Shirley L. Poole (New York: Stewart, Tabori & Chang, Inc., 1991), p. 49.

8. Dyer defines the utopian sensibilities as follows: energy, the capacity to act vigorously; human power, activity, potential (e.g. dance); abundance, the conquest of scarcity; having enough to spare without sense of poverty of other; enjoyment of sensuous material reality (e.g. spectacle); intensity, experiencing of emotion directly, fully, unambiguously, "authentically" without holding back (e.g. "incandescent" star performers); transparence, a quality of relationships—between represented characters, between performer and audience (e.g. sincere stars; love and romance); and community, togetherness, sense of belonging, network of phatic relationships (e.g. singalong chorus numbers). See Richard Dyer, "Entertainment and Utopia," in *Genre: The Musical*, ed. Rick Altman (London: Routledge and Kegan Paul, 1981), pp. 175–89.

9. George Mosse, *Nationalism and Sexuality: Middle-Class Morality and Sexual Norms in Modern Europe* (Madison, WI: Wisconsin University Press, 1985).

10. Here I am referring to Mulvey's "Visual Pleasure and Narrative Cinema." However, I will not attempt to engage in questions of spectatorship. At this point, I am interested in Lee's structuring of the male gaze. See Laura Mulvey, *Visual and Other Pleasures* (Bloomington, IN: Indiana University Press, 1989).

11. Reginald Hudlin interviewed in Marlaine Glicksman, "They Gotta Have It," *Film Comment* (May–June 1990), pp. 65–9.

12. Lisa Kennedy, "Wack House," *Village Voice* (March 13, 1990), p. 65.

13. Warrington Hudlin argues that this scene is anti-rape (*versus* anti-gay): "The point is the guy is in danger of being raped. We're not taking a position on homosexuality, we're taking a position on sex against someone's will." However, the confinement of the anti-rape discourse to a homosocial space of the prison cell directs the viewer not only to the potential of rape but also to rape as forced homosexuality; see Glicksman, "They Gotta Have It."

14. See Kennedy's reading of Bilial.

15. John Singleton interviewed in Thomas Doherty and Jaquie Jones, "Two Takes on *Boyz N the Hood*," *Cineaste* 18.4 (1991), pp. 16–19.

16. Jackie Bayars, *All That Heaven Allows: Re-Reading Gender in the 1950s Melodrama* (Chapel Hill, NC: The University of North Carolina Press, 1990), p. 8.

17. Bayars, pp. 217–26.

18. Jonathan Rutherford, "Who's That Man?" *Male Order: Unwrapping Masculinity*, eds Rowena Chapman and Jonathan Rutherford (London: Lawrence & Wishart, 1988), pp. 21–67.

19. Patrick Cole, "Cinema Revolution," *Emerge* (January 1992), pp. 36–40.

20. Jacqui Jones, "The New Ghetto Aesthetic," *Wide Angle* 13.3–4 (1991), pp. 32–43.

21. Ed Guerrero, "A Circus of Dreams and Lies: The Black Film Wave at Middle Age," *The New American Cinema*, ed. Jon Lewis (Durham, NC: Duke University Press, 1998), pp. 328–52.

22. Here I am using Judith Mayne's notion of the limit and horizon. See Judith Mayne, "A Parallax View of Lesbian Authorship," *Inside/Out*, ed. Daina Fuss (New York: Routledge, 1991), pp. 173–84.

23. For more discussion of this see Guerrero, "Circus of Dreams and Lies."

24. Films like *Panther* (Mario Van Peebles 1995); *Dead Presidents* (The Hughes Brothers 1995); *Clockers* (Spike Lee 1995); and *Devil in a Blue Dress* (Carl Franklin 1995), for example.

25. Guerrero, "Circus of Dreams and Lies," p. 349.

26. This is most apparent in the increased and increasing number of black male stars and celebrities: Denzel Washington, Will Smith, Eddie Murphy, Ice-T, Ice Cube, Samuel Jackson, Laurence Fishbourne, Roger Guenevere Smith, Savion Glover, Cedric the Entertainer, Bernie Mac, Steve Harvey, Chris Rock, Chris Tucker, Jamie Foxx, to name a few. And also the expansion of the role of the thug or the gangsta to that of the anti-hero in American film, for example Ice Cube's character in *Escape from Mars* (John Carpenter 2001) or XXX: *State of the Union* (Lee Tamohori 2005) and Snoop Doggy Dogg's character in *Bones* (Ernest Dickerson 2001).

27. Indeed, one can examine John Singleton's return to the hood film, a genre and black male narrative which he, arguably, formalized, and the closure of that genre and narrative in *Baby Boy* (2001). In this film Singleton rewrites the ambiguous and abject figure of the gangsta, Doughboy (Ice Cube) from *Boyz N the Hood* (1991), as threat, menace and impossibility in the imagined black community, through the annihilation of the gangsta character Rodney (Snoop Dogg) in the protection of family and class and economic mobility. The archetypal gangsta character, which functioned as the consciousness of the black community in so many hood films, is no longer viable and, instead, replaced by the conscientious, jobless, yet upwardly mobile, "baby boy" (Jody as portrayed by Tyrese Gibson), a figure of mockery and revision.

CHAPTER 3
MEDIA AND THE REPRESENTATION OF GENDER AND SEXUAL DESIRE

EDITOR'S INTRODUCTION

Our identity and how we present ourselves is critical to how we are received by others in the classroom, workplace, and as we participate in family and social occasions. Socially accepted behavior is expected. Family, teachers, religious leaders, and media images offer advice on both appropriate behavior and what is considered socially unacceptable.

Essential to this process is our sense of our sexual identity and how we present ourselves as gendered, sexual beings to others. Here the advice is far more confusing, inadequate, and sometimes goes against the very core of who we are. Understanding who we are and how media narratives and characterizations impact our sense of self is critical to our personal well-being.

Humans cry when in physical or emotional pain. That males are somehow considered less masculine for producing tears goes against our basic human need to express negative, painful experiences in a physical way. That a woman should not be president of the United States because of a stereotypical belief that hormonal shifts caused by menstruation or menopause would make her irrational under pressure is in itself lacking in proof or scientific explanation. Families and religious leaders who set down rules of conduct in gender-specific ways may not be serving well the children whose impulses do not follow the generalized rules.

Mediated gender models add information and tools for problem solving outside personal experience and the advice of those in our social circle. The power of narrative is in its ability to engage us both intellectually and emotionally within a safe context that does not require the exposure of our questions and insecurities. Narrative gratifies our need for order and explanation, a sense of cause-and-effect correlation that explains why things happen the way they do.

MALE TYPES IN POPULAR CULTURE

- Strong
- Brave
- Physical
- Resourceful
- Witty
- Violent

- Persistent
- Winner
- Sexually aggressive
- Sexually desirable
- Seducer
- Adventurer

Film and television programming portrays men in multiple roles and with varying degrees of complexity. Men in our capitalist society are expected to be successful in business in order to provide for themselves and their families. Young men are expected to fight wars, win at sports games, and to successfully bed fertile females in order to protect the country, win glory for their university or community, and keep the population growing. In order to be heroes men should be strong, energetic, and intellectually engaged in commercial innovation. Conversely men should not be afraid to fight or unable to earn a "respectable" living. Male characters in classic Hollywood films were active, adventurous, and victorious.

In *Stagecoach* (1939), though an escapee from jail, John Wayne's character fights to protect the non-heroic occupants of the stagecoach. His tenderness in relating to women and his offer to provide marriage and a home to a prostitute "with a heart of gold" identify a duality in his characterization. The Ringo Kid's ability to fight and successfully defeat the enemies of the community supersedes his past crimes and offers him the rewards of domesticity and a more peaceful future. But will this be enough for a person brought up on violence and competition? Will he follow a path toward further development of future domesticity and community involvement, or will this hero become restless and move off looking for the next fight, the next moment of glory, or the next woman to bed? Both westerns and action adventure films explore these questions as heroes age and as their families crumble. Ethan Edwards in *The Searchers* (1956) saves his family and the small community of which he is a part and then melts back into the wilderness from which he initially emerged. In *Die Hard* (1988) John McClane is having marital problems. His heroic behavior when taking on the evil Hans Gruber and his gang help his estranged wife come back to seeing his value, but will it last? *Fight Club* (1999) and *The Departed* (2006) take on the duality of the masculine persona and question the expectation that the "hero" in US cinema is both ready to fight and simultaneously ready to settle down and be a peaceful member of family and community.

OBJECTIFICATION OF THE FEMALE

The depiction of masculinity provides an array of societal types. Film and television producers, writers, directors, cinematographers, and editors are primarily male. As males they have the power to tell stories about worlds they understand. The tales they often tell are male centered, dealing with the anxieties and preoccupations of the male hero. The portrayal of women—like the portrayal of other subordinated groups in our society—is often secondary to the primary (usually white) male characters. Women are to gazed upon as we might look at an expensive new car. The most sexually desirable women are fought over and won. Ultimately women are to be consumed and controlled. Patriarchal culture producers often define women as sexual beings in very limited terms. The female protagonist in classic Hollywood cinema is often portrayed as either virgin or whore.

The self-imposed Hollywood Production Code complicated the depiction of the female in the 1930s and 1940s. A female protagonist was to be attractive to the male hero (and the audience), but if she gives in to their mutual sexual attraction before marriage, the woman must pay for her weakness. She must lose him, their "illegitimate" offspring, and her reputation. Just as the Hays Office decreed that crime did not pay, so too, sexuality did not pay. When the results of mutual desire were uncovered, it was the woman, not the man, who paid the price. Humphrey Bogart's Sam Spade sends Mary Astor's Brigid O'Shaughnessy "up the river" in *The Maltese Falcon* (1941). In *Double Indemnity* (1944) Fred MacMurray's Walter Neff and Barbara Stanwyck's Phyllis Dietrichson are both questionable characters, but she dies in ignominy while he lives long enough to tell the story and place responsibility on her seduction of his duped self. In *Gilda* (1946) Rita Hayworth's sexualized persona, Gilda Mundson Farrell, is saved from retribution by a last-minute revelation that all her apparent sexual encounters were merely a ruse to make her former lover jealous. When they decide to marry all is made right.

Laura Mulvey first identified the centrality of the male-dominated production team in terms of "the male gaze." In the essay "The Male Gaze," by Shohini Chaudhuri, the concept of the male gaze is explored and developed. In film and television it is usually the male who has agency, who does the looking at and positioning of the female. The female is shaped by the look of the male cameraman though his lens, by her subjective positioning by the male writers and director, and by the direct looking of the male actors who share the screen with her. The look may be adoring, it may be lustful, and it may be disrespectful. The audience, male and female, shares this constructed gaze and consumes the female as an object of male (and audience) desire, rather than as an agent unto her own right. For the male hero the consumption and the consummation is usually complete. She is the prize for the fairy-tale prince who has succeeded in his quest. She is both object of desire and reward for the cowboy, action hero, or gangster. But she is seldom the hero herself.

Women in television and film continue to be put on display, their physical attractiveness both glorified and demeaned.

FEMALE TYPES IN POPULAR CULTURE

- Mother
- Daughter
- Maiden aunt
- Evil witch
- Damsel
- Prize
- Waiting for prince
- Seeking prince
- Mean girl
- Nymphomaniac
- Whore
- Tomboy
- Career woman
- Consumer

Female Characters in Film and Television
- Looking for love
- Beautiful according to current cultural standards
- Active according to current cultural standards
- Sexually available/unavailable according to behavior of the male
- Predominantly Anglo women or women of different ethnicities whose features conform to a definition of beauty based on dominant white standards and limited ideas of the "exotic"
- Passive in most situations, deferring to the associated male
- Aggressive in terms of protecting children and home
- Of similar class or of lower class to the associated male
- Young

The early television program *I Love Lucy* (1951–1957) portrays a frustrated housewife longing to be out in the professional world. Her desires were familiar to many women in the United States and around the world who dreamed of balancing home life with a career. The spunky women of early television were met with considerable resistance. In the 1950s television show *The Honeymooners* (1955–1956) Ralph Kramden, played by comedian Jackie Gleason, frequently threatens his wife's challenges to his dominating behavior with the threat that he will "send her to the moon." His closed and shaking fist supports this promise.

Statistics indicate that between 2001 and 2012, American troops killed in Afghanistan and Iraq numbered 6,488; during that same period nearly twice that number of women were killed in the United States by a person with whom they shared a relationship. It is estimated that as many as 5 million women in the United States experience physical violence from an intimate partner every year. Over a lifetime one in four women and one in seven men are physically assaulted by someone they know. It is further estimated that as many as one in three women and one in five men in college are sexually assaulted, primarily by someone with whom they share an acquaintance.

Media's representation of women as sexual objects designed for the entertainment of men deserves scrutiny. The patriarchal construction of "good girls" and "bad girls" both presents women for male gratification and calls them out for being sexually attractive. "Slut shaming" and "stud praising" demean us as individuals and put us at risk of marginalizing and devaluing ourselves and others.

In their essay, "Are You Lonesome Tonight?" Mary Desjardins and Mark Williams explore the representation of male and female desire and seduction in post–World War II radio and television. The radio show *The Lonesome Gal* and the television show *The Continental* are programs that identify pre–social media singles "looking for love" as constructions of the desire of both character and audience to connect with another. The radio construction of *The Lonesome Gal* by disc jockey Jean King was carried by fifty-seven radio stations across the country in 1947. *Lonesome Gal* was carefully constructed to be both sexually alluring (in terms of voice and King's wearing a mask in public) and domesticated. Lonesome Gal spoke to her man as desired, and that desire was manifested in her careful preparation of their domestic space. Alternately, the persona of the Continental was direct and sexually seductive. His European accent gave him a sophisticated air that only marginally covered his lascivious intent. His invisible guest was a moth to the flame.

In "Men are from Marlboro Country, Women are from Wisteria Lane: Gender Perspectives" Dustin Kidd explores the binary of gender representation. *The Saviors and the Saved: Masculine Redemption in Contemporary Films* authors Amy Aronson and Michael Kimmel consider how to make a "bad boy" a domestically available individual. What does it take to tame Clark Gable's Rhett Butler (*Gone with the Wind*) or Bogart's hard-boiled detective Sam Spade?

READING 8
THE MALE GAZE

By Shohini Chaudhuri

In her article 'Visual Pleasure and Narrative Cinema', written in 1973 and published in *Screen* in 1975, Laura Mulvey argued that the controlling gaze in cinema is always male. Spectators are encouraged to identify with the look of the male hero and make the heroine a passive object of erotic spectacle. Mulvey's concept of the 'male gaze' subsequently became *the* main talking point of feminist film debate. This chapter begins with Mulvey's background in the Woman's Movement and charts her intellectual trajectory from politics to aesthetics. It then goes on to detail her arguments about the male gaze and how film is structured according to male fantasies of voyeurism and fetishism. The chapter will focus on 'Visual Pleasure and Narrative Cinema' but it will also draw on Mulvey's other essays from *Visual and Other Pleasures* (1989) and *Fetishism and Curiosity* (1996). Finally, it will consider Mulvey's 'Afterthoughts' on her arguments about visual pleasure in the light of the critical response to her work, which highlighted issues of female spectatorship.

SEXUAL POLITICS

> As I was lifted bodily out of the hall, three Miss Worlds came running up to me, a trio of sequinned, perfumed visions, saying 'Are you all right?', 'Let her go.' When the policeman explained we were from WL [Women's Liberation] and demonstrating against them, I managed to say that we weren't against them, we were for them.

(Mulvey and Jimenez 1989: 5)

At the 1970 Miss World Contest at London's Albert Hall, a group of feminists, hiding leaflets, water-pistols, stink-bombs, and bags of flour in their clothes, secreted themselves among the audience. When the signal was given, they hurled their missiles at the stage. Their protest was broadcast live, gaining the highest viewing ratings that year, before the demo was finally stopped. Among the demonstrators was Mulvey, who recounts the event in 'The Spectacle is Vulnerable: Miss World, 1970', an article co-written with Margarita Jimenez for

London's Women's Liberation Workshop journal *Shrew*. The demonstration went successfully, they say in the article, because 'the spectacle isn't prepared for anything other than passive spectators' (Mulvey and Jimenez 1989: 5).

As well as addressing some common misconceptions about what 1970s Women's Liberation was all about, this early article offers a good starting point for the concerns that Mulvey developed into feminist film theory. 'The Miss World competition', Mulvey and Jimenez declare, 'is a public celebration of the traditional female road to success', where women are defined solely by their physical attributes. For Mulvey and her cohorts, sabotaging the Miss World contest meant striking a blow against 'this narrow destiny' and crucially, 'a blow against passivity, not only the enforced passivity of the girls on the stage but the passivity we all felt in ourselves' (Mulvey and Jimenez 1989: 3).

Mulvey's passion for film predates her involvement in the Women's Liberation Movement. Yet it was the Women's Liberation Movement that gave the counterweight to her film theory and filmmaking, compelling her to look at film, especially Hollywood film, through critical eyes and, essentially, enabling her to *write*. Pieces in the journal *Shrew* were written and edited collaboratively and published anonymously, 'a political gesture against the ownership and authority implied by signature' and a way of giving women the 'collective strength ... to build new means of expression' (Mulvey 1989a: viii). In 'The Spectacle is Vulnerable', Jimenez's personal first-person account is merged with Mulvey's third-person commentary. Despite the dual voice, the specific preoccupations that would embroil Mulvey in the never-ending debates that indelibly bear her name are here in embryonic form: namely, the political campaign involving women's struggle to gain control over their own bodies and how they are represented; the notion of woman as passive spectacle; and the passivity of spectators.

Yet there is a wide gap between this piece and Mulvey's better-known work. In some respects it has more in common with the 'Images of Women' criticism we touched on in the last chapter, with its underlying idea that one can break through the alienating spectacle or façade to women's 'reality' hidden behind it, and that the action of a self-enlightened few are enough to destroy it. It cannot explain what keeps the spectacle in place and what puts women in positions of enforced passivity and moreover makes men and women accept this as natural and inevitable. In other words, it can offer a *description* of ideology but it cannot account for how ideology is *produced* and *perpetuated*. Mulvey's subsequent, more theoretical work takes this next step, drawing on Althusserian Marxism, semiotics, and—most of all—psychoanalysis.

While semiotics led to a way of understanding how images work as signs, psychoanalysis, Mulvey believed, was best placed to unlock 'the mechanics of popular mythology and its raw materials' (xiii). Reflecting on her work fifteen years later, she writes:

Psychoanalytic theory provided ... the ability to see through the surface of cultural phenomena as though with intellectual X-ray eyes. The images and received ideas of run of the mill sexism were transformed into a series of clues for deciphering a nether world, seething with displaced drives and misrecognised desire.

(Mulvey 1989a: xiv)

In 'Visual Pleasure and Narrative Cinema', she remarks on the 'beauty' of psychoanalysis in the way it renders the frustration women experience under 'the phallocentric order' (Mulvey 1989c: 15). The essay is heavily inflected by the theories of Jacques Lacan, who famously stated that 'the unconscious is structured like a language'. Mulvey sets out to uncover the ways in which 'the unconscious of patriarchal society has structured film form' (1989c: 14). This political use of psychoanalysis enables her to turn her focus from the mere description of woman as spectacle to the male psyche whose needs the spectacle serves.

LUST OF THE EYES

The 'magic' of Hollywood, argues Mulvey, lies in its 'skilled and satisfying manipulation of visual pleasure' (Mulvey 1989c: 16). Central to this is what Freud, in his 'Three Essays on the Theory of Sexuality', called 'scopophilia' or 'pleasure in looking' (Freud 1991b: 70). In its active aspect, scopophilia involves taking people as objects for sexual stimulation through sight, 'subjecting them to a controlling and curious gaze' (Mulvey 1989c: 16). An extreme example of this is a Peeping Tom, whose sexual satisfaction is wholly dependent on this activity. Although mainstream cinema is obviously designed for public exhibition, Mulvey suggests that it effectively positions its spectators as Peeping Toms: the darkened auditorium gives each spectator the illusion of being a privileged voyeur, peeping in on a private world, separate from the rest of the audience.

Mulvey adds that cinema also develops scopophilia 'in its narcissistic aspect', exploiting the viewer's desire to identify with a human face and form that they recognize as being similar to their own (Mulvey 1989c: 17). Here, she refers to Lacan, who proposed that human identity or the ego is formed during the Mirror Stage, when an infant first encounters itself as a separate entity, typically through its reflection in a mirror. The infant joyfully identifies with its mirror image. However, this identification is based on an imaginary misrecognition because the mirror presents an *ideal* ego—perfect, complete, and in control—at odds with the infant's actual experience of its body, which is at this stage uncoordinated and helpless as well as speechless (Lacan 1993: 2). Human individuals are haunted by this idealized image of themselves throughout their lives.

It is not difficult to connect this to cinema. Sitting in the auditorium, fascinated by the images on the screen, the spectator's awareness of themselves as a separate entity temporarily dissolves—forgetting who they are and the time and space they inhabit, they become like an infant, whose ego boundaries are yet to be formed. At the same time, the cinema re-evokes the moment at which their ego came into being. The spectator identifies with the glamorous stars on the screen—ego ideals who 'act out a complex process of likeness and difference' in an echo of the infant's misrecognition of itself as the Other in the mirror, who is more perfect, complete, and in control (Mulvey 1989c: 18).

The French film theorist Christian Metz likened the cinema screen to a mirror, in his 1975 article 'The Imaginary Signifier', published in *Screen*. But although he, too, draws links between the Mirror Stage and cinematic perception, it is Mulvey's groundbreaking analysis that spells out the implications for cinema's organization of sexual difference: 'In a world ordered by sexual imbalance, pleasure in looking has been split between active/male and passive/female' (Mulvey 1989c: 19). She argues that there are two forms of looking involved in the spectator's relationship with the screen. One is active scopophilia, which uses another person as an erotic object and in which the subject's identity is different from and distanced from the object on the screen. The other arises from narcissism and the formation of the ego, where the spectator identifies with their on-screen likeness (Mulvey 1989c: 18).

In narrative cinema, woman plays a 'traditional exhibitionistic role'—her body is held up as a passive erotic object for the gaze of male spectators, so that they can project their fantasies on to her. She connotes 'to-be-looked-at-ness' (Mulvey 1989c: 19). The men on screen, on the other hand, are agents of the look, with whom spectators identify to enjoy vicarious control and possession of the woman. We can see, in almost any classic Hollywood film, that the heroine is an object to be looked at: she is filmed in soft focus, 'coded for strong visual and erotic impact' (Mulvey 1989c: 19).

Narrative cinema, then, is not unlike other visual forms that display women as sexual objects, such as pin-ups or striptease. But what distinguishes cinema from other forms of female sexual display is that it incorporates permutations of the look into its very structure, predetermining how the woman is to be looked at, and thus placing all spectators in the 'masculinized' position of looking at her. Mulvey observes that there are three sets of looks involved in cinema: (1) the camera's look at the pro-filmic reality, (2) the audience's look at the final film product, and (3) the characters' looks at each other. The conventions of narrative cinema strive to make the audience forget the camera and the fact that they are watching a film. They work to deny both (1) and (2) in favour of (3)—all in the interests of creating a 'convincing' illusion of a world where the male protagonist acts as the spectator's surrogate (Mulvey 1989c: 26). In the narrative structure, too, the male drives the story forward, while the female has a passive role, linked to her status as spectacle. As well as identifying with 'the active power' of the hero's gaze at the woman, the spectator acquires the illusion of ordering and controlling the narrative themself (Mulvey 1989c: 20).

But, psychoanalytically speaking, woman poses a problem for the male who looks at her. Due to her 'lack' of a penis, woman evokes the unpleasurable threat of castration. This castration anxiety is related to the child's original trauma of discovering the mother does not have a penis; consequently, according to Freudian theory, the child assumes she is castrated. Films master this castration anxiety in two ways: first, by re-enacting the trauma through voyeurism, investigating the woman and revealing her guilt (i.e. her 'castration'), then either punishing or saving her; second, by disavowing castration through fetishism, i.e. endowing the woman's body with extreme aesthetic perfection, which diverts attention from her 'missing' penis and makes her reassuring rather than dangerous.

The voyeuristic strategy is typical of film noir, a genre known for its sexually alluring but deadly *femmes fatales*. In the process of investigating an intrigue or murder, the hero (usually a detective) ends up investigating *her*. The hero, who thus represents the Law, brings her crimes to light but, at an unconscious level, it is really the problem of her sexuality that is being resolved. Through his voyeuristic and sadistic control over her, the hero reaffirms his own mastery (and, by proxy, the male spectator's). *The Maltese Falcon* (1941) exemplifies this: it ends with the *femme fatale* being arrested, prison bar-like shadows cast across her as she is taken away in a caged lift.

Mulvey herself relates this strategy to Alfred Hitchcock's films. Technically, they do not belong to film noir, but they foreground voyeurism, putting the man on the right side of the Law, and woman on the wrong side. The protagonist of *Rear Window* (1954), for example, is a photojournalist, Jeffries (James Stewart), who has broken his leg in the line of professional duty and is confined to his flat where he spies on his neighbours through his window. The film clearly establishes his voyeurism and activity through his hazardous profession and the photographic equipment lying around the flat. At the same time, his accident, which immobilizes him in his seat, 'puts him squarely in the fantasy position of the cinema audience', who must also limit their activity

FREUDIAN FETISHISM

Fetishism is now commonly understood in a sexual sense, as overvaluing part of a sexual object as a substitute for the whole. Specifically for Freud, fetishism defends against castration anxiety arising from the awareness of sexual difference. In his view, a child's initial knowledge of sexual difference rests on the absence or presence of the penis. Boys assume that everyone owns a penis until they discover that the mother does not have one; then they believe she must have been castrated. The fetishist, however, refuses to believe the woman is castrated. He uses the fetish to cover over and disavow the sight of her 'wound', overvaluing other, more harmless parts of her body. This disavowal is such that it allows the fetishist to retain his belief that the woman has a penis and simultaneously acknowledge that she doesn't.

Mulvey initially explored the topic of fetishism in her essay 'Fears, Fantasies and the Male Unconscious or, "You Don't Know What is Happening, Do You, Mr Jones?"' (1973), where she demonstrates that, far from being 'the private taste of an odd minority', as most people think it is, fetishism pervades the mass media, mostly at an unconscious level (Mulvey 1989b: 13). Considering sculptures by Allen Jones, who produced ideas for the milkbar in A Clockwork Orange (1971), she argues that Jones's work is valuable from a feminist perspective because it clearly conveys how male castration anxiety comes to be projected onto the female form, which is then appropriated as a fetish—for example, how woman is represented adorned with phallic shapes. We can see this in many media images of women, where certain 'well-known phallic extensions', such as guns, cigarettes, and high-heeled shoes 'divert the eye' (Mulvey 1989b: 8).

to looking (Mulvey 1989c: 24). For most of the film, the audience is restricted to Jeffries's narrative and optical point of view. The window frame, for him, becomes like the cinema screen for the audience: a canvas onto which he projects his repressed desires and fantasies. Using binoculars and his long-lens camera to get a better view, he effectively becomes a 'Peeping Tom'—in fact his nurse Stella accuses him of being one.

Jeffries's girlfriend Lisa (Grace Kelly), a fashion model who is always flaunting her new clothes, is, according to Mulvey, an exemplary exhibitionist—typical of women in narrative cinema. However, Jeffries only becomes fascinated with Lisa when she crosses over from the space of the spectator to the opposite block, which corresponds to the space of the screen. Lisa climbs into a neighbour's apartment to find incriminating evidence of a murder and is surprised by the neighbour when he returns. Thereby, Jeffries is able to see her 'as a guilty intruder exposed by a dangerous man' who threatens to punish her (Mulvey 1989c: 23). This gives Jeffries the chance of saving her.

For Mulvey, Josef von Sternberg's films exemplify fetishism, especially those starring Marlene Dietrich, the fetishized female form *par excellence*. In its broadest meaning, fetishism disavows knowledge in favour of belief, conjuring up the superstitious beliefs of 'primitive' societies. It is a resonant concept for Mulvey, because—as she states in her later work *Fetishism and Curiosity*—it appears in the writings of both Marx and Freud; these thinkers used it to question the rationality of Western thought, which has supposedly overcome such beliefs (Mulvey 1996: 2). For both Marx and Freud, fetishism has to do with value or, more particularly, overvaluing.

Marx discussed commodity fetishism to try to understand how abstract values come to be invested in things, and how their origins as products of labour or social relations are disavowed. Freud, on the other hand, in his 1927 essay on the topic, explored how fetishism 'ascribes excessive value to objects considered to be valueless by common consensus' (Mulvey 1996: 2).

The Freudian and Marxist conceptions of fetishism coalesce in Mulvey's discussion of the dream factory of cinema. On the cinema screen itself, the woman as erotic spectacle is the perfect fetish. The camera fetishistically isolates fragments of her body (face, breasts, legs) in close-ups. The use of such close-ups for the heroine stresses that, unlike the hero, she is valued above all for what her appearance connotes, for her beauty and sexual desirability. One is unlikely to find similar sorts of shots of the male hero, unless the shots concern narrative events; for example, in *Rear Window*, the camera focuses on Jeffries's broken leg. The close-ups of parts of the female body, on the other hand, have the quality of a 'cut-out or icon', temporarily halting the flow of the narrative to invite erotic contemplation and shattering the illusion of depth rather than enforcing verisimilitude (Mulvey 1989c: 20).

The fetishization of women in cinema extends to the cult of a female star such as Dietrich. Here, too, over-valuation implies a refusal to recognize sexual difference, making the female form 'safe' for the enjoyment of the male gaze. The glamour of the star is emphasized and becomes pleasurable in itself, 'a perfect streamlined image of femininity' (Mulvey 1996: 8). Mulvey argues that Sternberg's films represent a special instance in narrative cinema as they bypass the male protagonist's controlling gaze altogether, facilitating a 'direct rapport' between the image and the spectator (Mulvey 1989c: 22). The woman in these films, she writes, is 'a perfect product, whose body, stylised and fragmented by close-ups, is the content of the film and the direct recipient of the spectator's look'.

Mulvey emphasizes the need for women to understand the mechanisms of voyeurism and fetishism that underlie the patriarchal unconscious of narrative film. At the time of writing 'Visual Pleasure and Narrative Cinema', her aims were iconoclastic: to break the codes and destroy narrative pleasure. At the end of her essay she calls for filmmakers to 'free the look of the camera into its materiality in time and space and the look of the audience into dialectics and passionate detachment' (Mulvey 1989c: 26). At that point, she imagined a feminist cinema along the lines of radical modernist practice, with its strategies of self-reflexivity, disruption, and defamiliarization, as exemplified by Bertolt Brecht's work in theatre, on the one hand, and Jean-Luc Godard's post-1968 films (such as *British Sounds* [1970]) on the other. She also went on to make her own films, including *Riddles of the Sphinx* (1977) (in collaboration with Peter Wollen), which, with its 360 degree pans and voiceover commentary, puts these ideas into practice. However, her stance on film and the possibilities for feminist filmmaking has changed a lot since then, perhaps most dramatically in her recent book *Death 24 × a Second* (see Mulvey 2005: 190), which will be discussed briefly in the final chapter.

THE FEMALE SPECTATOR

There have been countless reactions to 'Visual Pleasure and Narrative Cinema', countering—or at least confronting—Mulvey's view that narrative cinema positions its spectators as male, catering only for male fantasies and pleasures. The essay exerted such a strong impact on the direction of feminist film theory that many subsequent works constitute a direct response to it. In particular, it was felt to ignore the circumstances of the female spectator—is she *always* constructed by the film-text in the same way as the male spectator? If she identifies with the look of the male protagonist, is she, too, impelled to make the female protagonist into an object of erotic desire? What about the 'actual' women in the audience?

Such debates became the hot topic of feminist film theory during the 1980s. Critics pointed to the tradition of the 'Woman's film' and other types of melodrama, especially from the 1930s and 1940s, to demonstrate that films that specifically try to address female spectators have always existed. Films such as *Stella Dallas* (1937), *Mildred Pierce* (1945), and *Letter from an Unknown Woman* (1948) centre on a female protagonist whose viewpoint appears to guide the film and deal with feminine concerns and experiences (see Gledhill 1987; Doane 1987; Kuhn 1994). However, the need to create mass entertainment for female audiences gave rise to an irreconcilable gap between the patriarchal ideology at work in these films and female desires expressed in them. The movies' endings typically strived to resolve these contradictions—for example, at the end of *Stella Dallas*, the heroine realizes that her desire to be 'something else besides a mother' conflicts with her maternal duty. At the same time, the film lays bare this contradiction and permits women's lived frustrations to find a voice.

Mulvey herself anticipated these concerns in her 1977 essay on Douglas Sirk's melodramas where she argues that 'having a female point of view dominating the narrative produces an excess which precludes satisfaction … Hollywood films made with a female audience in mind tell a story of contradiction, not of reconciliation' (Mulvey 1989e: 43). In her 'Afterthoughts on "Visual Pleasure and Narrative Cinema"', inspired by *Duel in the Sun*' (1981), she reconsiders the role of the female spectator. Whereas before she had maintained that narrative cinema does not offer a place for female spectators, here she argues that the female spectator might enjoy the fantasy of control and freedom over the narrative world that identification with the hero affords and that she can cross the lines of gender in her identification with the male hero because her gender is itself divided.

At this point, Mulvey alludes to Freud, who identified a pre-Oedipal 'phallic phase' in girls (associated with activity), later repressed when they develop their femininity; during many women's lives, there are frequent regressions to this phallic phase, leading their behaviour to alternate between '"passive" femininity and regressive "masculinity"' (Mulvey 1989d: 35). It is this 'internal oscillation of desire' that lies dormant in the female spectator and awaits to 'be "pleasured"' in stories like *Duel in the Sun* (1946), a Western with a female protagonist, Pearl, who is torn between the path towards 'correct' femininity (becoming a 'lady'), and being a tomboy; these split desires are dramatized in the way she is caught between two men, Jesse and Lewt. Comparing the female spectator to Pearl, Mulvey argues that 'she temporarily accepts "masculinisation" in memory of her "active" phase', however, the film does not dramatize the success of masculine identification but its sadness. So, too, Mulvey suggests that the female spectator can identify with the active, masculine position, but this is a form of 'transvestite' identification that sits uneasily on her (Mulvey 1989d: 33).

The American feminist film theorist Mary Ann Doane has led debates on genres where the implied spectator is female and has expanded Mulvey's paradigm in several important ways. In 'Film and the Masquerade: Theorizing the Female Spectator' (1982), she defines the structure of the gaze in terms of proximity and distance in relation to the image rather than, as Mulvey put it, a distinction between 'male/active' and 'female/passive' and the female spectator's 'transvestite' oscillation between these two forms of identification. The particular problem posed by the female spectator, Doane claims, lies in the fact that woman functions as the image, resulting in a potential failure of distance between spectator and screen. The female spectator has two options. The first is to over-identify with the woman on the screen, becoming emotionally over-involved with the heroine. The other option, equally 'untenable' from a feminist perspective, is for the female spectator to take the heroine as her own narcissistic object of desire (Doane 1991: 31). In both, the spectator loses herself in the image.

Doane suggests that a way out of this dilemma is for the female spectator to read the on-screen image of her likeness as a masquerade. The psychoanalyst Joan Rivière addressed the topic of masquerade in her essay 'Womanliness as a Masquerade' (1929). Reflecting on women who flaunt their femininity in an exaggerated way, she suggests that such behaviour is a masquerade or mask adopted by certain women 'to hide their possession of masculinity and to avert the reprisals expected if she was found to possess it … The reader may now ask how I define womanliness or where I draw the line between genuine womanliness and the "masquerade". My suggestion is … they are the same thing' (Rivière 1986: 38). Here, Rivière deduced the socially constructed character of femininity. Doane appropriates the notion of masquerade to theorize the possibility of creating a distance between the female spectator and woman as image, making the latter available for viewers to critique. As she recognizes, however, within films, female characters who masquerade are often punished—for instance, *femmes fatales* who try to usurp the masculine activity of looking, or horror film heroines whose terrified gaze is mastered by the monster's gaze.

Finally, Doane analyzes a photograph, '*Un Regard Oblique*' (1948) by Robert Doisneau, to illustrate the way Hollywood integrates the male gaze into its narratives and at the same time denies the female gaze. The photograph depicts a man and a woman looking at a shop window. The woman stands in the centre and the photograph appears to emphasize her look. However, the real power of the gaze lies with the man, who stands in the corner of the picture. His gaze, cutting across and effectively erasing the woman's gaze, is aimed at a painting of a female nude. Unlike the picture that captures the woman's attention, which is absent to the viewer, the painting of the nude is prominently displayed in the photograph. Therefore, despite her narrative centring, the female *subject* is overtaken by the picture as *object* of the male gaze; the photograph is, in effect, a 'joke' at her expense. For Doane, the photograph exemplifies the sexually differentiated structures of looking inscribed in cinema: 'The fetishistic representation of the nude female body, fully in view, insures a masculinization of the spectatorial position' (Doane 1991: 29).

Feminist film theorists have also undertaken research to discover more about actual audiences and how they respond to films. Instead of looking at what kind of spectator is 'implied' by films, these theorists engage in 'empirical' studies of actual, historical, or current audiences by looking at exhibition practices, forms of reception, and the social composition of audiences. Ien Ang's *Watching Dallas* (1985) pioneered this approach in television studies. In both film and television studies, the shift has been accompanied by the recognition that audiences do not just passively absorb pre-given meanings 'forced' upon them by media texts but actively create their own meanings. However, many feminist critics working with this approach tend to combine it with psychoanalytic theorizing (Hansen 2000). Despite the incontestable value of empirical research, theory has never outlived its uses. One reason for this is that empirical audience research—for example, in the form of interviews with real spectators—cannot by itself help us understand the often-unconscious desires motivating people to watch movies. Another is that the notion of the 'real audience' in empirical audience research, with its parameters defined by the researcher, is just as much a construct as the textual spectator (Brunsdon 1992: 125).

Attempts to give the concept of the female spectator a historical and ethnographic specificity also led feminist theorists to explore differences between women, particularly as shaped by different experiences of race, class, and sexuality. For example, studies have suggested that the 'look' of lesbian spectators of mainstream films can override the male viewpoint constructed in those films, enabling the films to be read pleasurably 'against the grain' (Ellsworth 1990). In 'White Privilege and Looking Relations: Race and Gender in Feminist Film Theory' (1988), Jane Gaines extends these concerns to race, providing a critique of feminist film theory's use of psychoanalysis. This type of analysis, she argues, may 'lock us into modes of analysis' based on a male/female opposition that supports mainly white middle-class values and prevents us from understanding the position of women who suffer other sorts of oppression (Gaines 2000: 340). She illustrates her case with an analysis of a film about a black fashion model, *Mahogany* (1975), starring Diana Ross, chosen because it is tempting to read its themes of sadism, voyeurism, and photography psychoanalytically, in the manner of Mulvey. Yet, to do this, Gaines points out, is to 'step into an ideological signifying trap set up by the chain of meanings that lead away from seeing the film in terms of racial conflict' (Gaines 2000: 344). She also points out that, unlike the white man, the black male character in *Mahogany* and black males in other mainstream American films do not have the power or privilege of sexual looking. This makes race a determining factor in the male gaze. In the US, this can historically be traced back to power relations between blacks and whites during slavery. Gaines highlights the need for a theory of black representation that is sensitive to history. bell hooks has also explored these particular issues in her book *Black Looks* (1992).

Meanwhile other critics, for example D.N. Rodowick, have found fault with the binary logic of Mulvey's argument. But while her insistent use of oppositions, such as male/female, active/passive, scopophilia/narcissism, is often attributed to her dependence on psychoanalysis, Rodowick points out that Freud himself 'problematizes any strict binary division between "maleness"/"femaleness" and activity/passivity' in questions of desire and identification (Rodowick 2000: 192). Such criticisms have, in turn, led to a more precise use of psychoanalysis by the feminist film theorists discussed in this book, who all engage with these debates at some level.

SUMMARY

In her celebrated essay 'Visual Pleasure and Narrative Cinema', Mulvey proposes that narrative cinema produces the male as agent of the look and the female as the object of spectacle through mechanisms of voyeurism and fetishism. In this way, narrative cinema imposes 'masculine' viewing strategies on all of its spectators, irrespective of their actual sex. Her argument gave rise to a number of debates, particularly as to whether narrative cinema systematically excludes women and the 'female gaze'. To answer these questions, feminist theorists investigated films targeted at female viewers as well as studying the actual reception of films by female audiences. Mulvey herself modified her arguments in her 'Afterthoughts' to her essay, where she considers the role of the female spectator. She argues that, in accepting the 'masculinized' subject position offered to her by narrative film, the female spectator can engage in a form of 'transvestite' identification, which involves alternating between genders. However, the universalizing tendencies of Mulvey's psychoanalytic framework also came under scrutiny, including from black feminist theorists, who stressed the importance of integrating the role of history into the analysis of filmic representation, as well as of recognizing that women's oppression is not exclusively determined by gender.

READING 9

"ARE YOU LONESOME TONIGHT?": GENDERED ADDRESS
IN *THE LONESOME GAL* AND *THE CONTINENTAL*

By Mary Desjardins and Mark Williams

This essay examines representations of two broadcast media performers of the post–World War II era whose openly gendered direct address was considered blatantly suggestive but also complementary to each other. *The Lonesome Gal* was a radio show begun in Dayton, Ohio, in 1947 and transported to Los Angeles in 1949. It featured a female disc jockey of unknown identity who adopted the persona of a woman-in-waiting, patiently longing for her desired (male) listener. Interweaving complimentary patter, sponsor-supported asides, and personalized introductions to romantic and popular musical selections, she opened and closed each program with her admonition "I love you more than anybody else in the whole world." Listeners were routinely addressed as "muffin," "baby," and "dreamboat." At what appears to be the peak in her popularity, Renzo Cesana premiered on local Los Angeles television as *The Continental*, a suave European date for his (female) viewer, whom he flattered and embarrassed (via direct visual address) into a position as a sexual fetish.

Examined together, these shows are representative of certain tensions and contradictions in postwar American culture, especially when related to the social and gendered status of the private sphere, the rapidly changing postwar broadcast industries, and the relationship of these media to the construction of that private sphere. A close look at the competing radio and television institutions at this time, and the discursive strategies and positionings in examples of program texts of these shows, reveals that the textual meanings and ideological effects of *The Continental* and *The Lonesome Gal* are not based on neat reversals or "separate-but-equal" policy for seducing heterosexual male and female viewers and listeners. We will argue that although the conditions of reception of these programs include the possibility of affirming the "difference" of female desire, this possibility only arises through a struggle with conditions that worked to secure male mastery over the physical space of the home, where women had become ensconced.

Our analysis will suggest how media institutions, program texts, audiences, and other cultural discourses worked to construct conditions of reception that operate from what Christine Gledhill argues are "competing frames of reference and experience."[1] Meaning, according to Gledhill, arises "out of a struggle or negotiation" between these registers, which renders the hegemony or dominance of meaning unstable and subject to continual renegotiation. One central negotiation at stake in the historical reception of *The Continental* and *The*

Lonesome Gal is the postwar rejection of an effacement of difference allegedly characteristic of wartime "unity." This rejection was generally achieved through a defensive retrenchment within socially defined roles that served patriarchal consumer capitalism. Such retrenchments included the attempts to usher women back into the home, the massive movement to the suburbs (which were often stringently discriminating, characterized by several barriers of entry according to race, class, and religion), and the surveillance and persecution of people who blurred social, gender, and political boundaries.

JEAN KING AS THE "LONESOME GAL": INDUSTRIAL CONTEXTS

The Lonesome Gal went on the air in October 1947 as a local radio show in Dayton, featuring talk and recorded music. Within a year, "Lonesome Gal" host Jean King had won Billboard's award for Top Disc Jockey of the Year, and the press was claiming that the show had saved its sponsor (a local restaurant) from bankruptcy.[2] In 1949 King moved to Los Angeles, where she was at first unable to convince any local stations to give her show a try. With the help of a salesman and veteran radio producer Bill Rousseau (who became her husband), she was soon recording her program for syndication.

By June 1950, *The Lonesome Gal* was carried by fifty-seven stations throughout the country, with King recording 285 programs a week. (The show was heard five nights a week on each of the fifty-seven stations; King recorded programs with separate, personalized commercials for local sponsors in each city.)[3] She corresponded with local chambers of commerce in order to include hometown atmosphere, mentioning local streets and people in her chats. This marathon recording schedule necessitated a studio in her own home, where she lived with her husband/producer (who was also for a time the producer of the *Dragnet* radio program) and his two children from a previous marriage. To maintain her air of mystery and the illusion of her availability—not to mention her "loneliness"—King never mentioned her name, her husband, her two children, or her remarkably labor-intensive production process within the Lonesome Gal's pleasant patter.[4] However, she did recount anecdotes about personal concerns such as her garden and cats (i.e., preoccupations that fill the time between visits to or from her "desired" listener) as interstitial remarks between jockeying records chosen from her own collection.

The success of *The Lonesome Gal* can be situated within its negotiation of a number of major shifts experienced by the radio industry in the late 1940s and early 1950s. As a national advertising medium, radio had nearly reached a point of audience saturation, with limited potential for future growth. Rising production costs and a threatened loss of audience to television meant decreasing network revenues and profits. As a result, the industry as a whole began to reconfigure its policies and practices regarding national and local advertising, and the use of transcribed programming. The shows of many major stars were canceled because they were too expensive, and much performing and technical talent drifted to television.

Although radio talent had always performed tasks associated with disc jockeying, it was only in the late 1940s that such a role became central to the industry. Since the beginning of its existence as a mass entertainment medium, the radio industry had been discouraged from playing "canned music" by the FRC, FCC, ASCAP, and the AFM. There had been court battles over the copyright legality of playing records bought through retailers, and the FCC had mandated that stations identify to listeners the recorded nature of such music at regular intervals, helping to produce an ideologically informed "distaste" for seemingly less-genuine or less-"live" radio performances.[5] Consequently, it had been mostly small local stations that risked playing records as regular programming fare. King's first radio venue, for example, wing in Dayton, had recently disengaged itself from network affiliation and therefore had to produce more of its own original programming. By the late 1940s, larger stations and network affiliates also started to produce more shows with disc jockeys playing records. The FCC had let up on its restrictions for record playing after the Supreme Court ruled that once bought, a record could be played by a station at any time. These "record" shows were cheaper to produce and could also be tailored to reflect local tastes, an important advantage in selling advertising time to the local sponsors, who were now increasingly more important as supporters of radio programming.[6]

The production and distribution of *The Lonesome Gal* were compatible with these sorts of shifts in the industry. Because of the emerging gap between network and local station interests, and the changing valuation of transcribed recordings (from condemned, to condoned, to commended), King was able to independently produce and syndicate a popular, successful non-network program. Radio stations and advertisers were not paying for an expensive network personality. At the same time, King's practice of remaining a mystery behind *The Lonesome Gal* format, enhanced by her insistence on wearing a mask in public appearances or in photos, gave her persona the fetishistic and charismatic qualities of a star. Her commitment to weaving local information into her intimate chats complemented stations' attempts to create unique local identities in what was becoming a more decentralized industry, and also complemented local advertisers' desires to personalize their products.

The success of *The Lonesome Gal* must also be seen within the context of the changing role of women in the radio industry. Since the rise of radio in the 1920s, debates surrounding the aesthetics of radio broadcasts had often centered around the supposedly displeasing qualities of the female voice—it was alternately deemed too monotonous, too shrill, or displaying too much personality.[7] Yet even though no women became important announcers on a national level at this time, the popularity of radio homemakers, especially notable in the Midwest, suggests that many listeners had no problem with the voices of helpful women who eased listener isolation and shared some of the labor and scheduling burdens of the domestic sphere.[8]

Even though listeners—as opposed to scientists, critics, and broadcasters—did not seem to have a problem with the female voice, Michelle Hilmes has noted that the network-controlled radio industry confined programs that featured the female voice and expressed women's concerns to a schedule and a set of promotional discourses that associated them with the "disparaged commercialized form of the daytime serial" (a disparagement echoed by cultural critics in reviews and editorials).[9] By the 1940s, especially in cooperation with the propaganda efforts of the OWI to get women into the World War II home-front workforce, network radio did use women's voices in programs like *Listen Women* to expand notions of the female sphere beyond the domestic. Although such shows conveniently alternated stereotypes of the home-front superwoman with the housewife as "weaker sex," Hilmes argues that "wartime media succeeded in recasting the identity of the audience to whom they appealed."[10] Radio's wartime "success" in reaching women, then, involved its mass circulation of tensions between private domesticity and public achievement, making visible (or more precisely, audible) aspects of women's lives that had earlier been obscured by debates about the unsuitability of their voices or the relegation of their programming to less-esteemed daytime hours.

By the early post–World War II period, concerns about female pitch and voice quality had become selectively ignored. In an era when the recently "freed" FM band caused a proliferation of new channels, and some AM affiliates were cut loose as networks turned money and attention to television, local or syndicated programming was even more important.[11] The lady, or "glamour" disc jockey, was seen as an exploitable novelty in this competitive climate—a "novelty" status determined in part by an implicit mandate that women's voices be experienced as innocuous on U.S. radio, especially in contrast to the possibly dangerous qualities of the female voice exemplified in anti-American propaganda broadcasts by Tokyo Rose in Japan and Axis Sally in Germany. These women were tried for treason during the very period in which the glamour disc jockey was a successful experiment on American radio.

A perceived threat of, and desire to control, the encroachment of women in the domestic radio industry occurred within a broader context of anxiety about self-determined women in the postwar United States. This was not conceived as a problematic involving women's voices alone, however, and extended across institutional as well as industrial and textual matters. A 1948 issue of *Broadcasting* magazine rather bluntly evidences a nexus of anxieties regarding the movement of women into male-dominated (and typically male-exclusive) preserves of the communications field. In an article announcing the swearing in of Frieda Hennock, the first female member of the FCC,[12] commission chair Wayne Coy is described congratulating Hennock with the following welcome: the commission as always had "rectitude, fortitude, and solemnitude—but never before pulchritude."[13] A cartoon from a July 1948 issue of *Broadcasting* depicts members of the FCC in a nighttime meeting (Figure 9.1). As the newest member primps before her pocket mirror, her male colleagues are having what seems to be a collective misogynist dream of their "castrating" wives. Images of sour-looking old women appear over the heads of all the male members, prompting one to suggest, "By order of higher authority, there

"By order of higher authority, there will be no night sessions henceforth."

Figure 9.1 Cartoon from *Broadcasting*, 12 July 1948.
Sid Hix, from Broadcasting; July 12, 1948. Copyright © 1948 by NewBay Media, LLC.

will be no night sessions henceforth."[14] The professional working woman, as seen by the radio industry (or at least by this prominent industry organ), is thus depicted as narcissistic, a threat to what are assumed to be the concerns of domestic women, and a problematic object of desire for her male coworkers.

A few years later, a complimentary article about Hennock displays a different ambivalence about the power of professional women in the media. Seemingly oblivious to any threat she might pose to wives of FCC members, "The Lady from the FCC" suggests that men nevertheless fear her because Hennock's law career had focused on helping widows and orphans, and "the women and children still love her."[15] After an initial "quiet period" during her FCC tenure, Hennock's profile on the commission became that of an open advocate for more educational television programming to "develop the minds, the hearts … of our youth" (39). Such altruistic and socially minded goals are more indicative of an institutionalized sense of the maternal than a stereotypical feminine narcissism implied by the cartoon, though the article does assure readers that Hen-nock "is no less feminine now that she is a Commissioner. She wears gay, frothy gowns and the most frivolous hats." It goes on to claim, "she is a very attractive woman and as feminine as only a really good-looking woman can be, but she can be as dogged as the toughest Senator, and tougher than some of the male law-makers with whom she has to tangle" (39). Ultimately, then, the article works to portray/defend Hennock's "difference" in terms of a potential "threat," due not only to what it positions as her "essential" femininity but also to a strategic combination of femininity with more typically "masculine" tenacity and competitive spirit.

In depictions such as these articles and cartoon, industry publications display an anxiety over summoning a visual fantasy of Hennock to both demonstrate and contain her power. In the cartoon, the fantasy visualizes Hennock and the male members' wives to suggest that Hennock's public power threatens the private realm where traditional wives are supposed—but apparently fail—to satisfy male desires. In the articles, Hennock's "pulchritude" and concern for fashion are the visible manifestations of a femininity that is presumedly at odds with, or not readily discernible from, her "dogged" toughness as a professional woman.

Radio listening itself at this time had a similar fantasy status, one in which visible versus invisible, public versus private, invocatory ethereality versus imaged concreteness, dominated as tensions in its listeners' pleasures and psychic investments.[16] In its April 1949 issue, *Radio Best* presented "Mental Television," a feature by comic strip artist Mel Graf, in which his drawings of disc jockeys are placed alongside their photographs. Graf describes how his drawings reflect the fantasies inspired by the disc jockey's voices, and how those frequently clashed with the reality of their actual appearances. The feature was so popular that the magazine had Graf repeat the exercise—this time including a cartoon rendering and photo of the Lonesome Gal—in the next issue.[17]

As the portrayals of Hennock suggest, the tensions of visibility/invisibility and public/private had a particular valence when associated with women and radio. Jean King's use of a low, sexy voice in creating *The Lonesome Gal* had the potential to suggest the femme fatale, the stereotype used to link powerful women to personal downfalls and political subversiveness in both the immediate post–World War II and the HUAC periods. And although both industry and mass-market publications marveled at King's success, with her husky voice cooing sweet nothings to her special "guy," there is indication that the disembodied female voice was not entirely unthreatening and was best "enjoyed" if contained within a sexually defined female body.

Such a strategy of containment is exemplified in *Radio Best* magazine's 1948 contest to elect the "most glamorous" female disc jockey, with readers sending in votes.[18] The candidates are pictured in the contest announcement, ostensibly because the disc jockeys at this time were all on local stations (including King in this, her presyndication period), and so not familiar to all readers of the magazine. But it is significant that most of

Figure 9.2 "Who's Your Favorite Glamour Disc Jockey?" Contest, *Radio Best* magazine, May 1948. Library of American Broadcasting, Hornbake Library, University of Maryland, College Park.

Figure 9.3   Second page (ballot page) for "Who's Your Favorite Glamour Disc Jockey?" Contest, *Radio Best* **magazine, June 1948. Library of American Broadcasting, Hornbake Library, University of Maryland, College Park.**

these "glamour" pictures are cheesecake images, modeled on the poses and attitudes used in stills produced to accentuate the sexual allure of female film stars (Figures 9.2 and 9.3). Posing for the objectifying gaze of the presumed male reader, some of the disc jockeys are dressed in bathing suits, strapless gowns, tight sweaters, and, in King's case, wearing a facial mask that hides—and consequently fetishizes—the area around her eyes. Some have their chests pushed forward to appear "busty"; legs are posed to show off both calves and thighs; some have lips slightly open, or eyes looking off-camera. Of the sixteen candidates pictured, only one—one of two "cowgirl" disc jockeys—is posed in a relaxed, nonsexualized manner.

King won second place in *Radio Best*'s glamour contest, but she would ultimately prove to be the most successful in terms of airtime longevity and national fame (once her show was syndicated). In 1951 MGM bought the film rights to the Lonesome Gal personality and announced that either Ava Gardner or Lana Turner would star in her story.[19] Although MGM was promising the allure of one of two of their most glamorous stars, the studio never made the picture. Universal bought the rights from MGM in 1956, this time with King herself to write the story treatment, but once again the project was shelved.[20]

Despite King's frequent visual depiction in glamorous poses (especially when masked), and MGM's plan to approximate her appeal through casting sexy Ava Gardner or Lana Turner, over the ten years she was on the air, King was increasingly understood as a savvy businesswoman, and the Lonesome Gal as a devoted friend in her shows and publicity. The erotic qualities of King's performance as the Lonesome Gal seem to have been increasingly propped onto what can be recognized as a maternal address concerned with the every need of *The Lonesome Gal*'s man. This propping, while it diffuses the gendered nature of the addressee (i.e., allows her address to cast its net over the imaginary of female listeners as well), aligns *The Lonesome Gal* with more traditional female roles—ultimately closer to the "neighboring," interpersonal address of the radio homemakers than the aggressive, "treasonous," seductive address of Rose and Sally and the femme fatale.

TEXTUAL AND AUDIENCE ANALYSIS

On a textual and discursive level, the success of both *The Lonesome Gal* and *The Continental* is due in large part to each program's use of direct address—a strategy that compels the listener or viewer to enter into and identify with the program's gendered but porous fictive space. Such an invitation is immediately apparent from *The Lonesome Gal*'s opening line: "Sweetie, no matter what anybody says, I love you better than anybody in the whole world." The following is an excerpt of her continued opening address for one program (circa 1951):

(Singing, with accompaniment)
Lonesome, I'm a real lonesome gal.
I can't stop feeling lonesome. Heaven knows when I shall.

(over theme music)
Hi, baby. This is your Lonesome Gal. Are you as lazy as I am right this minute? Then keep on being lazy, and forget everything for awhile, except us. I have no profound knowledge to impart, but I sure do love ya and I want to tell you so. So light up a pipe full of Bond Street, lover, and relax.

(Singing)

Who knows what tomorrow may bring?
I wonder whether I'll know when my heart starts to sing?

(over theme music)

Cutie, this is a very special event for me, to be back with you again. Gee, I've missed you. And a lot of things have happened since I was with you last. But I won't try and tell you everything at once. I'll spread my news over a long period of time. Cause you know me—the more visits I get with you, the better I like it. (music out)

There's one thing I bet you didn't notice: my new winter window-box. Know what those plants are? Martha Washington geraniums. Just a little something for me to tend to when you're not here. But with you back, I'll have lots to do. And this time, baby, I hope it's for keeps. Nobody can break this up. Course anyone who'd think of trying that would be a cockeyed optimist.

(Recorded song follows immediately: "Cockeyed Optimist")

The seductive hailing of the listener as "sweetie," coupled with the declaration of an exclusive intimacy between them, is a strong draw into the fictive space of *The Lonesome Gal*'s world. But her musical lament (that she can't help feeling lonesome) contradicts the permanence of their intimacy and opens to question the power of female desire initially asserted with so much confidence: the show suggests that the seductive, unattached woman is fated to be lonely. In this way, it negotiates a maintenance of women's assumed desire for marriage, even as it acknowledges an uncontrollable melancholic desire that marriage won't necessarily appease. As a means of sustaining interest in the show's textual developments and encouraging regular listening, it intimates the necessity of an ongoing resolicitation of male desire, in order to help the Lonesome Gal overcome her loneliness. Within each show, the textual economy between her concluding phrases and the songs that follow them afford a forward momentum, a flow based on a kind of iterative wit—a pleasantly predictable rhyme between textual units. On an institutional level, the repetition and serialization of sexual desire is compatible with advertisers' needs to continually reopen the desire of the listeners to consume their products.

The facilitation of consumption also operates within the Lonesome Gal's positioning of her time with the male listener as a time to be "lazy," the leisure time so often fantasized by contemporary advertising discourses to create their products' appeal, to place them in the life schedule of postwar consumers. One of the most consistent characteristics of the textual operations of *The Lonesome Gal*'s chats is the smooth transition or slippage between the seductive descriptions of being lazy together with the listener and their constitution as a couple that enjoys his use of the sponsor's product:

Dreamboat, every girl likes to be with a man of good taste. And sweetie, I'm no exception. That's why I like being with you. I like the ties you pick, I like the clothes you wear, and the music you choose. And most of all I like the Bond Street tobacco you smoke. Good taste is just another name for Bond Street. Sweetie, I don't have to tell you about Bond Street tobacco. You smoke it, you taste it, you enjoy the full, rich, mellow pleasure that comes out of that wonderful Bond Street blend.

But what I do want to tell you is what it means to me, what it means to the girl you're with, when you're smoking Bond Street. It means the joy of seeing you happy. It means the pleasure of enjoying with you the gentle, delicate aroma that only Bond Street has. It means the good taste of a kiss between boy and girl. Maybe this isn't news to you, but it's good to know these things about Bond Street tobacco. The mild, clean, good-tasting tobacco that pleases not only you, baby, but the girl you're with. It's a man's tobacco that keeps a girl feeling good about the man who smokes it. You'll remember that, won't you baby? I know you will—you've got good taste. You're my everything.

(Recorded song follows immediately: "You're My Everything")

The Lonesome Gal's attraction to her male listeners is linked here to their possession of "taste." She takes pride and self-satisfaction in being associated with such good taste. Bolstering the male ego is thereby accomplished by persuading the listener that using Bond Street tobacco conforms to a dynamic in which both the product and women/a woman accessorize men/a man appropriately. This address is also open to women, ostensibly "overhearing" this conversation, who might share the Lonesome Gal's melancholic unattached status—or, even if married, share her loneliness—and who may be inclined to purchase such products for their own boyfriends, husbands, and so on. The threat of the single or lonely female subject is repositioned in a more commercially sanctioned space as "male accessory," sexual object, and/or retail conduit.

Although we do not have access to demographic figures for the program, there are some textual and extra-textual discourses (such as publicity, etc.) that suggest there were indeed numerous female "eavesdroppers" on these intimate conversations. In a 1985 interview, King said that many women wrote in to say she "made their ironing easier and to thank her for showing them how men liked to be talked to."[21] Over time, products advertised become less male centered (from tobacco and beer to restaurants, antique stores, and car dealerships), and the persona of Jean King in popular magazines shifted from a woman of mystery to a basically happy homemaker, whose overwork in radio production had caused her to occasionally collapse from exhaustion.[22]

The patter in the show also became less determinedly male directed, with comments more oriented to social observation, including the addition of a "food for thought" segment during which the Lonesome Gal read words of advice sent in from listeners, many of whom were women. The show continued to create a slippage between advertised products and suggested listening positions, but delivered by a persona now less constructed as an ideal sexual mate and more as an ideal oral/aural mother, a comforting fantasy figure promising pleasurable fusion for listening subjects of both genders. From this perspective, the Lonesome Gal as a radio mother exists as a voice that cannot be subordinated in visual spectacle, taken in by a listening ear. Even though promotion and publicity of King (and other women disc jockeys) attempted to "contain" the female radio personality visually, the actual vocal performance broadcast over the airwaves cannot be readily incorporated through the gaze, as the maternal body is by cinematic or televisual textual regimes. However, this fantasy projection of the maternal, whether constituted through visual or aural corporeality, generally supports a conservative subject positioning.[23]

The Lonesome Gal and its seductively maternal aural space can be seen to function as a trope for radio's shifting institutional, textual, and cultural identities circulating at this moment. In a post-atomic-bomb Cold War American culture, the annihilation of subjectivity not only was a genuine possibility but was often represented in popular discourses as virtually coterminous with aspects of female desire and subjectivity.[24] The fictive aural space offered by *The Lonesome Gal* manages anxiety through a sonorous envelopment of the listening subject, involving a pleasurable play with the desire of fusion/annihilation (with the maternal). One way for radio to survive in the age of television was by not competing with television's stars and narratives, which offered viewers a series of discrete identifications, but instead seeking new functions aligned with a fragmented and mobilized audience increasingly listening to the popular car radio, or the newly developed clock or transistor radios. By the mid-1950s, radios were imagined to be—and could increasingly be found—most everywhere in the urban and suburban topography. *The Lonesome Gal* offers one voice and format that suggests a pleasurable and soothing omnipresence. In this way, it harkens back to the "neighboring" of radio homemakers but also anticipates talk radio hosts and therapists, programming formats that have also responded to a specialized and dispersed audience through a slow development of ongoing intimacy between listener and host.

THE CONTINENTAL: *TEXTUAL AND INDUSTRIAL ANALYSES*

Conversely, an aggressive address is central to the discursive strategies of *The Continental*, a persona and format that Renzo Cesana appears to have borrowed and transposed from *The Lonesome Gal*. Premiering on local Los Angeles radio in February 1951, and directly following *The Lonesome Gal* in station KHJ's late-night schedule, *The Continental* found little success and was soon canceled. Cesana convinced local television station KNBH (channel 4) to air a visualized, direct-address fifteen-minute version of the show in June, which quickly gained considerable notoriety and national magazine attention,[25] propelling Cesana into a contract with Capitol Records and then a twice-weekly CBS network version of the show (Tuesday and Thursday at 11:15 P.M., running from January 22 to April 17, 1952; see Figure 9.4).[26]

Institutionally, Cesana's career rise can be positioned within industry economics and practices almost wholly reversed from those that King was taking advantage of in radio. Unlike the economically stalled radio industry, the television industry (in pursuing the established broadcast industrial paradigms) had an imperative to grow: to sell more sets, and to increase both local audiences and television's national saturation. To achieve this meant attracting more and different viewers, filling in and expanding broadcast schedules, and in general maintaining television as a topical and attractively "new" consumer purchase, while at the same time indicating that it could be both flexible and substantial enough to maintain viewer interest. As a result, there was a much greater tendency to take risks on formats and performers. For the networks in the East, this included seeking out talent from local markets. *The Continental*'s brief rise to national attention played a part in this dynamic.

Los Angeles had become a primary source market for such transplanted programs as networks assimilated locally successful shows and performers such as Mike Stokey's *Pantomine Quiz*. Even Hopalong Cassidy, whose career as a heroic cowboy was revived by television at this time, was first aired and rose to popularity on local Los Angeles television. In addition, enterprising local stations had syndicated some of their programs nationally, including *Time for Beany*, *Wrestling from Hollywood*, *Life with Elizabeth* (which starred Betty White), and the most successful of these shows, *Liberace*.

Cesana's success with *The Continental* was a notable if fleeting example of this trend. Premiering on the CBS network in January 1952, twice weekly in late-night spots, he received photo spreads in *Life* magazine the following month, and then *Look* magazine, which documented the various spoofs of his format that other network shows had performed: Jimmy Durante, Red Skelton, Robert Q. Lewis, Jackie Gleason, Alan Young, and Donald O'Connor had each parodied him.[27] The instant recognizability of his format, derived from a certain creative ingenuity in resolving budgetary limitations (e.g., the use of direct address), was combined with the show's inherent camp value in making opaque the sexual content latent in common stereotypes of swarthy Europeans. All of this was readily acknowledged and lampooned—an early example of television's self-referential humor, which has always served in part to elevate TV as a significant source of intertextual reference. In this way, the show was perfectly compatible with, and valuable to, the industry's agendas of growth.

But the degree to which such parodies critiqued or otherwise defused the implicit gender politics of the show (or of television at large) seems to have been slight. *The Continental* was parodied, but it was also considered to be in some way threatening to the security of heterosexual couplings, a response that we will discuss in more detail later. Institutionally, the show took part in a quite polarized depiction of televisual sexuality and desire, indicated by one industry response to the show's almost immediate popularity and notoriety. Counterprogramming in some local markets featured a five-minute seduction by a female "counterpart" dressed in a provocative negligee, wishing the (male) audience good night.

Such representations of women on early TV, though rarely so baldly suggestive, were actually not uncommon, as featured personalities such as Faye Emerson, Dagmar, Zsa Zsa Gabor, and countless dancers and chorus girls "entertained" in part via provocative attire and décolletage. Such renderings were often excused or even applauded for their function in providing (male) diversions from what were perceived to be incessant and increasing social pressures and threats. In other words, sexually suggestive programs were positioned as sites of leisure, in answer to what seemed to be growing "external" threats and personal pressures that the postwar consumer culture was suggested to be able to allay or resolve. *The Continental,* while seeming to, and in many cases undoubtedly succeeding to, genuinely address female desire, is a notable if partial exception to the general trend of such shows. We will suggest that although his attention to female desire is not wholly recuperable, the program's allegedly dystopian potential (as sexual rival) is not-so-subtly compromised, so that Cesana's gendered address was actually complementary to TV's general regime of sexual representation at this historical moment.

The suggestiveness of the direct address employed by Cesana as "the Continental" is virtually unchecked.[28] Cesana speaks for himself (and for his "guest") and tempers his aggressiveness only as it approaches a limit point of taste and propriety (he embarrasses "her"). *The Continental* directly attempts to induce a fetishization of women in their social existence via an evocation of some idealized, imaginary construct of the woman-as-fetish.

Especially in the network version of the show (which are, to our knowledge, the only kinescope copies available), the program has a distinctive and important "frame": it is sponsored by Burr-Mill Cameo stockings, which offer "the fashion advantage of face powder finish." Although we never see Cesana's "date" during the show, we do see, before and after his monologue, fetishized models raising a skirt, blowing on a powder puff, and exhibiting clothes, suggesting how a viewer might approximate the ideal fetish that the show evokes. Within one show, Cesana details his modes and practices of fetishization (saving lost gloves, charting the length of skirts, etc.), offering to the implied female viewer an identification with them. He offers an imaginary construct of his "guest" in a strapless, sleeveless, backless, "slightly frontless" gown, in a progressively shorter skirt, with exquisitely sized and formed hands, and so on.

Within his address, the Continental creates a space for women's sexuality but assigns it to the purpose of male desire: he opens the process of fetishization but presents it as a double bind of women's intentionality. Cesana's opening remarks in this undated CBS episode indicate that a woman's acceptance of a position of fetishization should be seen as a "gift" to men, which men have misunderstood as narcissism:

> You know, I've always wanted to thank you for making me so happy—with the pains you take to always look your best: so well-dressed, well-groomed, well-coiffed. And all for me. Oh yes, [there are] others that say that women are supposed to dress to please themselves. But you and I know better. That probably must have been started by a man, who wanted to blame you instead of himself for those little charge accounts you open with such gay abandon.

A woman's sexuality is flattered into a position of object status and also related to her activity to spend and consume—to actively pursue making herself into a fetish by investing monetarily into the suggested libidinal economy (for example, to buy Cameo stockings). Any contradiction or difficulty in assuming or maintaining this object status—especially in the form of traditional male complaints of feminine "irrationality"—is similarly flattered away. After Cesana breeches the assumed limit point of tact in his address, by virtually implying his "guest" is naked, he apologizes:

> Oh darling, now you're unhappy? Oh, I've embarrassed you; I'm sorry. Well then, you know, you might be unhappy for no reason at all. That's what makes you women so fascinating. You see, to have a reason for being happy or unhappy, well, that is a superfluity to which I, a mere man, still cling. But you—you're a woman, darling, you are above all sorts of reasons or causes or anything.

We do not have figures that describe the viewership of *The Continental*, either locally or nationally, but it seems significant to consider the program in relation to the postwar generation of married couples who were progenitors of the baby boom, especially in addressing housewives tied to, and largely defined by, their (asexual) domestic responsibilities. The few newspaper and magazine articles about the show that we have located indicate a half-joking dystopian threat perceived via its attention to female desire.

Hal Humphrey, television columnist for the *Los Angeles Mirror*, titled his review of *The Continental*'s local L.A. premiere "Comes Now 'The Other Man,'" offering a corrective to his previous day's column, in which he had warned housewives in TV homes of the danger they run by getting careless about their appearance while their husbands ogle the beauty parade on the video screen. *The Continental*, Humphrey suggested, is "a program which is designed to put another strain on family ties," and he concluded that "if you catch the little woman turning to channel 4 tonight at 11, break her arm. At 11:15 it will be too late."[29]

An article in *TV-Radio Life*, a local Los Angeles publication, suggested a decidedly gendered split of affection for Cesana. In the article, Cesana is described as evidencing during an interview an awareness of, and appreciation for, the domestic chores previously mentioned:

> Renzo, with great waving of hands and in his inimitable and fascinating accent, carried the typical American housewife through a whole day's activities. And very accurately done it was. He finished

with a beam of pride for all American femininity ... "and at the end of this day's work they are as gracious and lovely as no other woman in the world can hope to be!"

Certainly the husbands of America can't disagree with him on this. But while they are out working calculators, riveting with machines, or swinging golf clubs, Renzo is working in TV toward entertaining their wives. And they loathe him for it![30]

The husbands reportedly offended and enraged were doubtless disturbed that the show offered to women the opportunity to identify with the position of a mistress in an extramarital, if not adulterous, affair. (At the conclusion of one episode, when Cesana requests that his "guest" bring a friend along next time to accompany a friend of his—"He's not particular, as long as it's a woman"—he does stipulate that she should be "unattached.") This reaction to a program so thoroughly engrained in patriarchal positionings of women is a sign of just how repressive this system can be regarding female sexuality.

In conclusion, we would suggest that the relative failure of The Continental to achieve lasting popularity (none of Cesana's various local and national shows appear to have stayed on the air at one station for more than a year), as opposed to the approximately decade-long run of The Lonesome Gal, is less due to media specificity than to differences in the way the two shows sustained and serialized the gendered desires they evoked.[31] Whereas The Continental offered only an unrelated series of seduction ploys and scenarios, which ultimately repeated with little variation from week to week, The Lonesome Gal not only shifted from a more sexually seductive address to one that facilitated a sense of emotional well-being but also forged an intimacy with listeners that developed gradually over time, on the basis of shared experiences and a past history together. Such an intimacy over time did not threaten the appeal of the show for men and also agreed with reading competencies more likely to be cultivated by, and socially induced in, women. By examining these shows and formats across industrial, institutional, and programming contexts, we hope to have suggested a more complete understanding of the goals and stakes implicit in what may appear to be merely complementary texts—and complementary media—especially as they illustrate historically specific valences of gendered media practices.

NOTES

Thanks to Ron Wolf of the Pacific Pioneer Broadcasters and John and Larry Gassman of SPERDVAC for making available several episodes of The Lonesome Gal found in their respective collections of transcribed radio programs. Thanks also to Ned Comstock at the USC Cinema-Television Library for research assistance.

1. Christine Gledhill, "Pleasurable Negotiations," in The Female Spectator, ed. E. Deidre Pribram (New York: Verso), 68.
2. "Lonesome ... by Choice," TV-Radio Life, 14 July 1950.
3. "How Are You Baby," Time, 26 June 1950, 47–48.
4. The Lonesome Gal was revealed to be Jean King as early as 1948 in a variety of magazines, both specialized radio-TV publications and mass-market general-readership magazines (such as Time). However, she never mentioned her name or marital status on the air, nor did she show her face unmasked in either photos or personal appearances.

5. In December 1946 the FCC had allowed transcription recordings of less than one minute to go unidentified as such, which led to a boom in transcribed ads. Bing Crosby, whose 3M Company pioneered various recording technologies, had begun to transcribe his ABC network show that same year. While NBC and CBS initially refused transcribed shows, ABC and Mutual relished them, and independent syndicators such as the Keystone Broadcasting System (a transcription quasi "network") and Frederick W. Ziv, who would go on to great success in television, flourished. See "Transcription Boom," *Newsweek*, 19 January 1948, 58. Regarding another transcription company, see Linda L. Painter, "The Rise and Decline of Standard Radio Transcription Company," *JEMF Quarterly* 17, no. 64 (winter 1981): 194–200. On a related topic, Robert Vianello has detailed how major U.S. radio networks used an enhanced, expensively produced rendering of (national) "live" programming, which demarcated their address from that of the qualitatively less spectacular (local) "live." See Robert Vianello, "The Power Politics of 'Live' Television," *Journal of Film and Video* 37, no. 3 (summer 1985).

6. Arnold Passman, *The Dee Jays* (New York: Macmillan, 1971). Typical of most historians of radio, Passman does not discuss the female "glamour" disc jockeys, even though radio and general readership magazines of the time frequently mention them. Passman does discuss the economic, industrial, and cultural factors that led to the predominance of DJ-oriented and Top 40 radio programming in the postwar era.

7. The debates about radio and the female voice are discussed by Anne McKay in "Speaking Up: Voice Amplification and Women's Struggle for Public Expression," in *Technology and Women's Voices: Keeping in Touch*, ed. Cheris Kramarae (New York: Kegan Paul, 1988), 187–206; and Michelle Hilmes, *Radio Voices: American Broadcasting, 1922–1952* (Minneapolis: University of Minnesota Press, 1997), 141–45. See also Amy Lawrence, *Echo and Narcissus: Women's Voices in Classical Hollywood Cinema* (Berkeley: University of California Press, 1991), 29–32.

8. See Jane Stern and Michael Stern, "Neighboring," *New Yorker*, 15 April 1991, 78–92; Robert Birkby, *KMA Radio: The First Sixty Years* (Shenandoah, Iowa: May Broadcasting, 1985); and Evelyn Birkby, *Neighboring on the Air: Cooking with KMA Radio Homemakers* (Iowa City: University of Iowa Press, 1991).

9. Hilmes, *Radio Voices*, 141.

10. Ibid., 264.

11. See Hilmes, *Radio Voices*, 272–73, for an excellent discussion on the impact of these changes on the development of African American programming.

12. Erik Barnouw suggests that President Truman had put Hennock forward as a nominee to the commission in order to invite an uncooperative Congress "to go on record as anti-feminist or anti-Semitic. They risked neither and confirmed her quickly." *The Golden Web: A History of Broadcasting in the United States, Volume II, 1933–1953* (New York: Oxford University Press, 1968), 293.

13. "Madame Commissioner," *Broadcasting*, 12 July 1948.

14. *Broadcasting*, 12 July 1948.

15. Saul Carson, "The Lady from the FCC," *TV Screen*, August 1951, 38.

16. For a discussion of radio's invocatory ethereality, see Susan J. Douglas, *Listening In: Radio and the American Imagination* (New York: Times Books, 1999), 40–54. Douglas argues that radio has historically had a special relationship to the male listener.

17. Mel Graf, "Mental Television," *Radio Best*, April 1949, 36–37; and Mel Graf, "Mental Television," *Radio Best*, May 1949, 40–41.

18. Coverage of the contest is found in the May through August 1948 issues of *Radio Best*. Pictures of the various candidates accompany the contest announcements (May issue, p. 21, and June issue, pp. 32–33); King's masked image as the Lonesome Gal is present in all four issues.

19. "Radio's 'Lonesome Gal' Acquired for MGM Film," *Hollywood Reporter*, 27 September 1951.

20. "'Lonesome Gal' Will Be Biopictured by UI; MGM Project Off," *Variety*, 6 July 1956. It is not clear from any of the blurbs about the "Lonesome Gal" film in the industry trade press whether the narrative would detail the life of Jean King or her alter radio ego, the Lonesome Gal persona. An unpublished interoffice memo at Universal-International Pictures dated 23 February 1954 indicates that the MGM project had been based on the Lonesome Gal character (USC Cinema-Television Library, Universal Collection, Box 719, Folder 22972). Apparently Jean King was hired by MGM to do voice-overs for some of their film trailers. Her voice is recognizable in the trailer for the 1956 MGM film *Diane*.

21. See Richard Lamparski, *Whatever Became Of … ?* 9th series (New York: Crown Publishers, 1985), 100–101.

22. See especially "Put Legs to Your Prayers," *TV-Radio Life*, 28 October 1955, 6.

23. Of course, recent critical theory about audience/spectators/listeners reminds us that responses are unpredictable and open to multiple positionings. That *The Lonesome Gal* offered a conservative subject positioning—or, for that matter, primarily a maternal projection—was not necessarily the position or fantasy of every listener. In Lamparski's 1985 interview, King recounts how one woman had a distinctly sexual, lesbian fantasy regarding *The Lonesome Gal*. She would write King passionate letters, send yellow roses, and was persuaded by police to desist from such practices after she wrote a detailed letter describing the lovemaking she expected to share with King/Lonesome Gal (Lamparski, *Whatever Became Of … ?*).

24. This relationship between the atomic threat and female desire/subjectivity literally climaxes in *Kiss Me Deadly* (Robert Aldrich, 1955), one of the most pointed critiques of masculine narcissism and the Cold War context to appear during the period. At the end of the film, Gabrielle, one of the transgressive female characters in the film, sets off an apparent atomic explosion via her curiosity about "the Great Whatsit." Significantly, a radio show with an address very similar to that of King is playing on protagonist Mike Hammer's car radio during the opening scene of the film. For an example of nonfiction televisual disclosure that relates atomic blasts and an image of women, see Mark Williams, "History in a Flash: Notes on the Myth of TV 'Liveness,'" in *Collecting Visible Evidence*, Visible Evidence Series, ed. Jane M. Gaines and Michael Renov (Minneapolis: University of Minnesota Press, 1999).

25. See "Latin Lover," *Time*, 5 November 1951, 104–5; and "Lonesome Guy," *News-week*, 5 November 1951, 58. Cesana had begun his career in his native city of Rome, Italy, where his father was publisher of a newspaper, *Il Messaggero*. As a youth Cesana wrote and produced experimental plays and was a schoolmate of Roberto Rossellini. MGM brought Cesana to the United States in the mid-1930s to help adapt their films for Italian audiences. After a failed promotion as a budding star ("The Shark of the Tiber"), he appeared on radio in San Francisco, and later became U.S. advertising director for a prominent Italian wine company, and also started his own advertising agency. After Rossellini invited

him back to Italy to appear as the priest in the film *Stromboli* (Rossellini, 1950), Cesana appeared as a priest in several more films before returning to radio as "the Continental." See "Give Him Paradise," *Fortnight*, 24 December 1951.

26. Jack Gould's *New York Times* review of Cesana's network premiere wryly suggests that CBS was attempting a strategy toward network parity with station-rich NBC, by hiring "the first electronic gigolo." It is intriguing to note that both Gould and Philip Hamburger (is this a pseudonym?) in *The New Yorker* figure their gendered resistance to *The Continental* in class terms, by reporting their desire for a bottle of beer. See Jack Gould, "Radio and Television," *New York Times*, 1 February 1952; and Philip Hamburger, "Television," *New Yorker*, 16 February 1952.

27. See "Woo-Pitcher Gets Network," *Life*, 11 February 1952; and "Kidding the Continental," *Look*, 22 April 1952.

28. Cesana would sometimes phone female viewers in response to their letters to him, a practice that apparently could disturb the fetishization process for at least some viewers. See Jack Gould, "Radio and Television," *New York Times*, 1 February 1952.

29. Hal Humphrey, "Comes Now 'The Other Man,'" *Los Angeles Mirror*, 14 June 1951, 27.

30. Jane Pelgram, "Husbands Loathe Him!" *TV-Radio Life*, 14 September 1951, 39.

31. Cesana was subsequently featured in two short-lived series: *First Date*, on which he spoke to couples taking part in the show's titular activity, ABC (and possibly syndication), 1952–1953; and a program called *Love Story* (several programs have shared this title; it is unclear which one Cesana appeared on). He also briefly reprised his most famous role in a new format, in which he interviewed women, *Ladies! The Continental* on local Los Angeles station KTLA in 1961. Over his career, he appeared in dozens of films in the United States and Italy, and a great many more television shows, including hits such as *Mission Impossible* and *That Girl*. See "The Continental: 15 Years Later," *TV Guide*, 21 November 1970, 49.

WORKS CITED

Barnouw, Erik. *The Golden Web: A History of Broadcasting in the United States, Volume II, 1933–1953*. New York: Oxford University Press, 1968.

Birkby, Evelyn. *Neighboring on the Air: Cooking with KMA Radio Homemakers*. Iowa City: University of Iowa Press, 1991.

Birkby, Robert. *KMA Radio: The First Sixty Years*. Shenandoah, Iowa: May Broadcasting, 1985.

Carson, Saul. "The Lady from the FCC." *TV Screen*, August 1951, 38.

"The Continental: 15 Years Later." *TV Guide*, 21 November 1970, 49.

Douglas, Susan J. *Listening In: Radio and the American Imagination*. New York: Times Books, 1999.

"Give Him Paradise." *Fortnight*, 24 December 1951.

Gledhill, Christine. "Pleasurable Negotiations." In *The Female Spectator*, ed. E. Deidre Pribram. New York: Verso.

Gould, Jack. "Radio and Television." *New York Times*, 1 February 1952.

Graf, Mel. "Mental Television." *Radio Best*, April 1949, 36–37.

____. "Mental Television." *Radio Best*, May 1949, 40–41.

Hamburger, Philip. "Television." *The New Yorker*, 16 February 1952.

Hilmes, Michelle. *Radio Voices: American Broadcasting, 1922–1952*. Minneapolis: University of Minnesota Press, 1997.

"How Are You Baby." *Time*, 26 June 1950, 47–48.

Humphrey, Hal. "Comes Now 'The Other Man.'" *Los Angeles Mirror*, 14 June 1951, 27.

"Kidding the Continental." *Look*, 22 April 1952.

Lamparski, Richard. *Whatever Became Of … ?* 9th Series. New York: Crown Publishers, 1985.

"Latin Lover." *Time*, 5 November 1951, 104–5.

Lawrence, Amy. *Echo and Narcissus: Women's Voices in Classical Hollywood Cinema*. Berkeley: University of California Press, 1991.

"Lonesome … by Choice." *TV-Radio Life*, 14 July 1950.

"'Lonesome Gal' Will Be Biopictured by UI; MGM Project Off." *Variety*, 6 July 1956.

"Lonesome Guy." *Newsweek*, 5 November 1951, 58.

"Madame Commissioner." *Broadcasting*, 12 July 1948.

McKay, Anne. "Speaking Up: Voice Amplification and Women's Struggle for Public Expression." In *Technology and Women's Voices: Keeping in Touch*, ed. Cheris Kramarae. New York: Kegan Paul, 1988.

Painter, Linda L. "The Rise and Decline of Standard Radio Transcription Company." *JEMF Quarterly* 17, no. 64 (winter 1981): 194–200.

Passman, Arnold. *The Dee Jays*. New York: Macmillan, 1971.

Pelgram, Jane. "Husbands Loathe Him!" *TV-Radio Life*, 14 September 1951, 39.

"Put Legs to Your Prayers." *TV-Radio Life*, 28 October 1955, 6.

"Radio's 'Lonesome Gal' Acquired for MGM Film." *Hollywood Reporter*, 27 September 1951.

Stern, Jane, and Michael Stern. "Neighboring." *The New Yorker*, 15 April 1991, 78–92.

"Transcription Boom." *Newsweek*, 19 January 1948, 58.

Universal-International Pictures memo, dated 23 February 1954. Universal Collection, Box 719, Folder 22972. University of Southern California Cinema-Television Library.

Vianello, Robert. "The Power Politics of 'Live' Television." *Journal of Film and Video* 37, no. 3 (summer 1985).

Williams, Mark. "History in a Flash: Notes on the Myth of TV 'Liveness.'" In *Collecting Visible Evidence*, Visible Evidence Series, ed. Jane M. Gaines and Michael Renov. Minneapolis: University of Minnesota Press, 1999.

"Woo-Pitcher Gets Network." *Life*, 11 February 1952.

READING 10
MEN ARE FROM MARLBORO COUNTRY, WOMEN ARE FROM WISTERIA LANE

By Dustin Kidd

GENDER PERSPECTIVES

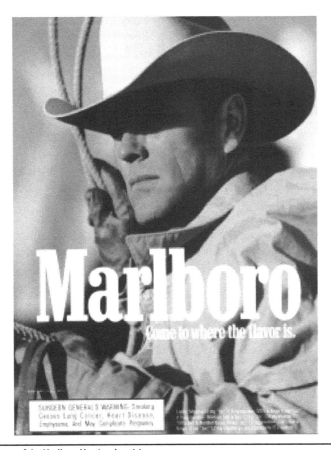

Figure 10.1 One of many images of the Marlboro Man in advertising
Source: Everett Collection.

GENDER NEVER GOES DOWN SMOOTHLY

Have you ever been in a conversation about a work of art, a song, or a poem, and heard someone say something like "meaning is open to interpretation; it could mean anything depending on the observer"? There is a common perception about cultural objects that they have no inherent meaning, that the meaning is always open. Let's ponder that in the context of a Belvedere vodka ad that appeared online in March 2012. The ad shows a smiling man holding onto a woman from behind, as the woman, with eyes opened wide, eyebrows raised, and mouth open in an O shape, leaps away.[1] The caption above the photo reads, "Unlike some people," and the copy overlaid on the photo says, "Belvedere always goes down smoothly." Aside from some blinds and wood paneling behind the two figures, there's nothing else recognizable in the image. If I told you that this ad, as described, is a social commentary on globalization, I think you would raise your eyebrows. If I told you that this ad depicts two puppies playing in the park, you would think me crazy. But if I said that I saw this image, with the accompanying text, as an offensive joke about rape, I think people's reactions would vary. Some might quickly agree, whereas others would say that I am reading too much into an advertising image. In either case, people are not likely to think that I am insane, as perhaps they would if I said this image displays puppies or globalization. In other words, the possibility that I could interpret this image as an offensive rape joke is structured into the content. A man is grabbing a woman from behind; she looks frightened or alarmed as she tries to get away. He is smiling in a way that might be taken as sinister; the text implies that she is the kind of person who does not go down smoothly. Clearly, in this ad, going down smoothly is preferable to the kind of refusal that she is making. "Going down smoothly" is a common way of talking about alcohol. "Going down" is a common way of talking about oral sex. In short, this image tells a story about a man who is pulling a woman into a sexual assault, and she is refusing. He would get less resistance from his glass of vodka than he is getting from this assault victim. It is not irrelevant that alcohol is estimated to be a factor in two-thirds of sexual assaults and date rapes among adolescents and college students.

Are there other ways that we can read this image? Maybe they were watching a movie, cuddled next to one another during a date, when she reacted with fear to a scary scene, and he is comforting her. But if that is the case, the line about not going down smoothly does not fit. The line implies that there are people who do not go down smoothly, so an alternative explanation would have to make clear what such a person would be (outside of the context of a rape joke) and how such a person figures into this image. Maybe we are meant to interpret this male as creepy, and therefore as someone who does not go down smoothly, so we should identify with this woman and choose a glass of vodka instead of this creepy guy. Maybe that's what Belvedere intended, or maybe now we are reading that into the image in an attempt to let Belvedere off the hook for an offensive ad.

The ad was only on Belvedere's Facebook page for one hour before it was pulled down. The company apologized and promised an investigation. And that is where the story gets even more interesting. The image was created by an ad agency called Last Exit, which was hired to spur Belvedere's online and social media promotions. The image used in the ad was actually stolen from a user-generated video called "AWKWARD MOMENTS: The Baby Picture," posted to the website Funny or Die, a popular site for watching short humorous videos, many of which feature celebrities. But users can also post their own videos. "AWKWARD MOMENTS"

---

1 The ad is easy to find online, using search phrases such as "Belvedere vodka ad controversy."

was posted by an actress named Alicyn Packard, who does voice work for Cartoon Network programs, and it features Packard and her boyfriend acting out a comedic sketch in which a woman's parents pressure her to reenact a scene from a baby picture (Gardner 2012). To do this, she has to climb onto her boyfriend's lap. The video implies that he develops an erection, which he claims is really just his cell phone. In the climactic moment of the video, just as the parents snap the photo, she jumps in response to something that she feels beneath her. That's the moment that they make the very faces we see in the Belvedere ad. The boyfriend then apologizes, saying, "Sorry, that was my voicemail," to which she replies, "Why is your voicemail wet?" Packard has since sued for damages in response to the theft of the video still.

It is tempting to dismiss the Belvedere vodka ad. A rogue midlevel advertising executive stole an image, gave it a whole new and very disturbing context, and released it in an ad for his client. Belvedere isn't the problem; advertising isn't the problem; it was just a "bad apple," which was handled appropriately with an apology and a retraction. Problem solved.

But the problem is not solved if the Belvedere ad is indicative of the kinds of images that we see in advertising across the board. Consider the ways that women are typically posed in advertising (see Figure 10.2). Again, the meaning is open to multiple interpretations, but it is difficult to avoid recognizing that women are often placed in vulnerable poses in which they are sexualized and objectified. These kinds of images appear again and again across advertising and throughout popular culture. Jean Kilbourne explains why this matters in the documentary *Killing Us Softly 4*:

> We all grow up in a culture in which women's bodies are constantly turned into things and objects, here she's become the bottle of Michelob. In this ad she becomes part of a video game. And this is everywhere, in all kinds of advertising. Women's bodies are turned into things and objects. Now of course this affects female self-esteem. It also does something even more insidious—it creates a climate of widespread violence against women. I'm not at all saying that an ad like this directly causes violence, it's not that simple, but turning a human being into a thing is almost always the first step towards justifying violence against that person. We see this with racism, we see it with homophobia, we see it with terrorism. It's always the same process. The person is dehumanized and violence becomes inevitable. And that step is already and constantly taken against women. (Kilbourne 2010)

The goal of this chapter is to explore the ways that gender impacts the production, content, and audience of popular culture. Popular culture tells many stories about women and men, including many different kinds of women and many different kinds of men.

CULTURE AND THE AWAKENING OF GENDER

Why is popular culture so full of disparaging images of women—images that belittle, berate, and sexualize women? To answer this question, I turn first to Beatrice Potter Webb, whose work spanned from the late nineteenth century into the twentieth. Webb was a self-taught sociologist who was deeply connected to the reform movements of her time. She published her own analysis of gender relations in 1913, in the introduction

Figure 10.2 A selection of ways that women are portrayed in advertising in popular magazines.

to a special issue of *The New Statesman*, a magazine that she founded along with her husband, Sydney Webb. The special issue was entitled "The Awakening of Women," and it sought to understand the development of the women's movement of the time. In her introduction, Webb argues that the women's movement developed hand-in-hand with both the labor movement and the movement of "subject people's" seeking liberation from their oppressors. She asserts that movements of liberation advance out of deep intersections of race, class, and gender. Her explanation for these forms of oppression, and for the growing movements against them, is largely economic:

> For good or for evil, the capitalist system has forced millions of women out of a position of economic dependence on husband or father into the position of independent wage-earners, often responsible for the livelihood not of themselves alone, but also of family dependents. The tragedy of the situation is that, whilst we have forced these millions of women to walk along the wage-earning road, we have not unbound their feet! (Webb 1998, 304)

Webb's observation is that the economic situation had changed, pushing more women into the economic realm through work and making them major and even primary breadwinners for their families.

But even as this economic change occurred, the cultural system lagged behind by devaluing the status of women:

> By continuing to brand the woman as the social inferior of the man, unworthy of any share in the direction of the country, upon the economic development of which we have made her directly dependent; by providing for her much less technical training and higher education than for the boy; by telling her that she has slighter faculties and smaller needs, and that nothing but toil of routine character is expected from her. (Webb 1998, 304)

Webb wrote this essay a century ago, yet many of her claims still seem to describe the relations of women and men in the twenty-first century. Women are still branded as the social inferiors of men in many ways, and most of that branding happens through the mechanism of popular culture. Every female and every male whom we see on television, in film, in music, in books, and on the Internet presents us with a story about gender. There are currents and countercurrents in this ocean of stories, but when they are all added up, we find that women are overwhelmingly presented as *less than*, whether it is through sexual objectification, stereotypes, or underrepresentation.

Contemporary sociologist Judith Lorber helps to explain the powerful and persisting role of culture in *Paradoxes of Gender* (1994), which focuses on the ways that gender is socially constructed. The idea that gender is a social construction pushes against deep-seated and taken for granted ideas that gender is simply the mechanical outcome of divergent human biologies. Lorber provides two useful axioms for understanding the social construction of gender. First, "for individuals, gender means sameness." For men, the multitude of differences between all of the males in the world is collapsed, so that the category "male" can invoke one list of meanings for all of those men. That's the sameness involved. Gender implies that all men are somehow the same as all other men, and that all women are somehow the same as all other women. Lorber explains that studying the effect of gender on individuals means studying sex categories, gender identities, gendered marital and procreative statuses, gendered sexual orientations, gendered personalities, gendered processes, gender beliefs, and gender displays.

Second, Lorber says that "for society, gender means difference." As gender collapses individual differences into two categories of sameness, it also marks those categories as fundamentally different, with a gulf between them that cannot be bridged. Woman is "night to his day" to use Lorber's phrase. Or as the popular author John Gray says, "Men are from Mars and women are from Venus." That phrase implies that men and women are alien to one another and come from radically different parts of the solar system. That extreme level of difference cannot be rooted in biology, because men and women are the same species and share the same DNA. The idea that men and women are fundamentally and radically different from each other is a cultural phenomenon. It is part of the beliefs of contemporary American society, and in one way or another, it has been part of the beliefs of nearly all human societies in history. In many societies this idea is undergoing some renegotiation, but it is far from disappearing. According to Lorber, studying gender's effects on society means examining gender statuses, the gendered division of labor, gendered kinship, gendered sexual scripts, gendered personalities, gendered social control, gender ideology, and gender imagery. This chapter looks primarily at gender imagery and the ways that this imagery is used to construct gender ideology and gendered sexual scripts. But it also examines the division of labor as it pertains to the production of popular culture.

GENDER IN THE SOCIAL WORLD

The majority of Americans are female. According to the US Census, 50.8 percent of Americans are "female persons."[2] When discussing gender in the contemporary United States, we often draw on the same language we use to discuss minorities—racial minorities, ethnic minorities, sexual minorities, and so forth—but women are not a minority. They may have a minority of the available social **power**, but in terms of numbers, women are a majority.

The **privilege** that men receive in this country is of course not new, and it is not unique across the planet. But the exact character of male privilege does vary across time and among societies. Understanding how male privilege is maintained, negotiated, and reproduced seems especially relevant when examining a society like the contemporary United States, where in some ways we have attempted to unpack that privilege. First-wave feminism produced the women's suffrage movement and led to women receiving the right to vote in 1920. Second-wave feminism focused on educational and occupational equality, emboldened by the inclusion of gender discrimination in the Civil Rights Act of 1964, as well as Betty Friedan's discussion of "the problem that has no name" in her famous *The Feminine Mystique* (1963). Third-wave feminism has brought greater attention to women of color, poor women, queer women, and the diverse experiences of women around the globe. And yet men still dominate in many occupational spheres, outnumber women in the political arena, and make more money than women for doing the same work with the same level of experience.

GENDER DEMOGRAPHICS IN THE MASS MEDIA

Despite comprising just over half of the population, women are underrepresented on television. Martha Lauzen's report on prime time television analyzes women's representation on TV from a number of years. In the 1995–1996 television season, female characters comprised only 37 percent of prime time television roles. This percentage rose steadily, eventually reaching 43 percent for 2007–2008 (Lauzen 2008). My own analysis of the 2010–2011 season found that women characters comprised only 39.4 percent of credited roles on prime time for the major broadcast networks.

We do not see a lot of trans men and women in popular culture, except as rare one-off characters who are often the butt of the joke. But that is changing. When Mac, on *It's Always Sunny in Philadelphia*, met a trans woman named Carmen, it initially seemed that the story would be used solely for goofball humor. But things became more interesting as Mac started dating Carmen and struggled with the tension between his feelings of attraction and the pressures he felt from his friends to reject her.

I really enjoyed the character Alexis on the show *Ugly Betty*, played by Rebecca Romijn. The show only occasionally focused on her identity as a trans woman and did not hesitate to make her beautiful and powerful. It did explore her dating life in one episode, as well as her friendships with other women, but in a fairly nuanced

---

2 http://quickfacts.census.gov/qfd/states/00000.html.

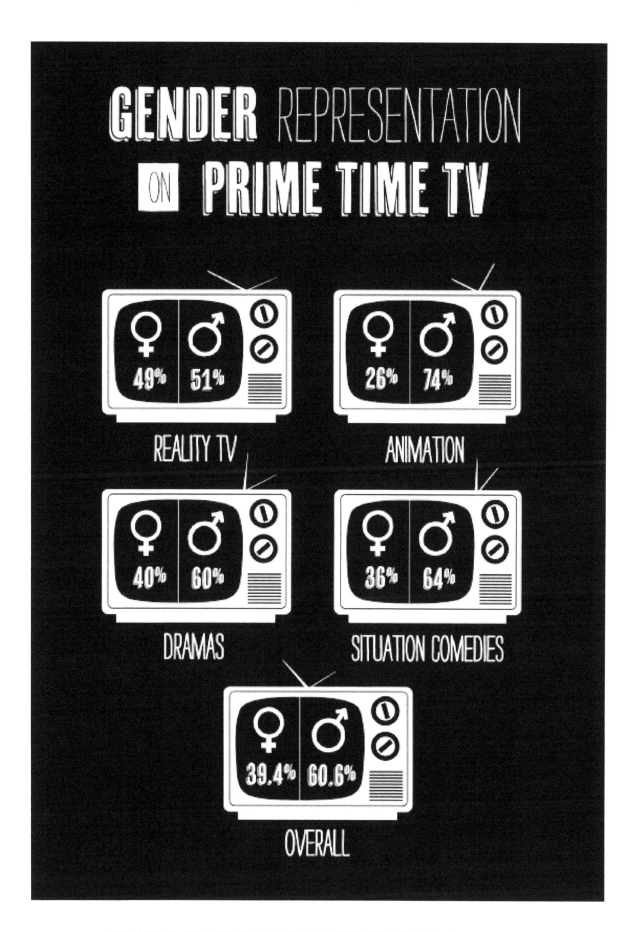

and interesting way. She felt three-dimensional in ways that other trans characters do not. Her gender identity was only one aspect of her role on the show, and her status as a professional in a family company trumped the issue of gender.

However, trans characters make very few appearances on television or in other forms of popular culture. Some trans representation has occurred regularly since news coverage in the 1950s of the Christine Jorgensen story, about a woman who returned from Denmark after undergoing surgery to reassign her to a female gender (now referred to as gender confirmation surgery). We really cannot say that the frequency of trans representation has increased significantly, but the quality of trans representations may be improving.

Comparing gender representations by genre, for 2010–2011, as shown in "Gender Representations in Prime Time Television," I found that reality TV offered the most gender parity, 51 percent of roles going to men and 49 percent to women. That is not to say that reality TV is especially progressive when it comes to gender. On the contrary, the major reason for the even split in gender roles is that reality television remains deeply committed to gender divisions, demonstrating this by frequently pitting men against women for at least a portion of the season. Shows like *The Biggest Loser*, *The Apprentice*, *Hell's Kitchen*, and *So You Think You Can Dance* usually begin their seasons with even numbers of male and female contestants. On other shows, the contestants are made up of either all men (*The Bachelorette*) or all women (*America's Next Top Model*). These single-gender shows roughly balance each other out. So the gender parity in reality television is actually quite carefully constructed in a way that tends to affirm, rather than challenge, gender divisions. In addition to the contestants, a small number of roles on each show are given to hosts, judges, and coaches or other support staff. These roles comprise both men and women, with a slight overrepresentation of men.

Shifting from quantitative to qualitative analysis, we could argue that the *types* of roles played by women are in fact progressive. There is seemingly no logical reason for contestants on *Hell's Kitchen*, a cooking show, to be divided by gender—and as the show progresses into the season, the gender division loses significance as new teams are forged. But regardless of the persistence of gender division, the show still presents a model of women as successful chefs, and in a way that makes their success look no different from the success that men have in the same field. Other programs demonstrate that women excel in professional and amateur fields, or that women are capable of great feats, such as dramatic weight loss.

Turning to dramas, we find a world where there is less gender parity than on reality TV but also less gender division. Only 40 percent of prime time dramatic roles are performed by women. Despite the underrepresentation, many of these women are presented in roles very similar to the men's: lawyers, police officers, doctors, and other types of professionals. The major exceptions are on shows that focus on the home, which are more likely to feature women who are "housewives," desperate or otherwise. Although women are presented as powerful and respected in occupational dramas, their numbers are usually well below those of men. So the story told about these settings indicates that these occupations are primarily male spaces that accommodate a limited number of women.

Women are even less visible in the genre of situation comedies, where they comprise just over 36 percent of characters. This may seem surprising, because many sitcoms over the years have focused on family settings, in which women would seem to be about half of the characters. An increasing number of sitcoms are now situated in nonfamily settings, focusing on particular workplaces (*The Office*, *30 Rock*) or on groups of young singles (*How I Met Your Mother*, *Big Bang Theory*). Though women play key roles in these newer types of shows, they are nevertheless a numerical minority in most cases. On *30 Rock*, Tina Fey's character Liz Lemon offers a model of a successful and creative woman working in the television industry. She is the star of the show, but she is surrounded by several men and very few women. Although we might *perceive* that shows like *30 Rock* offer heightened visibility for women in strong roles, as women move to the central roles on these shows, they are surrounded by an ever-growing gaggle of men.

Animation, the sitcom's little cousin, is the most masculine space on broadcast television. Less than 26 percent of characters on animated prime time shows are women. At first glance these shows appear to focus on families, like *The Simpsons*, where men and women are roughly equal in number. But the patriarch in these families—Homer Simpson, Peter Griffin, Cleveland Brown—dominates the story lines, which means we meet far more of his male friends than his wife's female friends.

We find a similar picture when we shift our attention to the cineplex. Many popular films, from comedies to dramas, focus on heterosexual relationships, which would seem to require a male and a female lead, and perhaps some gender parity for supporting roles as well. Many action movies, including the buddy cop genre, tend to feature only male leads and present environments that are predominantly male. These films are balanced, though, by "chick flicks," which focus more on female leads and female environments. In sum, we might expect that the content of films would be a 50/50 split between male and female characters.

Not so, says the research on film characters. Consider the evidence from reports by lead author Stacy L. Smith, a scholar at the University of Southern California's Annenberg School of Communication. Smith and her co author examined the one hundred top-grossing films of 2009 and found that only 32.8 percent of speaking characters were female (Smith and Choueiti 2010), as shown in "Percentage of On-screen Roles Held by Women." This is the same percentage of women characters they found in a study of 2008 films, and it is only slightly higher than their findings from 2007, when 29.9 percent of film characters were women. The authors also counted the number of films that had gender parity in 2009. These are films in which girls or women appear in 45–54.9 percent of the speaking roles. They found that only 17 percent of 2009 films achieved this gender parity.

The authors compared male and female characters in terms of the quality of their characterizations. They found that women are frequently sexualized in these roles, much more so than men. Of female characters, 25.8 percent were shown in "sexy attire," compared to only 4.7 percent of male characters. Some 23.6 percent of female characters were shown at least partially naked, compared to only 7.4 percent of male characters. Finally, 10.9 percent of female characters were explicitly identified by other characters as attractive, compared to 2.5 percent of male characters. That 10.9 may seem like a small percentage, but most characters are presented as attractive in ways that do not involve having another character state the attractiveness. In addition, female characters are more likely than male characters to be shown in a committed relationship, conveying a message that women's identity is more dependent than men's on romance and monogamy. Women's roles cluster more toward the lower end of the age spectrum than men's roles do. Although young adulthood is the most common character age for both genders—48.7 percent of males and 56.6 percent of females—women begin to disappear in older age groups. More than a third of male characters, 35.2 percent, are aged forty to sixty-four, compared to only 22.2 percent of female characters. At the other end of the spectrum, 10.7 percent of female characters are teenagers (ages thirteen to twenty), compared to only 6.4 percent of male characters. A smaller number of male and female roles are preteens, and an even smaller number are elderly,

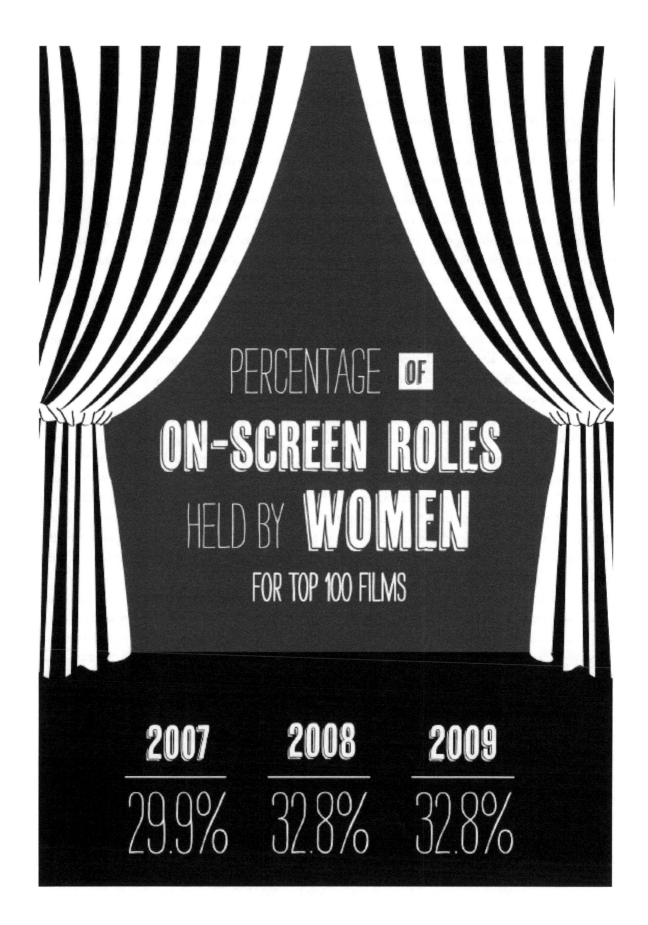

PERCENTAGE OF
ON-SCREEN ROLES
HELD BY WOMEN
FOR TOP 100 FILMS

2007	2008	2009
29.9%	32.8%	32.8%

but women outnumber men in the preteen category, and men outnumber women in the elderly category. This is especially interesting because men typically die at younger ages than women, and women outnumber men among the elderly in the real world.

One of the most popular mechanisms for analyzing women's relevance to the world of film was developed not by a sociologist, but by a cartoonist. Alison Bechdel presented the **Bechdel test** in her 1986 comic book *Dykes to Watch Out For* (Bechdel 1986). A film has to meet three criteria to pass the Bechdel test, which only moderately certifies the film as progressive on gender. The film must have (1) at least two or more female characters who (2) have names and (3) talk to each other about something other than men.[3] This seems very simple and in many ways outdated, but Hollywood is still struggling to produce films that pass this test. Anita Sarkeesian, a media critic who runs the blog Feminist Frequency, ran the Bechdel test on the 2011 Best Picture Oscar nominees:[4]

The Descendants: Passes the test because a few named female characters do have some limited conversations.

Money Ball: Fails the test because there is never a moment when two female characters speak to each other.

The Tree of Life: Fails the test because in the only scene of two women speaking to each other, they are speaking about the death of a male.

Hugo: The test is inconclusive. There is a very brief (five-second) scene of two females talking about film, but otherwise the females only speak to each other about males.

Extremely Loud and Incredibly Close: Fails the test because the women characters only speak to each other about a male character.

Midnight in Paris: Fails the test. Although there is a scene of two women speaking to each other about a possible furniture purchase, there are also two men involved in that discussion. Even the presence of poet Gertrude Stein as a character in the film does not manage to help the film pass the test.

War Horse: Fails the test because it centers on male characters.

The Help: Passes the test and features many conversations between women about topics other than men. However, it has been criticized for its treatment of race.

The Artist: Fails the test. This is a silent film, so Sarkeesian looked for any nonverbal communication between women about something other than a man, but could not find any.

Out of nine films nominated for the 2011 Best Picture Oscar, only two passed the test, and only one of those films is actually focused on female characters. As Sarkeesian points out, many excellent films may fail the test, which is why the test is best administered on a grouping of films such as award nominees or box office hits.

Beyond the quantitative demographics, we can find some consistencies in the depictions of gender in American films. In 1987 sociologist Stanford M. Lyman published a qualitative analysis of major American films released in the years 1930–1980, focusing on the types of roles played by women and men and the ways their characters develop. He found that the purposes of women characters are largely presented as conquering

---

3   The rule about the characters needing to have names is not actually in the original comic book presentation of the test, which is discussed by an unnamed character. The name rule was added in popular use at some point thereafter and has stuck.

4   Available online at http://www.feministfrequency.com/2012/02/the-2012-oscars-and-the-bechdel-test.

and taming men, undermining men's individuality, and knitting rebellious men back into the social fabric. "Women chasten misanthropic men, repair their social, psychic, and self-or-war-inflicted wounds, and wind them back to the world of everyday American reality—that world of competitive coexistence, compulsive conformity and driving incentives to success" (Lyman 1987). What is most striking about Lyman's observation is that women are defined entirely in terms of men, not on their own terms. Obviously this does not account for all films. It is simply a generalization about the overall pattern in American film. By comparison, the story presented about men in American film is that their "true traits of masculinity" emerge only when they reject society and escape into the wilds (the desert, the ocean, outer space). In many films, some balance is forged when men rebel and conquer and then marry. The man must leave society to conquer it, but he is restored to the perfected society through marriage to a woman.

Lyman's interpretation of gender in American films can also be used to analyze gender in advertising images. Historically, advertising's archetype of the powerful, solitary male is the Marlboro Man, a rugged, cigarette-smoking cowboy. The Marlboro Man defines life on his own terms and cannot be tamed by women or society. More recently, some images of men have poked fun at what we might call **hypermasculinity** (see Figure 10.3). For example, Old Spice has run a series of very popular ads featuring Isaiah Mustafa declaring to women: "Anything is possible when your man smells like Old Spice and not a lady." The line, and the ads, are so over the top that most viewers laugh. But the Old Spice man is still a masculine man who is selling a

Figure 10.3   A selection of ways that men are portrayed in advertising in popular magazines.

product. As one commenter warns: "The commercials in effect say, 'Isn't it silly how we pull stunts to get you to buy our product? Silly, but still—buy it'" (Sherwood 2010). Susan Bordo reviews the changing images of men in advertising in *The Male Body* (Bordo 1999). She suggests that images of men have experienced a bifurcation in recent years, as increasingly male bodies have become elements of spectacle. She refers to the two leading images as "rocks" and "leaners." Rocks are active, muscular, and powerful men. They are like the Marlboro Man if he were to rip off his shirt and reveal six-pack abs and intimidating biceps. Leaners are feminized, more passive, more inviting to the viewer. They are posed in ways that have been more common for women for decades. Their bodies are less muscular but very lean.

The leaner is a profoundly new image of men, but it is not a profoundly new image. Women have been posed this way in advertising for years. As Bordo explains, leaners are not the result of feminism, and these images are not the result of new attention to male desire; quite the contrary. Gay men have taken on powerful roles in both advertising and fashion and have found a space in which they are able to express their own desires through advertising imagery without ever having to deeply discuss the sexual politics behind the image. But surprisingly, as a result some men are now subjected to the same kinds of sexual objectification that has typically been targeted only to women.

If we turn to the world of books, we find that the best demographic work has focused on children's books. A team of authors led by Janice McCabe published a study looking at gender in children's books throughout the twentieth century (McCabe et al. 2011). The first important point to understand about gender in children's books is that many children's books have no human characters. Many nonhuman characters, such as animals, *are* gendered, but some are not. McCabe and her coauthors analyzed 5,618 children's books across a span of 101 years, divided into three categories: all Caldecott Award winners, all Little Golden Books (from the main series, but ignoring those in side series), and all books listed in the *Children's Catalog*. Of these, only about half had gendered characters, either human or animal.

How do representations of females compare to those for males? The analysis of the titles of books is shown in "Male and Female Characters in Children's Books." The authors find that males appear in titles about twice as often as females. On average, 36.5 percent of books include a male in the title, compared to only 17.5 percent that include a female. Focusing on the actual characters, the authors find that the gender pattern depends on the type of character in question. When the type of character is human children, boys outnumber girls, but not by much, appearing in 26.4 percent of books compared to girls at 19 percent. Animals show the least amount of gender parity. Male animals appear in 23.2 percent of the books analyzed, compared to female animals appearing in only 7.5 percent. This study indicates that from a very young age, boys and girls are presented with a cultural landscape that "symbolically annihilates" women.

As boys and girls become older, their attention may shift from books to music and music videos. Sut Jhally's documentary series *Dreamworlds* offers a gendered critique of music videos from the perspective of cultural studies. *Cultural studies* is an interdisciplinary field of academic scholarship that draws on the methods of textual analysis long used by literary scholars and historians and applies them to a wide variety of texts that were previously ignored by these disciplines. A growing number of sociologists engage in cultural studies as well, but the method is quite different from other sociological practices because of the focus on tracing narratives across cultural texts rather than relying on strict sampling methods. In *Dreamworlds*, Jhally never tells us how or why he chooses the videos that he discusses, but it is presumably because of the way these videos

MALE [AND] FEMALE CHARACTERS [IN] CHILDREN'S BOOKS

Male and Female Characters in Major Children's Books

5,618 TOTAL NUMBER OF BOOKS

36.5% WITH MALE IN TITLE

17.5% WITH FEMALE IN TITLE

26.4% WITH BOY CHARACTERS

19.0% WITH GIRL CHARACTERS

23.2% WITH MALE ANIMALS

7.5% WITH FEMALE ANIMALS

56.9% WITH MALE CENTRAL CHARACTERS

30.8% WITH FEMALE CENTRAL CHARACTERS

allow him to tell a very particular story about the presentation of women's bodies. Had he conducted a random sample of music videos, he likely would not have been able to present the same narrative. Jhally made the first *Dreamworlds* documentary in 1990. He was threatened with legal action by MTV but managed to avoid it by insisting that his clips were within the realm of fair use laws. He released a second version in 1995 and a third in 2007. Jhally claims that music videos systematically reduce women's lives to the roles they play in men's sexuality. He points to videos in which women seem disabled by the absence of men and driven by their sexual need for them. Jhally concludes that is not a problem of too *much* sex in music videos, but rather of too *little*: only one story about women's sexuality is told in these videos, while many alternative stories are suppressed.

Jhally's claims are supported by a 2011 analysis by Cara Wallis (2011). She compares the behaviors of male and female performers in music videos. She finds that women are much more likely than men to childishly suck on their fingers, to touch themselves delicately, to give sultry looks, and to touch their hair. A similar study of music was performed a few years earlier by Rana A. Emerson (2002), who looked specifically at black women's performances in music videos. Emerson offers neither a comparison to white women, nor a comparison to men. Instead, she engages in a descriptive analysis that focused on discovering how black women are presented, and present themselves, in music videos. She divides her findings into three categories: (1) stereotypes and controlling images, (2) counter-controlling images, and (3) images of ambivalence or contradiction. The term *controlling images* refers to the work of Patricia Hill Collins, who has a chapter titled "Mammies, Matriarchs, and Other Controlling Images" in her book *Black Feminist Thought* (1990). Emerson's goal is to identify the controlling images in music videos, as well as the alternatives to those controlling images. The main controlling images that she finds are the focus on women's bodies, the reduction of women's lives to a one-dimensional need for men and romance, and the presentation of female performers as the protégées of male producers and DJs. The counterimages she discusses include videos that focus on blackness as a marker of empowerment, that feature sisterhood and black women working together, and that focus on women's independence. Emerson also examines a set of videos that seem to fall between the two extremes of controlling and counter- controlling images. These ambivalent videos may focus on male/female collaboration in music production, women objectifying and sexualizing male bodies, or women who sing about autonomy even as the visual aspect of the video continues to objectify their bodies.

METHODOLOGY MOMENT

DESCRIPTIVE ANALYSIS

The world of popular culture can present an incredibly large universe for asking social science questions. Although this book demonstrates that a wealth of social scientific inquiry has already analyzed many corners of the pop culture universe, there is still far more that we need to explore. It can be difficult to ask precise questions about the social world if the specific territory that we are examining has not been mapped out carefully. When we turn our attention to an understudied topic, we often need to begin with projects focused on descriptive analysis.

Descriptive analysis is a form of inquiry that allows the researcher to map out the prominent landmarks of a given social world. Although it is important to read as much relevant literature on the topic as possible, with descriptive analysis the literature review would not yield a set of hypotheses, because such hypotheses can bias us toward seeing patterns that may not actually be present or are present but not significant. Rana Emerson's study of how black women are presented in music videos is an excellent example of descriptive analysis. Emerson describes her research as follows: "This study explores Black women's representation in music video through the analysis of a sample of videos by African American women singers, rappers, and musicians produced and distributed at the end of the 1990s." The key word here is *explore*. Descriptive analysis is a kind of exploratory study. Emerson was turning her scholarly gaze on a subject—black women in music videos—that had been theorized and discussed, but not empirically researched. She knew from her examination of the existing literature on cultural representations that both controlling images and counterimages are important focal points for analysis, and she added some question about videos that might be positioned between those two extremes, which she calls ambivalent images. What she did not know going into the study is what it actually looks like to fit into any of these three types of images. Her exploration allowed her see what kinds of controlling images appear in music videos, what kinds of counterimages appear, and what kinds of ambivalent images appear. Although she lacked a detailed map of the territory when she began, she at least had some guideposts based on the work of previous scholars studying similar topics.

Beginning a descriptive analysis requires asking an exploratory question that focuses on a sociological issue. Consider the following question: *What is happening on reality television?* I hear that question often from folks who are dismayed or overwhelmed by the seeming bizarreness of reality TV. Although it is an interesting question, it is not sufficiently sociological. A stronger version might be: *How do depictions of men compare to depictions of women in reality TV?* Now we have a thematic focus for the question that is social in nature. We could perhaps start with the kinds of depictions in which men and women are presented as the same, and compare those moments to depictions of men and women as dramatically different. That would give us some sense of how reality television draws lines of humanity (male and female), femininity, and masculinity. We would then choose a sample of shows to see what kinds of depictions we find when keeping our attention trained on this question about gender.

GENDERED PRODUCTION

To understand the representations of women and men in the content of popular culture, it is important to look behind the scenes to see how gender shapes the workforce of the culture industries. Here we find that women are even more underrepresented than they are in the content.

Martha Lauzen (2012) has studied the role of women in television production for several years. Examining the 2010–2011 TV season, she found that only 25 percent of behind-the-scenes professionals on prime time shows were women. There is significant variation by the type of work performed, but women are underrepresented in all occupations. Lauzen's findings paint a bleak picture for women's involvement in television (see Table 10.1).

Table 10.1 Percentage of Women-Held Occupations on Prime Time TV Shows, 2010–2011 Season*

Occupation	Percent
Producers	37
Executive Producers	22
Editors	20
Creators	18
Writers	15
Directors	11
Directors of Photography	4

*On the major broadcast networks
(Source: LAUZEN 2012.)

These numbers highlight the fact that television is an overwhelmingly male field, even more off-screen than on. Women's voices, visions, and interests are underrepresented across the scope of television production. These numbers suggest that most female characters on television are authored, framed, and photographed by men. Many of the women we see on TV are actually voicing the imaginations of men, rather than offering new visibility for women's perspectives.

Lauzen and her colleague David Dozier have studied the relationship between television content and women's participation in televisual storytelling from a number of angles. One study in 2004 compared shows made by all-male teams to shows made by mixed-gender teams, finding that when women are involved in the storytelling process, the stories told on TV are more likely to show Occupation Directors of Photography equity between men and women (Lauzen and Dozier 2004). By comparison, when the story is told only by men, the male characters have much higher levels of power and occupational prestige than the female characters. Another analysis by the same authors in 2006 found that on scripted shows, women's involvement behind the scenes has the effect of increasing women's numerical representation and their likelihood of being featured in moments of conflict and resolution (Lauzen and Dozier 2006). Conflicts are an important marker of the centrality of a character, because conflict so often drives plot. But surprisingly, this pattern does not hold up when the authors turn to reality television. Reality, which has more gender parity than any other genre, is less likely to feature women characters, including within central conflicts, when women are involved in the storytelling process. Lauzen and Dozier can only speculate about this anomaly:

> Perhaps the often-macho environs of reality programs, which often include the mean streets of large metropolitan areas on crime shows (e.g., Cops), the rugged settings of survival contests (e.g., Survivor), and the base contests pursued on "can-you-top-this" gross out programs (e.g., Fear Factor) attract women storytellers who hold more traditional perceptions of appropriate gendered behavior. (2006, 453)

The gendered patterns for scenes of conflict and resolution are given more detail in a 2008 report, which found that women's involvement off-screen decreases male-male physical conflicts, but has no significant effect on mixed-gender or female-female physical conflicts. These physical confrontations are then compared to "verbally competitive interactions" (arguments) and "verbally cooperative interactions" (debates/discussions). For most forms, there is no significant difference between all-male storytelling teams and mixed-gender teams. But mixed-gender teams do feature significantly more use of male-male arguments and fewer male-male debates (Lauzen and Dozier 2008).

Two other patterns are worth noting. First, when women are involved behind the scenes, female characters are more likely to "break the fourth wall" by speaking to the camera (Lauzen and Diess 2009). Overall, men dominate this unusual but powerful storytelling technique, but the involvement of women makes it more likely that female characters will employ this convention as well. When female characters break the fourth wall on shows that have female involvement off-screen, they are more likely than male characters to use that moment to comment on issues of competition, as compared to shows with all-male storytellers. Second, when women are involved off-screen, male and female characters are both more likely to be featured in interpersonal settings and roles, rather than in work roles, than in shows with all-male storytellers (Lauzen, Dozier, and Horan 2008). The inverse is also true: when women are not present off-screen, both male and female characters are more likely to be featured in work roles, rather than in interpersonal roles. Overall, men are more likely to dominate work roles, whereas women dominate interpersonal roles.

We return to the work of Stacy L. Smith to examine the influence of gender in the film industry. Smith and her coauthor look at the demographics behind the camera and find that, for the one hundred top-grossing films of 2009, only 3.6 percent of directors, 13.5 percent of writers, and 21.6 percent of producers are female (Smith and Choueiti 2010). (See Table 10.2.) Most films are crafted almost entirely by men, who seem unlikely to give many roles to women or to reduce the stereotypical ways that women are portrayed. When women *are* involved behind the scenes, the number of on-screen roles for women increases. Whereas films with no female writer presented women in only 29.8 percent of on-screen roles, films with a female writer (even when she was just one among several men) featured women in 40.0 percent of on-screen roles. Films with no female director presented women in only 32.2 percent of on-screen roles, compared to films with a female director, which featured women in 47.7 percent of on-screen roles. However, the authors are quick to point out that only four films in 2009 had female directors, so we cannot conclude much from this finding. In a study published in 1996, Denise Bielby and William Bielby found that women writers in the film industry experience a cumulative disadvantage whereby the gap between their incomes and those of men grows across the span of their careers, so that men benefit financially from accumulating experience far more than women do. Similarly, sociologists Anne E. Lincoln and Michael Patrick Allen (2004) have found that women suffer more from the detrimental effect of age on acting careers than do men. They also demonstrate that although the gender gap in the number of film roles is lessening, the presence of women as prominent cast members still lags behind men in significant ways.

Table 10.2 Percentage of Women-Held Off-screen Occupations for Top 100 Films

Year	2007	2008	2009
Off-screen Occupations	16.7%	17.0%	18.1%

(Source: Smith and Choueiti 2010.)

Male privilege also permeates the music industry, at least as much as it does the other segments of the mass media. In 2003 *Rolling Stone* magazine formulated a list of the top 500 albums of all time by surveying music professionals and critics. The compilation of this list created an opportunity for two sociologists—Vaughn Schmutz and Alison Faupel—to examine the dynamics of what they call "cultural consecration," the process by which certain cultural objects are given a privileged status. Schmutz and Faupel (2010) used a mixed-method approach to answer the question of why so few women made the list. Only 38 (7.6 percent) of the 500 consecrated albums were made by female solo performers or all-female performing groups, compared to 415 albums by male individuals and groups (the remaining 47 albums were by mixed-gender groups). The authors question whether album sales, Grammy awards, and critical reviews offer any predictors of consecration and use logistic regression analysis to find that positive critical recognition is the best predictor. Female musicians are actually more likely to achieve popular success or to receive a Grammy than they are to receive positive recognition from critics. So the most important predictor of consecration is also the professional tool that is least available to women. The authors turn to qualitative methods to see if the reviews that accompany the *Rolling Stone* list reveal any important patterns of gender difference. They find that reviews of male artists tend to focus on the performer's role in history, artistic vision, and solitary creativity. Women, by contrast, are discussed in terms of their authenticity, honesty, emotionality, and placement in extended social networks. Unlike men, who are described as singularly following their visions to achieve artistic success, women are presented as dependent on the fortune of relationships, often with men (fathers, husbands, producers), to secure professional success.

METHODOLOGY MOMENT

INTERVIEWING CREATORS

The best way to find out why culture looks the way it does is to ask the very people who create it. Surprisingly, we have very few studies that do just that. There are a number of reasons for this lack. First, for most of us the production of popular culture happens in far away places like Hollywood, New York, or Nashville. Second, as we saw in Chapter 1, the bulk of popular culture is produced within massive private corporations that are very protective of their products and their production processes. Third, many researchers (myself included) succumb to the ease with which we can study cultural content, rather than cultural production, because the content is usually freely available and we need no special permissions to study it. Whatever the reason, many sociologists of popular culture have chosen not to go to the source of those cultural goods to find out why the content is what it is.

An important exception to this quandary is Todd Gitlin's groundbreaking work on the production of prime time television (Gitlin 1983). Gitlin began with a question about how television handles power, politics, and social issues. Initially, his inquiry started with an examination of television itself, but then, he explains, "It began to dawn on me that I could not hope to understand why network television was what it was unless I understood who put the images on the small screen and for what reasons" (13). As a result of this realization, Gitlin shifted his attention to interviewing the folks who create prime time television. That forced him to take the bold step of reaching out to the executives who seemed to be locked away inside corporate studios. Luckily for Gitlin, he was able to live in Los Angeles during the time the interviews were conducted.

Beginning the process of interviewing cultural creators can be challenging, as Gitlin explains:

> I had started cold, with a University of California, Berkeley, letterhead and the names of a few friends of friends and onetime colleagues of colleagues. One name led to another. . . . From January through July 1981, some 200 industry people were decent enough to let me interview them about why they do what they do. Only half a dozen refused outright to speak to me, all of them high-level. (1983, 13)

Because Gitlin actually accomplished this feat of speaking to network executives, many of whom he discovered were only too eager to talk about what they do, he was able to discover that they operate in a field of tremendous uncertainty, not knowing how their newest projects are likely to fare. He calls this "the problem of knowing."

Reaching out to network TV executives was not easy, but Gitlin tried it, and it paid off. A lot of important sociological knowledge has never been gathered simply because no researcher has been bold enough to reach out and ask the questions of the right people.

GENDERED AUDIENCES

One final issue to consider is how gender shapes cultural consumption. This actually opens up a host of important questions. Do men and women watch television and film differently? Do they prefer different types of shows? Do they have comparable tastes in music? Do they use the Internet for the same reasons and at the same rates? Why do they align with different genres of literature?

Unfortunately our knowledge of audiences is quite limited, and gender-specific information is even more limited. For television, Nielsen collects data on audiences by gender, but their data are not publicly available. Scholars who study audiences primarily do so through focus groups, interviews, or ethnographies, which are quite time consuming and typically involve very small sample sizes. Cultural studies scholars, particularly in Great Britain, have given more attention to audience analyses than American sociologists, but their findings on gender are still quite limited.

David Morley (1992) has produced some of the best television audience research in England. One of his major assertions is that television watching should be analyzed in terms of household patterns rather than individual patterns. Unlike cell phones or laptops, televisions are used collectively by entire households, particularly by families. Morley's research examines the way that gendered family roles shape television watching patterns. For example, he finds that fathers typically control the television remote, giving them control of what the family watches, when, and for how long. He also finds that men think of television as a focused individual experience, even when they watch TV with their families. So they tend to prefer watching in silence, and they are more likely to change channels without any discussion. Women, he finds, view TV watching more as a social experience and are more interested in processing what they watch through conversation. He notes that mothers will sometimes watch programs they have no interest in simply as a way to connect with their children. Women also report talking about their viewing experiences with their peers, whereas men are much less likely to do so. Finally, he also notes that the television set is often viewed as an appliance and is therefore coded as masculine. There is an expectation for men to understand the mechanics of television setup and to show an interest in television technology.

Regarding film, the Motion Picture Association of America claims that half of all movie tickets are purchased by women. On average, women go to the movies 4.0 times per year, compared to a slightly higher number for men, 4.2.[5] Surprisingly, we have very little data on how men and women interpret the films they consume, so we do not really know whether there are key gender differences in film reception. Clearly, many genres include some subtle gender coding. Drawing from the genre list on filmsite.org,[6] as well as the associated list of subgenres,[7] I code "chick flicks," dramas, melodramas, and romance films as all associated primarily with women—highlighting the ways that female representations in popular culture emphasize women's need for relationships. The list of genres associated with men is much longer: action, adventure, comedy, crime and gangster, horror, science fiction, war films, Westerns, disaster films, guy films, road films, sports films, and thriller and suspense. But the female audience for male-associated films is very high, whereas the male audience for female-associated films is quite low. (See Table 10.3.)

Table 10.3 Genres and Subgenres by Association with Gendered Audiences

	Male Audiences	Female Audiences	No Strong Gender Association
Main Genres	Action Adventure Comedy Crime & Gangster Horror Science Fiction War Westerns	Dramas Musicals/Dance	Epics/Historical
Subgenres	Disaster Fantasy Guy Films Road Films Sports Films Supernatural Thriller/Suspense	Chick Flicks Melodramas & Weepers Romance	Biopics Detective & Mystery Film Noir

The main genres and subgenres are found at http://www.filmsite.org/genres.html and http://www.filmsite.org/subgenres.html. The claims of gendered audience association are purely my own.

---

5   MPAA (2012).

6   http://www.filmsite.org/genres.html.

7   http://www.filmsite.org/genres.html.

How does gender influence the consumption of popular music? According to a study by Gregory T. Toney and James B. Weaver III (1994), men and women have very different reactions to music and music videos. These authors showed a series of popular rock videos to a sample of sixty-nine females and ninety-six males, then asked the participants to complete a survey about their reactions to those videos. The survey questions included indicators of how much the participants *enjoyed* each video as well indicators of how much they found the video to be *disturbing*. For women, there was an inverse relationship between disturbance and enjoyment. The more disturbing the women found the video, the less they enjoyed it. The less disturbing they found the video, the more they enjoyed it. For men, the researchers found there was a direct relationship between disturbance and enjoyment, because men actually linked disturbance to enjoyment. The more disturbing they found the video, the more they enjoyed it. The less disturbing they found the video, the less they enjoyed it. According to these findings, it seems clear that gender plays a shaping role in the experience of musical consumption. From a sociological perspective, that is unlikely to be a result of biological differences and instead is probably a consequence of very different socialization experiences as well as differing social roles, norms, and expectations.

Gender can function not just as a standpoint from which we consume culture, but also as a set of **interpretive strategies**, mechanisms by which we make meaning out of the culture we consume. *Interpretive strategies* is a social science concept that in many ways parallels the humanities notion of aesthetics. Both concepts refer to the ways that we make judgments about cultural objects. Whereas aesthetics pays more attention to the nature of the object itself, the concept of interpretive strategies focuses more on how we incorporate cultural objects into social action. Sarah M. Corse and Saundra Davis Westervelt (2002) have demonstrated the ways that changing ideologies about gender have in turn changed the ways that society critiques popular literature. They focus their analysis on the critical reception of the Kate Chopin novel *The Awakening*. Chopin's novel was published in 1899 and followed another successful novel and two books of short stories, but *The Awakening* was received less favorably. Corse and Westervelt examine critical reviews of the novel in three historical periods: (1) the initial release of the novel, characterized by unfavorable reviews; (2) the years 1950–1979, described as a liminal period for the novel, with somewhat improved reviews; and (3) the years 1980–1994, in which the novel was presented as a taken-for-granted member of the American literary canon. How does a novel go from being ridiculed as immoral and poorly written to becoming canonized? Corse and Westervelt use the term *valorization* to describe this process of a cultural object moving upward through the cultural stratification system. They find that the growing influence of feminism as an interpretive strategy is the best way to explain the valorization of *The Awakening*. Some feminist analysis began to appear in the middle period, but the feminist perspective was largely taken for granted by the later period. This raises questions about how contemporary social movements may one day lead to a reevaluation of the culture we currently consume or reject.

Feminism is just one of many ways that gender can construct interpretive lenses through which we might make sense of culture. The cultural studies scholar Janice Radway discovered this in her ethnographic study of women who read romance novels (Radway 1984). Romances have often been critiqued by feminists as mechanisms that celebrate and reproduce patriarchy by glorifying the story of the damsel in distress. But Radway discovered that romance readers can be far more discerning than feminist scholars might suspect and are making careful choices about the kinds of romance novels they read. She asked her forty-two participants, a semi-organized group of women in the pseudonymous town of Smithton, to identify their three main reasons for reading romance novels from a list of eight possible reasons. She combined the top three choices to get the rankings shown in Table 10.4.

Table 10.4 Combined 1st, 2nd, and 3rd Choice Responses

Question: Which of the following best describes why you read romances?	
a. To escape my daily problems	13
b. To learn about faraway places and times	19
c. For simple relaxation	33
d. Because I wish I had a romance like the heroine's	5
e. Because reading is just for me; it is my time	28
f. Because I like to read about the strong, virile heroes	4
g. Because reading is at least better than other forms of escape	5
h. Because romantic stories are never sad or depressing	10

(Source: Radway 1984, 61.)

What do these numbers tell us? First and foremost, they reveal that neither the romance nor the men are the main draw of these novels. Instead, the books provide a refuge for these women. Reading relaxes them and provides them with a way to carve out time to focus on themselves. In addition, the historical settings of the books can also provide an educational experience. Radway demonstrates that romance readers are not mere pawns of a patriarchal publishing system. They make their own demands upon the text, even if these demands do little to transform the patriarchal world in which these women live. As Radway explains:

> When the act of romance reading is viewed as it is by the readers themselves, from within a belief system that accepts as given the institutions of heterosexuality and monogamous marriage, it can be conceived as an activity of mild protest and longing for reform necessitated by those institutions' failure to satisfy the emotional needs of women.... When viewed from the vantage point of a feminism that would like to see the women's oppositional impulse lead to real social change, romance reading can also be seen as an activity that could potentially disarm that impulse. (1984, 213)

The centerpiece of Radway's argument is that we must study audiences ethnographically to understand how they consume cultural objects and put them into play in social action.

Gender also influences the ways that we engage with the Internet and social media. Eszter Hargittai and Gina Walejko (2008) refer to this difference as the *participation divide*, a play on the more established notion of the **digital divide**. The concept of the *digital divide* refers to perceived and real differences—by class, race, and gender in particular—in the extent to which people have access to computers, the Internet, and the skills needed to succeed with these digital tools. Hargittai and Walejko's concept of a participation divide shifts

METHODOLOGY MOMENT

STUDYING CONTROVERSY

Culture causes wars. The stories that we tell ourselves through the culture that we produce and consume are sometimes heavily disputed. Across the territories of popular culture we can find a number of war-torn front-lines, and culture that addresses issues of identity and inequality is usually the ground zero for these conflicts. The term *culture war* has been coined to describe these spaces in which symbolic battles are being fought over notions of national identity, public policy, and shared morality. James Davison Hunter's book *Culture Wars* (1991) explores five major fields in which such wars are taking place: the family institution, education, the legal system, electoral politics, and media and the arts. I have written about the culture war of the arts in a book published in 2010, *Legislating Creativity* (Kidd 2010). In that book I define a culture war as "a media-grabbing multi-vocal conflict within and across institutions that has consequences for the kinds of demands that institutions make on public policy" (147). Recent battlegrounds in the culture wars range from the uproar over the 2004 Super Bowl incident in which Justin Timberlake ripped open Janet Jackson's shirt, exposing her breast, to the 2012 election discussions of PBS and *Sesame Street*, resulting in the Million Puppet March on Washington.

Studying controversy is a kind of *ethnomethodology*, which is the study of everyday folkways, and it is most associated with the sociologist Harold Garfinkel, who published *Studies in Ethnomethodology* in 1967. Folkways are everyday norms and practices that we take for granted. These norms are brought to the surface and made visible when they are violated, such as when introductory sociology students are asked to breach a norm as a class assignment. Folkways exist at all levels of society. Cultural controversies reveal the folkways of major institutions, from art worlds to politics to the media.

One of the most striking battles in the culture war over gender centers on the underreported controversy over Sarah Jones's song-poem "Your Revolution." Inspired by Gil Scott-Heron's "The Revolution Will Not Be Televised," Jones crafted a performance poem around the line "Your revolution will not happen between these thighs." Her poem is a lament that many men in the hip-hop world are making music about dominating and belittling women, rather than focusing on racial revolution. She takes the actual lyrics of these male performers and spins them on their heads:

> With LL, hard as hell, you know doin' it and doin' it and doin' it well,
> Doin' it and doin' it and doin' it well, nah come on now.
> Your revolution will not be you smacking it up, flipping it, or rubbing it down
> Nor will it take you downtown or humpin around
> Because that revolution will not happen between these thighs.
> (Jones 2000)

Continued...

Just in this short selection of lyrics, Jones draws from LL Cool Jay's song "Doin' It," Bell Biv DeVoe's "Do Me," and Bobby Brown's "Humping Around." Jones's goal is not to verbally assault black male artists, but rather to hold some artists accountable for the choices they have made and to turn the attention of artists and audiences back to the issue of revolution.

Jones performed "Your Revolution" on HBO's *Def Poetry Jam* to great acclaim and then worked with DJ Vadim to craft a more musical version of the poem. When Portland, Oregon, radio station KBOO played "Your Revolution" in May 2001, the Federal Communications Commission levied a $7,000 fine for the airing of a song with "indecent content." Once that fine was imposed, no other station would touch "Your Revolution." The indecent content stems entirely from the lyrics that Jones quotes from songs by men—songs that have all played on the airwaves without dissent from the FCC. With the help of People for the American Way, Jones sued the FCC. Initially the suit was thrown out of a federal court for lack of jurisdiction, but Jones appealed. While awaiting the appeal, which some commentators thought she would win,[1] the FCC reversed its ruling and declared that "Your Revolution" is not indecent. The conflict over "Your Revolution" became a battle over gender, corporate versus artistic authority in the hip-hop world, and the legitimacy of external regulation of creative content.

---

1   See Marjorie Heins (2003), "The Strange Case of Sarah Jones," on the Web site for the Free Expression Policy Project: http://www.fepproject.org/commentaries/sarah jones.html.

attention to the capacity for Internet and social media users to go beyond accessing culture into actually creating it. They surveyed 1,060 first-year college students about their creation of content using digital tools as well as their experience with sharing their self-produced content online. Initially, it appears that men and women create content at similar rates: 62.3 percent of men and 60.0 percent of women claim to have made content in the form of music, artistic photography, poetry/fiction, or film/video. But disparities arise when we focus on each of the specific types of content. In the sample, 42.6 percent of men have created musical content, compared to only 27.4 percent of women. Men also surpass women in creation of film and video: 26.6 percent of men in the survey claim to have made film or video, compared to 16.9 percent of women. Women surpass men in creation of artistic photography and poetry/fiction: 29.6 percent of women in the sample have created artistic photography, compared to 25.2 percent of men, and 30.3 percent of women in the sample have created poetry/fiction, compared to only 20.5 percent of men. So men and women create different kinds of cultural content, but they are equally involved in cultural creation overall. When it comes to hitting the "publish" button and uploading that content online, another disparity emerges: 60.3 percent of men say that they share the cultural content they create online, compared to only 50.6 percent of women. If we shift the focus to the specific type of content—music, artistic photography, poetry/fiction, or film/video—men outpace women in sharing for all types. This is even true for the types that are produced at greater rates by women.

WRAP-UP

The term *annihilation* might be the best way to make sense of how gender works in popular culture. Gender's influence is to symbolically annihilate women and girls from children's books, television, and film. Women's bodies are annihilated in advertising images that use sexual assault as a comedic premise to sell liquor. Women's multidimensional identities are annihilated in music videos that reduce women's lives to the need for romance and sex from men. Some women are annihilated more than others. Women of color, lesbians, trans women, poor women, and older women seem to be particularly at risk, as are political women, tough women, and radical women.

Male privilege, a key aspect of how gender works in the social world, is produced in part by the mechanisms of popular culture. Men—or at least *some* men—can take for granted that when they turn on their televisions or open their books they will see people like themselves who are empowered and successful, in a variety of possible life outcomes. Men can assume that other men are the authors of the stories that are told about men and about human life in general. Male privilege is particularly beneficial to wealthy and upper-middle-class men, white men, and straight men, as well as manly men, strong men, and men with guns.

RESOURCES

Resources for Examining Gender in the Social World
- US Census Bureau, Main Page on Age and Sex: https://http://www.census.gov/population/age.

Resources for Examining Gender in Popular Culture
- Video: *Killing Us Softly 4*, from the Media Education Foundation.
- Video: *Tough Guide*, from the Media Education Foundation.
- Video: *Dreamworlds 3*, from the Media Education Foundation.

READING 11

THE SAVIORS AND THE SAVED: MASCULINE REDEMPTION IN CONTEMPORARY FILMS

By Amy Aronson and Michael Kimmel

During her reign as resident feminist on the op-ed page of the *New York Times*, Anna Quindlen once asked her women readers which man they'd prefer for a mate: a short, thin, reedy man, careful, committed, and chivalrous, always sexually faithful; or a dark, roguishly handsome, self-interested scoundrel who would never be faithful. Readers, of course, chose the former (though when posed to our students, several women always note that they wouldn't mind having sex with the latter before they got married).

But what if, Quindlen asked, you gave them names. Call the first one Ashley Wilkes, the second Rhett Butler. Now whom would you choose?

"Well, that's different," said one woman student. "Rhett Butler's never been loved by me. When I love him, he'll change."

In a heartbeat, Quindlen had exposed the consequences of women's romantic fantasies: a woman's love can change a bad man into a good man. When Rhett is loved by that woman, he may physically remain Rhett (indeed, he'd better), but emotionally he'll become Ashley.

This romantic fantasy—"the angel in the house," in Virginia Woolfs famous phrase—is the centerpiece of feminine fiction;[1] Charlotte Bronte's *Jane Eyre* (1847), which many see as the great mother of all women's novels, is a *locus dassicus*. And it's been a Hollywood staple for decades: *Eyre* itself has been made into a film an astounding eight times. Think of *Magnificent Obsession* (1954) in which Rock Hudson renounces his wastrel ways and dedicates himself to medicine for the love of Jane Wyman. (And this was a remake of the 1935 film with Robert Taylor and Irene Dunn.) Or *San Francisco* (1936), where the bad gin-joint proprietor (Gable again) is transformed in his battle with the saintly priest (Spencer Tracy) for Jeanette MacDonald's soul (and other body parts).

Like Gable, Humphrey Bogart made a virtual career out of this transformation. In *Casablanca* (1942) his infernal abiding love for Ingrid Bergman leads him to act heroically, the renunciation of love as its ultimate confirmation. In *African Queen* (1951), it's Katherine Hepburn who elicits the move; in *To Have and Have Not* (1944), it's Lauren Bacall (who is also the vehicle for the plunge into depravity and ruin in *The Big Sleep*[1946]).

The transformative power of women's pure love has been one of America's most resilient cultural tropes. Except it doesn't work anymore. Because it wasn't really femininity that transformed those bad guys. It was innocence. And once upon a time, women embodied that innocence—on screen and in real life.

Not anymore. Feminism changed all that.[2] In the movies, feminism changed good girls, innocent and pure, into worldly women—corrupted by power (*Disclosure*, 1994), tainted by greed (the bony climber Sigourney Weaver compared to the zaftig wannabe Melanie Griffith in *Working Girl*, 1988), inured to the needs of their children (*Kramer vs. Kramer*, 1979). Some have even become murderous (*Thelma and Louise*, 1991.)

And they've got better things to do with their time than changing bad men into good ones. In *An Unmarried Woman* (1978), Jill Clayburgh opts to stay that way, while in *Waiting to Exhale* (1995), the ensemble waits for men who are already good. In *She's Gotta Have it* (1986), girls just wanna have fun too.

About the only recent movie in which good women turn bad men into good men is *The First Wives Club* (1996)—but that's after they've been dumped, and against the men's wills. About the best today's women can get from men is grudgingly ethical behavior, which, fortunately, is more than compensated by sisterly solidarity.

So what's a bad man to do? What force is innocent and virtuous enough to change him? In Hollywood these days, it's a little child who will lead him.

Only young children embody the virtuous innocence that can change bad men into good men.[3] This is easily observable in several recent Hollywood hits. In *Liar Liar* (1997), for example, it is shyster corporate attorney Jim Carrey's revelation that he's a bad father to his five-year-old son that leads him to the righteous path. His Dantean descent into the depravity of unbridled honesty, occasioned by Justin Cooper's birthday wish that his father couldn't lie for twenty-four hours, transforms a bad father into a good man, literally overnight.

And the pivotal scene in *Jerry Maguire* (1996), an Oscar-nominated smash hit, comes not through a magical romantic moment or ecstatic sexual passion between Tom Cruise and Renee Zellweger, and not even in the racial healing generated by his friendship with Cuba Gooding Jr. It's when Cruise is sitting on the sofa with Jonathan Lipnicki, Zellweger's adorably bespectacled and nerdy son, that he realizes the meaning of life and the importance of acting like a mensch.

It's doubly significant that in both cases, the guy then gets the girl. Not only must he prove himself worthy as a father figure to her children, but he can only accomplish that, only be changed, by the boys.

And what about some other recent "classics," like *Vice Versa* (1988) in which Judge Reinhold is changed from a demanding workaholic to an understanding boss, and a bumbling boyfriend into a loving mate, by walking a mile in his son's moccasins and listening to his sage advice. Or *Made in America* (1993) in which the conniving cracker used-car salesman Ted Danson becomes a smoke-free, teetotaling, virtuous father to his part-black daughter. And what about *Bye Bye Love* (1987), in which three divorced dads (Randy Quaid, Paul Reiser, and Matthew Modine) suffer more from being away from their children than from their divorcees, and after painful revelation, become better fathers, and therefore better men. Even Oscar Schindler (*Schindler's List*, 1993) is haunted by that little girl in the red dress, whose terror transfixes and then transforms him. (In case viewers missed the point, Spielberg colorizes her image in the stark black and white world of the Holocaust.) Spielberg has made a virtual cottage industry celebrating childhood innocence against the corruptions of adulthood. In his *E.T.* (1982), only the love and faith of children enables that elfin extraterrestrial to escape from the prodding and poking invasions of grownup researchers. And then there's another film, *Three*

Men and a Baby (1987), in which gurgling infantile innocence tames three devoutly philandering bachelors the way no women ever could.

This trope shows no signs of fading out. One of the first big summer movies of the new millennium was *The Kid* (2000), starring diehard action hero Bruce Willis. In this film, he plays a middle-aged jerk who gets his shot at redemption when he meets a ten-year-old boy who reminds him of himself.

In a sense, *Kramer vs. Kramer* is the touchstone text of this new genre. There, Dustin Hoffman, an absentee landlord of domestic patriarchy, is converted to devoted daddydom by making breakfast and sitting by the playground, while his ex-wife, Meryl Streep, is climbing the corporate ladder. Not only can men be nurturing fathers, the film suggested, but they can be better *mothers* than modern women.

And *Kramer* evokes another timeless theme: it is the sons who will heal the pain of the fathers. Fatherhood is thrust upon the Hoffman character unwittingly, and he gradually transforms himself in the role to become a nurturing parent. Far more than in *Tootsie* (1982), it is in *Kramer vs. Kramer* that Dustin Hoffman "learns to do it without the dress." He learns not to be a woman, whom he can merely imitate, but to be a "mother." As, of course, does Robin Williams, in *Mrs. Doubtfire* (1993), although he also needs the asexuality of the frumpy British nanny in order to get in touch with his "feminine" side.

Nowhere is this theme of the son healing his father's wounds, and, in the process healing his own "father wound," clearer than in *Field of Dreams* (1989) a film that ushered in a new genre, the male weepie. (This film was a perfect cipher for the sexes, a John Gray interplanetary gender difference moment: women watched, almost stupefied, at the ending, saying, "I don't get it, they're having a catch?" while their husbands/dates/ boyfriends/friends wept openly and said, "They're having a catch!") It is through baseball, America's game, that father and son are reconciled, that the pain of both father and son is finally healed.

Taken together, these fatherhood fables can be read as part of the "backlash-bind" against women. Women have abandoned their role as nurturing mother in their rush toward self-fulfillment professionally or sexually. If women would only leave the workplace and go back home, where they belong, they could do their job of taming men and raising children, who would not be placed at such risk that they have to transform men themselves. (Of course, women can keep working and being independent, but they'll never get a man that way.) Women can either be powerless, long-suffering saving graces (as of old), or powerless, manless figures on the margin—ultimately to be rescued by their children as well. Writing men in can mean writing women out.

Women can no longer be counted on to transform bad men into good men, since they have abandoned their natural roles. So who is going to help them return to innocence, to their naturally virtuous state which they abandoned when they left the home and went off to the workplace? Men obviously can't do it: they're programmed to be violent rapacious beasts until some force constrains them. And children failed at the task, or at least they can't be counted on since feminism—the glamorous world of work, sexual fulfillment, and individual identity—has seduced women away from their families, homes and most important, motherhood.

To be sure, there are exceptions, such as *Baby Boom* (1987), the yuppie-becomes-mommy confection starring Diane Keaton. There, the necessity of child care transforms a corporate career climber into a nurturing mother substitute, whose business savvy suddenly makes her more successful than she could ever have dreamed earlier. Kids are good for business when you make kids *the* business.

But these days, children can be counted on to help teach bad men to be good men, but not bad career women to be good nurturing maternal figures. That task would have to go to someone who really knows the values of domesticity, someone who can really express feelings and has his or her priorities right. Of course, it's gay men! Gay men have stepped into the breach and are teaching straight women how to hold onto their men, their families and reset their priorities so that domestic bliss takes priority over career hustles.

In Hollywood's current rendition, gay men are not the sex-crazed near-maniacal predators of *Cruising* (1980), nor even the genuinely maniacal female-wannabes of *Silence of the Lambs* (1991). Gay men are kind, considerate, nurturing, and, most important, domestic. They like the home, they know how to decorate it, and they know that domestic bliss is the only real happiness. Gay men have become today's women.[4] And like women, they may be an object of desire, but they are not its subject—these gay men do not have gay sex. Their goal is not to change men—men are far too homophobic for that!—but to help women realize the errors of their ways and to come back to the home.

This is evident in several recent films.[5] In *Four Weddings and a Funeral* (1993), while the feckless Hugh Grant stumbles toward amorous rapprochement with Andie MacDowell, it is the caring, committed relationship between the two gay male characters that illustrates the kind of love and caring that straights can only envy.

But in that film, gay male intervention is only indirect, by way of illustration. In *My Best Friend's Wedding* (1997), it is Rupert Everett (an openly gay man playing an openly gay man) who shows the relationship-phobic Julia Roberts that she can balance work and family. Only with his guidance can Roberts, portraying a food critic, have her (wedding) cake and eat it too.

The gay man—straight woman model pairing appears to be a cinematic match made in heaven. Or at least the act won't be breaking up soon. In *The Next Best Thing* (2000), Everett teams up with Madonna, who portrays a thirtysomething single woman who convinces her best friend, Everett, to be the father of her child before time runs out on her biological clock. Alas, five years later, she falls in love with another man. (This is said to be a work of fiction, and not at all based on the life of the pop diva.).

In the hit comedy *In and Out* (1998), after her fiancé, Kevin Kline, comes out as gay, Joan Cusak is helped by another gay character, a television reporter played by Tom Selleck, to find a man who loves her for exactly who she is—without myths, lies, or diets. And in *The Object of My Affection* (1998), Jennifer Aniston learns what she really needs in a husband and father for her child—someone with whom she won't have sex!

It is interesting, and perhaps not coincidental, that the emergence of gay men as the nurturing role models who can teach heterosexual women how to keep their priorities straight, almost always takes place in anticipation of a heterosexual wedding. Every one of these films centers on a forthcoming nuptial ceremony, in which the bride's ambivalence, or some other equally contrived plot device, signals the need for gay male intervention. (Even in *The Birdcage* [1996], Robin Williams's son's impending wedding leads to the relationship crisis—in which, as we find out, it is the amorous lovebird relationship between Williams and Nathan Lane that provides the real role model to the young couple, not the upper-class chill between Gene Hackman and Diane Wiest.) What gay men represent is clear priorities—relationships always come first, before commitment to work.

Even television, long a holdout against gay characters that were remotely sympathetic, has jumped on the gay bandwagon. Several spinoffs of the very successful *Will and Grace* are in the pipeline—each one pairing a confused heterosexual career woman and her happy, healthy gay male roommate. Whereas gay men and lesbians were virtually invisible only a few years ago, today there are thirteen gay men (one lead, seven regular, and five recurring) characters on major television shows, and nine lesbians (one regular and eight recurring).[6]

Of course, in order for Will (played by Eric McCormick) to be a credible lead, he must play off his far more flamboyant sidekick, Jack (played by Sean Hayes), who so exaggerates camp stereotypes of gay masculinity that Will seems, well, normal. That normalization is crucial to his ability to transform Grace—or at least provide ongoing relationship counsel. Will is quite close to the man of Grace's dreams, which explains why she can't seem to find a straight man who has all of Will's virtues.

What makes gay men such good advisors to straight women is that they know the pleasures of the home, and are uncorrupted by lust for women, which, as we all know, is the major thing that makes men behave badly.

Of course, making children and gay men the repository of Rousseauian innocence and virtue may make plots simpler, but also blurs the politics. Gone are the little monsters of Puritanism, whose wills must be broken; gone, too, the Freudian bundles of sexual energy and infantile aggression. In the depoliticized world in which everything you really needed to know you learned in kindergarten, compassionate politics has become a form of infantile regression. And the costs for gay men are simple: they can never fall in love or have sex. In order for gay men to reorient heterosexual women's botched priorities, they must, themselves, be as virtuous as children, innocent and asexual.

Such fables thus fit snugly into a right-wing family values agenda, almost suggesting that children need fathers more than they need mothers (if not fathers, at least patriarchs). There are no "feminist" marriages here, with two good parents balancing career and family, working as equals for the good of all concerned. And as the Christian Coalition counsels, we're able to "love the sinner and hate the sin," separating homosexuals from homosexuality, because we don't ever allow them to express their own sexuality.

Of course, *Ellen* (with Ellen DeGeneres in the title role) breaks that mold, and, in so doing, reinforces it. It is permissible (with much right-wing squawking, of course) for a woman to kiss another woman. But a passionate kiss is a long way off for two men in a major television show.

In these films and TV shows, both heterosexual women and heterosexual men are in desperate need of transformation. Women have been seduced by the workplace and have abandoned their natural nurturing roles; men never had those roles to begin with and have no way to get in touch with their feelings. Yes, it's true that such films show that men can love children and even do housework and child care, without sacrificing their masculinity. And they also show that women can remember that it is love and family that provide the center of one's life.

But they also show that men and women require some external agent to prompt the transformation, something outside themselves. Men and feminist women won't get better unless they are pushed, we're told; left to themselves, they can barely manage a nudge toward being better fathers and mothers, husbands and wives. Nary a whiff of compassion or nurturing wafts upward from these men or women on their own. In the world of Hollywood masculinity and postfeminist femininity, ethics seem still to reside in some mythic Other, waiting to be inhaled.

NOTES

1. See Virginia Woolf, "Professions for Women," in Michele Barrett, ed., *Virginia Woolf: Women and Writing* (New York: Harcourt, Brace, Jovanovich, 1979), 57–63. A definition appears on 58–59.
2. One book that in some ways anticipates this discussion is Tania Mod- leski's *Feminism without Women* (New York: Routledge, 1991).

3. Vivian Sobchack, discussing the role of the child within the genres of contemporary horror film and the family melodrama, argues that the child in the horror film "shows us the terror and rage of *patriarchy in decline* …," while the "popular family melodrama shows us a sweetly problematic *paternity in ascendance.*" See Sobchack, "Child/Alien/Father: Patriarchal Crisis and Generic Exchange." *Camera Obscura* 15 (1986): 7–36. See also Thomas DiPiero, "The Patriarch Is Not (Just) a Man." *Camera Obscura* 25–26 (1991): 101–24.

4. The literary critic Leslie Fiedler has elaborated a related theme, wherein gay men function as a form of female surrogate, thus releasing straight men from the confines of marriage and letting them off the hook for generations of oppressing the Other. Several other literary scholars have usefully explored this theme, particularly Richard Slotkin, *Regeneration through Violence: The Mythology of the American Frontier, 1600–1800* (Middletown: Wesleyan University Press, 1973); and Richard Volney Chase, *The American Novel and Its Traditions.* (Baltimore: Johns Hopkins University Press, 1980).

5. Sharon Willis further elaborates Fiedler's theme, and does so in terms of contemporary film genres. In her chapter, "Mutilated Masculinities and Their Prostheses: Die Hards and Lethal Weapons," she argues that "what these films put forward as the central figure of masculinity in crisis is really white heterosexual masculinity desperately seeking to reconstruct itself within a web of social differences, where its opposing terms include not only femininity but black masculinity and male homosexuality." See Willis, *High Contrast: Race and Gender in Contemporary Hollywood Film* (Durham, NC: Duke University Press, 1997), p. 31.

6. Tallies come from GLAAD. Web site, www.GLAAD.org

CHAPTER 4
POLITICS OF REPRESENTATION AND IDENTITY

EDITOR'S INTRODUCTION

GAY, LESBIAN, AND TRANSGENDER REPRESENTATION

Film and theater have long toyed with the idea of gender fluidity and transformation. Binary presentations that portray male and female as oppositional forces invite critique of those who cross the line. So when Mademoiselle Amy Jolly, played by Marlene Dietrich, dresses in male formal attire for a nightclub act in *Morocco* (1930), she attracts attention from both the audience and Légionnaire Tom Brown, played by Gary Cooper. Shockingly Jolly passes by the handsome Légionnaire and flirtatiously hands her favor to a woman. This transgression of the male/female binary was both scandalous and inauthentic as Jolly quickly fell into the arms of Légionnaire Brown. But the scene is not forgotten. Classical Hollywood cinema supported hints of gender fluidity as well as the spectrum of diverse sexual expression, but primarily supported the dominant cultural trope of gender separation and privileged male-female sexual attraction. Gay and lesbian characters were stereotyped and kept to minor roles or identified as villains. In films such as *Some Like It Hot* (1959), *Tootsie* (1982), and *Mrs. Doubtfire* (1993), cross-dressing is a subject of humor. Men who dress as women lose status and are bedeviled by the trappings of the "feminine." In these films, clearly identified heterosexual males dress as females out of absurd necessity, and through the antics of trying on the dress and life of the female manage by the end of the movie to become better men. In *Victor Victoria* (1982), Julie Andrews plays Victoria Grant who, near starvation, becomes embroiled in a ruse where she pretends to be a gay man who cross-dresses as a woman to entertain in gay nightclubs. The film is both humorous and tragic. While Victor gains fame and financial gain; the issue of not being able to be truly herself weighs heavily on Victoria.

More recently *Boys Don't Cry* (1999), *Paris Is Burning* (1990), and *Orange Is the New Black* (2013–), *The Danish Girl* (2015), and reality show *I Am Cait* (2015) take a serious approach to gender identification and transgender issues, deconstructing the narrow definitions of the male and female prevalent in our society as represented and reinforced by our media. Recent representation of the lives of gay, lesbian, and transgender people and the exclusion experienced by those who do not comfortably fit into the binaries offered by social sexual norming offer alternatives to the limitations of our traditional definitions and representations.

New films and television programs offer somewhat more fully developed depictions of gay and lesbian characters than the old stereotypical characterizations of past generations. Ellen DeGeneres revealed that her character on *The Ellen Show* (2001–2002) preferred women to men as sexual partners. *Will & Grace* (1998–2006) and *Modern Family* (2009–) feature gay characters in prominent roles. *The L Word* (2004–2009) focuses on the lives of a group of lesbian friends, and *Looking* (2014–2015) features gay friends as they sort through everyday situations.

Dustin Kidd examines sexual identity in "Not That there is Anything Wrong with That." In "'I Know What I Am': Gender, Sexuality and Identity" from his book *Imagining Transgender*, David Valentine delves into a careful and thought-provoking description of the transgender community and the issues they deal with in terms of identity. Media representation of gender identities are considered by Martha Gever in her essay "Going Public: Star Wars in the Liberation Movement" and by Steven Cohan in his essay "Queer Eye for the Straight Guise: Camp, Postfeminism, and the Fab Five's Makeovers of Masculinity."

READING 12

NOT THAT THERE IS ANYTHING WRONG WITH THAT, SEXUALITY PERSPECTIVES

By Dustin Kidd

Figure 12.1 Logo for the It Gets Better Project, which began in 2010 as a campaign to reduce suicide among LGBT teens. (Courtesy of It Gets Better Project.)

Source: It Gets Better Project.

WE LOST A LITTLE MONSTER THIS WEEK

On May 4, 2011, fourteen-year-old Jamey Rodemeyer took to his YouTube video blog[1] to send an important message to the world. Jamey was an openly bisexual student who faced constant bullying in his school for his

---

1   http://www.youtube.com/user/xgothemo99xx.

sexuality. He knew that many other teens faced the same problem, and he wanted to inspire them to persist and survive:

> Hi, this is Jamey from Buffalo, New York and I'm just here to tell you that it does get better. Here's a little bit of my story. December 2010 I thought I was bi and then I always got made fun of because I virtually have no guy friends and I only have friends that are girls and it bothered me because they would be like "faggot that" and they caught me in the hallways and I felt like I could never escape it. And I made a Formspring, which I shouldn't have done, and people would just constantly send me hate telling me that gay people would go to hell.

> And I just want to tell you that it does get better because when I came out for being bi I got so much support from my friends and it made me feel so secure. If your friends or family isn't even there for you I look up to one of the most supporting people of the gay community that I think of, that I know, Lady Gaga. She makes me so happy and she lets me know that I was born this way and that's my advice to you from her. You were born this way, now all you have to do is hold your head up and you'll go far because that's all you have to do is just love yourself and you're set. And, I promise you it will get better.

> I have so much support from people I don't even know online. I know that sounds creepy but they are so nice and caring and they don't ever want me to die and it's just so, so much support for me. So, just listen here, it gets better. And look at me I'm doing better, I went to the Monster Ball and now I'm liberated so it gets better.[2]

Jamey titled the video "It Gets Better, I Promise!" It was his contribution to the It Gets Better Project (see Figure 12.1), a YouTube-based initiative that was started in 2010 by the columnist Dan Savage in response to a slew of suicides by lesbian, gay, bisexual, and transgender (LGBT) teens.[3]

Savage's column Savage Love has provided weekly sex advice to readers of the Seattle-based weekly, The Stranger, since 1991, and to the many readers who follow the syndicated column in other outlets across the country. His podcast has offered similar advice since 2006. When the media began to pay particular attention to LGBT suicides in 2010, Savage decided to address what seemed to be a growing problem by sending a message to LGBT teens that they are not alone and their lives are going to get better. Savage and his partner Terry Miller posted one of the first It Gets Better videos on YouTube and began recruiting other celebrities to do the same. They also invited non-celebrities to upload their own It Gets Better videos. In their video, Savage and Miller talk about how difficult their own childhoods were as gay youths whose sexuality was not accepted by their parents and peers. But their families came around in time, they both found success in their careers, they met each other and fell in love, and they started a family with the adoption of their son. Things started out rough, but they got better.

---

2   Jamey Rodemeyer's video can be found on YouTube at http://www.youtube.com/watch?v=-Pb1CaGMdWk.
3   http://www.itgetsbetter.org.

It Gets Better videos have been posted by nearly three thousand people and groups, including Barack Obama, Perez Hilton, Ellen Degeneres, Hillary Clinton, and Google.

And Jamey Rodemeyer. Four months after posting his video, Jamey Rodemeyer took his own life. He hung himself outside his suburban Buffalo home, a day after sending his last message to the world via Twitter: "@ladygaga bye mother monster, thank you for all you have done, paws up forever." "Mother monster" is a term of endearment for the pop singer Lady Gaga, who calls her fans Little Monsters. The word *monster* highlights the way that fans of Lady Gaga see themselves as freaks and misfits, even as they find community and solidarity with one another. The limited release Super Deluxe version of her album *Fame Monster* included an art book stating the Manifesto of Little Monsters:

> There's something heroic about the way my fans operate their cameras. So precisely and intricately, so proudly, and so methodically. Like Kings writing the history of their people. It's their prolific nature that both creates and procures what will later be perceived as the "kingdom." So, the real truth about Lady Gaga fans lies in this sentiment: They are the kings. They are the queens. They write the history of the kingdom, while I am something of a devoted Jester.

> It is in the theory of perception that we have established our bond. Or, the lie, I should say, for which we kill. We are nothing without our image. Without our projection. Without the spiritual hologram of who we perceive ourselves to be, or rather to become, in the future.

> When you're lonely,
> I'll be lonely too,
> And this is the fame.[4]

A week after Rodemeyer's death, Lady Gaga took to the stage at the iHeart-Radio music festival in Las Vegas and dedicated her song "Hair" to him, saying, "We lost a little monster this week," and posting a photograph of Jamey on a large screen for the audience to see. "I wrote this record about how your identity is really all you've got when you're in school ... so tonight, Jamey, I know you're up there looking at us, and you're not a victim ... you're a lesson to all of us."[5] The song "Hair" (Lady Gaga 2011b) is about a seemingly rebellious teenager who wants to express himself (or herself) through his hair, and how he wants to be loved for being who he is. The central message of the song is "I am as free as my hair. I am my hair."[6] After Jamey's death, even as messages of sadness and support came pouring in to Jamey's family, his parents went on the *Today* show to ask that cyber bullies stop posting hateful messages online about their son.

---

4   http://ladygaga.wikia.com/wiki/Manifesto_of_Little_Monsters.
5   http://www.youtube.com/watch?v=MpHSWMQwovA.
6   The song stands in contrast to India.Arie's song "I Am Not My Hair," (India.Arie 2006), even though both songs present messages of liberation and self-acceptance.

SEXUALITY, SUICIDE, AND POWER

Why do LGBT youths turn to the Internet to share their voices, at the risk of providing more ammunition to bullies? Why do adult leaders in the LGBT community turn to YouTube to try to stop teen suicide and the bullying of LGBT youths? Why do kids like Jamey Rodemeyer take pop stars like Lady Gaga so seriously? It is not just the Internet or Lady Gaga; LGBT activists are increasingly focusing their attention on cultural outlets like television and film as driving forces for change, rather than just focusing on the political system. This gives us the opportunity to explore the functions that popular culture serves in contemporary society.

Emile Durkheim, one of the early founders of sociology in Europe, might seem an odd person to turn to at this point. He certainly is not known as a theorist of sexuality; rather, his theories are much more general and can be used to understand all sorts of social boundaries and the mechanisms that we use to construct them. Durkheim is well known for his study *Suicide* (1951), which presents a sociological perspective on suicide rates. We typically think of suicide in psychological terms. A person experiences depression or loss and cannot cope, and a suicide may result. But Durkheim takes the stance that suicide *rates* are social facts, which vary from one society to the next and from one time period to the next and tell us something about the social world. Durkheim argues that suicide tends to increase during periods of **anomie**, or normlessness. If society is in flux—economically, politically, culturally—then people may feel disconnected from it or uncertain of how to live, and this in turn can lead to an increase in suicide. According to Durkheim, two factors are important for reducing anomie: integration and regulation. Individuals must be woven into the fabric of society—through relationships, contracts, associations, and so forth—and society must provide some moral authority that gives its members a sense of direction and purpose. That moral authority can be the church or pop music, as long as it is a strong authority.

Durkheim turned to the question of social functions in *The Rules of Sociological Method* (1938). Despite the perception that all crime is bad, Durkheim took the stance that crime is normal, is unavoidable, and serves positive functions for society. Today, popular culture performs many of the functions that Durkheim attributed to crime. Crime and its punishments have become so routinized and obscured from public observation that they simply are unable to play the same role that they did when trials were held in the public square and executions were spectator events. Occasionally a major hearing, such as the trial of O. J. Simpson, will capture public attention, but that is only because of the mediating role of commercial media. I contend that popular culture serves five major social functions.[7]

First, popular culture generates basic social norms. Although no American consumes all of American popular culture, most Americans consume quite a lot of it. In *The Dominant Ideology Thesis*, Nicholas Abercrombie, Stephen Hill, and Bryan Turner (1980) identify popular culture as the key means by which the ideas of the dominant classes might be transmitted to the whole of society in the era of late capitalism. Today, in the realm of sexuality, popular culture is becoming a vehicle for new ways to think about sexual orientation. The new visibility of gay characters and artists is providing LGBT youths with more images of people like them. When Joe Biden stated his support for gay marriage, he cited *Will and Grace* as an important factor in changing American minds about gay people.

---

7   For an expansion on this discussion, see Kidd (2007).

Second, popular culture produces social boundaries. The clothing we wear, the music we listen to, and the television we watch not only constitute our identities, but also help to separate our identity categories from others'. My love of Willie Nelson and Emmylou Harris helps me to find others who are "like me." People who listen to Billy Ray Cyrus or Eminem are not "like me," at least not musically. Maybe there is an Eminem fan who really should be my friend; fashion, television, film, and literature may yet bring us together.

Paul Willis (1977) finds that popular culture in the form of fashion is an important tool for boundary maintenance among working-class adolescent males in Britain. In *Learning to Labor*, Willis takes as his subject population a group called the "lads," who actively resist the authority of the school system. The lads define their identities in contrast to the "ear'oles," who embrace school culture, and in contrast to the school itself:

> As the most visible, personalised and instantly understood element of resistance to staff and ascendancy over "ear'oles," clothes have great importance to "the lads."' The first sign of a lad "coming out" is a fairly rapid change in his clothes and hairstyle. The particular form of this alternative dress is determined by outside influences, especially fashions current in the wider symbolic system of youth culture. (1977, 17)

Fashion is a shorthand for a distinctive set of values, goals, and practices. Willis uses the phrase "coming out" in a generic way, not in reference to gay kids acknowledging their sexual orientation. But it is also true that young people often use fashion as a marker of coming out of the closet and embracing gay identity. There is no inherent reason for gay youths to change their hair, clothes, or appearance. But as Lady Gaga says in her manifesto and in her song "Hair," these are among the few tools that young people have to declare their individuality.

Third, popular culture produces rituals that generate social solidarity. People who share identity categories have solidarity with one another, thanks to the rituals of popular culture. Teenagers are united by rhythms at the rave and the club; college students come together to watch "Must See TV" on NBC; Harry Potter fans become friends at book release parties or while standing in line for the movies. As a college student in the 1990s in the small-town South, I used to go to The Round Up on Friday nights for line dancing with the locals. These rituals produce feelings of shared sentiment—the excitement and love for Lady Gaga as a role model and mother figure, for example—and these feelings produce social cohesion by bonding members of society together in relationships of trust and shared purpose. When Lady Gaga declared, "We lost a little monster," her fans took it as a very personal loss to their community.

Why does solidarity matter? Based on the work of Durkheim, it is clear that solidarity is the basis of social cohesion; the sense of trust that solidarity engenders is a necessary precondition before members of society will take the risky step of investing their resources, time, and selves in their societies. Without solidarity, humans are purely biological—and not social—entities. In contemporary capitalist societies, popular culture is one of the most important sources of the rituals that produce solidarity, because of its widespread and frequent consumption.

Fourth, popular culture generates innovation. It is an outcome of technical innovations, such as the printing press and photography. But the market value of popular culture has produced a race for new technologies whose benefits extend beyond the realms of the popular and the cultural. Arguably the most important area of technological progress as a consequence of popular culture is the Internet. The World Wide Web is largely driven by one of the most financially successful areas of popular culture: pornography. We can thank the porn industry for such important technological advances as e-commerce and streaming videos (Barss 2010). These technologies are now widely used for nonpornographic purposes of business and leisure. Americans consume pornography at very high rates, and many Americans spend a fair amount of money on it. The financial stakes have allowed pornography to take risks in technological advancements that have offered tremendous benefits to the rest of the online commerce world.

Fifth, and finally, popular culture generates social progress. Books in particular have been very important. Upton Sinclair's *The Jungle* (1906) led to significant reforms in the American food industry. Harriet Beecher Stowe's 1852 publication of *Uncle Tom's Cabin* prepared America for massive reorganization of its racial structure and is credited as at least a partial cause of the Civil War. Contemporary spaces of popular culture that lead, or may lead, to social change are numerous and varied. Dan Savage's It Gets Better project is a prime example of using the Internet to effect social change—not just a decline in suicide rates among LGBT youths, but also a transformation in how Americans treat gay people. The weighty role that popular culture performs in social change makes it an important element in the dynamics of contemporary social life.

This extension of Durkheim's functionalism helps us understand some of the roles that popular culture plays in contemporary social structure. But Durkheim offers us very little when it comes to accounting for **power**. I turn now to the work of Michel Foucault, who wrote very explicitly about power and its relationship to sexuality. Foucault's definition of power differs substantially from the top-down model that most other scholars use:

> It seems to me that power must be understood in the first instance as the multiplicity of force relations immanent in the sphere in which they operate and which constitute their own organization; as the process which, through ceaseless struggles and confrontations, transforms, strengthens, or reverses them; as the support which these force relations find in one another, thus forming a chain or system, or on the contrary, the disjunctions and contradictions which isolate them from one another; and lastly, as the strategies in which they take effect, whose general design or institutional crystallization is embodied in the state apparatus, in the formulation of the law, in the various social hegemonies. (1990, 92–93)

This is not an easy statement to follow, to be sure. But Foucault's influence on theories of both power and sexuality is enormous, and this statement captures much of his position on the topic, so it is worth spending some time to unpack what he says. Foucault's approach to power is rooted in microlevel relationships. Every relationship is a power relationship. From Foucault's perspective, there are no powerless people. Every person who has one or more relationships contends with power. But power is not something held by individual people; it is a property of the relationship itself. Power is found both in the prevalent patterns of society *and* in the counterpatterns that push against the current. Laws and "social hegemonies" like racism, homophobia, and sexism are crystallizations of power relationships.

Applying power to the story of Jamey Rodemeyer's life and tragic death, we may be tempted to focus on the power that Jamey's bullies seem to hold. But Foucault would instead have us focus on the relationship

between Jamey and his bullies, not just on the bullies themselves. They were engaged in a sort of "ceaseless struggle" that is actually very common in American middle and high schools. Bullying is a relationship of power that is often linked to other power relationships in the bully's past. Many bullies were themselves the victims of bullying, and still others come from abusive homes. Moreover, bullies often target kids who are subject to discrimination in the larger social world. In Jamey's case, a homophobic culture made him seem like a legitimate target to the bullies in his school. Those bullies were not acting in isolation; they took their cues from the "social hegemonies." Jamey was not a powerless victim. His video blog gave him a voice to speak against his bullies and to speak up for kids like himself. His video "It Gets Better, I Promise!" has received nearly two million views. Jamey was active in confronting and transforming the multiplicity of force relations that were immanent in his own life. The actions of a seemingly powerless fourteen-year-old boy influenced a wealthy and powerful pop singer, Lady Gaga, to arrange a meeting with President Barack Obama to begin a discussion about crafting federal antibullying legislation. As of this writing, that legislation has not passed, but it is still being debated, and it is generally referred to as Jamey's Law. From Foucault's perspective, we have a "Chain of Power Relations."

SEXUALITY IN THE SOCIAL WORLD

We are only beginning to learn to measure sexual identity. One measure of sexuality is offered in the Centers for Disease Control and Prevention's (CDC) report *Sexual Behavior and Selected Health Measures* (Mosher, Chandra, and Jones 2005). In this study, just over 90 percent of men and women identify as heterosexual. (See "Sexual Demographic of the United States.") But that does not mean that nearly 10 percent are gay or lesbian. For men, 2.3 percent identify as homosexual, 1.8 percent identify as bisexual, 3.9 percent identify as "something else," and 1.8 percent did not report their sexual identity. The respondents who did not report, or chose "something else," are not necessarily queer. We simply do not know what their sexualities look like. They may be straight people who have internalized a message that sexual categories are limiting or socially constructed. So only 4.1 percent of men in the study identified themselves as gay or bisexual. For women, the numbers are similar: 1.3 percent identify as homosexual, 2.8 percent identify as bisexual, 3.8 percent identify as "something else," and 1.8 percent did not report. Although queer women were more likely than queer men to identify as bisexual, we still find a total of 4.1 percent of women claiming a lesbian or bisexual identity.

WARNING: SEXUAL CONTENT

The metaphor of the closet, out of which gay people must emerge to reveal their sexuality in a world that presupposes straightness, has been adapted for the film industry as the celluloid closet, referring to the compound that was used to capture early films. Film historian Vito Russo coined this term in a book of the same name (Russo 1987). The "closet" that gays come out of is of course a metaphorical and symbolic closet, which begs the question of how exactly it is constructed as a kind of psychic structure, not only for gay people—many of whom find the idea ridiculous—but also for an entire society that struggles with comprehending the emergence of sexual identity. The notion of a *celluloid* closet highlights both the deep-seated though surprising

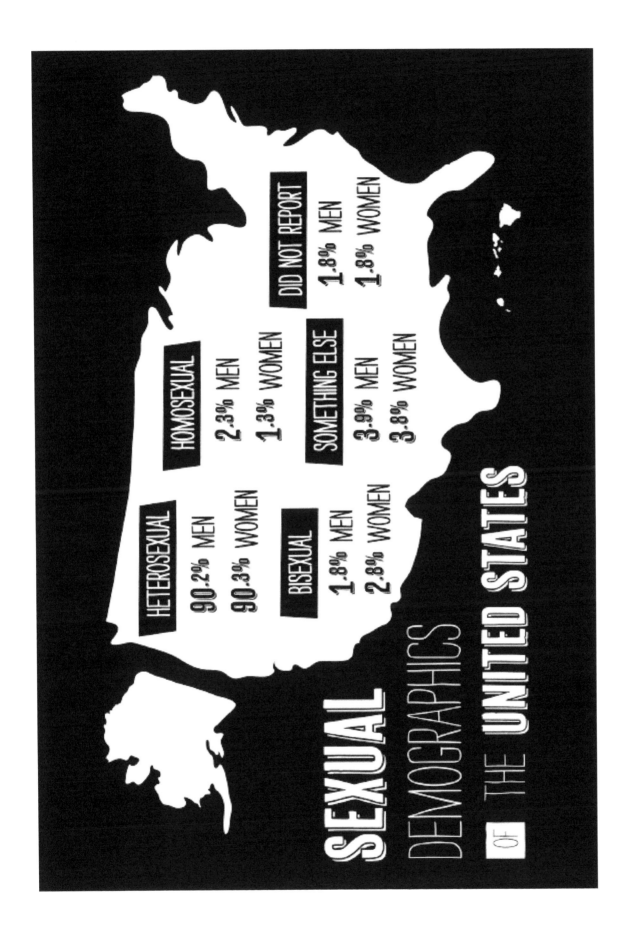

homophobia of the film world and the role that film plays in forcing many gays and lesbians into hiding an important part of their identities.

It is not uncommon to associate Hollywood with gay people. The world of theater has often been a refuge for young gay people who felt rejected in other career paths or found that acting gave them a valuable way of exploring sexuality and identity and of passing in a world that rejected them. Certainly there have always been gay people involved in the film industry, at all levels. But Hollywood has its own closets, and the film industry has to be responsive to moviegoers and theater owners all across the country.

Consider the case of *Brokeback Mountain*, the 2005 film by director Ang Lee. The movie was considered "groundbreaking"—a term used in reviews in the *LA Times*, the *New York Times*, and many other outlets—because of its mainstream presentation of same-sex romance between two male sheepherders. The film's director is a straight man, it was adapted from a short story written by a straight woman (Annie Proulx), and its lead male and female actors were all straight. The film appeared on 2,089 cinema screens and made just over $83 million in domestic gross receipts, making it the twenty-second highest grossing film of 2005. This was thirty-six years after the Stonewall Riots. Though many gay historians dispute using the Stonewall Riots of 1969 as the opening of the gay liberation movement, no one argues that it started later than that. So if Hollywood's groundbreaking moment came thirty-six years after the latest possible start of the political organization of gays and lesbians in the United States, then we can hardly say that film is leading the way for progress. Indeed, we have to recognize that film is often far behind the political currents of society.

Russo's *Celluloid Closet* examines why and how Hollywood has lagged behind for so long. The book offers close readings of a slew of films with important, if coded, messages about sexuality, as well as an analysis of the industry itself and its off-screen aspects that account for the on-screen lag. In Russo's estimation, even when Hollywood has shown queer characters, those characters have been far removed from the realities of gays and lesbians. He distinguishes the bulk of Hollywood images as films about homosexuality, not films about gay people. He appeals for change in the afterword of his revised edition: "So no more films about homosexuality. Instead, more films that explore people who happen to be gay in America and how their lives intersect with the dominant culture" (1987, 326).

One of Russo's chapters is subtitled "The Invisible Years," referring to the earliest years of film, up to the 1960s. Are gays and lesbians still invisible in film today? The issue can be considered in many ways. How many gay characters appear in film? How many gay-themed films reach the cinema screens? How large is the audience for gay-themed films? I address this last question by looking at Box Office Mojo's list of the Top 100 gay/lesbian movies, which is ranked in order of the lifetime gross of each film.[8] The number 1 film on this list is *The Birdcage* (1996), which has grossed over $124 million. When we scroll down to the number 10 film on the list, *To Wong Foo, Thanks for Everything, Julie Newmar* (1995), the gross drops tremendously, to $36 million. The number 20 spot is held by *The Kids Are All Right* (2010), which comes in at just under $21 million. Jumping all the way down to 50, we find *Personal Best* (1982), coming in at $5.6 million. The last film on the list, *My Summer of Love* (2005), has made only $1 million. Based on this list, even with what seems like a recent explosion of gay films, we have to conclude that broad audiences simply are not seeing many gay-themed films. None of the Top 100 gay/lesbian films has earned enough to make it into the Top 100 US films.

---

8   http://boxofficemojo.com/genres/chart/?id=gay.htm.

Turning to the small screen, one of the largest demographic changes on television in recent history is the emergence of many characters who are gay, lesbian, or bisexual. Shows like *Ellen* and later *Will and Grace* gave heightened visibility to this American demographic. This is not the first time that queer characters have appeared on television. Steven Capsuto's historical analysis of television, *Alternate Channels* (2000), finds that the earliest acknowledgments of homosexuality came in the form of unscripted programs like sports and news. Wrestling's Gorgeous George was an implied gay character in the late 1940s, though the sportsman behind the character, George Wagner, was a married heterosexual. In the 1950s, variety and news shows took an interest in Christine Jorgensen, a transsexual woman who had returned from sex reassignment surgery in Denmark. When the McCarthy hearings of 1954 added homosexual "perverts" to their list of targets alongside communists, the news media were forced to at least acknowledge gay sexuality on television.

In the many years since then, televisual portrayals of queer identities have transformed from one decade to the next, with a focus on gay politics in the 1960s, disco in the 1970s, AIDS in the 1980s, gay mainstream visibility in the 1990s, and gay civil rights in the first decade of the twenty-first century.[9]

The most consistent analysis of LGBT representations on television is conducted by the Gay and Lesbian Alliance Against Defamation (GLAAD), which publishes two annual reports that assess the presence of queer roles on TV. "Where Are We on TV?" reviews the new television lineup every fall, as announced by the networks (Gay and Lesbian Alliance Against Defamation 2011a). The "Network Responsibility Index" (NRI) provides a follow-up to "Where Are We on TV?" by looking back at the preceding year of television and grading networks on their inclusion of queer characters and themes (Gay and Lesbian Alliance Against Defamation 2011b).

The 2011 NRI looked back at the 2010–2011 television season, examining any programming that aired between June 1, 2010, and May 31, 2011. The NRI counts hours of LGBT impressions. If an hour of television includes a major character who is queer, that hour counts as one major impression. If the hour includes only a discussion of gay issues or the presence of a minor character who is queer, that hour counts as a minor impression. The main goal of the NRI is to compare networks, and from year to year. Networks are given one of four grades, based on the percentage of LGBT-inclusive hours of programming, as well as the quality of the representations that are offered and the diversity of those representations: excellent, good, adequate, or failing. For 2010–2011, GLAAD ranked the broadcast networks as follows:

1. The CW: Good (33% of prime time hours LGBT-inclusive)
2. Fox: Good (29% of prime time hours LGBT-inclusive)
3. ABC: Good (23% of prime time hours LGBT-inclusive)
4. NBC: Adequate (15% of prime time hours LGBT-inclusive)
5. CBS: Adequate (10% of prime time hours LGBT-inclusive)

In terms of racial diversity among LGBT characters, GLAAD's NRI found that black LGBT characters were the most underrepresented group in number of programming hours (not in number of characters). Hispanic and Asian LGBT characters fared better than blacks, but still had quite limited representation compared to whites.

---

9   These eras are covered in detail in the Media Education Foundation documentary *Off the Straight and Narrow.*

Most LGBT impressions on TV are of gay men. Lesbians are significantly underrepresented, and queer women are more likely to be presented as bisexual than lesbian.

In my own analysis of the same season—shown in "Sexual Demographics in Television"—which focuses on characters rather than hours of programming, I found that lesbian, gay, and bisexual characters accounted for 5.1 percent of prime time characters whose sexuality was clearly identified. (Many characters are never identified sexually, either because of their age or because of the small scope of their roles.) That leaves 94.9 percent of sexually identified characters as straight. The characters who are queer are mostly gay males: 3.6 percent, compared to 0.7 percent lesbians, 0.2 percent bisexual males, and 0.6 percent bisexual females. In other words, 70.1 percent of queer characters are gay males. Also, 82 percent of queer characters are white; 3.3 percent are Asian, 8.2 percent are Hispanic, and 6.5 percent are black. Some 93.5 percent of queer men on prime time TV are gay, whereas 6.5 percent are bisexual. By comparison, 53.3 percent of queer women on prime time TV are lesbian, and 46.7 percent are bisexual.

Comparing queer representation across genres, we should first start with the special case of animation. Animation on prime time for the major broadcast networks really just means Fox on Sunday evenings. It is a very small subset of prime time television. At first glance, animation appears to be quite progressive when it comes to sexuality, given that 16.9 percent of animated characters in 2010–2011 were queer. That is much higher than the overall average of 5.1 percent. But many of these characters are minor, and they often serve as the butt of jokes. As GLAAD points out, "FOX's greatest problems with LGBT representation have typically been during their Sunday animation block" (Gay and Lesbian Alliance Against Defamation 2011b, 12). On sitcoms, queer roles constitute 6.1 percent of sexually identified characters, compared to 4.7 percent of characters on reality shows and 3.6 percent of characters on dramas. Across all genres, gay white men occupy most of the queer roles.

In the world of music we find a very different pattern. Although there are some prominent gay men in the popular music industry—Elton John, George Michael, Ricky Martin—nearly all avoided coming out until after their fame was well established. The same has been true for lesbians in the music industry, with some of the most prominent being Melissa Etheridge, The Indigo Girls, and K. D. Lang.[10] But unlike men, many women in music have become very successful while identifying as bisexual. A review of the *Billboard* Top 100 from 2010 reveals that two bisexual women—Lady Gaga and Ke$ha—each had four hits on that year's Top 100 list.[11] Katy Perry, who does not identify as bisexual but hit fame with the bisexually charged "I Kissed a Girl," had two of the Top 100 songs of 2010. There are no lesbian women in the Top 100 from that year, and there is only one gay male: Adam Lambert. Lambert has one song in the Top 100, which we can combine with the four each from Lady Gaga and Ke$ha to conclude that 9 percent of songs in the 2010 Top 100 are by queer performers. Not bad, but that's only three different performers. It is true that there is some fluidity to sexual identity, especially in a world where queer people are pressured to stay in the closet and may only come out later in their careers or never at all. What I analyze here in the case of musicians refers to the *public* sexual identity, which tells us something about how these performers are understood by audiences.

---

10   http://lesbianlife.about.com/od/lesbianmusicians/a/TopLesbianBands.htm.
11   http://www.billboard.com/charts-year-end/hot-100-songs?year=2010#/charts-year-end/hot-100-songs?year=2010.

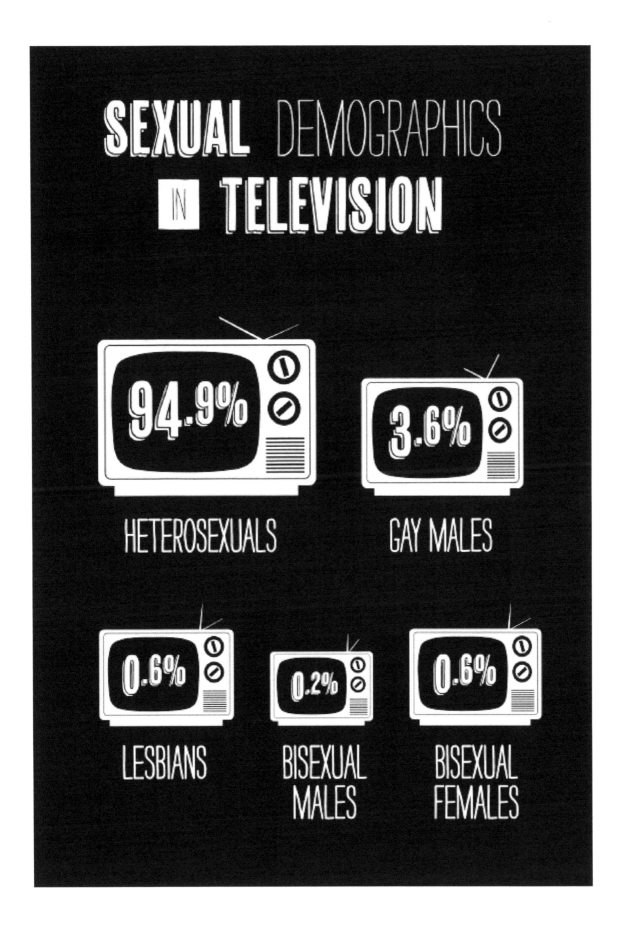

Figure 12.2 Batman and his sidekick Robin both dressed in unusual ways, but we could argue that Robin is significantly more flamboyant than the superhero he assists.

Source: Everett Collection.

The field of literature would seem to be the richest space for research on gay representations. Thus far, however, sociologists have largely left that work to their colleagues in the English department. Although literary analyses of gay characters can help us to better understand the role of sexuality in literary history, we need to apply the methods of sociology to really make claims about the frequency of different types of representations, the practices through which these representations are produced, and the deployment of these representations by audiences engaged in the process of meaning-making.

Neil Shyminsky (2011) offers a queer analysis of comic book heroes and their sidekicks. He begins with the premise that the many male superheroes are gay enough that they produce queer anxiety, from their S&M-themed costumes to the superpowers that make them mutants and freaks. But the superhero must be affirmed as the very model of modern masculinity, which is where his sidekick comes in. Although the sidekick creates an ambiguous homosocial relationship, he also serves as a foil for the failed masculinity of the superhero. The ambiguity of the superhero/sidekick relationship is comedically celebrated and mocked by the *Saturday Night Live* animated shorts "The Ambiguously Gay Duo." Shyminsky pays particular attention to the relationships between Superman/Clark Kent and his "cub reporter" sidekick Jimmy Olsen, and between Batman and the three men who stepped into the Robin role over the years of that comic. Both Jimmy and Robin are presented as feminized men, which allows them to affirm the masculinity of the superheroes they serve. Jimmy Olsen frequently wears drag to go undercover to investigate a story, but just as frequently puts himself in danger's way and needs Superman to save him. Robin foolishly wears the flamboyantly red, green, and yellow costume and arrogantly thinks he can take down the villains on his own (see Figure 12.2). The role of Robin, the sidekick, has been played by three alter egos over the years since he was first created in 1940. The original Robin, Dick Grayson, eventually went to college. The second Robin, Jason Todd, was killed by the Joker. The most recent

---

METHODOLOGY MOMENT

QUANTITATIVE CONTENT ANALYSIS

Quantitative content analysis is the act of counting characters, plot elements, and other kinds of representations in a carefully chosen sample. It allows us to make very broad, but often not very deep, claims about the kinds of representations that appear in cultural content. Quantitative content analysis allows for breadth because, when carefully made, a coding sheet facilitates most analyses happening relatively quickly, so that a larger sample can be reviewed. It does not allow for depth, because it usually separates specific representations from the context in which they occur. For example, I stated previously that 5.1 percent of sexually identified characters in the 2010 season of prime time programming on the major broadcast networks are gay, lesbian, or bisexual. If you were to ask me whether those representations were largely positive or negative, or what kinds of jobs the characters had, or how multidimensional their lives are, I could not tell you, because none of those were codes in my analysis. I can certainly add codes, but there will always be layers of meaning that are missed in a quantitative content analysis. By comparison, if you asked Neil Shyminsky (cited in reference to comic book characters) to comment in depth about Jimmy Olsen or Robin, he certainly could. But if you asked him what percentage of superheroes have sidekicks, or how many sidekicks serve as gay foils, he certainly could not answer that question based on the research he conducted for the article I cited. That article offered a deep analysis of the meaningful relationships within a small handful of comics, whereas my study offered a broad overview of television representations. Although deep issues of meaning are tremendously important, it is just as important to examine the broad context of cultural representations. I like to think of qualitative content analyses as landscape paintings of one particular perspective from within a scenic location, and of quantitative content analyses as maps drawn from above.

Quantitative content analyses need to begin with a research question. *What is the racial breakdown of prime time television? What is the ratio of men to women in film? How many television programming*

Continued...

hours include gay characters? How many children's book characters are disabled? The research question should help to determine what the unit of analysis needs to be. If the question is about characters, then the unit of analysis is each individual character (perhaps limited to speaking roles). If the question is about programming hours, then the unit of analysis is an hour of television programming. An hour of television programming should not be confused for an individual television program, as many programs are only thirty minutes long, and others (such as movies, extended episodes, and sporting events) last longer than an hour. In a study of music, a research question about songs has a different unit of analysis than a question about albums.

The research question should also clarify the important variables being counted, such as the race of an author, the gender of a singer, or the sexuality of a character. Of course we also have to determine how we will know the answer to this question. This can actually be quite tricky. How would we know if a television character is gay? Do we presume the character is straight until there is an indication otherwise? If a character is shown in a same-sex relationship, do we presume he is gay or she is lesbian? How would we know the character is not bisexual? Identifying the sexuality of nonfictional people is hard enough. When the person is fictional, it becomes even tougher.

Here is how I answer those questions. I argue that a character has no more substance than what the creator of the character has actually shown. The creator has the right to reveal more later, but until that time all we have is what has been shown. If a character explicitly states his sexuality, then we have to assume that the statement is accurate until we are given some indication otherwise. If a male character dates a female, but then declares to her that he is gay, then we have to code him as gay in our analysis, even though we've only seen him in a straight relationship. If a character does not identify his own sexuality, then we have to look to his relationships for an indication. So a character in a straight relationship would be coded as straight, up until the specific episode when he declared his gay identity. A character having relationships with both men and women would be coded as bisexual until a moment when the character declares otherwise. Any character who is not shown in a relationship or with an interest in a relationship, and who does not declare her or his sexuality, must be coded as "unknown," meaning the character's sexuality has not been identified.

The process for making each determination is written up in a code-book, which is a set of protocols used in completing each coding sheet. We start to see quite quickly that quantitative content analysis can offer a number of difficult research complexities. The best resource for anyone preparing to engage in quantitative content analysis is Kimberly A. Neuendorf's *The Content Analysis Guidebook* (2002).

Robin is Tim Drake, who operates as the Red Robin. According to Shyminsky, these sidekicks serve as the less ambiguous half of the gay superhero/sidekick duos, distracting queer anxiety from the superhero.

GAY HOLLYWOOD

We know very little about queer participation in the production of television behind the cameras. Unlike gender and race, sexuality is not a category for which we regularly collect labor market data. So we know nothing about the percentages of actors, writers, directors, producers, or camera technicians who are gay.

Given the possibility of sexual nondisclosure, we should assume that gender patterns influence the opportunities faced by queer men and women in television production. That pattern means that gay men are likely to have many more opportunities off-screen than are lesbian women. Gay men have played key roles as creators, producers, and directors for some of the most watched shows. Key figures in this list are Greg Berlanti (*Dawson's Creek*; *Dirty, Sexy Money*; *Brothers and Sisters*), Ryan Murphy (*Glee*; *Nip/Tuck*), and Andy Cohen (*The Real Housewives* series; *Project Runway*). These prominent gay men have few lesbian counterparts. Lesbian women *are* working in television—Allison Adler's work on *Chuck* and *Glee* is an example—but they are fewer and less prominent.

Gay actors report having a very difficult time breaking into and succeeding in the film industry, although that is starting to change. In the essay "'I Saw You Naked': 'Hard' Acting in 'Gay' Movies," the actor Christopher Bradley discusses his struggles as a gay actor in the 1990s. His concerns were brought into focus one evening while he was working as a waiter at an event and was recognized by someone who remembered a nude scene that he had been in:

> I thought about the huge risk I'd taken in making that movie—being gay and starring in a gay independent film, something that just wasn't done at that time. A film with a nude love scene, no less. There were casting directors over the years who had refused to call me in just because they'd heard that I *might* be gay. If this risk didn't pay off, things were going to be far worse in that regard.

> I thought about the cover story interview I'd done for *Genre* magazine in which I'd spoken openly about being gay, when everyone would have understood (and even supported me) if I'd lied and said I had a girlfriend. How many actors have taken that route over the years? I thought about how my agent told me not to do *Leather Jacket Love Story* because it would ruin my career, and how I'd refused to budge. I thought about my bold plan to be the first gay actor to make it big while telling the truth right from the start, rather than after years of lying. (Bradley 2009, 42)

Although Bradley made a choice to be out and may have paid a price for it, many other gay and lesbian actors choose to keep quiet about their sexuality or to come out only after achieving significant success. In 2012 Matt Bomer and Jim Parsons, who both act on TV and in films, acknowledged their sexuality publicly. In both cases, the actors were said to have "come out," even though both were already open about their sexuality with their friends and families. The coming out in question was a matter of media acknowledgment, which also means standing up publicly as a gay figure. Christopher Bradley says things have become much easier in the new millennium: "I told this new manager I wasn't going to lie about it. She looked at me with some confusion and said, 'No one cares about that anymore.' Thirty years of tightness went out of my body" (2009, 52).

The emergence of gay- and lesbian-themed culture happened much earlier in the music industry, even if that industry still struggles to bring queer culture into the mainstream. Before the small art house music studios were swept up by the massive culture industry conglomerates, some gay and lesbian artists found safe havens in boutique recording studios. One such studio was Folkways Records, founded in New York City in 1948 by the recording engineer Moses Asch. As Cindy Boucher (2008) documents, Folkways produced four important gay- and lesbian-themed albums in the 1970s. Boucher argues that these albums were able to emerge in the 1970s, and not sooner, because of how the politics of the 1969 Stonewall Riots and the creation of the Gay Liberation Front helped to solidify queer community in America. Prior to the coming out of queer politics, gay and lesbian musicians hid their sexuality in innuendo and double entendre. Although other minority groups, from African Americans to working-class whites, were making protest songs several decades earlier, the only openly gay music existed in camp and parody songs, many produced in the 1960s by a company called Camp Records. But many of the musicians on Camp Records albums did not reveal their identities, which allowed the sexuality of the music to be out of the closet although the singer stayed in.

By contrast, the Folkways albums of the 1970s were openly gay, and most of them clearly identified the artists involved. The first was Michael Cohen's 1973 album *What Did You Expect? … Songs About the Experiences of Being Gay*. That is about as clear as an album title can be. The album is a mix of songs about gay romance and dating as well as protest songs against repressive Christianity. The 1979 Kathy Fire album *Songs of Fire: Songs of a Lesbian Anarchist* was even more radical and political, with songs like "Mother Rage" about lesbian pride and community among women. The other two albums were collaborations. *Walls to Roses: Songs of Changing Men* (Various Artists 1979) was an exploration of new ideas about masculinity, including many gay-themed songs such as the opening track, "Gay Spirit." *Gay and Straight Together* (Various Artists 1980) seemed to anticipate the creation of the national version of Parents and Friends of Lesbians and Gays (PFLAG) just one year later, as Boucher points out.[12]

If gay and lesbian artists in the 1970s had small labels like Folkways Records to find a voice, where do gay musicians turn today? Some go mainstream, usually hiding their sexuality until their careers are established. Others find a home in the dance music industry. The gay hip-hop artist Cazwell has been with the dance label West End Records since 2006. In comparison to the protest songs of the Folkways Records albums, Cazwell's songs tend to be more sexually charged and kitschy, such as his 2006 debut song "All Over Your Face" and his 2010 song "Ice Cream Truck." Cazwell has largely relied on YouTube to make his music videos available to his audience.

Although a number of artists have been out in the world of pop music, we are only now beginning to see more artists coming out in both hip-hop and country. Country singer Chely Wright came out in 2010. She was the first major country star to come out since K. D. Lang did so in 1992, and her experience is chronicled in the documentary *Wish Me Away* (Birleffi and Kopf 2011). In 2012 hip-hop artist Frank Ocean released a letter on his Tumblr account that detailed a same-sex relationship that had influenced his music, essentially revealing himself

---

12 Three of the four Folkway Records albums discussed here can be found on Spotify. Only Kathy Fire's is not available there. Some of her songs can be found on YouTube.

METHODOLOGY MOMENT PRODUCTION SURVEYS

Surveys allow us to ask important questions of a broad spectrum of people. Whereas interviews require sitting down with one person at a time, which also means adding in travel time and interview transcription time, surveys can often be conducted with far less human resource time, especially when done online. Very few surveys have been conducted that focus specifically on creative workers in the culture industries of film, television, publishing, music, and the Internet. This is because of the sense that workers in these industries are difficult to access, being geographically isolated in a small handful of cities and working for private corporations that do not make a lot of employee information publicly available. By comparison, most employees in small nonprofits are named on their organizations' websites, usually with contact information.

When it comes to issues of identity and inequality, there are two ways to approach conducting a survey of workplace experiences. The first is to survey a broad sample of workers, using demographic variables as a tool for comparing the experiences of different groups. For example, a survey researcher who is interested in how sexuality impacts job satisfaction may ask respondents to identify their sexual orientation in a set of demographic questions, perhaps along with age and race, then ask a series of questions about workplace experiences. This would allow for a comparison between straight employees and LGBT employees. The downside of this type of survey is that it does not allow us to find out much about a specific minority group, and often that group will represent only a small proportion of respondents. If gays, lesbians, and bisexuals only represent 5 percent of the population, then a survey of one hundred workers in a given industry may only have five respondents from the gay community. The data from those five respondents will be far less useful than the data from ninety-five straight respondents. Also, if we are asking gay and straight people to answer the same questions, then we have to account for the different ways they experience their sexual identity and the intervening role of privilege.

It may seem valid to ask a gay person: "What is it like to be lesbian, gay, or bisexual in your industry?" But a straight person could only speculate. The question is worded in a way that presumes a gay respondent. We could reword the question to make it more neutral: "How well does your industry handle issues of sexual identity diversity?" But heterosexual privilege is likely to yield very different perceptions. Those differences are very interesting, but if most respondents are heterosexual, then their responses may skew the kind of conclusions reached by the survey.

The alternative approach is to design a survey about the experiences of the minority group within the industry. To continue the example at hand, that could be a survey about gay, lesbian, and bisexual experiences in an industry, or even a survey that just targeted one of those groups. This approach offers the possibility of building a sample that is entirely made up of the minority group, although it may also be quite difficult to build a large sample of an underrepresented group. It also offers the opportunity to ask a particular group detailed questions that would be irrelevant to the larger

Continued...

Methodology Moment Production Surveys *Continued*

population. For example, you can ask gay people about their experience revealing their sexual identity to coworkers, but heterosexual people do not have to "come out" to coworkers. The pitfall of this approach is losing the chance to make comparisons between groups, such as comparing gay and straight workers.

One major survey that examines issues of sexuality in the workplace is the Out & Equal Workplace Survey, conducted collaboratively by Out & Equal Workplace Advocates, Witeck-Combs Communications, and Harris Interactive.[1] The survey follows the first approach discussed here, asking neutral questions of both straight and gay respondents, and the data are summarized in an online press release. They survey 2,775 workers, only 362 of whom identify as lesbian, gay, or bisexual. At 13 percent of respondents, gay people are actually overrepresented. They find important differences between gays and straights on a number of issues, including the importance given to nondiscrimination policies, the role of diversity in recruitment, and the extent of belief that employees are entitled to equal benefits regardless of sexuality. Just to highlight one of their findings, 92 percent of LGBT respondents agree with this statement: "How an employee does his or her job should be the standard for judging an employee, not their sexual orientation." By contrast, 78 percent of straight respondents agree with that statement. To be clear, a majority of both groups agree that performance matters in employee assessment, not sexuality, but many more LGBT people agree. So that is an interesting difference in worker perceptions.

The Out & Equal Workplace Survey does not focus on a particular industry. If we were to focus a survey on creative workers within the culture industries, we would have the opportunity to expand our questions beyond workplace experience to broader questions about the influence of sexual identity on the process of creative production. How often do gay writers get the opportunity to include gay characters in their scripts? How much do gay songwriters think about the opinions of fans when deciding what kinds of songs to write or how open to be about their sexuality? Workers can tell us about the workplace, but they can also give us important information about the creative process.

---

1   http://www.harrisinteractive.com/NewsRoom/PressReleases/tabid/446/ctl/ReadCustom%20Default/mid/1506/ArticleId/577/Default.aspx.

as gay or bisexual.[13] Ocean received more open support from the hip-hop community than Wright did from the country music community.

On rare occasions the corporations of the culture industry play a direct role in identity politics. Google is one company that has chosen to weigh in on gay politics, at the risk of alienating more conservative customers. It

---

13   http://frankocean.tumblr.com/post/26473798723.

issued its position statement, "Legalize Love," in the summer of 2012.[14] The statement not only boasts of Google's sponsorship of gay pride events around the world, but also features a discussion of Gayglers, Google's network for LGBT employees. This kind of open stance about issues of sexual politics is relatively rare. Even conservative organizations that have supported antigay causes have tried to keep those activities relatively secret.

VIEWER DISCRETION

Little is known about how sexuality shapes the experiences of receiving and interpreting films. As with television, there is a long history of queer readings of film, but such readings have lent themselves more to the kind of episodic character development found in TV. Cultural studies scholars have presented their own queer readings of some films. James R. Keller's *Queer (Un)Friendly Film and Television* (2002) offers queer readings of *Gladiator* and *The Usual Suspects*, among others. Although we know that some queer audiences may become invested in queer readings and may be actively involved in constructing queer meanings for seemingly hetero films, we do not actually know that straight people are not just as interested in "discovering" queerness in straight films. Moreover, many gay audiences reject the notion that sexuality is the primary lens through which they choose and consume culture. After all, gays and lesbians are also people who are identified by their race, class, gender, and disability status. They are individuals and are also part of the collective social fabric.

---

14   http://www.google.com/diversity/legalise-love.html.

Figure 12.3   The characters on *Will and Grace* provided many Americans with their first gay "friends" (Source: Everett Collection).
Source: Everett Collection.

We still have much to learn about how sexuality shapes audiences. Most of the attention paid to this issue has focused on queer interpretations of shows that seem to feature straight narratives. These are discussed in one segment of the excellent documentary *Off the Straight and Narrow*, which examines lesbian, gay, and bisexual images on television. Some queer interpretations involve reading into certain ambiguities about character relationships. Along these lines, Batman and Robin, Captain Kirk and Mister Spock, and Cagney and Lacey have all been read as secret queer couples. Other queer readings lean into the campiness of characters like Dominique Devereaux from *Dynasty*, described by a commentator in the documentary *Off the Straight and Narrow* as "TV's first black bitch!"

If queer readings offer a window into queer interpretations of straight story lines, then shows like *Will and Grace* offer an opportunity to understand how straight audiences comprehend gay story lines (see Figure 12.3). Sociologist Evan Cooper (2003) has offered such an analysis, examining how his straight college students engage with the very different gay images presented by the characters Will and Jack, as well as the straight image of Grace and the widowed-but-somewhat-queer image of Karen. Cooper found, for example, that men are most likely to identify Grace as their favorite character, whereas women divide somewhat evenly among the characters, leaning somewhat more in favor of Jack. Yet both men and women identify Jack as the funniest character. This indicates some level of discomfort among men with identifying a gay male as their favorite. Only 13.3 percent of men thought Grace was the funniest, whereas 44.2 percent said she was their favorite. Although 48.9 percent of men said Jack was the funniest, only 20.9 percent identified him as their favorite. Clearly, gender shapes the ways that men and women are able to engage with queerness on television.

Another sociologist, Thomas Linneman (2008), offers even further audience analysis using the show *Will and Grace*. Linneman focuses on a very particular rhetorical element in the show—moments in which gay male characters are feminized linguistically using feminine pronouns and names. Linneman produced a thirteen-minute tape containing twenty-five clips of these sorts of references. He showed the tape to six focus groups: one drawn from a gay and lesbian youth group, one group of straight high school students, a group of gay and lesbian college students, a group of straight college students, a group of gay and lesbian adults, and a group of straight adults. He found three key responses to the feminizing moments presented in the clips. The first response was obliviousness, which he found in both straight and queer groups, but more often in the straight respondents. The second response was anger. This was also found in all groups, but seemed more pronounced in the gay and lesbian adults. The third response was acceptance. Gay, lesbian, *and straight* respondents indicated that gay men frequently feminize each other in everyday life and therefore felt that this plot element was a necessary reflection of the social world.

Sexuality, it seems, is one of many influences on the ways that we interpret the culture we consume. Business professor Gillian Oakenfull has studied the influence of gay identity on reactions to advertising. In a study published in 2007, she compared gay and lesbian responses to print advertisements that target gay consumers. Her research design allowed her to compare the experiences of gay men to lesbian women in a world that tends to privilege the gay male experience as *the* LGBT experience. She also examined what she calls "degrees of gayness," using Vanable and colleagues' "Identification and Involvement with the Gay Community" scale (Vanable, McKirnan, and Stokes 1994), but modified in a way that accounted better for lesbian participation. Ranking her respondents on this scale, she then used the median scores to designate "high gay identity" and "low gay identity" gay men and lesbians. Categorizing her respondents in this way allowed her to compare within gay and lesbian groups to find additional audience differences.

Oakenfull showed respondents from all four of her groups (low and high gay identity men; low and high gay identity women) a set of three advertisements, all for alcoholic products. One of the ads relied on implicit imagery, using recognizable gay symbols (rainbow flag, pink triangle) and language (coming out) to signify the gay character of the ad and, by extension, of the target audience. One of the ads used explicit placement of lesbian women to signify gayness, while the third ad relied on explicit placement of gay men. Oakenfull hypothesized that the association of visual stimuli with male sexuality would lead gay men to prefer the ads featuring explicit imagery, and that the association of lesbian identity with gender politics would lead lesbian women to prefer implicit imagery. But the introduction of high and low gay identity made the study more complex. Oakenfull found that women of low gay identity generally preferred images with explicit lesbian imagery, whereas their high gay identity counterparts preferred images with implicit imagery. Men with low gay identity generally preferred images with implicit imagery, whereas their high gay identity counterparts preferred images with explicit gay imagery. The influence of level of gayness pointed in opposite directions for men and women.

Another study that examined the intersections of gender and sexuality is Mimi Schippers's (2000) ethnography of the world of alternative rock music. She studied the gendered and sexual interactions within the community of "active participants" in the alternative rock scene of Chicago. What makes this scene so interesting is that the participants have internalized a lot of messages from feminist and queer politics. Schippers notes that men avoid making overt comments about women and women's sexuality, and that there is a subculture norm of taking great offense to homophobia. Women, on the other hand, are much more comfortable making overt sexual statements, often about other women. Although none of the men or women in her study identified as gay, lesbian, or bisexual, Schippers identifies the women as queer because of the ways they sexualize each other as well as the ways they sexualize the music. Schippers provides a model for extending queer analysis to people other than gays, lesbians, and bisexuals.

Online, the construction of sexual identities becomes very complicated and very interesting. Sociologists Margaret Cooper and Kristina Dzara (2010) used participant observation to explore the ways that Facebook mediates the identity process for LGBT users, focusing on three key issues: identity construction, identity management and negotiation, and collective identity. They conclude that Facebook offers new possibilities for identity construction, especially for young people. Every aspect of a Facebook profile, from the initial "about" information to the ongoing status updates, is a form of identity construction. For LGBT users, this form of public identity construction also raises issues of sexual identity disclosure. A young person who wishes to be very open about sexual identity has a number of tools for making that identity very clear, from posting pictures to liking organizations, to using status updates to focus on gay-themed issues. But a young person wanting to limit sexual identity disclosure has to struggle with these same tools. He may be tagged unwittingly in a photograph that suggests his sexuality. He may have to think carefully about whose friend requests he accepts. He may have to delete comments from friends who are not sensitive to his disclosure concerns. This raises a host of issues for identity management. Cooper and Dzara list some hypothetical scenarios:

METHODOLOGY MOMENT

AUDIENCE INTERVIEWS

Interviews provide an exciting way to probe deeply into the process by which audiences of consumer culture make meaning out of that culture, then act on that meaning in the social world. A social researcher wishing to use interviews needs to begin by formulating a clear research question that can be clearly answered by interviews. Let's consider a few possible questions:

Question 1: Are gay television characters placed in more prestigious roles than straight television characters?

This is a good research question, but it is best answered through examination of content, not audiences.

Question 2: Do gay audiences look more favorably than straight audiences on shows featuring major characters who are gay?

This is also a good research question, and it is best answered through a focus on audiences. However, this is not a question that needs to be answered through interviews. The researcher answering this question could devise a simple survey question and deploy the survey to a wide range of audience members. There is no need to answer this question by speaking face-to-face with one person at a time.

Question 3: How do straight audiences compare to queer audiences in terms of the kinds of television that they watch, the ways they make sense of television, and the ways they act on television?

This is an excellent research question for using interview methods. This would be very difficult to reduce to a set of survey questions. Even if a survey could be devised, the researcher would lose the opportunity to ask follow-up questions and probe respondents in depth.

Let's imagine creating a research proposal to answer this question. Note that the question, as phrased here, does not presume gay-themed television or even a particular genre of television. We are leaving it to the audience members to tell us about the kind of television they consume. Because we are interested in comparing gay and straight audiences, we are going to need to recruit respondents by their sexual identity. If we decide that we want equal numbers of gay men and lesbian women, then we will also want to recruit equal numbers of straight men and straight women. That will allow us to investigate the intervening role of gender.

How many people from each group do we need to recruit? Obviously just one or two from each group is far too few. How can we make claims about gay male TV watchers based on just two gay male respondents? Even a pool as large as twenty will give us limited capacity to make claims about the much larger population, but it lets us make *much* safer claims than a pool of just two. If we decide that twenty in each category is a good number, that actually means recruiting eighty respondents.

If our interviews are an hour each, that is going to mean eighty hours of interview time, and those interviews have to be transcribed. When I first began conducting interviews in graduate school, I learned that each hour of interviews would be followed by six to eight hours of transcribing. At that time (I completed my PhD in 2004, so we are not talking about ancient history), transcription meant listening to the playback of an audio recording and pausing frequently to type up whatever was heard, then reviewing the document for errors. Now, thanks to much improved dictation and transcription software, the transcription process for an hour of interviews can take an hour or less. Still, eighty hours of interviews plus transcription time will add up very quickly. That level of work seems appropriate for a collaborative project among a few researchers or for a graduate student dissertation or a faculty member's ongoing project. But eighty interviews is probably too many for a smaller project by a single scholar. We may need to reduce the number of people in each category to fifteen or ten. For now, we will work with fifteen. We can illustrate our desired respondent pools with Table 12.1.

TABLE 12.1 Sample Respondent Pool

	Male	Female	Total
Gay	15	15	30
Straight	15	15	30
Total	30	30	60

As a shorthand, sociologists often talk about the number of people they need for each "cell" of their research, referring to the cells in a table like this one. Now, how do we find these people? Because straight people significantly outnumber gay people, we cannot simply dial random telephone numbers and hope to get a good balance of gay and straight. We may need to reach out to a gay organization to see if its e-mail listserv can be used to recruit additional gay respondents, or we could post requests for participants in gay and straight coffee shops. It is important not to rely on personal networks to find respondents. We are studying the larger social world, not just our own microcosm within that world.

Before we sit down with our participants, we need to devise a list of interview questions that are directly connected to the research question. It can be tempting to make a long list of questions that we want to ask, but if we want respondents to answer our questions in depth, assuming we have limited time with them, we have to limit ourselves to a few broad questions. Our main research question divides neatly into three sets of questions: (1) about television consumption, (2) about television interpretation (meaning-making), and (3) about social action. So our interview questions might look like these:

Continued...

Methodology Moment *Continued*

Question 1: Please list the television shows that you watch and how often you watch them.

Prompt: Any other genres of shows that you like?
Prompt: Are there other shows that you watch during the off-season?
Prompt: What about morning or daytime shows?

Question 2: For you, what makes a TV show "good"?

Prompt: What about the characters?
Prompt: What about the themes?
Prompt: What about the genre?

Question 3: Can you think of a time when something you saw on TV helped you decide how to act on an issue in real life?

Prompt: Has TV ever influenced the way you act at work?
Prompt: Has TV ever influenced the way you act in a relationship?
Prompt: Has TV ever influenced the way you think about social or political issues?

If we were to carry out this interview, I suspect that these three questions, with three prompts apiece, would actually generate a lot of information from each respondent. Once the interviews were complete, we would analyze the transcripts looking for key differences between demographics (gay/straight, male/female), as well as interesting similarities. We should also look for important differences within our demographic categories.

- Rob is "out" to friends in real life. He is not out on Facebook, however, because not all of his family members know. He plans a secret trip with his new boyfriend, who posts that he can't wait for their romantic European vacation.
- Sarah is also "out" in everyday life, but has not posted this, or any indicator of this, on Facebook, because she may face discrimination at work. Several coworkers have added her to their friends list. She states in a status update that she can't wait to go to a movie on Saturday night. One real-life friend posts, "Can't wait to meet your new lover!" Another friend posts, "You guys will like her! She's really nice!"

- Cary is out to friends and family, yet some of his family members are conservative and uncomfortable with public displays of affection between Cary and a partner. A friend of Cary's posts pics of him and his boyfriend in an embrace at a party. Another pic posted shows Cary's boyfriend in drag at a fund-raiser. (2010, 104–105)

Some readers may be wondering why Rob, Sarah, and Cary do not just update their privacy settings. But longtime Facebook users know that privacy settings have evolved over several years and have occasionally reset without warning to users. That means that LGBT Facebook users, like all kinds of teens in various ways, have to be very careful about disclosure even as they use social media to practice with identity construction and the presentation of self. Finally, Cooper and Dzara point out that many LGBT young people use causes and likes and other formats on Facebook to align with LGBT activism, finding collective identity in addition to creating individual identity. This can be particularly powerful for young people who are isolated from such activity by geography.

WRAP-UP

Jamey Rodemeyer did not live his life in the closet. The world of popular culture—from Lady Gaga's music to the It Gets Better campaign on You-Tube—gave Jamey the tools to leave the closet behind at a very young age. But the world of popular culture also provided Jamey's tormentors with the tools they needed to keep rebuilding that closet, if not around Jamey, then around their own notions of sexuality. Even with a growing emergence of gay characters in film and television, gay popular culture is still pressed into a closet in many ways. Gay visibility is allowed only to a few, who are often white, male, and economically privileged. Gay musicians continue to turn away from mainstream music to find accepting and eager audiences. Gay Facebook users find that the Internet provides as many tools for coming out as it does for "staying in." The metaphor of the closet continues to haunt gay, lesbian, and bisexual representations in popular culture. It continues to be a very real and powerful force for gay, lesbian, and bisexual workers in the culture industries. The closet still matters for audiences, too, but they at least are reminding us that there are many far more interesting metaphors for gay life that popular culture needs to draw from. Gay audiences, through the act of queer readings, are taking the raw materials of Hollywood, New York, Nashville, and our other cultural production centers around the world and twisting these resources into new imaginings, not only of the gay experience, but also of the human experience.

RESOURCES

Resources for Examining Sexuality in the Social World
- The Trevor Project: http://www.thetrevorproject.org.
- It Gets Better: http://www.itgetsbetter.org.
- Films: *Before Stonewall* (1984) and *After Stonewall* (1999), from First Run Features.

Resources for Examining Sexuality in Popular Culture
- No Homophobes, a website that tracks homophobic language on Twitter: http://www.nohomophobes.com/#!/today.

- AfterElton, a website of gossip and media posts about gay representations in popular culture: http://www.afterelton.com.
- AfterElton's Top 50 Gay Men in Music: http://www.afterelton.com/people/2011/02/top-50-gay-musicians.
- AfterEllen, a website of gossip and media posts about lesbian representations in popular culture: http://www.afterellen.com.
- GLAAD, the Gay and Lesbian Alliance Against Defamation, posts a variety of media resources on its website. Perhaps the most useful is the annual Network Responsibility Index. http://www.glaad.org.
- Video: *Off the Straight and Narrow: Lesbians, Gays, Bisexuals and Television, 1967–1998*, from the Media Education Foundation.
- Video: *Further Off the Straight and Narrow: New Gay Visibility on Television, 1998–2006*, from the Media Education Foundation.
- Video: *The Celluloid Closet*, from Sony Pictures.
- Video: *Fabulous!: The Story of Queer Cinema*, from IFC.

READING 13
"I KNOW WHAT I AM": GENDER, SEXUALITY, AND IDENTITY

By David Valentine

"I am a woman of trans ..." Tara pauses: "trans*African* experience!" she laughs. Later, while Nora is interviewing her on video, Tara says with more confidence: "I am a woman of transAfrican, transgender experience." I am again in the conference room at New York Hospital for the semi-monthly support group for HIV-positive transgender-identified people. My way into this group has been through Nora, an HIV-positive Latina heterosexual transgender woman (her own definition) who also works at the Gender Identity Project as a peer counselor and safer-sex outreach worker. However, while Nora has a similar history to those in the room—she is a person of color, a former sex worker, and HIV-positive—they do not say the same kinds of things about themselves.

Today Nora is interviewing Tara and the other group members about their experience with "transgender sex work" for a conference presentation she will be making. Tara's declaration of self gets my attention precisely because I have never heard her or any of the other group members use such a formulation before. As with the Clubhouse ball participants and the Meat Market sex workers, it is more common to hear participants refer to themselves as gay, fem queens, girls, and sometimes (though often jokingly) as women. I do not know how long Tara has used this formula to describe herself, but I'm pretty sure I know the origin of the "of transgender experience" construction. Rosalyne Blumenstein, GIP's director, formulated "woman of transgender experience" to describe her own identity and experience about a year before I started doing fieldwork.[1] Rosalyne's position at GIP has resulted in the distribution of this term in many contexts in New York and nationally, so that it has become widely used not only in GIP materials but in outreach work, in print, and increasingly in people's self-identifications. So Tara's statement is not just a statement of self but also indicates her location in a web of relations in which identity labels become distributed and simultaneously intelligible.

It seemed to me that Tara's statement that morning was elicited by the formal situation of a videotaped interview in the context of a hospital-sponsored support group, for at no other time did I hear her or any of the other group members use such an identity label about themselves or others. How is it, then, that Nora or Tara can access—strategically, and in different ways—the language of "transgender" while others who are assumed by social service agencies to *be* transgender often have never heard of the category at all? Moreover, what does it mean that Tara can employ—and creatively extend—"woman of transgender experience" in this context while using different terms in others, some of which resonate with "transgender" and some of which do not? Finally, how does her creative assertion of "transAfrican" modify what "transgender experience" can mean?

In much of the literature about transgender, transsexual, or gender-variant people, the concept of "identity" (or its kin in a family of concepts—subjectivity, personhood, selfhood) is generally an organizing principle, a chapter heading, or a theme that runs through the text. Indeed, "transgender" is culturally unintelligible without a concept of "identity." In these accounts, transgender identity tends to be invoked in standard ways. First, psychological and psychiatric approaches seek to explain how and why the process of gendered development works differently (or, in many accounts, *fails*) in transgender-identified people. Sociological and ethno-methodological investigations tend to focus on gendered practices, careers, and strategies, looking at how transgender-identification both subverts and upholds binary gender. And different arms of feminism take up this latter point, seeing on the one hand the embodied performativity of transgender identity as a site of radical gendered possibilities, or, on the other, the manifestation of false consciousness and the assertion of patriarchal gendered norms in the individual body. For transgender-identified people themselves, identity, whether understand as internal and eternal or as socially produced and contingent, is deeply felt indeed. However, I am not particularly interested in exploring any of these approaches, questions, or debates. Rather, I want to examine the idea that there is a transgender identity that can be located in a distinct domain called "gender."

The title of this chapter is drawn from a common assertion—"I know what I am"—professed by many study participants. When these participants described what they knew about themselves, however, their explanations moved out of the realm of what is usually understood by "transgender" in contemporary mainstream LGBT politics. In this chapter I want to look more closely at those who are included on the "transgender spectrum" by activists, scholars, and others but who do not usually use "transgender" to talk about themselves and their peers or who may not even know that it is a term which applies to them. In particular, I focus mostly on the talk of African American and Latina fem queens of the balls and Meat Market. Some of the people I discuss below claim to "know what I am," and others claim not to know who or what they are. But, I will argue, none of these people's understandings of themselves or their desires are intelligible in political categories of collective agency, because of the gap between their understandings of personhood and the political categories of identity which claim to represent them. However, I do not want to simply conflate this process with racial and class differences. I complicate the picture by looking at the organization of gendered/sexual identity across lines of class, race, age, and embodiment.[2] I want to look at the margins of the collective "transgender" rather than at its center. Thus, I will not discuss at any length the experiences of self-identified transsexual women or men, about whom much has been written.

Moreover, in analyzing this talk, I foreground not only what people said about their gendered/sexual practices and identities—their knowledge of "what I am"—but also what I made of this talk. I ask the reader to pay close attention to the questions I felt compelled to ask. That is, I want to consider how I myself was reproducing a theoretical understanding of transgender identity—and of gender and sexuality—which itself threatened to produce these accounts as incoherent and unintelligible.

My concern in this chapter is thus to document the instabilities of the category transgender when it is applied to individual lives, and how individuals' use or non-use of the category complicates the terms in which it has become institutionalized. In turn, it shows how the institutionalization of transgender produces these selves as unintelligible. The broader goal of this chapter is not to call for a more accurate representation of these lives or the elaboration of new categories to account for them. Rather, I will argue that the goals and logics of identity politics themselves produce this apparent unintelligibility and erase an analysis of the entrenched inequalities that underpin them.

THE MEAT MARKET

The Meat Market is only one of several "strolls" in New York City to which fem queen—or transgender-identified—sex workers come to meet their clients.[3] Whatever the language I, the GIP, or the sex workers themselves use, in the sexual marketplace of New York this niche is usually referred to as "chicks with dicks." Almost all the girls (as they call themselves most often) who walk these streets are African American or Latina; some are immigrants to the United States from Latin America or the Caribbean; and many of them have an affiliation with a ball House.

The Meat Market is particularly popular with clients who come from New Jersey and the outer boroughs. Even today, on a Friday and Saturday night, cars can be seen crawling past the curb as their occupants (mostly white men) observe the girls on the sidewalk. A pickup is made by a man coming to a stop and hailing a girl. Most sexual encounters take place in parked cars, though with increased policing and the presence of many bargoers, finding a quiet venue is hard. Sometimes a motel room may be hired, which the girls like because they can charge more. The girls do not live in or around the Meat Market; rather, they come from different parts of the city to congregate here. Some live in low-income public housing, others have their own apartments in lower-rent areas in the city. The Meat Market, then, is a space in which they work, exchange information, gossip, socialize, and come to understand themselves as constituting a group.

Talking about the Meat Market regulars as "sex workers," though, is complicated by the different experiences that people have of doing sex work. Some, like Sugar, have been out here for years—nineteen in Sugar's case. But there are also those like Mona, out for the first time, and others like Tamara, who sometimes works, sometimes doesn't. There are also several core groups of younger girls who work the cars intermittently, hanging out at Dizzy Izzy's bagel store or on the Ninth Avenue loading docks. India, Charity, Rita, Yolanda, Sybil, and others will chat and ki ki (or laugh) together for hours, often spending more time talking, it seems to me, than working.

Groupings in the Meat Market draw on social networks developed at the balls or in the Meat Market itself. Some girls, like Julip or Anita, who are in their twenties, are rarely if ever in a group, tending to walk alone in the quieter streets further west. They are not here to socialize but to make money. Anita does not like hanging out in groups because she hates to be gossiped about, and gossip is a major activity here. In the even darker corners, I meet girls like Giana. Giana has a serious drug habit about which she is very frank. Sometimes she is willing to be drawn into conversation, but more often not. Other girls stray into the areas north and south of the Meat Market proper, working alone on quieter, more residential streets. They do not have much contact with other workers, tend to be older, non-English speaking immigrants, and are outside the social networks of the younger girls on Ninth Avenue. But if the cops are actively rounding up, then the younger ones will also scatter north of 14th Street (the boundary of the sixth precinct) or along 14th Street to Eighth Avenue where they can blend into the larger crowds of pedestrians and subway users. It is here that I usually lock up my bicycle and begin my evening's participant-observation and outreach.

Among those people who hang out with the core group of fem queen sex workers on the stroll are a range of others: their butch queen friends, boyfriends, and other gay- and lesbian-identified youth of color. As well as the fem queens and butch queens, there are also some butches, most of them African American, who hang out on the loading dock or at the corner of Ninth Avenue. Some of them are boyfriends to the fem queens or to female-bodied femmes, but they are rarely willing to talk to me. Often, they hang out with the male-bodied masculine people—those people who, outside this study, might be understood unproblematically as "men"— who are also boyfriends to the fem queens.

The fem queens' experiences on the street are not always distinguishable from those of their peers and friends. Here, as in many U.S. urban centers, young people of color are frequently targets for police action, whatever their identities or appearance. The public space of the street can be dangerous simply because one is African American or Latina/o, since nonwhite racial identification in the United States is heavily coded by assumptions about criminality, drug use, and excessive sexuality. And as the realm of the public has contracted under neoliberal economic policies, evident in the gentrification and redevelopment of much of New York's public space in the 1990s, the pressure on poor youth of color from police and other authorities has become increasingly severe (Chesluk 2004; see Davis 1992 [1990]). The fem queens out in the Meat Market, though, have the added stigma of being male-bodied feminine persons, a fact well known to police, their clients, sightseers, and potential assailants (see Manalansan 2003: 80–81).

Among the array of people who engage in different forms of sex work here, virtually all were born as male-bodied people but present as feminine on the stroll. For some of them, their feminine presentation may be a part of their daily lives; for others, it is guided by the requirements of the work. One summer evening, I was handing out GIP safer-sex kits in the Meat Market when I came across a group of three young African American male teenagers hanging out by a car. To my surprise (since they had not seen me giving kits to anyone else), one of them asked for a kit. Sorry, I said, they're only for the girls, invoking my instructions that the kits only be distributed to those I could read as "transgender."

"I'm Tamara!" said the boy who'd asked for the kit. "Don't you recognize me?" He and his friends laughed as recognition dawned on my face. He said that he wasn't working tonight, just hanging out.[4] Some weeks later, I saw Tamara again, still dressed as a boy. He told me he had stopped working the stroll, though he still hung out there as a "butch queen." And though he was a butch queen in appearance, he told me she had started taking feminizing hormones. A few weeks later still, I saw her dressed as Tamara again, but a week after that Tamara was dressed as a boy once more. When I asked him why, he showed me a mark on his face: she was robbed, he said, and she's scared of being robbed again.

Other fem queens in the Meat Market may shift back and forth between butch queen and fem queen style (or identification) on the streets, but as at the balls, this distinction is often unclear and style in and of itself does not necessarily indicate an internal "gender identity." Sybil—twenty-something and Puerto Rican—for example sees herself as a "butch queen," even though she also sees herself as "real" and lives full time in her feminine presentation. When I asked her why she called herself a butch queen, she said it was because she was not on hormones. For Sybil, even living full time as a feminine person made her neither a fem queen nor a woman. Sybil's claims about herself, Tamara's shifting presentations, and his/her reasons for such shifts and use of hormones indicate that for at least some of the girls in the Meat Market, being a "fem queen" is more complex than the ball categories would imply.

This presented me with some practical, ethical, and epistemological problems. From the beginning of my fieldwork, I adopted the claim of activists and social service providers such as Melissa and Rosalyne that people should be addressed with the pronouns and descriptive gender categories appropriate to their gendered presentation. Indeed, sensitized as I was to these claims, when I first started fieldwork in the Meat Market I referred to the girls as women in conversation. However, this was frequently contested by the girls themselves. On another evening in the Meat Market, while hanging out with Monica and Sugar, I referred to Monica as a woman. Sugar said: "You call her what you want, but I'll call her a man." This did not seem to faze Monica, who laughed and retorted with a comment about Sugar's penis. "Yeah, well, yours is bigger than mine," she shouted, causing more laughter yet. This encounter left me feeling very uncomfortable. It seemed, again, to reduce Monica's gender identification to genitals, precisely the kind of claim that social service providers like Rosalyne would hotly contest. Yet I would also note that the description of themselves as "men" offended neither Monica nor Sugar.

But even here, I am unwilling to make broad claims about fem queen identity and their understandings of self through conventionally gendered terms. On another warm summer's evening on Little West 12th Street, I bumped into Julip, to whom I had given a safer-sex kit earlier. She was walking past me, ignoring me (as the girls often did when we had had an interaction and they were now working), when she suddenly turned to me and asked: "Do you think I look like a man?" "No," I said, caught off guard, "you don't. Why do you ask?" I added, thinking of a group of men whom I had earlier seen taunting her out of a car window. She told me that she had just taken a photograph of herself and some friends with a Polaroid camera, and in the photo something in her face had told her she looked like a man. She said she was hollow-cheeked and looked "hard." "Do I have a round face?" she asked. "No," I admitted, "but you have a nice face." I added: "The light is bad, and Polaroids aren't the best kinds of photos." She nodded, turned away, and marched off down the quiet street, wounded.

Julip's concern over "looking like a man" complicates Sugar's and Monica's jokes about each other's penises. While there is not the same articulated differentiation that I heard among white, middle-class transexual women between being a man and being a woman, there are also clear investments on the part of many of the girls out here in being "soft." The distinction between "hard" and "soft" is one of the most important in the Meat Market (and at the Clubhouse balls too, where "softness" is a major criterion for winning a fem queen face category). Hardness and softness—with their clearly gendered implications—have no easy correlate to any physical or sartorial appearance, though suppleness of skin, smoothness of features, and perceived femininity in facial and bodily contours count for a lot. The softer you are, the more "real" you are. "Softness" also applies to perceived femininity in style, body movement, and language use. And while the use of feminizing hormones is seen as essential for developing softness, girls often deny that they are using them, claiming that their softness is "natural." In moments of gossip and tattling, someone may be described disparagingly as "hard" or admired for being "soft." Pussy, out in the Meat Market one night, told me that the "hard" girls are the ones who will fuck, that is, the ones who will be the penetrative partner in anal sex, something many clients desire but girls may not want—or may not be able—to do. For many of the girls who are taking hormones, the capacity to sustain an erection is often impaired. This is a complex condensation: "hardness" is a general term for the visible signs of masculinity but also the capacity for sustaining an erection for the purposes of anal sex, and the desire or willingness to be the penetrative partner.[5]

The cross-cutting forms of identification, presentation, desire, and style in the Meat Market make it hard for me to justify the characterization of "fem queen sex workers" any more than I could that of "transgender sex workers." My use of the former term is, then, as much a selection of certain meanings to the exclusion of others as the latter one is. Next, I will draw on taped interviews to show how fem queens' (and butches') understandings of self resist any easy form of identification in the terms of the organizations which do outreach to them.

I KNOW WHAT I AM

The Meat Market is also a space (represented by my own presence there) where the fem queen sex workers will meet outreach workers from a variety of social service organizations who offer condoms, safer-sex literature, and information about services to which they are entitled as transgender-identified people. The same outreach workers (again, myself included) are also likely to be found at the Clubhouse on a Wednesday, at the Christopher Street Piers on a weekend, or at some of the bars, like Sally's, where older fem queens tend to congregate. As such, Meat Market regulars like Tamara, Julip, or Sugar are likely to know that they are considered transgender but, as with Tara at the New York Hospital group, it is rare to hear them use it in conversation about themselves.

If I and other outreach workers were giving safer-sex materials to trans-gender sex workers, our work was made more difficult by people like Tamara who shifted back and forth between masculine and feminine presentation, or by Sybil, who loudly proclaimed that she was a butch queen and not "a transgender." In interviews with some of the Meat Market girls, this attempt to define fem queens as "transgender" became even more difficult as they situated themselves in terms of this category and others.

In my interview with Anita (Puerto Rican, age twenty-four), for example, she told me she had been on feminizing hormones since her teenage years. This practice marked her as "transgender" in my understanding, one which was borne out in the first part of our interview:

3.1
ANITA: I identify myself as a drag queen, you know, and [laughs] and you know this is my lifestyle. I live my lifestyle like this twenty-four hours a day.
DV: You live as a woman.
ANITA: I live as a woman everyday, you know. (Interview, June 26, 1997)

It is notable that I read Anita's statement that she "identif[ies herself] as a drag queen" as "you live as a woman." Later in the interview, though, Anita complicated my assumptions. I asked her:

3.2
DV: Do you know what this term "transgender" means?
ANITA: No.
DV: You never heard it before?
ANITA: No.
DV: Um, but, OK do you know what transexual means?
ANITA: Transexual means a sex change right?

DV: Uh, yeah. You don't consider yourself to be transexual?

ANITA: No.

DV: No, OK. But, and do you consider yourself to be a woman?

ANITA: I consider … yes, yes, but I *know what I—I know what I am,* but I … I … you know, I treat myself like a woman, you know I do everything like a woman. I act like a woman, I move like a woman, you know. I do everything like—everything like a woman. [My emphasis]

Later still, shortly after I explained the collective meaning of transgender to Anita, she talked about herself as "gay." In return, I asked:

3.3

DV: You do you consider yourself to be gay then?

ANITA: Yes!

DV: Yeah.

ANITA: Yes.

DV: Yeah. Um.

ANITA: Yes.

DV: Even though you live as a woman.

ANITA: Yes.

DV: Right, OK.

ANITA: I know I'm gay and I know I'm a man.

Like Rita (who I quoted in the introduction), Anita claims a number of different identities: gay, drag queen, man. While she did not claim to be a transexual or a woman, she did not dispute my characterization of her as "living as a woman" (3.1) and noted that she does "everything like a woman" (3.2). In other words, being on hormones and living as a woman did not make her either transexual or a woman. But later in the interview, she said: "I don't wanna go back to a man, you know," implying that even if she is not a woman, she is no longer a man, despite her earlier assertion that "I know I'm a man" (3.3).

Anita's long experience on the stroll might account for some of these claims, but others such as Mona who have not been out here as long say similar things. Mona was new to the Meat Market when I met her and had not spent much time socializing (or being socialized) by the other girls. She had heard about the Meat Market from some friends and had gotten dressed up—rather androgynously compared to the more extravagantly fem style of Sugar or Julip—to see if she could make some money, but she had not been too successful. The visual economy of sex work in this context requires a certain constellation of clothing, embodiment, and style to be successful.[6] Despite this, her statements resonate with Anita's. In our interview, she began by saying:

3.4

MONA: My name is Mona, I'm a butch queen up in drags, I live my life as a woman, I'm twenty-two years old, African American, born and raised in Brooklyn. (Interview July 18, 1997)

Mona's simultaneous identification of herself as a "butch queen up in drags" and her claim to "live my life as a woman" raises questions about what these categories might mean. When we started discussing "transgender," Mona said that she wasn't sure what it meant but that she had "heard the girls you know, talk about transgender, you know, like talk about like fem queens, you know, female impersonators." Clearly, "transgender" is not entirely absent from the vocabulary of the Meat Market girls but it is compounded with others like "fem queen," "female impersonator," and "girl." Moreover, when I asked her about her experiences with social service agencies, Mona said: "I would like to participate in a lot of gay activities," indicating that this was also a category she understood herself to be part of. During the interview, as with Anita, I explained to Mona the meaning of "transgender" in its collective sense as used by the GIP, and then asked her to position herself in relationship to it:

3.5
DV: Given that description that I've just told you, would you consider yourself to be included under that category?
MONA: Exactly.
DV: Yeah? Um, so do you consider yourself to be gay?
MONA: Exactly.
DV: You are? OK. So what—what does that mean to you to be gay?
MONA: What does it mean to me to be gay?
DV: Uh huh.
MONA: It's not just only having feelings for someone of the same gender but also being turned on by the same gender.
DV: But you say that you're a woman as well?
MONA: Exactly.

Note that Mona's initial lack of certainty—about what "transgender" means—is the only thing she is not sure of in these extracts: she is certain that she's a woman ("exactly"), that she's transgender ("exactly"), and that she's gay ("exactly").

Similarly, Anita's exasperated "yes!" to the same question—"You do you consider yourself to be gay then?" (3.3)—as well as the confusion apparent in the questions I ask, indicates a more complex system of identification than I was bringing to the interview. The significant point is that for both Anita and Mona, "liv[ing] as a woman" does not preclude being "gay" where "gay" indexes erotic desire for someone who is male-bodied. My attempts to get Anita and Mona to define themselves in terms of one category or another speak to how powerfully this distinction had structured my research questions. Just as significantly, on a nightly basis, outreach workers from social service agencies across the city must decide whether the clients they meet are "transgender" or "gay" (like Jay at the Clubhouse ball), a product of the institutional and funding requirements of their agencies. Like me, they often find it difficult to enumerate on their outreach reports how may of their clients are "gay male" and how many are "transgender, MTF."

These modes of identification are not the only ones in the Meat Market, however. Other young people of color in this context are very clear about the differences between themselves and gay men and were much easier to count in outreach reports. Cherry (African American, age twenty), who often hangs out in the Meat Market and at the Piers, is adamant that she is a woman, that she has never been "gay," and she embraces transgender as a category to describe herself. Unlike Anita or Mona, though, Cherry is a regular attendee of GIP support groups, as well as other social services around the city which are organized around the category transgender. Cherry responded to my "how do you identify" question in our interview as follows:

3.6

CHERRY: I identify as female. I mean just because I have this penis doesn't mean that I consider myself a man. I don't even consider myself being born male, like I mean, I was just born with a penis, that's the way I look at it. And I consider the penis a clitoris. (Interview April 12, 1997)

Unlike Anita or Mona, Cherry also was able to give me a definition of "transgender" which excludes homosexual identification:

3.7

CHERRY: I know transgender can mean a person who may or may not go through the sexual process, the sexual reassignment surgery. A transexual can mean that a person who's already had it done but may or may not be totally happy with it.

Cherry explicitly rejects "fem queen," "gay," "drag queen," or "butch queen in drags" as terms that could apply to her. She spends a lot of time informing her peers that they are "transgender" and not "gay," and had she heard Monica or Sugar referring to one another as "men," she would no doubt have told them they were wrong. Indeed, she argued "as I have gone through my process," she has been able to resist these labels by insisting on her femaleness and by using the term "transgender" (or "transexual") to describe herself. Cherry's narrative and her employment of identity categories is very similar to many (usually white, middle-class) transexual women's stories of transition that I heard: an explicit rejection of homosexual identity, a repudiation of their maleness, and an identification as a heterosexual woman.

The significant difference between, on the one hand, Cherry and Tara, and those like Anita and Mona is not so much their class, racial identification, or age but their contact with those formalized contexts of community—support groups, social service agencies, clinics, and so on—which employ the understandings of "gay" and "transgender" that I am analyzing here. Both Tara and Cherry, for example, access services through GIP and have had individual counseling with Rosalyne. Both make use of a variety of services throughout the city which are part of a network of agencies and events—GIP, Positive Health Project, Harlem United, the annual Transgender Health Conference, and others—that provide services under the framework of transgender. That is, these contexts have provided for Tara and Cherry a language through which to interpret their experiences outside the more commonly distributed categories in the communities through which they move—fem queen, butch queen, drag queen, transvestite, and so on—much as the New York Hospital group provided Tara with the language of "woman of transAfrican, transgender experience."

For Cherry, this has given her a way of conceptualizing herself that few of her peers do. Cherry frames her own life experiences in terms of "my process," a common metaphor for transition employed in transgender discourses. This framework draws on a broader processual model in mental health, twelve-step programs, and support group settings and one deeply rooted in middle-class American understandings of self-transformation and remaking. For Cherry, her process involves a repudiation of those terms which imply homosexual identification and a movement toward eventual surgical transition and identification as a heterosexual woman. As such, she is able to see her penis as a clitoris (3.6) and to elaborate upon the differences between transexual and transgender (3.7). This is in sharp contrast to those like Anita or Mona—neither of whom access such services—who see themselves, simultaneously, as gay, as drag queens, as transgender, as men, as "liv[ing] as a woman," and so on.

Even so, this is not to say that involvement in such formalized contexts of social service provision necessarily results in a radical split between these two conceptual organizations of identity. Certainly, as I pointed out at the beginning of this chapter, Tara much more frequently refers to herself as gay, as do other members of her group. Likewise, peer outreach workers in the employ of social service organizations, like Renee or Jade (whom I discuss below), are quite aware of the use of transgender, yet they will often use a different model to describe themselves and even the people to whom they do outreach. Renee, who was a peer outreach worker for Harlem United, spoke of doing outreach to "transgenders in the Meat Market" but later in our interview she said, of herself and these same "transgenders":

3.8

RENEE: I really think we're all in the gay community [....] But I don't really think that we're all united, the transexuals are kinda off on their own. And that's why, you know, the transexuals have to come together and start their own shit up because of the—I mean a lot of the gay organizations, they don't give us any support. (Interview June 11, 1997)

For those like Renee, Cherry, or Tara who involve themselves in such organizations, "transgender" is a discourse through which they can mount demands of the "gay" community that in their view should respond to their needs and concerns. And it is through recourse to "transgender"—and the assumptions which underpin it—that these demands are made, a process which, almost inevitably, requires the participants to position themselves in relation to "gay." But this positioning, in turn, complicates what "gay" and "transgender" can mean, blurring the lines that seem so solid on outreach reports.

All the people I have discussed so far have been male-bodied feminine people. As I wrote above, butches—female-bodied masculine people—also hang out in the Meat Market, and they too become incorporated into the institutional terms of transgender. One example of this was Harlem United's hiring of Jade as a peer outreach worker to the butches in the summer of 1997. A Harlem United staffer, Jay (the same person who was pointing out "the transgenders" to me), told me that Jade was an African American "transgender man" and suggested that I interview him. But some weeks later, at the Clubhouse, Jay informed me—rather sheepishly—that Jade was not transgender-identified; rather, she was a "butch lesbian." Like the butch queen in drags he had pointed out to me at the Clubhouse ball as "a transgender," his initial identification had been wrong. However, even the latter appellation turned out not to be entirely accurate.

Jade's story is one which is indicative of the complex land between "gay/lesbian" and "transgender," and how institutionalized categories come up against personal experience. Jade's experiences and narratives are both different from and similar to the claims of people like Mona or Anita. Jade explicitly does not identify as transgender, but not because her experience does not match those of the set understood as transgender.[7] Now approaching fifty, Jade had worked for twenty years as a man in the postal service, dating women and socializing with her co-workers as a man. Though she has never taken testosterone shots, she passed as a man and was accepted as such by her co-workers and friends.

In our interview, Jade initially defined herself as both "gay" and as "a butch," but these claims were also complicated by other things she said about herself. In ways structurally equivalent to Anita and using the same terms, she saw herself as a woman (that is, an identification framed by her embodiment) but simultaneously understood herself in some ways as a "guy":

3.9

JADE: *I know what I am.* I know that I'm an aggressor, a very aggressive-thinking woman. I think just like a guy thinks. (Interview, November 6, 1997, my emphasis)

Jade's use of "transgender," like Cherry's and Renee's, has been framed in terms of her contact with social service agencies, in particular her employer, Harlem United. When I asked Jade what her understanding of "transgender" incorporated, she replied:

3.10

JADE: Well I heard the word when I came to Harlem United. I had never heard it before. I was like transgender? Transgender, the word "trans" was only used in "transexual," meaning that you were flipping over, changing your organs. That's the only time that I was familiar with the word "trans." Then when I came to Harlem United and I started coming down here on the West Side, I started hearing gay guys talk about being transgenders. I'm like, what the hell's a transgender? And that if you go to a ball, it's live like a woman, walk like a woman, eat like a woman, you know. And I guess—their description of a transgender is what I am or what I was.

Here, Jade seems to see herself as describable through "transgender," but a short time later she also said: "Do I consider myself a transgender? No." To complicate matters further, though, Jade returned to the question of transgender at the end of our interview, saying:

3.11

JADE: I think it's [the use of "transgender" at Harlem United] great, I think it's great, it opens up Harlem's eyes that there are gay men here, we're right here, and we ain't going nowhere.

In the latter quote, Jade makes the most complex statement of all, seeing "transgender" as making people aware that "there are gay men here, we're right here." This is a dense claim in which she seems to include herself in the category "gay men," but even more interestingly she equates "transgender" to "gay" as she also did earlier in the interview (3.10). Moreover, Jade's understanding of transgender—and her relationship to it—is complicated (at least for me) by her experience as a mother to her fifteen-year-old daughter. To her daughter, she is Mommy, "the best mommy she could ever get," and at one point she noted that her daughter was the only reason that she would not transition to living as a man. Indeed, she noted that prior to motherhood, she would have considered it:

3.12

JADE: I did then! I would have, yeah, back in the days if I would have had the money or the knowledge. I don't know if the knowledge was that good then. I would have did it, I would have did it.

DV: Right, so but what's um—what's different now. Why not now?

JADE: I've gotten older. Um—your ideas change. Society is more accept—they accept the gay life. It is a gay life.

Here again, Jade confounded my attempts to understand her as either a transgender man (someone who would have transitioned if they'd "had the money or the knowledge") or as a butch lesbian ("It is the gay life"). In the end, in my attempt to get Jade to position herself in my terms, I asked, somewhat desperately:

3.13

DV: Tell me about your gender in ten words.

JADE: My gender.

DV: You—I mean—I know you've been very eloquent about it but I just want you to give like some—like if you could just do it in ten.

JADE: I'm a hard daddy. I'm a hard daddy. At times, more times I think I'm a man than not. Um … my demeanor is very aggressive.

There are other apparent incoherencies in Jade's account that make me strive to get a statement of "ten words" about her gender: she is a mommy to her daughter and a hard daddy to her lovers; she is a woman, but "more times I think I'm a man than not"; the reason she used to want surgery was that the "gay life" was difficult and it would have been easier to be a man; yet even though she claims it is acceptable and easier to be gay now, she says she would still like the surgery if it weren't for her daughter. She recognizes that others may see her as transgender, but she says she's "gay." Overall, she is just a hard daddy.

Jade's statements clearly draw on a vocabulary of masculinity available to butch lesbians, as well as a long history and vocabulary of masculine-identified passing women, and invoke the "border wars" between FTMs and butches (see Halberstam 1998b; Hale 1998; Kennedy and Davis 1993; G. Rubin 1992; H. Rubin 2003). At the same time, Jade's understanding of herself is not equivalent to the self-conscious appropriation of "transgender butch" that Halberstam (1998b) describes. Rather than drawing on the possibilities of "transgender" to elaborate her identification, she positions herself simultaneously against and through its terms. Again, "transgender butch" certainly captures some of those qualities and experiences that Jade describes, but Jade's identification is more complex still, since she explicitly states that she does not see "transgender" as a category that describes her even as she recognizes that others may see her as such.

My difficulty in pinning down Jade's relationship to identity categories is not in the different ways she identifies as butch, as a hard daddy, or as a masculine female-bodied person. Rather, it lies in the fact that we are operating from different perspectives about two broader categories: "gay" and "transgender." Jade sees herself defined by a variety of characteristics: her attraction to women, as a "hard daddy" or "an aggressor," as a mommy to her daughter, as a guy, and as a woman. I am attempting to get Jade to talk about her gender apart from her sexual desire, about some kind of internal desire to be a man: that is, I am trying to get her to pin herself as *either* a butch-lesbian-hard-daddy ("gay/homosexual") *or* as a (straight) man ("transgender"). Consequently, my confusion is less about those descriptors of "female masculinity" (Halberstam 1998a) than about how to account for this masculinity in terms of the primary categories through which it can be understood in *institutional* terms.

While Jade's experience is clearly different from Anita's or Mona's—they are younger, male-bodied, have experienced sex work—their experiences come together insofar as their ways of understanding themselves escape easy classification through broader, more powerful discourses about possible identifications. There is no room at Harlem United for simply a "hard daddy." Jade was hired to do outreach to "the transgenders." This is the category through which her salary is funded via HIV/AIDS funds, the newly developing epidemiological category which captures the girls and guys she gives condoms to, and which organizes the support groups, social services, and funding (minimal as they might be) which support the nascent attention to this group.

Jade's account is marked by apparent incoherencies and contradictions that obviously, from my line of questioning, were making no sense at the time of my interview. To others, Jade's claims could be gathered into one of several opposing stories: that she is really a butch, who used to want SRS because of the homophobia she experienced; or that he is really a transman who, in other circumstances and with more education, would have made that choice and lived happily as a man. Yet it is also clear that Jade, in her own words "know[s] what I am." When I pay attention to the context of those answers, to their place on the map that I am drawing her into, it becomes apparent that it is my questioning that is producing the incoherence. Like Anita, Jade's claim to "know what I am" is the key to my mapping here.

These different accounts—drawn from interviews and social interactions—are intended to make the broader point that despite the differences between Jade and those like Anita or Julip or Tamara in terms of embodiment, age, gender identification, and sexual practices, all these individuals can be incorporated into the explanatory force of the collective mode of transgender, even as they contest some of its basic assumptions. Julip's concern that she "looks like a man," Sugar's and Monica's joking about being "men," Tamara's masculine dress (though having just started feminizing hormones), Mona's androgynous style, Sybil's description of herself as a butch queen, Jade's seemingly contradictory relationship to transgender, and Cherry's rejection of "gay" and adoption of "transgender"—all complicate any assertion of a stable identity for those on the Meat Market or at the Clubhouse. By this I do not mean that these individual fem queens, butches, or transexual women do not have "stable identities." Rather I am making two other points: first, even using locally derived terms for people does not capture the range of (sometimes contested) meanings that animate people's understandings of themselves in particular contexts. More importantly, though, the complexity of these identifications *does* lead to some social service providers seeing them as having "false consciousness," of shifting between apparently stable categories of identification because of a lack of education or an adherence to outmoded systems of meaning.

So what happens to those like Anita or Mona or Jade who have not taken on the understanding of "transgender" as something different from "gay" or even for those like Renee or Tara who employ it in strategic moments to make particular demands? One could argue that Anita or Mona are using "the master's tools," and that they should be "educated" into the new language and meanings of transgender as a liberatory and "true" description of their identities and experiences. But this implies that the new tools—those subsumed into "transgender"—are free of the social power relations that my colleague sees condensed in these people's statements about themselves as, simultaneously, woman, man, drag queen, gay, and transexual; or as woman, guy, butch, hard daddy, and mommy. Moreover, such an "education" also implies that what Mona or Anita or Jade know—about themselves and the world—is inherently false.

I heard many of these claims to and statements about knowledge of the self on the streets of the Meat Market and at the balls phrased in just these terms: "I know what I am." I am arguing that these are politically significant claims. At the same time, if at least some of the Meat Market girls (like Cherry) can understand themselves through transgender, it might seem that my concerns are cautionary at best. But what happens when people try to mount these claims about the self in particular social contexts? Next, I want to look at how, in conversation, competing claims over what counts as identity—what counts in knowing about oneself—become adjudicated.

THE ALTERNATIVE LIFESTYLES GROUP: "SOMEONE LIKE ME"

The Communities Together Services Center (CTSC) is about a ten-minute bike ride from the Meat Market, on the Lower East Side.[8] This center offers services for residents of the low-income housing in the area and in 1996 included an "Alternative Lifestyles" group. The participants were a group of friends from the projects—mostly young African American or Latina/o people who could be described as gay, lesbian, bisexual, and transgender—who came to the group weekly to talk about their experiences. Like the mix on the loading dock of the Meat Market, they included female- and male-bodied people with differing identifications. Though I never met any of the group's participants at the Meat Market, some of them told me that they attended the balls, and, like the fem queens there, some had engaged in sex work.

My way into this group, as with the New York Hospital group, was through Nora. Though Nora shares common life experiences with group members (as she did with the New York Hospital group), the way she and group members talked about themselves was quite different, underpinned by Nora's experience in social service settings both as a client and as a counselor. In the analysis that follows, based on exchanges during an Alternative Lifestyles group meeting in October 1996, I focus on this difference in the escalation of Nora's attempts to get one of the group members to identify as *either* transgender *or* gay.

While this was not a transgender-specific group, Nora was called upon to define the term at the beginning of the meeting, to which she gave the standard response of contemporary New York City social service providers. Transgender, she said, is an "umbrella term which includes […] transexuals, pre-op, post-op, uh, transvestites, drag queens, female impersonators." We had not been talking long when Miss Angel entered the room, late as usual. Miss Angel—African American and in her mid-twenties, a former drug user and sex worker—was one of the central participants in the group, the acknowledged linchpin of the core group of friends in the group. Like Mona in her interview with me, Miss Angel felt the need to give a brief narrative for my tape recorder:

3.14

MISS ANGEL: My name is Angel, I'm a pre-op transexual. I dunno *what* I am, I'm a woman, simply ... OK? I'm HIV-positive.

As such, Miss Angel seems to be reiterating the central tenet of transgender identity: that she is a woman, despite her male embodiment. However, later Miss Angel talked about her experience at high school in ways that complicated this assertion:

3.15

MISS ANGEL: I had to get to know new friends when I turned gay and it's not easy being gay.

NORA: How was your experience when you became a woman, a transexual woman?

MISS ANGEL: I was thirteen years old when I did everything.

NORA: Was it even harder?

MISS ANGEL: Was it harder? No.

NORA: Did it go from bad to worse?

MISS ANGEL: No [...] Um, when I was thirteen. It was hard, I went to school—

BEN: With breasts.

MISS ANGEL: The breasts.

Nora's questions to Miss Angel (3.15) are significant because she is proposing to Miss Angel two different states of coming out: as "gay" when she was thirteen, and as a "transexual woman" at a later date. Miss Angel, however, dismisses this: she was thirteen, she said, when she did "everything." This becomes clearer still in a later exchange between them, when they were discussing Miss Angel's sexual history:

3.16

MISS ANGEL: I went to bed with my own kind. I tried it once.

BEN: How was it?

MISS ANGEL: How was it?

BEN: Uh huh.

NORA: Now what is your own kind mean by definition, because you're always telling us—

MISS ANGEL: I'm a woman, well you know.

NORA: You're a woman, transexual, you're gay, you're homosexual.

BEN: A man.

MISS ANGEL: Look, me, like me, someone like me. Someone like me ... Someone like me.

NORA: [Who] changes sexuality, uh huh.[9]

BEN: With breasts.

MISS ANGEL: With breasts.

NORA: OK.

MISS ANGEL: I went out with someone like me. Her name was Billie Jean, she lives in Coney Island.

In both 3.15 and 3.16 Ben offers "breasts" by way of explanation of Miss Angel's being, which Miss Angel affirms. This reference to Miss Angel's breasts—the result of hormone therapy—is the final word in both cases. The reference to her body is particularly instructive, for Miss Angel's changing body shifts her—in contemporary understandings—into the category of "transgender" or, more specifically, "transexual," the latter category which she indeed uses to describe herself. Yet, as is clear from the preceding conversation, Miss Angel does not always stick to this definition of self. Indeed, Nora implicitly recognizes this in her attempts to get Miss Angel to define what her "own kind" is. She lists the identity categories that Miss Angel has used about herself in this group and in others (woman, transexual, gay, homosexual) (3.16), implying that she cannot be all these things. To this, Miss Angel insists: "Look, me, like me, someone like me. Someone like me … Someone like me." In the end, Nora leaves it there: "OK."

Toward the end of the meeting, Nora told us of her days of sex work when non-transgender men who were her clients would ask her what their desire for her meant for their own sexual identity:

3.17
NORA: And they're attracted to that [a feminine person with a penis] So they would tell me, "Well, what am I? I said, Well, I can't tell you what you are unless you know and I can't not tell you this is what you are and this is what you're gonna be, you know, because it's not my life." My life, *I know what I am*.
MISS ANGEL: ⌈*I'm a woman with a large clit.*
NORA: ⌊*I know what I am.* [My emphasis]

Nora's and Miss Angel's talk overlaps in the last two lines of 3.17: they speak at the same moment. Both profess, simultaneously, a knowledge of the self, but what they know is rooted in different ideas about *how* to know oneself. Nora's attempts to get Miss Angel to pick one of the definitions of self that she has used in the group fail precisely because they do not share the same understandings of how gendered and sexual identity works. Miss Angel claims to be gay, but also a transexual, and a "woman with a large clit." Like Cherry, she has reread parts of her anatomy to claim an identification as a woman, but like Anita or Mona, she also claims other kinds of identities, including "gay." Nora, as I have noted, shares much of Miss Angel's history and experience but she has an understanding of gendered and sexual identity gained through social service agencies, defined by a distinct split between gay identities on the one hand and transgender identities on the other. Miss Angel has no such model of personhood. All she can respond when Nora puts her on the spot is: "someone like me" (3.16). In the final quoted passage, Nora states, "I know what I am" (3.17). Like Anita, Mona, and many others, Nora asserts a knowledge of the self that is mounted against conventional understandings of bodily sex and gender identity. But, unlike those people, her statement of self never varies: she is a heterosexual transexual woman.

Miss Angel, at one point claims "I dunno *what* I am" (3.14), but it becomes clear that, in fact, she has a strong idea of "what I am": simultaneously gay, homosexual, transexual, and "a woman with a large clit." Even in the friendly atmosphere of a peer-led support group, certain statements of identity and experience can become interpreted—by Nora, by myself, and by others—as inconsistencies, but only because we are interpreting them within a theoretical framework which cannot make sense of them unless they are dismissed as false consciousness or a lack of education.

However, as I wrote above, I do not want to turn this into a simple story of how young, poor people of color are excluded from dominant discourses and practices around "transgender." Indeed, it is not that easy to make such a case, as Tara, Nora, and Cherry make clear. Moreover, the kinds of complexities I have discussed above are not restricted to the young kids hanging in the Meat Market or the Clubhouse. In other places around the city, I also met people whose understandings of self, practices, and identifications similarly confused an easy distinction between gay and transgender.

AT KARALYN'S: ONE OF THE GUYS

From the Lower East Side and the Meat Market, let's go back to Karalyn's, the bar on 10th Avenue and 55th Street frequented mostly by white male cross-dressers, though it has its share of transexual women, admirers, and some people of color too. It doesn't take me long to get up there from the Village—it's about a twenty-minute bike ride. Here, one of the regulars is Sherry. Sherry is white, in her mid-thirties, and lives in Pennsylvania, traveling into the city on the weekends in her Porsche to come to Karalyn's or Tranny Chaser.[10] She used to own and run an insurance company but has retired, partly because she is HIV-positive. Despite these markers of upper-middle-classness, Sherry has lived frugally since her retirement. She cross-dresses on weekends and has been on hormones for a year or so but does not believe she is transexual; and indeed, while she was quite aware of the concept "transgender" and all it implies, she most often referred to herself as "gay" in our conversations. One evening she told me "I'm going up to P-town with two other guys," indicating through this structure that she also understood herself at times as a "guy."

After talking over this issue—being gay, being transgender—over drinks at Karalyn's in the summer of 1997, I received this e-mail from Sherry:

You asked about the differences between someone like myself and the […] queens [a category to which she had opposed herself in our conversations]. Well, for one, none of them take hormones. They like using their penises, while myself i prefer impotence. So in that regard, our identity and gender are somewhat different. They consider themselves gay drag queens, and to a degree i suppose i consider myself gay as well, although a post op-TS friend of mine thinks i should go thru the change, and that i'd be more happy living as a straight woman. That's HER opinion. I really don't know. I do know that i love men, and that i could be quite happy living fulltime as a woman, but i also accept the fact that physically i don't think i can pull it off. Therefore i feel like i'm trying things like hormones, and i'm planning on having some cosmetic surgery done to see just how far i can take this. (E-mail, May 9, 1997) A few months later, this time at Tranny Chaser, I saw Sherry again. We caught up on news, and she told me a bit more about the visit of a non-transgender woman friend from Germany, whom I had met the last time I had bumped into Sherry here. She divulged the fact that they had had sex the evening I had seen them together at the bar. I was rather startled at this: how did it feel to have sex with a woman? I asked. She shrugged: it was fine. It wasn't the first time for Sherry, whose fourteen-year-old son lives with her.

A month after this, I cycled up to Karalyn's for the last time, as it was about to close down. Karalyn had lost the battle to keep open a bar that only really had a weekend crowd, a business not sustainable with New York rents. At the bar, I leaned over to say hello to Tina the barmaid and caught sight of a half-familiar face to my right. Half-familiar because it was Sherry, but she was in masculine clothes—jeans, a loose shirt, and a vest—and was sporting a goatee. I was startled again, and she was amused at my surprise. There was some reason for the goatee that I couldn't quite make out, something to do with a cut on her chin, which had led to her coming to Karalyn's in her male persona.

We settled down to a long talk, occasionally greeting other people we knew as they came in. She told me she was still having electrolysis on her cheeks and repeated that she was on hormones, but her beard still sprouted powerfully. I asked her how it felt being on hormones, and she startled me once more by taking my hand and placing it on her chest, visible under the loose cotton shirt she was wearing. Her breasts were soft. She used to have a lot of muscle mass there, she said, but it has all gone due to the hormones. I asked her how she would like me to refer to her as a man, and she said simply "Shay" would do, as it would work for both Sherry and Shane, her male name. Despite the hormones and electrolysis, Sherry still had no plans for surgery and shuddered when I mentioned it.

Unlike Anita or Miss Angel, Sherry does not claim to "know what I am." In fact, her e-mail claimed that she "really do[esn't] know" whether she is a gay man or a transexual woman. The indeterminacy of Sherry's identity and presentation seems to make sense in the collective mode of transgender, yet Sherry was clear that "transgender" could not describe her experiences, especially since she was attracted to gay men as a man. And at other times, Sherry told me that she was content not to know. Indeed, Sherry's lack of certainty could be understood not as a function of an innate uncertainty about who she is but because of the way she feels compelled to describe her desires through a set of discourses that do not make sense of them. While Sherry is white, upper middle class, and in most ways shares very few of the social experiences of Jade, Anita, or Miss Angel, like them she is hard-pressed to align her self-understandings with discrete categories of identity.

Sherry is just one of a heaving crowd of regulars who come and go at Karalyn's. There are plenty of others who easily fit into "transgender" here, and who understand its boundaries and see themselves as incorporated within it in different ways. But far more often, the boundaries of categories—transgender, gay, transexual, transvestite, and others—blend and blur around the bar. Often, the regulars simply refer to one another as "trannies," a useful catchall, like "transgender," but one which can incorporate the gay male cross-dressers who sometimes come and hang out. There is Chris, who says she likes men and used to think she was gay, but now she's not sure what she is. Her psychoanalyst believes she is just too homophobic to come out, but Chris rejects this analysis. "I have one self, but two lives," she says. And Gwen likes being a gay man most of the time, but sometimes she gets the urge to dress and hang out at Karalyn's. "I can't do this downtown," she told me, referring to gay male bars in the Village and Chelsea. "What gay man would want to fuck someone in a dress?" Here, she might score with a heterosexual cross-dresser.

What I describe here may seem to be a reiteration of the power of transgender—to incorporate many different kinds of gendered expression and desire under its umbrella. But the point is that for many of the people at Karalyn's, "transgender" (in its implicit opposition to "homosexuality") cannot make sense of the way they experience their desires and selves precisely because they see their desires fueled by their "sexuality." Whether these people are secure in their knowledge of "what" they are (like, in very different ways, Cherry or

Miss Angel) or not (like Sherry), none of their experiences are easily accounted for through the categories of either homosexuality or transgender.

FRACTIOUS FRACTURES

The critique of identity politics is certainly not new and has been developed in feminism, queer/LGBT studies, critical race theory, and other bodies of critical theory (e.g., Moraga and Anzaldúa 1981, Epstein 1987, Warner 1993, Scott 1993). The stories that I have told above demonstrate the usefulness of those critiques which point out that "identity" can erase the intersections of different kinds of social experiences, more often than not asserting the experience of white, middle-class U.S. American social actors as the implicit exemplary center. The basic argument that animates these critiques is that in privileging one "identity" ("woman," "gay," "American"), the intersections of these social differences are erased, disabling those who are multiply engaged by racial, ethnic, sexual, gendered, and other kinds of differences. Identity politics also, as Scott (1993) points out, simply affirms the differences between groups and extends those differences back into history.

However, these stories are useful not simply to show how identity categories such as "gay" or "transgender" cannot account for the complexity of people's desires, understandings of self, and experience (though they do this too). Rather, they are most useful in showing that the complexity of experience can disrupt the very analytic categories by which social theorists and others attempt to describe the intersections of different forms of lived experience. That is, Anita or Jade do not simply demonstrate the ways that gendered and sexual experiences escape the boundaries of identity categories: rather, they show how that which counts as "gender" or "sexuality" is itself the contested ground.

The point of these ethnographic anecdotes and theoretical discussions of "identity," then, is not to reveal "transgender" or "person of transexual/transgender experience" as empty categories. Rather, they show that the *category* of transgender is (as much as the category of "homosexuality") an *effect* of the distinction between what "gender" and "sexuality" have come to mean in much contemporary politics, theory, and social service provision. What I am after here is the increasing institutional power of "transgender" to order certain experiences, even as it erases their complexity. If someone like Nora or someone like Jade argues that "I know what I am," that knowledge becomes differently understood—and judged—in terms of a categorical system where Nora's knowledge is intelligible in institutional contexts but Jade's is not. For Jade, being gay, a woman, a hard daddy, and a guy are equally and simultaneously possible. And for Mona, there is no necessary conflict between being gay ("exactly") or a woman ("exactly") or transgender ("exactly"). That is, for Mona, knowing you are a gay man does not exclude the possibility of knowing that you live as a woman, in the same way that for Jade, being a hard daddy and "thinking like a guy" does not mean you can't be a mommy to your daughter and a woman. This, I would argue, is *not* the same understanding which underpins dominant ideas about gender and sexuality in the United States, the "master's tools" version of gendered and sexual personhood in which cross-gender identification is a restricted possibility for people who are "really" homosexual. Nor is it evidence that homosexual identification among those perceived as "transgender" is the result of not being "educated" into the possibilities of transgender identification. If the emergent idea of gender and sexuality as separable and separate entities has been opposed to the conflation of these experiences in mainstream U.S. society, then Mona or Jade's or Tara's understandings are different again. That is, in their view of the world, *any difference sets you apart from heteronormativity, a difference which can be named in a variety of ways*: for Mona, as gay, a butch queen up in drags, or as transgender; for Jade as a woman, a guy, a hard daddy, a butch, or as gay; and for Tara as both a gay girl and a "woman of transAfrican, transgender experience."

The significant difference between Mona's or Jade's or Tara's understanding of "gender" and "sexuality" and that employed in mainstream LGBT organizations is that in mainstream gay and lesbian politics, difference from heteronormativity is that which is to be elided. That is, contemporary mainstream gay and lesbian politics works to minimize the difference between homosexuality and heterosexuality, precisely by removing the visibility of (class-inflected and racialized) gender difference from the category "gay," part of the dynamic that Lisa Duggan neatly captures with the term "homonormativity" (2003: 50). This is possible only through a conceptual shift which produces gender and sexuality—and the identities that are seen to flow from them—as radically different domains and experiences. And it is for this reason, I have argued, that "transgender" has been able to emerge as a distinct category of being, predicated on an autonomous sphere of "gender." However, because Mona, Jade, Tara, and a host of others do not share in this binarized conception of their experiences or identities, their statements of self become unrepresentable—and incoherent—to those who claim to represent them. To "know what I am," in other words, is not enough to be accounted for in mainstream identity politics.

Moreover, this is not simply a story that can easily be made along lines of race, age, or class. While Anita, Mona, and Jade are people of color, poor, working class, and in many ways disenfranchised, Sherry is white and middle class. Cherry—Mona and Anita's peer—hangs out on the Meat Market but explicitly rejects the idea that she was ever "gay" and employs "transgender" as a category which makes sense of her experience. The white, middle-class gay male drag queens of the Imperial Court discussed in chapter 2 are very clear about the differences between themselves and transgender-identified people, even though they are described as transgender in many contexts. Jade is approaching fifty and has a long experience in the butch/femme communities of color in New York City, while Mona—male-bodied and identifying simultaneously as gay, transgender, and a woman—is just twenty-two. And Tara condenses racial, gendered, and sexual identity by claiming to be both "gay" and "a woman of trans-African, transgender experience."

By noting these divergences and convergences, I want to resist any attempt to reduce my analyses here to one simply about class, race, or age. Rather, if there is a commonality, it is one of involvement in formalized institutions which employ transgender as a category for the purposes of community building and social service provision. Cherry is distinguished from her peers by her heavy involvement in GIP and other organizational support groups. Sherry, Julip, Anita, and Mona do not participate in these contexts. But even this does not fully explain all these differences, for Jade and Renee, who work for a social service agency as "transgender peer outreach workers," shift between seeing themselves and their clients as "transgender" and "gay."

After reading this chapter, one might justifiably ask: so what if Jade or Mona or Miss Angel or Sherry come to understand themselves as—or are understood through—transgender? If, as it seems, at least some of them are comfortable with using the category about themselves at least part of the time or can make sense of the category as incorporating them (for example, Jade, Mona, Renee, or Anita), then doesn't it make sense to educate them into a distinction that enables them to organize their selves in this way? In the end, I would say that this is not necessarily a negative outcome. For some, like Cherry, this has proved a powerful tool of self-understanding.

Yet, at the same time, I have some cautions. First, from a purely utilitarian perspective, one of the central tenets of the kinds of public health–oriented social service outreach I have been invoking here—a central site for the production of transgender as a category—is to pay attention to the experiences and identifications of those to whom such outreach is done. That is, in order to reach people you wish to help, you need to understand and use the categories by which they understand themselves. As such, instrumentally, it makes sense to think about the implications of these stories for the kinds of public health models being developed under the rubric of "transgender."

But second, from a more abstract but still political perspective, the "education" of Jade or Anita or even Sherry in the meanings of transgender ignores the fact that for someone like Sherry the category simply does not make sense of who she feels she is. And, for Jade or Anita, it implies that the way they understand themselves now is inherently false, and that to "know what I am" is, in fact, not really to know at all. Sherry, motoring down to New York in her Porsche, may not in the end have to choose between being gay or being transgender. Jade or Anita, on the other hand, may not have this luxury, dependent as they are on social services and (dwindling) institutionalized social safety nets, institutions which operate through discrete categories of identity. So, while I have argued above that I do not want to reduce this analysis to race, age, or class, my concern here finally is that the young, the poor, the people of color who are understood as being transgender are increasingly having to un-know what they know about themselves and learn a new vocabulary of identity.

And even here, there is nothing inherently—ethically, morally—wrong with this. Culture is produced in the constant, shifting emergence of meaning as people engage with one another as social actors in particular contexts. That is, I am not invested in romanticizing Jade or Anita as "natives" whose "culture" should be left alone or "preserved." But simultaneously, I am cautious about the other possibility, where for them to become "transgender" requires a recognition of another organization of their identities as being, inherently, false and outmoded.

In writing about her experience of being subject to surgeries at an early age because of an intersex condition, Cheryl Chase (1998) writes that her genitalia—understood in popular and medical discourses and practices as "ambiguous"—were not, prior to surgical intervention, ambiguous at all. They were exactly what they were. Rather, a powerful system of binary gender and sexed bodies produced them *as* ambiguous. Chase's point is similar to one of the earliest observations in American anthropology. In his classic article "On Alternating Sounds" (1889), Franz Boas contests the claims of Euro-American observers that Native American languages were "primitive" because there was no consistency in the pronunciation of words in those languages. Boas's counterargument was revolutionary. He proposed that it was the investigators' inability to understand the phonemic distinctions of those languages, rather than the speakers' imprecision, which resulted in the interpretation of primitivity.

With the stories I've told above, what struck me most while they were being told to me was how ambiguous and shifting they were, an impression not dissimilar to those held by Chase's doctors and the nineteenth-century linguists Boas took on. And, like those linguists, the call to "educate" fem queens into the language of transgender and the repudiation of their homosexual identification as outmoded smacks of an implicit claim about their primitivity. Yet one can make the same discursive move here that Chase or Boas makes: in their own terms, these stories are entirely coherent. They are ambiguous only in a binary system where primary "gender" or "sexual" identity must be conceived as two distinct arenas of one's experience. As Mark Johnson writes: "there is nothing ambiguous about ambiguity, sexual or otherwise. Rather, ambiguity is the specific product or effect of different historical relations of power and resistance through which various cultural subjects are created and re-create themselves" (1997: 13–14).

If, as I argue, these professions of self exceed identity categories, another way of reading these interview excerpts and ethnographic anecdotes is to celebrate them as queer, indeed to see them as breaking down or resisting the solidity of identity categories. Jacob Hale, writing of what he calls genderqueer positions which contest a strict division between FTM and butch identities, argues that "our dislocatedness provides us with subject positions. This might sound paradoxical but it is not, for dislocatedness is not the absolute absence of location. Because borders between gender categories are zones of overlap, not lines, our dislocatedness is constituted by our locations in the overlapping margins of multiple gender categories: we bear Wittgensteinian family resemblances to people who occupy multiple gender categories" (1998: 336). However, while Hale's argument is convincing for the subject positions he is discussing, it does not necessarily account for the experiences of the people I have discussed here. A perspective which celebrates dislocatedness in the Meat Market would ignore the fact that in this context, fem queens, butches, and others are highly active in maintaining categorical boundaries such as at the Clubhouse balls or in the Meat Market where being called "hard" is itself a form of categorical policing. That is, I do not believe that these stories demonstrate a system outside representation itself. Rather, it is still a system of categorical orderings, but one that is differently organized from, and cannot be accounted for in, the relatively more powerful terms of mainsteam identity politics.

It is true that even though they may not identify as "transgender" as such, people like Jade, Miss Angel, or Anita nonetheless benefit from the outreach done in its terms. Yet, from both a theoretical and utilitarian perspective, "transgender" cannot account for the complexity of their understandings of self. It is important to note that I am not calling for "better representation" of those I discuss above, or the simple elaboration of new categories, but rather a reexamination of a system which, in both practical and theoretical terms, marks Miss Angel, Anita, or Jade as "other." This is the case whether they are understood as suffering "false consciousness" or as representative of a queer, subversive selfhood beyond categories. I am suggesting, in short, that their claims about themselves should be taken seriously, in their own terms. Indeed, as I will argue in more depth in Part III and especially in the conclusion, this suggestion is only the beginning of a broader analysis of a system of identity politics where "representation" as a trope itself erases more complex analyses of political and economic injustices.

Having laid out some of the institutionalized politics of identity and community that are shaped by—and shape—the category transgender and its differences from homosexuality, I want to move, in Part III of this book, to consider three realms in which this category has become institutionalized: academic and popular literature, the contexts of political activism and social service provision to which I have alluded throughout the previous chapters, and the recourse to narratives of violence in making claims for the state's attention to transgender lives. Here, I want to consider how the development of a body of knowledge around the category transgender, shaped by an ontological distinction between gender and sexuality, is doing similar work in contexts as diverse as literature reviews, social justice activism, and telling stories of violence suffered. And again, my analysis—and my political concerns—revolve around what these orderings achieve, for whom, and what the implications are for the increasing use of transgender in these contexts, even as they produce remarkable social achievements.

NOTES

1. Rosalyne explains that this phrase—drawing on similar constructions such as "person of African descent"—foregrounds her identity as a woman first and foremost while acknowledging her transexual/transgender history.

2. The majority of the people I discuss were ascribed male at birth. The one extended case of a female-bodied person—Jade—that I discuss below further complicates the gay/transgender distinction, but there are clear differences between Jade's experience and those of the male-bodied feminine people I am discussing. I must stress that I do not intend to simply conflate Jade's experience with the experiences of the other (male-bodied feminine) people I discuss. Rather, I want to point to the place where many kinds of differences—gender, sexuality, class, race, age—become smoothed out through the assumption of common transgender identification and experience.

3. During my fieldwork from 1996 through 1998, the Meat Market was still an active semi-industrial space. Nowadays, it is better known for its art galleries, boutiques, and upscale bars and restaurants which have replaced most of the meat industry in the eastern blocks of the district, pushing the sex-work industry into the as-yet-undeveloped area between Washington Street and the Hudson River. The development of the Hudson River Park and the Christopher Street Piers bordering the Meat Market to the west has accelerated the process of gentrification. The descriptions which follow draw on my experience in the late 1990s.

4. Tamara corrected me when I referred to him as "she" to one of his friends, indicating that when dressed as a masculine person, he preferred masculine pronouns.

5. In many ways, this set of meanings around hardness, softness, and penetration are similar to those that Kulick (1998) discusses for Brazilian travestis. The majority of the girls in the Meat Market do not desire genital surgeries (at least in their response to my questions). Like Kulick's informants, the fem queens often turn to unlicensed practitioners for body modifications; one of them, India, told me of her plans to have breast and hip silicone injections from a person in Brooklyn who did such procedures in her apartment, a procedure I later attended.

6. I have adapted this from Henry Goldschmidt's (2006) phrase "visual economy of race," itself adapted from Wiegman (1995).

7. The choice of the feminine pronoun here is one I agonized over, and it speaks both to the power of binary gender and the assumptions underlying the categories "gay" and "transgender" I am analyzing. As the following interview excerpts make clear, Jade does identify as masculine in many ways, but she

also insists that she is a woman. Consequently, I use Jade's own gendering of herself, as I have with all the people I discuss in this study.

8. I use a pseudonym for the center's name.

9. Given my argument, one might imagine that Nora would have said "gender" rather than "sexuality" here. At the same time, however, her use of "sexuality" indicates the slippage between these categories in talk and practice and points to the gaps produced by needing to talk about erotic desire and gendered practices in discrete categories.

10. Again, my use of "her" and "she" to describe Sherry is a conscious decision, based not necessarily on Sherry's understandings of herself (which, as I discuss below, are not easily understood in terms of binary gender) but rather on the fact that I interacted with Sherry mainly in her feminine persona.

READING 14
GOING PUBLIC: STAR WARS IN THE LIBERATION MOVEMENTS

By Martha Gever

From the outset, the gay and women's liberation movements that burst forth on the public stage in the late 1960s looked forward to a world transformed by political and cultural revolutions, but members of these movements also forged historical arguments to counter the idea that homosexuality was unhealthy and socially pernicious. Where lesbians were concerned, famous women—from Sappho to Gertrude Stein—whose homosexuality had been practically erased, were posthumously recruited as distinguished forebears. The justification for the attention given to eminent lesbians of past eras was similar to that most frequently encountered today: role models. This was not a novel argument, insofar as the homosexuality of distinguished individuals has been a consistent feature of organized efforts to obtain social approbation and decriminalization of homosexuality. Magnus Hirschfeld, who founded the Scientific Humanitarian Committee in Berlin in 1898 and later established the Institute for Sexual Science to promote sexual reform and tolerance of homosexuality in particular, compiled lists of famous homosexuals to promote his cause. However, the difference between the rationale for these earlier efforts and those made since the 1960s is that Hirschfeld and his contemporaries believed that this information would change social mores in a population they considered largely heterosexual, while members of liberation groups were more concerned with problems of self-regard among gay men and lesbians.

In 1969, Dick Leitsch, executive director of the New York City chapter of the Mattachine Society, called for research into and publication of information about notable lesbian and gay men by members of the nascent gay liberation movement:

> Homosexuals, like everyone else, need people to identify with. We need heroes, homosexuals who have "made it", to show what we can do if we try…. Increased interest in homosexual heroes and homosexual histories would help solve the identity crisis so many homosexuals feel by bringing home the realization that we are not "freaks", but part of a group that has always existed and contributed its bit toward civilization and culture. (Leitsch 1969)

For Leitsch and like-minded comrades, a parade of accomplished cultural and political figures who could be identified as lesbian or gay offered psychological benefits for shame-ridden gay men and lesbians who were potential members of the movement. Awareness of these dead heroes would instill pride, which quickly became the watchword of the gay liberation program.

Living lesbian and gay heroes were another matter, all famously occupying more or less transparent but securely guarded closets. And, although it might seem inconsistent with efforts to identify noteworthy representatives, any lesbian who became renowned due to her involvement in the women's or gay movement was suspected of using politics for self-aggrandizement.[1] In other words, the concern with celebrity in lesbian cultural milieus was treated as a political problem as often as it was interpreted as an achievement. Documents from the extremely volatile and often contentious late 1960s and early 1970s confirm the difficulties presented by lesbian celebrity, which could be summarized as one general question: how to deal with the media. At that time and from the perspective of the young radicals who constituted the first gay and women's liberation groups, television and the mainstream press were not looked upon as neutral publicity vehicles. Instead, these media were assumed to be ideological instruments of repressive patriarchy and capitalism, an assessment amply supported by much of the coverage they offered—or neglected to give—about these movements. Women's liberation fared slightly better in this regard, although its more radical contingents were routinely treated as extremists. Gay liberation activists and actions, on the other hand, were either ignored completely or rendered as eccentric curiosities. The uprising in New York City sparked by a police raid of the Stonewall Inn in June 1969, for example, either was given little mention in the local news media or treated as an amusing escapade with little political import (Alwood 1996).

The gay and women's liberation movements, like other radical political and countercultural groups active in the 1960s and early seventies, regarded media that did not emanate from friendly quarters—alternative, noncommercial media—with deep suspicion. In addition to general skepticism about the ideological slant given to reports on events and issues by dominant media, members of radical organizations resented its power to authorize spokespeople and leaders. The ideals of democratic decision making often upheld by these groups, combined with an effort to incorporate Maoist principles of self-government in North American oppositional politics, created an atmosphere of mistrust concerning leaders or any structures that reproduced and institutionalized power differentials among individuals. The Gay Liberation Front (GLF), the name chosen by the first militant gay liberation organization formed in New York City in the wake of the Stonewall Rebellion, is indicative of its political principles, which consciously aligned this group with the popular national liberation struggles in Asia, Africa, and Latin America that emerged in the post–World War II period.

SHOOTING STARS

Another source of gay and lesbian activists' ire regarding the press was the common journalistic practice of seeking conventionally attractive members of these groups as de facto representatives. The chosen spokespeople were almost uniformly white and middle-class, often conservatively attired and well mannered by bourgeois standards. The gay press of the era, which consisted primarily of locally distributed, inexpensive newsprint periodicals, routinely registered antagonism to what was viewed as the commercial media's imposition of an individualistic ethic on fundamentally collective efforts. Anyone quoted as a spokesperson was likely to be castigated for her or his cooperation. For example, a feminist gay man, writing in the pages of the New York GLF newspaper *Come Out*, disparaged an article on gay liberation in the *New York Times* in a typical fashion: "[W]e can tell who are those among us who had the lowest consciousness—the straight identified homosexuals who compete with each other for access to the pig media." More optimistically, he added, "All the media in the world cannot erase the products of a gay consciousness" (Gavin 1972).[2]

The same theme was taken up most vigorously by lesbians involved in both the feminist and gay movements, so it is not surprising that lesbians were among the most vociferous media critics. A regular contributor in both contexts, Martha Shelley, was particularly contemptuous of a new phenomenon she designated the "Women's Liberation Media Star," who she profiled for *Come Out* readers:

> Generally a college-educated, white, well-heeled woman who knows a great deal about publicity and publishing but who never has the time for consciousness raising, she is prone to make apologetic statements to the male press, prone to waste her time arguing with Hugh Heffner or Dick Cavett when she could be organizing women. "I have a wonderful relationship with my husband," says one denying her lesbian relationships in *Life* magazine—when only a week before she brought tears to the eyes of gay women with the stories of her ill-fated lesbian affairs. (Shelley 1970–71, n.p.)

Shelley goes on to explain the political repercussions that will ensue from efforts to use mainstream media to publicize feminist and gay arguments for liberation: "These media stars, carefully coifed and lathered with foundation makeup, claim to represent all women. In actuality they are ripping off all women.... These women will betray us when the *cock* crows.... If large numbers of women are going to passively depend on a few stars to liberate them, instead of getting themselves together to do it, the movement will surely fail" (ibid.). According to Shelley's logic, efforts to secure media coverage were distracting, at best, if not utterly antithetical to the principles and purposes of liberation.

Shelley's decision to omit the name of the offending woman featured in *Life* is curious and deserves further reflection. On one hand, it could be interpreted as a refusal to acknowledge someone the media chose to shine a spotlight on as worthy of additional publicity. Or it might be construed as recognition of that woman's claim to membership in the movement, despite her willingness to be singled out for attention. Therefore, not indicating her proper name may have been an effort to spare her embarrassment. (Shelley was less circumspect when she dealt with Betty Friedan in this article, perhaps because condemnation in this instance was directed at a feminist who had publicly distanced herself from radical feminists and lesbian activists, and attempted to do so in the name of the entire women's movement.) But there was little mystery concerning the reference for anyone involved in radical feminist or gay politics, at least in New York City.

She was clearly identifiable as Kate Millett, whose 1970 best-selling *Sexual Politics* gave feminists conceptual ammunition for a full-fledged attack on patriarchal, sexist culture as represented by Sigmund Freud, D. H. Lawrence, and Norman Mailer, among others. However, Millett didn't count on—nor could she have predicted—her elevation to media stardom as the result of her book's popular success. Her portrait was displayed on the cover of the August 31, 1970, issue of *Time*, which devoted eight of its pages to a feature on "the politics of sex," including a sidebar profile of Millett, "Who's Come a Long Way, Baby?" She was, as Shelley noted sarcastically, interviewed at length by a reporter from *Life* for its September 4, 1970, feature on women's liberation (Wrenn 1970). She appeared on radio and television talk shows. All of this attention might have been lapped up greedily by someone trying to make a career as an actress or politician, but Millett was a literary scholar and artist, and her much-touted book was her Ph.D. thesis. She was also an avid participant in a political movement that distrusted all such fanfare.

Not that mainstream media univocally praised Millett. She was lampooned viciously in an *Esquire* illustration; her work was also dismissed as unnecessarily strident and poorly documented by a reviewer in the same issue of *Esquire*, as well as in *Harper's*, the *New Republic*, and *Commentary* (Decter 1970; Howe 1970; Lawrenson 1971; Malcolm 1970). Indeed, she became the symbol of everything that opponents of feminism despised. On top of that, a subsequent *Time* article cited a statement concerning her bisexuality that Millett had made to a gathering at Columbia University in November 1970, using this as evidence of her writing's dubious value. "The disclosure is bound to discredit her as a spokeswoman for her cause, cast further doubt on her theories, and reinforce the views of those skeptics who routinely dismiss all liberationists as lesbians," the article stated matter-of-factly ("Women's Lib" 1970). The New York City chapter of the National Organization of Women (NOW) immediately set out to dispute the underlying argument that a lesbian is automatically disreputable at a demonstration for child care and abortion rights held several days after the *Time* article appeared. Demonstrators wore lavender armbands and distributed leaflets declaring support for Millett and condemning *Time* for trying to undermine their movement. When the press failed to cover this aspect of the event, a group of feminists called a press conference to state plainly once again the solidarity between women's and gay liberation, with Millett prominent among the speakers. This time, the media took note. According to Sidney Abbott and Barbara Love's account of this affair, "Media coverage was excellent.... It virtually halted dyke-baiting" (Abbott and Love [1972] 1985, 125).[3]

For Millett, however, this display of sisterhood could not offset entirely the effects of the treatment she received from within movement ranks. The attacks began as soon as *Sexual Politics* was published and an unsigned leaflet denouncing Millett for grandstanding was distributed at a meeting of Radicalesbians, a group formed in response to homophobic statements by prominent members of the women's movement like Friedan and Susan Brownmiller. Friedan had become infamous within U.S. lesbian circles as the author of the remark that lesbianism was a "lavender menace" as far as women's liberation was concerned. Nor did she stop there, but later engineered a purge of lesbian officers in NOW. Brownmiller echoed Friedan when she dismissed lesbians' presence within women's liberation as a "lavender herring" in a piece she wrote for the *New York Times Magazine* (Brownmiller 1970). Taken together, these condescending comments by leading feminists inspired the militant Lavender Menace action by Radicalesbians at the Second Congress to Unite Women in 1970 in New York City (Abbott and Love [1972] 1985, 108–116). And it was a member of Radicalesbians who challenged Millett to admit her lesbian affairs at the Columbia event (Jay 1999, 232–233).

In *Flying*, Millett's autobiographical account of the year following her publishing success and her anointment as a women's liberation luminary, she writes about several grueling months on the college lecture circuit, after which "you come home to find everybody in New York invents scandalous legends while you're gone, and three purists have just put forth an edict on your treason" (Millett 1974, 93). Shelley could be counted as one of these purists, but so too could any of a number of radical feminists, such as the authors of "What Can We Do about the Media," a set of resolutions proposed by a feminist collective called the Class Workshop at the 1970 Congress to Unite Women. Among the tenets the group advocated were the following:

> Women's Liberation is getting popular enough that the media needs us as much as we need them. We can and must dictate our terms to them: present prepared statements and refuse to give personal information.... From now on anyone who refuses to follow this policy must be assumed to be doing so for her own personal aggrandizement.... No member of a group can appear as an independent feminist—whether for fame or for money.... No individual or group can earn a living by writing or speaking about women's liberation.... Anyone who wants to write should write for the movement, not for the publishing industry.... Any individual who refuses collective discipline will be ostracized from the movement. (Class Workshop 1970)

Millett was guilty on all counts. But the resolutions were not endorsed by those attending the conference. These were extreme and ultimately impractical guidelines for a political movement with a constituency as broad as women's liberation. The publishing industry was eager to cater to a growing audience for writings by feminists and about feminism, and the movement counted a goodly number of members with literary ambitions among its active members. However, such sentiments were very much in line with the antiestablishment stance characteristic of the more radical segments of both gay and women's liberation.

In many respects, disdain for the media and the fear that it would dilute radical messages by transforming movement spokespeople into celebrities had been a feature of American radical politics since the mid-1960s. The civil rights, Black Power, and anti–Vietnam War movements had all grappled with the problem but were never able to resolve it. As Todd Gitlin explains in his classic study of the relationship between the New Left and the media, *The Whole World Is Watching*, movement leaders like Mark Rudd of Columbia Students for a Democratic Society, Abbie Hoffman and Jerry Rubin of the Yippies, and Stokely Carmichael of the Student Nonviolent Coordinating Committee became so newsworthy that they often ignored the principles of egalitarian decision making officially endorsed by the groups they represented. As the result of the media attention, Gitlin says, "Narcissistic motives, once negligible or contained, inevitably flourished, fattened by rewards, while more cooperative impulses withered" (Gitlin 1980, 161). In his analysis, the feminists who built the women's liberation movement in the late 1960s reacted against such preening ambitions and macho posturing with efforts to guard against this phenomenon, although they, too, could not control journalists' compulsive focus on individual personalities. Kate Millett captures well the impossible situation that faced any feminist who was singled out as a public figure: "[T]he movement is sending out double signals: you absolutely must preach at our panel, star at our conference ... at the same time laying down a wonderfully uptight line about elitism. Why can't we stick by what we knew was right to start with—no bloody leaders?" (Millett 1974, 92–93).

OUTER SPACE

Unlike feminists, gay liberation groups rarely faced the need to deal with the possibility of their leaders becoming media stars, because at this time outspoken members of this political constituency were automatically deemed objects of scorn and derision. The mainstream press never seemed eager to identify gay or lesbian leaders, or even to acknowledge that homosexuality could be a political identity, as opposed to a shameful condition. Even a sympathetic article, such as a profile of the recently radicalized Daughters of Bilitis (DOB) that appeared in a 1971 issue of the *New York Times Magazine*, devoted considerable space and little criticism to theories concerning the psychopathology of lesbianism (Klemesrud 1971). No one who believed that the mass media pursued a repressive social agenda would be surprised by the repeated insinuations of perversion among lesbian activists in so much of the reporting on feminist and gay politics. But for revolutionaries like Rita Mae Brown, a leading radical lesbian feminist polemicist in the early 1970s, this kind of treatment could be interpreted as a political advantage. "For those who build toward a new world, women's liberation is a dead movement twitching its limbs in the vulgar throes of establishment recognition," she wrote. "Women-identified women will not sell out" (Brown [1972] 1992, 195). Like many others at that time, Brown believed that radical lesbians possessed the political analysis and revolutionary resolve necessary to bring about the liberation of all women.

However, there was at least one American lesbian, beside the ambiguous Kate Millett, who attracted abundant notice from the press due to her outspoken advocacy of lesbian issues and her unrepentant sexual identity. This was Jill Johnston, known mainly as regular contributor to the *Village Voice* and author of one of the first books to champion the new radical lesbian politics, *Lesbian Nation* (1973). Many lesbians expressed their admiration for Johnston's work, for the courage exhibited by an established, albeit avant-garde, art and dance critic publicly proclaiming her lesbianism and writing about her lesbian life. But she also encountered extreme animosity from lesbian feminist militants, which she also chronicled in her weekly column, reprinted in *Lesbian Nation*, and recalled in a 1998 republication of much of this material. Looking back on the hostile reception she often received from members of both women's and gay liberation, Johnston credits the media for producing her "new giantess misshapen profile rigged up in the glare of national publicity" and the "'false self' of stardumb" (Johnston 1998, n.p.) that resulted. Still, she remained mindful of how she abetted the production of her own notoriety and therefore put herself directly in the line of fire.

The kind of high jinks that landed Johnston in this predicament were often designed to garner attention from journalists who couldn't resist a juicy tidbit, although precedents can be found in the dadaesque prose she had been producing for the *Voice* for years. Starting out as a fairly conventional critic of avant-garde art and dance in the late 1950s, she developed a quirky, rambling, sometimes whimsical, often intimate writing style by the mid-1960s. Her columns could be described as the literary equivalent of the happenings, Fluxus performances, and similar aesthetic attacks on the pretensions of high art that she championed as a critic— "an art of high amusement and contempt for authority," as she put it (ibid.). Predictably, in the early days of women's liberation, Johnston ran afoul of more respectable feminists like Friedan, who was interested in press coverage of the movement but not the kind generated by outrageous behavior. In summer 1970, Women Strike for Equality, a coalition made up of various women's liberation groups and headed by Friedan, held a fundraising cocktail party at the East Hampton home of avant-garde art collectors Ethel and Robert Scull.

But Johnston upstaged representatives of the feminist group by taking a topless swim in the hosts' pool while society reporters from the *New York Times*, *Newsweek*, UPI, and others took notes and snapped photos. "Have gun, will travel. See pool, will swim," she wrote in her gleeful account of the episode, "Bash in the Sculls" (Johnston 1998, 10). Later she explained that she had not planned the action to "protest the discrimination of lesbians by feminists" because, in her words, "I wasn't nearly so organized" (Johnston 1973, 16).

Then, in the spring of 1971, Johnston published a piece in the *Voice* entitled "Lois Lane Is a Lesbian," no more impassioned than her previous writings but unusual in that she no longer mentioned lesbianism in passing but explicitly aligned herself with gay liberation and offered a theory of lesbian feminist politics. One would assume that such an unvarnished statement of affiliation in a widely read newspaper would be welcomed by gay and lesbian activists. But Johnston was too eccentric for many involved in either women's or gay liberation. As she noted in the same article, "I'm persona non grata with every 'group' in the country.... The women's lib people don't like the way I swim. The Gay Liberation Front says I wouldn't get any support from *them*.... Gay newspaper says I'm an exhibitionist" (Johnston 1998, 31). The last count of the indictment, at least, seems justified, although *Gay*'s coverage of Johnston could also be attributed to their overall tendency to dismiss or belittle women's liberation and anyone associated with it.[4] *Gay*'s sexism aside, Johnston's performance at Town Hall in New York City in May 1971, a media circus staged as a confrontation between Norman Mailer and his feminist critics, could easily be put down as exhibitionist. Indeed, Johnston did not shy away from this characterization but saw her public buffoonery as classic *épater-le-bourgeois* theatrics meant to upset well-heeled supporters of fashionable radical causes. As far as she was concerned, her antics were also intended as a critical commentary on the event's premise—that "women's liberation is a debatable issue" (Johnston 1973, 17). She refused the terms of the debate and also its format when she rose from the conference table to join a couple of friends in sexual horseplay on stage.

But she did not repeat her performance or otherwise disrupt a local television talk show on which she and DOB president Ruth Simpson were scheduled to appear along with two conservative psychiatrists. Simpson and other members of her organization left in protest after attempting to oust the male guests and host, while Johnston stayed behind and attempted to contradict the doctors' ideas about sexual perversion (Johnston 1971a; "Lesbians Zap Bandy" 1971). And when she teamed up with author Germaine Greer, feminist media star of the moment and copanelist at Town Hall, on another TV talk show, Johnston was outspoken but not particularly raucous (Johnston 1971b). In a way, though, it didn't matter whether she played the game or not, whether she answered the interviewers questions or turned the tables on them. She was invited to participate in these discussions because of her notoriety for being colorful, which included being unbashful about her lesbianism, and if she lived up to her reputation the producers got what they were after. For Johnston, as well as other lesbians, a coherent, effective strategy for being taken seriously by the dominant media at this time was structurally impossible. As a result of these and similar skirmishes with the media, Johnston adopted an analysis similar to Shelley's and other movement critics of the time, even though she was vulnerable to the charge that her high visibility made her a collaborator with the enemy.[5]

Jill Johnston's clown persona may have allowed her to overcome the strictures that prevented the mass media from creating gay and lesbian liberation icons (n.b. there were no lesbians on covers of major national news magazines until 1993),[6] although it permitted them to dismiss this newly open and prideful lesbian as a kook. On occasion, a relatively conservative, not at all amusing gay spokesman like Dick Leitsch was quoted as a representative of the old-guard homophile activists in the Mattachine Society, and serious DOB officials like Ruth Simpson in New York or the group's founders Del Martin and Phyllis Lyon in San Francisco would be called upon for authoritative lesbian viewpoints. But none of these political leaders became as widely identified with the movement as did Johnston. Nowadays her or Millett's notoriety would be celebrated as a milestone in the contest for visibility. Then it was a millstone that each had to drag around from speaking engagement to speaking engagement on the lecture and talk show circuit that constituted movement stardom.

TALKING TRASH

Johnston and Millett may have been media stars, emblems of the women's and gay liberation movements that provoked major press coverage at the end of the sixties, but they were also objects of what became known as trashing by feminist and lesbian activists critical of celebrity. Johnston even engaged in a bit of this activity, accusing Millett of "posing as 'straight' for the media" prior to *Time*'s outing of the *Sexual Politics* author, although that didn't spare Johnston the same treatment when the media nominated her as the representative for lesbian liberation and she didn't decline.[7] In her case, the charge was that she was male-identified, because she boasted of her sexual exploits in print (Johnston 1973, 132–133), and elitist because, as she put it, "the entire dyke community from coast to coast was not invited" to a meeting she tried to organize on the intersecting interests of lesbians and feminists (Johnston 1974, 189). Similarly, Jo Freeman, a women's liberation activist based in Chicago, was shunned and surreptitiously denounced by supposed "sisters" in Chicago in the early seventies. Some years later she published an article in *Ms.*, using her movement *nom de guerre* Joreen, that analyzed trashing as an unacknowledged enforcement of traditional concepts of proper feminine behavior (Joreen 1976). In another article on the subject Freeman examined how the charge of elitism was used as a wrong-headed attempt to adhere to democratic ideals but led inevitably to covert power plays (Joreen [1972] 1973). When these bitter struggles over media representation were taking place, however, few were prepared to speak up or write publicly about this form of callous behavior because the tactic left them estranged from the movement they were accused of betraying.

Rita Mae Brown, who was willing to antagonize anyone, undertook a critique similar to Freeman's in an essay entitled "Leadership vs Stardom" (1972), written while she was a member of the Furies lesbian collective in Washington, D.C. But this didn't prevent her doing a bit of trashing of celebrity spokeswomen herself. In Brown's analysis, "The rule of thumb for stars is this: she gets money from the white, rich, male world.... [T]hese tokens will in no way change the structure of government nor of the economy" (Brown 1972, 20). Having taken swipes at sellouts, she did assert that attacks on stars from within the movement, although motivated by justifiable animosity, "play into the hands of the male supremacists who then use these attacks to illustrate the 'fact' that 'women hate each other and can't work together'" (ibid.). The more important point for Brown was that a star should not be mistaken for a leader, "a woman who comes from the ranks of the movement.... She is not receiving rewards from male supremacists to divert our movement" (ibid.). What worried her is that the trashing of stars had spread to the trashing of leaders, which threatened to destroy the movement by driving away the most dedicated and talented organizers and thinkers.

The implicit assumption of this argument is that leaders never become stars and vice versa. The two categories—which could be distinguished as (deserved) political reputation opposed to (arbitrary) entertainment celebrity—were deemed utterly incommensurate, although, as Brown herself demonstrated in her own career, the wall between the two could be and was breached within a decade and crumbled altogether within two. Perhaps because she proceeded from cultural notoriety to political activism, and not the other way round like Brown, Johnston remarked in her contribution to this debate—an essay irreverently titled "Delitism, Stardumb, and Leadershit"—that "a star is not necessarily *not* a leader and vice versa" (Johnston 1974, 193, emphasis added). Johnston wasn't putting herself forward as a candidate for leadership in the movement (although it's possible to read Brown's comments in this light) but seemed less willing to rebuke those who abjured all contact with the mainstream media.

Distrust of stars, and the media in general, may have been a hallmark of radical gay politics in the late 1960s and early 1970s, but that did not preclude dreams of recruiting closeted celebrities whose support would speed liberation—of all gay people, including the stars in question. The president of one of the first gay liberation groups in the country, Homosexuals Intransigent! (HI), a student organization founded at the City College of New York in April 1969, advocated just such a project in an issue of *Gay Power*, another alternative, "underground" paper. "Celebrities who are homosexual could do a lot to change public attitudes towards homosexuality," he wrote. "Any *one* celebrity publicly declaring himself [*sic*] homosexual would risk retaliation, but if dozens or hundreds of thousands of gay public figures declared themselves at the same time, their declaration would *force* the public to change its attitude toward homosexuality more than toward themselves" ("HI!" 1971). The plan was to draw up a list of famous gay people and write letters asking them to allow their names to be used in ads or, if they were uneasy about this option, to donate money that would be used to recruit others who might be bolder.

Needless to say, the proposal never got off the ground. What it does indicate, however, is that from the beginning coming out was the central tenet and strategy of gay and lesbian liberation politics. Given their apparent faith in the persuasive power of celebrity, it is curious that representatives of HI described the group as "leaderless," and the article cited above has no byline. The contradiction between engaging in fantasies about gaining support from rich, famous homosexuals and disavowing any differences in status among individual members indicates how the logic of visibility politics created blind spots in the radical gay movements as they grew and attracted supporters. But the main contradiction this produced emerged almost immediately, when gay and lesbian activists recognized and set out to exploit the political implications of coming out. Although the effects did not become manifest for some time, it is at precisely this juncture that lesbian celebrity and politics intersect.

THE PERSONALITY IS POLITICAL

Although much has changed in the decades since the concepts entailed in lesbian/gay liberation first took shape, the axiom that coming out is an essential requirement for viable lesbian or gay politics has not. Indeed, coming out quickly became the cornerstone around which the movement was built—its most important feature—and the closet its most influential metaphor, to the point that both terms have been applied in all types of contexts that have nothing to do with homosexuality.[8] Coming out also drew celebrities into the liberation project because of their emblematic significance within mainstream culture. The political valence of such notables shifted from their position as questionable agents of social conformity—since their silence served as a reminder that homosexuality was reprehensible—to potential role models if (but only if) they were willing to assert their homosexuality publicly. Coming out became the defining feature of the new politics of homosexuality, which logically generated and accelerated interest in lesbian and gay celebrities, both in the ranks of the liberation movement and in the culture at large.

A typical argument for coming out as a political strategy was made in the early days of gay liberation by New York GLF member Martha Shelley: "The worst part of being a homosexual is having to keep it *secret* ... the daily knowledge that what you are is something so awful that it cannot be revealed.... [T]he internal violence of being made to carry or choosing to carry the load of straight society's unconscious guilt—this is what tears us apart, what makes us want to stand up in the offices, the factories and the schools and shout our true identities" (Shelley 1970). Significantly, *Come Out* was the name of New York GLF's newspaper, first published in November 1969. Although the political implications of coming out seem to have been first publicized by local media produced in New York City, these ideas quickly proliferated around the country. For instance, Shelley's remarks on coming out appeared first in the East Village radical newspaper *Rat* and then in the *Detroit Gay Liberator*. The *Chicago Gay Liberation Newsletter* reproduced excerpts of a speech given by GLF founding member Michael Brown at the first New York City Gay Pride rally in June 1970: "[W]e'll never have the freedom and civil rights we deserve as human beings until we stop hiding in closets and in the shelter of anonymity. We have to come out into the open and stop being ashamed or else people will go on treating us as freaks" (Chicago Gay Liberation 1970, 1).

The implication of the rapid diffusion of these ideas is not that New York City was the source of all lesbian/gay liberation theory and propaganda during this era. In many respects the movement's dynamism as a national phenomenon can be attributed to conditions that were not specific to any particular locale. On the other hand, local formations were not uniform nor were there any national organizations that could claim to represent lesbians and gay men on a national level. For example, issues of the *Detroit Gay Liberator* offer evidence that the socialist contingent in GLF in that city was even stronger than in New York, which could be attributed to the history of working-class militancy in Detroit's auto industry. Likewise, the *Chicago Gay Liberation Newsletter* carried more and longer articles about racism within the movement than any of the New York gay liberation papers. However, a loose communications network existed among the various gay/lesbian groups and their constituents, who stayed in touch largely through the publications that circulated among them. Thus, reprinted remarks made by New York GLF members signaled that affiliated groups understood themselves as part of a national movement and generally endorsed the sentiment that coming out should be placed high on the gay liberation agenda.

The provocation to come out quickly enlisted supporters outside the active membership of gay liberation organizations as well. Inspired by the radicals in GLF and other lesbian/gay liberation groups, Johnston amplified previous references to herself as a lesbian she had made in print and alerted *Village Voice* readers that such deeds were political acts: "Gay people are now expecting and demanding the same sanctified regard for their sexual interests and unions as they have rendered for so long as they can remember to the weird forces that endowed them with life in the first place. Now there is *only one way* for this social change to take place. And that is for all gay people, those who know it and accept it, to stand up and speak for themselves" (Johnston

1998, 29; emphasis added). In her own coming out statement, Johnston encapsulated what became the prevailing wisdom among champions of gay and lesbian liberation: coming out will precipitate social recognition and respect, thus liberation.

As mentioned previously, GLF groups were modeled on the national liberation movements that sought freedom from colonial domination in the post–World War II period, armed conflicts that were still raging in areas of Asia and Africa at the end of the 1960s.[9] In this context, coming out was advocated as a means of declaring an oppositional identity as a member of the oppressed group, thereby taking the first step toward building a militant gay political movement. Although making a public declaration of one's homosexuality was less frequently mentioned as a method for achieving a sense of personal self-worth, this, too, was sometimes described as a side effect of collective organizing. Like the radical factions of the women's liberation movement of that period, GLF and affiliated groups advocated consciousness raising, which they believed linked self-awareness and self-respect to solidarity with others who shared one's social marginality. According to GLF's philosophy, the primary goal of the process was to understand how the oppression of lesbians and gay men was related to that directed at others on the left and to forge alliances with them on the basis of a common interest in overthrowing all systems of discrimination and exploitation.

From the start, though, gay liberation groups included activists who weren't interested in GLF's socialist and feminist theories but wanted to "obtain political power … by working within the present system rather than trying to destroy it" (Owles 1970). This was the rationale behind the formation of the reform-minded Gay Activist Alliance (GAA), created by disgruntled GLF members in late 1969. GAA and its supporters at *Gay* had no argument with capitalism and were not interested in making connections between social injustices like racism or sexism and the political-economic system. Nor did they want to participate in unstructured, leaderless groups, since they deemed these ineffective for planning and carrying out political lobbying, legal challenges, or fund-raising activities. For adherents of this position coming out was the *primary* organizing principle of their political program, because, as the group's first president stated, they believed, "Before a gay is willing to fight for anything he [sic] has to be aware of his own repression" (ibid.). However, this dispute was not confined to differences in political ideology between the rival organizations, since a number of GLF members endorsed the idea that a vibrant, open homosexual counterculture, not political revolution, should be the movement's top priority. Coming out figured prominently in strategies for realizing such a community. And the same split between political and cultural activists could be found in the ranks of GAA (Jay 1999, 89; Marotta 1981).

For a fleeting moment, the political/cultural split within the movement placed differing emphases on the interpretation of coming out. In early 1970, *Gay* published a letter in its advice column that epitomized the disagreement:

Q. I am a lesbian belonging to the *Gay Liberation Front*. We have had some internal dissension over a question of priorities. Which is more important, do you think, political liberation or mental liberation?

A. Liberation of the head, of course…. If we do not *feel* free inside, where we *really live* most intensely, we are not free anywhere. (Kaiso 1970)

The schism between gay liberals and revolutionaries, as well as between political versus cultural interests, in New York City was replicated in cities around the country. Around the same time many lesbians deserted both camps to form separate, often separatist, lesbian-feminist groups. Within three years, champions of a unified, revolutionary gay and lesbian politics with ties to other liberation movements had retreated and their organizations had all but disbanded, while the ascendant liberals transformed the gay movement into a campaign for civil rights, in contrast to the sweeping social transformations the radicals had envisioned.[10]

In the process of this political displacement, an emphasis on *individual* self-knowledge and well-being became the predominant rationale for coming out, compared to the *collective* goal of organizing a substantial oppositional movement informed by revolutionary consciousness. This is often interpreted as fallout from the implosion of left radicalism in the United States, due to disillusionment with the ultramilitant rhetoric and violent methods championed (and actualized in rare instances) by frustrated revolutionaries, coupled with important political victories for the right in the national political arena (Nixon's election as president in 1968, for starters). This is the commonsense explanation of the disintegration of many radical left political organizations that occurred in the mid-1970s. Yet, gay politics and culture indicate that there is a more compelling argument that accounts for the success of what were considered reformist strategies for achieving liberation. The connecting link is the practical production of new kinds of gay and lesbian identities after 1968, which rendered coming out the most potent weapon in the liberation arsenal.[11]

Although the conflicts that erupted in GLF were real and often bitterly fought, in several important respects the cultural/political, liberal/radical factions did not differ significantly. Indeed, many defining elements of the branches of the reform movement that succeeded that contentious period were informed by theoretical and strategic approaches advocated by the revolutionary faction. And these, in turn, were linked to broader developments in social practices and technologies having to do with permutations in definitions of personhood, what Nikolas Rose describes as "identity projects" (N. Rose 1998, 157).[12] The term "technology" is also borrowed from Rose, who elaborates concepts introduced by Michel Foucault in order to analyze the historically contingent production of particular kinds of persons and notions of selves. Technologies in this sense are not physical instruments or institutional systems but practical and technical methods for administrating populations and individual subjects. Rose explains, "Technologies of the self take the form of elaboration of certain techniques for the conduct of one's relation with oneself, for example requiring one to relate to oneself epistemologically (know yourself), despotically (master yourself), or in other ways (care for yourself)" (N. Rose 1998, 29). Coming out is such a technology.

UNLIKELY BEDFELLOWS

Advocates of gay and lesbian liberation or, later, gay/lesbian civil rights conceived coming out as a means to counteract social conformity and complacency in matters related to sexuality and gender. Where the public was concerned, coming out was intended to precipitate two effects: (1) exposure of homosexuality as a trait of seemingly "normal" individuals, which would unsettle assumptions about definitions of normalcy, and (2) demonstration of prideful gay and lesbian identities. Having been pigeonholed for the better part of a century throughout the West as both unfortunate and dangerous aberrant creatures, anyone who thought of her- or himself as a homosexual person (not everyone who engaged in homosexual practices did, or does) was encouraged to take part in overthrowing the various mechanisms that guaranteed the odium meted out to homosexuality and homosexuals. Thus, rationales for coming out frequently invoked socialization and social roles, usually gender roles, to explain how homosexuality has been defined as deviance and how it might be reformulated as a positive identity.

Consider, for instance, how GLFers Allan Warshawsky and Ellen Bedoz introduced the problem in *Come Out*: "We are all the products of an oppressive society.... The institution of the nuclear family socializes us to meet the inhuman needs of the system. It defines our roles and pressures its members into fulfilling them. These roles no longer serve the needs of the individual" (Warshawsky and Bedoz 1970). "The Woman Identified Woman" manifesto issued by Radicalesbians, a New York group made up of dissident members of both women's and gay liberation organizations (including Martha Shelley and Rita Mae Brown), struck a similar note and described how socialization and roles affect lesbians in particular:

> [A lesbian] may not be fully conscious of the political implications of what for her began as personal necessity, but on some level she has not been able to accept the limitations and oppression laid on her by the most basic role in her society—the female role.... To the extent that she cannot expel the heavy socialization that goes with being female, she can never truly find peace with herself. For she is caught somewhere between accepting society's view of her—in which case she cannot accept herself—and coming to understand what this sexist society has done to her and why it is functional and necessary for it to do so. (Radicalesbians [1970] 1973, 240–241)

In the latter call to arms, attention shifts from statements about how social forces conspire to impose normative heterosexuality to explanations of why individual opposition to these processes promises social and political liberation.

Yet, despite their interest in revolutionizing family structures and sexual-gender norms, advocates of gay and lesbian liberation frequently employed the terminology and concepts used by adherents of the dominant social theory at the time, structural-functionalism, which proceeds from the premise that societies are integrated systems that tend inherently toward equilibrium, with internal mechanisms that contain any disruptive elements. The primary architect of this influential branch of American sociology was Talcott Parsons. His book *Family, Socialization, and the Interaction Process* (1955), coauthored with Robert Bales, is the classic structural-functionalist treatise on the relationship between family structures and socialization, defined as the process of internalization of norms and values that produces individuals who perform given social roles. According to Parsons, the family in modern societies serves the function of ensuring the differentiation of gender roles. Although not inborn, these roles are nonetheless natural, because they are products of the public-private dichotomy in social life, which Parsons sees as evidence of objective increases in social differentiation and complexity. In Parsons's words, this is a "positive 'progressive' development" (Parsons and Bales 1955, 51). Thus, sexual and gender norms are socially necessary. For instance, Parsons avers that "the prohibition of homosexuality has the function of reinforcing the differentiation of sex roles" (103), which is precisely the dynamic lesbian and gay critics aimed to dismantle.

Although they clearly did not endorse Parsons's belief that the taboo against homosexuality was socially "progressive" or similar structural-functionalist justifications for bigotry, the arguments made by

Warshawsky, Bedoz, Radicalesbians, and various like-minded analysts of homosexuality were informed by functionalist reasoning. In other words, they accepted the basic tenets of functionalist theory, which treats social phenomena in terms of each one's contribution to overall social stability (e.g., definitions of crime function as demarcations that limit collectively approved behavior). Rather than challenging the basic premise of functionalist theory, that social structures require and ensure consensus, these lesbian and gay theorists advocated establishing a different consensus. They hoped that exposing the operations of this system would spur proliberation forces to counteract its effects and pave the road to a new set of cultural norms.

Take, for example, socialization, perhaps the most significant concept appropriated by gay liberation from this strain of social theory (although this term has come to dominate the vocabulary used to talk about the relationship between individuals and social structures to such an extent that its theoretical lineage has become obscure). Socialization is at heart a theory of social reproduction. It explains how individual participants in the social world—that is, everyone—are integrated into it and therefore guarantee its continuity. The theory of socialization depends on the bedrock assumption that most humans will adapt to the world as given to them because they will be rewarded for doing so; social norms are learned by means of an overlapping system of frustrations and gratifications (Parsons and Olds 1955, 193). Briefly stated, this integration is achieved through the internalization of norms, which begins at birth for every individual within the family circle. The theory of socialization is antithetical to disorder or antagonism, other than as instances of pathology, and neglects questions of power. In theory, socialization produces individual selves that mesh neatly with the requirements of an orderly society.

Closely related to socialization is the concept of social roles, the positions individuals occupy within the social order. Structural-functionalism employs the concept of roles to explain the allocation and performance of the diverse individual undertakings that constitute the social system, and sex roles provide an all-purpose shorthand for how gender identity is taken up and lived. Similarly, the concept of sex roles provided the theoretical framework used within both the women's and gay liberation movements to explain conventional gender and sexual behavior and attitudes. However, sex role theory, like socialization, supports an integration-oriented functionalism that promulgates normative ideals about social relations and structures. Moreover, the most influential theoretical support for sex roles is that provided by Parsons's writings on the nuclear family. In this context, roles divide responsibilities and personalities found within that institution into two categories: "instrumental" and "expressive." Each of these complementary attributes conforms to a gender role, with the husband-father characterized by the former and the wife-mother by the latter (Parsons and Bales 1955, 22). Once again, a normative imperative is engraved indelibly on the theoretical model.

Curiously, the role paradigm, which emerged in the 1930s and flourished in the 1950s and 1960s, had been roundly criticized and largely rejected by social theorists as early as the mid-sixties. But, as R. W. Connell notes, the concept of sex (or gender) roles survives in sociology and social psychology textbooks, and continues to inform applications of those discourses in myriad practical settings: education, corporate and industrial management, and social work, as well as popular social commentaries produced by news and entertainment media. Connell's explanation for why role theory was widely embraced in the first place and has remained prevalent is that it "attempted to show the functional necessity (for social survival) of role performance." It was, he writes, "the classic illustration of social determinism" that offered a scientific rationale for social hierarchies (Connell 1979, 11), "a theoretical ideology developed to cope with the stresses in the cultural order *created* by movements of resistance," including political activism in favor of sexual liberation (14). To quote Connell again, "Role theory plainly appeals to those who like to think that the social order works by mutual agreement; that people ought to do what they are told; and there is something wrong with those who don't.... This association of role theory with concepts of 'deviance' and programmes of therapy is thus not accidental at all" (15).[13]

Conflict presents a dilemma for role theory, as it does for socialization, since the model presumes an efficient, integrated, self-regulating social system. In other words, a functionalist approach assumes that conformity and consensus are essential, intrinsic features of social life. Roles are not freely chosen nor subject to idiosyncratic manipulation. They merely define the various interrelated positions that individuals occupy within the social system. Proponents of role theory believe that its scientific basis can be substantiated further by the statistical methods used to ascertain role definitions, so that what most people do and believe becomes synonymous with objective imperatives of the social system. Harnessed to the apparently scientific truth provided by statistical evidence, roles take on an objective, coercive quality, even when contradictory roles and role performances are acknowledged. This entire theoretical edifice consists of a grand tautological argument for adaptation to social norms.

Again, I don't want to imply that lesbian and gay liberation activist-authors, along with other members of the gay liberation movement, endorsed the conservative positions held by structural-functionalists like Parsons. Quite obviously, they did not. They hoped to create new models of sexuality and gender, doing away with oppressive concepts of normalcy. They adamantly opposed the roles and processes of socialization that were said to inculcate these, as well as the structures of domination that rely upon the inferior status of femininity and homosexuality. Some advocated destroying the entire system, doing away with all roles, all authority. The antidote to oppression they recommended was the demolition of the structures that secure social domination and control. For example, the Radicalesbians imagined eliminating categories of sexuality (but not gender), entirely: "In a society where men do not oppress women, and sexual expression is allowed to follow feelings, the categories of homosexuality and heterosexuality would disappear" (Radicalesbians [1970] 1973, 241).

I doubt that very many, if any, of the movements' polemicists had studied Parsons's or others' structural-functionalist texts firsthand. If they had, they might have been less inclined to reiterate the key words used in this discourse: socialization, sex roles, et cetera. It is more likely that they picked up the basic structural-functionalist idiom and ways of thinking about social processes by virtue of the theory's translation into nonacademic descriptions of social life (think, for instance, of the everyday use of the word dysfunctional, another borrowing from the structural-functionalist lexicon). Moreover, the normative dimension of structural-functionalism gave its descriptions of social phenomena the authority of realism, so that sex roles, say, were understood as empirical forms of acting and thinking imposed by an impersonal, objective culture.

It's important to recall, one more time, that constructing a critique of gender and sexuality without these dominant concepts would have been quite difficult, since popular as well as academic discourse concerned with sexuality and gender was so thoroughly saturated with structural-functionalist assumptions about how social life is organized and how people operate within it. That doesn't mean, however, that the effects of hewing to this theoretical legacy are inconsequential. By reiterating the interpretation of Parsons's theory of social organization and operation, the gay and women's liberation movements endorsed unwittingly a conceptual framework that posits norms and consensus as essential features of social order. If this order is not thoroughly obliterated, if the revolution doesn't occur, the social system established and supported by functional imperatives will remain firmly in place. The ideal of liberation around which resistance was to be rallied demanded a romantic belief in the elementary antagonism between individual fulfillment and social constraint, or a variation on Freud's thesis about civilization's discontents. But those who took up such arguments—reformers along with revolutionaries—also borrowed from the despised discourse of social control—allying themselves with theories that assumed the calculability of all human actions, which if adequately analyzed and rationally criticized can be reengineered.

The gay and women's liberation projects preserved vestiges of structural-functionalism at the core of their critique and retained these in various practices intended to develop it further. Two widely embraced attempts to rationalize structural solutions to sexism and heterosexism were: consciousness-raising groups, which consisted of rule-governed and highly controlled discussions about shared personal experiences intended to reveal the larger political hierarchies and constraints underlying them; and separatist collectives founded by lesbians in order to devise mechanisms that would foster new forms of subjectivity, as well provide incubators for vanguard revolutionary activities. Not even the dissolution of many of these groups and disillusionment of many of their participants would undermine the powerful currents of functionalist thinking, which survive in various concepts bandied about in lesbian political analysis to this day.

One is the idea of role models, which is so frequently invoked that the roles to be modeled seem to be objectively determined. Another is the belief in and reliance on quantitative data, usually the results of opinion surveys, used by lesbian and gay journalists and policy analysts to plot political progress (or regress), and by lesbian and gay political organizations to set agendas and formulate strategies. This is the distinctively twentieth-century form of objective knowledge about social phenomena, which, as Rose observes, "takes a very material form—diagrams, graphs, tables, charts, numbers—[and] which materializes human qualities in forms amenable to normalization and calculation" (N. Rose 1998, 120).[14] A related development is the technical interpretation of and justification for coming out: an increase in the number of self-declared lesbian and gay men will strengthen advocates' claims for greater recognition and less discrimination, based on irrefutable measures of scientific fact. But perhaps what this almost casual citation of a dubious theoretical paradigm bespeaks most of all is social science's authority in shaping commonsense beliefs concerning social reality.

Proponents of gay and women's liberation may have taken what Parsons and others had to say about socialization and sex roles at face value, but that didn't mean that they were willing to become compliant social subjects. It isn't surprising, then, to find the authority of social scientists responsible for promoting functionalist explanations of social behavior endorsed implicitly by Warshawsky and Bedoz in one paragraph of their *Come Out* article—"The institution of the nuclear family socializes us to meet the inhuman needs of the system. It defines our roles and pressures its members into fulfilling them"—and vigorously challenged in the next:

Divergence is labelled "sick", "deviate", "unhealthy", "abnormal" by the establishment's social scientists who function as the system's official agents of guilt and shame. They establish arbitrary norms so that those who differ can be made to feel "abnormal"....

Thus the pressure for "deviates" to camoflage [sic] their differences to avoid scorn: the Black passing as white, the clean shaven Jew ... , the homosexual who leads a double life. These people have sacrificed their selfhood for the safety of acceptance. They have victimized themselves. (Warshawsky and Bedoz 1970)

This is where the activists outline their oppositional stance regarding prevailing approaches to "social problems," one critical of the structural-functional maxim that defines deviance as evidence of defective socialization, which the social system will necessarily correct, or as role conflict that may trouble an individual but not affect the social order. Either account provides support for the diagnosis of homosexuality as a psychological disorder—embodied by a dysfunctional kind of person. Of course, it was this psychiatric definition of homosexuality that gay liberation was most intent on dismantling, and which coming out was intended to vanquish. However, by hewing to structural-functionalist paradigms, activists and theorists of the gay and women's liberation movements lay the groundwork for the ambivalence about celebrity that can be found in lesbian and gay contexts to this day—proud embrace of those the mainstream media treats as movement representatives on one hand and disdain for or ridicule of media stars on the other.

EXPERT TESTIMONY

Numerous historians contend, with ample archival support, that medicalization superseded morality as the primary mode of the social regulation of sexuality over the course of the twentieth century (Davidson 1987; Foucault 1978). By the 1960s, the understanding of homosexuality as a matter best handled by medical professionals had become ubiquitous, and various psychological therapies were applied in attempts to control, if not "cure," those who were diagnosed as homosexual. One remedy regarded as promising in the sixties was a type of behavior modification called aversion therapy. A patient would be given an injection of apomorphine, which produced nausea while he (less frequently she) was shown images of individuals of the same sex. Or the patient received a jolt of electricity after reading a series of descriptions of homosexual behavior, followed by reading passages describing heterosexual behavior without any shock (Nathaniel McConaghy, quoted in Alinder [1970] 1992, 143). In effect, the doctors who practiced this therapy hoped to reconfigure what they understood to be a neurological stimulus-response mechanism.

More conservative—and more common—treatments were various talking cures, which may have been more insidious than the overt cruelty of electroshock or injections of noxious chemicals because the patient was expected to assume responsibility for failure if homosexual desires could not be eradicated. In all but a very few instances they could not. Feelings of guilt and shame were oft-cited consequences of such ordeals. While it is quite likely that many gay men and lesbians may not have believed that they suffered from mental illness, the heterosexual imperative was so rigorously enforced through a variety of cultural and legal mechanisms that self-perceptions became moot. Personal narratives from the preliberation era in twentieth-century North America and Europe are riddled with accounts of gay men and lesbians seeking professional help to rid themselves of homosexual desires and of minors whose parents imposed psychiatric treatment upon them.[15]

Homosexuality, it can be said, was (and in some places, still is) a disqualified identity, at the same time that it was an illicit practice. This was addressed cryptically in the founding principles and purposes of GLF, which asserted, "We are going to be who we are" (*Come Out* 1970, 2). While indicating the importance of self-definition to the movement, strategists never questioned accepted concepts of what a *self* is, assuming that it is (we are) unified, governed by self-awareness, author of its (our) own desires and actions. Instead of encouraging debate about such fundamental notions of the self, they concentrated on redefining homosexuality as a *valid* category of personhood. To accomplish this, the enemy was identified—psychologists, psychiatrists, and the media that popularized their ideas—and scientific expertise on homosexuality was forcefully challenged.

One of the most dramatic actions taken by gay liberation activists was an invasion of the annual meeting of the American Psychiatric Association (APA) in 1970 (Alinder [1970] 1992). The intruders declared solidarity with the antipsychiatry movement spearheaded by former patients in mental hospitals and inspired by the writings of radical psychiatrists like the Marxist–humanist David Cooper (1967; 1968) and R. D. Laing (1967), whose approach was based on phenomenology. Jill Johnston, for one, applauded this development, which she predicted would result in a "comprehensive political-psychological theory and counter consciousness that will be a more effective subversive deviation from the patriarchal authoritative hierarchical law enforcement reality oriented materialistic sexually repressive fucked up culture in which we live" (Johnston 1974, 256). In the short term, this promise was actualized, since challenges to the psychiatric profession provided gay liberation with one of its first victories: in 1973 the APA agreed to remove homosexuality from its list of approved diagnoses in the *Diagnostic and Statistical Manual*. And in 1980, gay activists and sympathetic professionals defeated an attempt to reintroduce a comparable diagnostic category.

Therapists began to advertise their acceptance of homosexuality almost as soon as the movement was launched, and a number of lesbians and gay men established professional practices geared specifically to helping others regard their homosexuality in a positive light. The gay press ran columns dealing with psychological issues. For example, *Gay* regularly published commentary and advice by psychologist Dr. Stephen Kaiso under the heading "The Well of Possibility," signaling the movement's rejection of Radclyffe Hall's conclusion that loneliness is the inevitable consequence of homosexuality. In addition, many of the activities sponsored by the newly constituted lesbian and gay organizations—the recitation of individual coming out stories in writings by members of the movement, and in less formal settings, as well as cultural events intended to instill pride in lesbian/gay identity and camaraderie—can be understood as therapeutic. Talk shows and magazine articles offered opportunities for lesbian and gay liberationists to confront their psychiatric foes in public forums, since mental health was the preferred frame for media coverage of homosexuality, even after gay liberation proclaimed the rejection of medical expertise.[16]

Retrospective accounts of gay liberation have described the first organizations as riddled by divisions. Histories of the movement recall how lines were drawn and positions staked out that pitted politics against culture, street demonstrations and militant confrontations against social companionship and pleasure—dancing and psychedelic drugs being two of the favorite diversions offered, in addition to opportunities for sex, at GLF social events—and political revolution against tolerance of gay and lesbian lifestyles (Jay 1999; Marotta 1981).[17] But, from the start, the political rationale for coming out entailed cultural justifications, and both promised to promote personal well-being, conceived as self-awareness and self-expression. The Radicalesbians summed up the goal as "realness, feel[ing] at last that we are coinciding with ourselves," leading to "a revolution to end the imposition of all coercive identifications, and to achieve maximum autonomy in human expression" (Radicalesbians [1970] 1973, 245). The slogan "gay is good," echoed the Black Pride movement's "black is beautiful." And Warshawsky and Bedoz underlined the political effects that would follow: "We will no longer mutilate our true self-potential in an attempt to measure up to false 'norms'. In liberating ourselves from our shame we make our first attack upon the system" (Warshawsky and Bedoz 1970). It doesn't seem an exaggeration to say that the new gay politics and the cultural counterpart made self-esteem a first principle.

Paradoxically, this kind of rhetoric connects the objectives of gay liberation with what Foucault designated "governmentality" or "mentalities of government," which characterize liberal modernity (Burchell, Gordon, and Miller 1991; Foucault 1994). In his elaboration of this concept, Rose points out that governmentality does not refer to state power alone but can be applied to any ethical system that seeks to "act upon the lives of each and all in order to avert evils and achieve such desirable states as health, happiness, wealth, and tranquillity" (N. Rose 1998, 152). Although we may be inclined to interpret any notion of liberation as inherently opposed to the coercive practices of government, Foucault and Rose argue that the kind of subjectivity characteristic of modern Western democracies—the autonomous self—is itself an exercise of disciplinary authority that places ever more responsibility on individuals to monitor and regulate their own deeds and beliefs, to know and improve themselves, to become self-governing. How is this achieved? Major resources for governmentality are what Rose refers to as the "psy" disciplines and technologies—psychology, psychiatry, psychotherapy, psychoanalysis, "through which self-governing capabilities can be installed in free individuals in order to bring their own ways of conducting and evaluating themselves into alignment with political objectives" (155).

The gay liberation movement attracted notice for its scandalous impulses and intentions, with provocateurs like Shelley throwing down the gauntlet to straight folks with such statements as "We want to reach the homosexual entombed in you, to liberate our brothers and sisters, locked in the prisons of your skulls" (Shelley [1970] 1992). In settling on strategies that emphasized psychological factors, though, movement strategists were mainly concerned with shifting the realm of expertise from accredited professionals to individuals. In Rose's analysis this is characteristic of modern subjectivity in general: "[E]ach of us has *become* a psychologist, incorporating its vocabulary into our way of speaking, its gaze into our ways of looking, its judgments into our calculations and decisions" (N. Rose 1998, 123). Likewise, the significance of coming out, routinely explained as an individually accomplished antidote for internalized guilt, fear, shame, and the lack of integrated sense of self, situates this practice as a "therapeutic technology of the self," which involves techniques for cultivating self-respect and developing a suitable identity narrative (195).

Self-image assumes an central position in such projects. The very first issue of *Come Out* featured a piece entitled "A Positive Image for the Homosexual." Written by psychologist Leo Louis Martello, who became a regular contributor to the paper, the article offers a vision of gay liberation that reflects concerns about its symbolic representation: "Homosexuality is not a problem in itself. The problem is society's attitude toward it. Since the majority condemns homosexuality, the homosexual minority has passively accepted this contemptuous view of itself.... The greatest battle of the homosexual in an oppressive society is with himself [sic], more precisely the *image* of himself as forced upon him by non-homosexuals" (Martello 1969).

Thus, the demand that media institutions replace negative stereotypes with positive images emerged as a central feature of lesbian and gay liberation politics early on. The importance accorded positive images stems from their presumed truthfulness, as opposed to the pathological depictions of lesbians and gay men the liberation (later, civil rights) movement deemed malicious falsehoods. The first candidates for exemplary standard-bearers might include such bohemian, countercultural icons as Johnston, but once the heyday of confrontational liberation politics had passed—by the mid-1970s—the ideal positive image took on a more respectable cast. And the argument for such images became more specific: wide publication and broadcasting of positive images would render homosexuality socially legitimate.

Underlying both approaches, though, a more important kind of realism was at stake: all famous lesbians and gay men were called upon to endorse the truth of self-knowledge attained through coming out and crafting a self-image that reflects pride and self-possession. These positive images were defined as realistic representations of self-affirming lesbians and gay men, who then provide role models worthy of emulation by the next generation. Once again, however, the influence of functionalist paradigms of socialization and roles can be detected in the efficacy accorded positive images, as well as the related idea of role models. What, exactly, is modeled as the result of exposure to an image (visual or linguistic) of a self-proclaimed lesbian? Is it simply that the role model is not closeted, and therefore not ashamed of her lesbianism? Is that a role? What possible function could such a role serve? An obvious place to look for an answer might be Mary MacIntosh's article "The Homosexual Role" (1968), which explains how this deviant role enforces hetero-masculine norms and is not a social position accepted by all, or even most men who actually engage in homosexual practices. MacIntosh criticizes the normative function of the disreputable and marginal role she describes, confirming the connection between role theory and functionalist ways of thinking. In contrast, subsequent discussions about role models and positive images have overlooked the linkage between these concepts and their conservative sources, and are thus limited to attempts to pour new homosexual wine into old structural-functionalist bottles.

Another, more productive way to think about this question is to consider the pressures brought to bear on social norms, for instance by women who do not conform to feminine standards. Add to that the emergence in the nineteenth century of what Ian Hacking calls "a particular medico-forensic-political language of individual and social control," which employed the newly developed scientific technique of statistical analysis to define forms of deviance and rendered norms meaningful (Hacking 1986, 226). In this environment, a new kind of person, a new social identity was minted, the lesbian. Now, the process of making up people that Hacking describes is dynamic, neither wholly the contrivance of forces of social control nor an innovation by nonconformists. Instead, both interact and react in the process of producing the definition of a lesbian person. This approach allows for improvisations for which the static and determinist logic of role theory cannot account.

Commenting on how the generation of new kinds of people affects individuals, Hacking remarks, "Who we are is not only what we did, do, and will do but also what we might have done and may do. Making up people changes the space of possibilities for personhood" (229). For instance, at the beginning of the twenty-first century we can define ourselves as transgendered, transsexual, lesbian, female homosexual, bisexual, heterosexual, or any combination of these. And we do not require a medical expert to verify the definitions. A self-determined categorization carries sufficient authority. But, in spite of these proliferating options, Hacking reminds us, "our possibilities, although inexhaustible, are also bounded" (ibid.), bounded, first of all, by prevailing concepts of how subjectivity can be achieved and lived, how person-hood is constituted.

By the end of the 1960s, lesbians, along with gay men, created a political movement that promised to remove all barriers that cordoned them off from participation in social institutions. Talk of liberation was not just a rhetorical gesture; activists of this period were committed to the ideal of freedom and their ability to realize it. But one of the most formidable boundaries they didn't take into account was precisely that imposed by notions of personal freedom, which were then and remain central to the concept and practice of coming out. Intended as a technique for achieving personal liberation through collective identification, coming out became contingent upon and supported by a paradigm of subjectivity—self-knowledgeable and self-assured—that emphasizes "mental health" above all. The privileging of coming out suggested that political solidarity with other lesbians can only be attained by ridding oneself of any trace of self-loathing, which is assumed to be characteristic of the condition of being a lesbian in the first place.

The type of lesbian person who would be produced through a combination of self-examination and self-approbation was seen as the antidote to the despised and therefore depressed, self-hating lesbian described by definitions of homosexual pathology. The vocabulary and techniques of psychological diagnoses and treatment could be used to convince the leery that release from self-contempt is worth the risk of being regarded as deviant. Moreover, coming out has been undertaken not only as a project of self-validation but also self-fashioning. Rose describes this process as becoming an entrepreneur of the self, "seeking to maximize its own powers, its own happiness, its own quality of life, though enhancing its autonomy and then instrumentalizing its autonomous choices in the service of its life-style" (N. Rose 1998, 158). It wasn't that lesbians were supposed to become "normal," co-opted by the culture that had disparaged them, but the gay and women's movements crafted an approach to lesbian identity that can be interpreted as the fullest, most ambitious realization of this entrepreneurial character.

However, the idea of lesbian identity itself has produced a welter of theoretical challenges from feminist and gay thinkers, who point out the problems that accompany any fixed notion of this kind of person. As Judith Butler, one of the most thoughtful and provocative among such theorists, asks, "If to be a lesbian is an act, a leave-taking of heterosexuality, a self-naming that contests the compulsory meanings of heterosexuality's women and men, what is to keep the name of lesbian from becoming an equally compulsory category? What qualifies as a lesbian? Does anyone know?" (Butler 1990, 127). The category may not be clear-cut, and attempts to give it definitive meaning have produced as much political rancor as unity. Yet, the dilemmas created by the notion of lesbian identity have been taken beyond the subcultural level, to the pages of large circulation print and broadcast media, occasioned by the trickle-up effect of coming out. The logic of coming out, which rests on the belief that sexuality is a basic—perhaps *the* basic—dimension of subjectivity, combined with an entrepreneurial concept of individual existence, made lesbian celebrity feasible.

INDIVIDUAL INITIATIVE

What lesbian celebrity would become, or that such personages were possible in the first place, was anticipated in the career of one veteran of the militant lesbian liberation movement I have mentioned several times—a prime mover in the Lavender Menace action and coauthor of the clarion call for radical lesbian revolution,

"The Woman-Identified Woman"—as well as one of the vociferous critics of celebrity in its ranks: Rita Mae Brown. By the end of the 1970s, Brown had moved from the underground success of her first novel, *Rubyfruit Jungle* ([1973] 1977), issued by the small feminist press Daughters Inc., into the world of major publishing houses, mainstream publicity, and widespread notoriety. Never shy, Brown encouraged her racy reputation by identifying herself as the model for *Rubyfruit* bad-girl, hot-lesbian protagonist Molly Bolt. Although it seems accurate to say that her subcultural reputation acted as a springboard to the larger public stage, this move was not generally duplicated by many of her contemporaries from the lesbian liberation days.[18] Nor could Brown's celebrity have been predicted by her political history or the writings she produced as a movement firebrand: essays that castigated respectable, middle-class feminists (1976) and a collection of poems with the incendiary title *The Hand That Cradles the Rock* (1971). In 1972, she had proclaimed in print that "star rip-offs must be stopped." By 1978, she and her supporters were knocking on the doors of Hollywood studios with hopes of bringing *Rubyfruit* to the big screen, presumably with a star or starlet playing the leading character based on Brown herself (Rubyfruit Jungle Productions n.d.).[19] And by 1980, her status as a famous lesbian, in the United States anyway, focused the attention of the tabloid press and their paparazzi stringers on the lesbian sexuality of a rising star in another cultural arena: tennis player Martina Navratilova.

Despite the fact that the affair between Brown and Navratilova was made public when they were spotted together at the Wimbledon tournament and photographed by reporters from British tabloids, then made the object of much broader publicity that reached readers around the world, this liaison did not manage to render Navratilova a lesbian celebrity—yet. Eventually, she became the most famous lesbian in the world, a prototype of lesbian celebrity.

As a conclusion to this one, suffice it to say that radical lesbians may have railed against stars, but eventually celebrity culture caught up with the movement. Or, it could be said, the movement's politics of coming out converged with cultural definitions of celebrity. None of this occurred overnight but over several decades, nor has it proceeded without dispute—legal, political, cultural. But the seeds of this development were sown in the initial formulations of what liberation would mean.

NOTES

1. For gay men, media celebrity seemed less dangerous for those singled out, perhaps because public lesbians were often associated with the women's movement and feminist issues, which attracted much more press attention than gay and lesbian political organizing and action in the late 1960s. At times, however, condemnations of gay male activists who were featured in media reports could be just as nasty.

2. The epithet "pig," frequently used in the writings of radicals in this period, was borrowed from the Black Panther Party. For a discussion of this influence, see D'Emilio (1992, xxxv).

3. For a description of the entire sequence of events, see Abbott and Love ([1972] 1985, 119–125).

4. In support of this assessment, I offer the evidence of *Gay*'s routine neglect of feminist activities and viewpoints, save a regular column by pseudonymous lesbian Lily Hansen (Lilli Vincenz), who wrote almost entirely about her personal life (family, girlfriend, dog). The only exception to such gestures toward lesbian inclusion were *Gay*'s infrequent profiles of lesbians who became famous long ago and were either dead (Radclyffe Hall) or living in obscurity (Djuna Barnes). Pieces by men in *Gay* often

evaluated their female peers in terms of their attractiveness and were disdainful of any who were old, overweight, unfashionably dressed, or otherwise not glamorous. It's not too difficult to figure out why lesbians deserted the gay movement to form separate organizations. In one issue (March 1, 1970), they illustrated the token lesbian column with a soft-porn type image of a naked woman, which prompted a public protest by Martha Shelley at a panel on gay liberation and the media. For *Gay's* rebuttal to Shelley see Ogren (1971), which avers that women's liberation and gay liberation share no common ground. In another issue of *Gay*, art critic Gregory Battcock (1970) expressed support for the Panthers, the anti–Vietnam War movement, and opposition to police harassment while refusing expressly to support women's liberation. The pattern continues in Sorel David's lukewarm review of Johnston's first book, *Marmalade Me* (1971), a selection of her dance and art criticism from the *Village Voice*, where the critic states, "I used to like Jill Johnston, but that was before she became a professional lesbian." *Gay's* disinterest in lesbian issues can be contrasted with coverage in *Come Out*, the publication of New York GLF. Significantly, *Gay* was affiliated with the Gay Activist Alliance, formed by (mostly male) members of GLF who objected to the original group's gestures of solidarity with the Black Panthers and its sympathy with and support for women's liberation.

5. Johnston's views on this topic can be found in the two *Voice* articles cited previously (1971a and 1971b), as well as in *Lesbian Nation* (1973). One difference between her position and Shelley's was that she didn't condemn other feminists who were singled out for media attention. In addition, her first two books were published by established presses like Dutton (*Marmalade Me*) and Simon and Schuster (*Lesbian Nation*), which was unacceptable for the strictest adherents of the radical (lesbian) feminist code of conduct in relation to the media.

6. The cover story on Martina Navratilova in the June 30, 1982 issue of *Newsweek* does not contradict this observation, since it appeared during the period when she vociferously denied that she was a lesbian. (See chapter 6.)

7. See, for example, two articles on gay liberation that appeared in mass circulation magazines in 1971, both of which included photographs of Johnston: "The Militant Homosexual" (1971) in *Newsweek*, and "Homosexuals in Revolt: The Year that One Liberation Movement Turned Militant" (1971) in *Life*. In the former, Johnston is the only woman depicted, and she is one of three lesbians who appeared in the eight heavily illustrated *Life* magazine pages devoted to the new gay movement.

8. During the past decade or so, "coming out" and "the closet" have become generalized metaphors applicable to an increasingly broad range of situations and people. Nowadays, one can "come out" as a previously "closeted" wife beater, depressed person, National Rifle Association supporter, you name it. But, I would argue, associations with being closeted and coming out as a homosexual remain embedded in these expressions.

9. From the outlook of 2003, when "rights" is the word generally associated with gay/lesbian politics, the assumption is that this movement arose out of African-American struggles for civil rights and related campaigns for social justice. Such precedents are not irrelevant, but the first gay liberation groups self-consciously aligned themselves with socialist revolutionaries in the Third World and more militant supporters of the Black Power movement in the U.S., who believed that equality and justice would result only after the edifice of capitalist imperialism was demolished. This perspective

can be gleaned from the numerous writings from this time that contain idiomatic spellings like Amerika, a rhetorical trademark of the Black Panther Party, and closed with the slogan, "All Power to the People!" See, for example, Chicago Gay Liberation ([1970] 1992) and Third World Gay Revolution ([1971] 1992).

10. Lesbian-feminism developed in a number of directions and survives as a distinct cultural formation in enclaves around the country. In addition, successful agitation for recognition within the women's movement offered a more agreeable environment for work on lesbian issues and ideas for many lesbian activists. Still, a goodly number of lesbians remained allied with gay politics and have been particularly prominent within it since the AIDS epidemic erupted in the early 1980s.

11. I use 1968 as the temporal demarcation of gay politics' decisive turn away from the homophile political model, based upon programs designed to promote tolerance and acceptance, toward a more defiant stance, not 1969, when the Stonewall uprising took place. Although the latter is an important landmark, the forces that it has come to represent had already taken root, as the formation of groups at various colleges in 1968 indicates.

12. Rose defines identity projects in this way: "Contemporary individuals are incited to live as if making a *project* of themselves: they are to *work* on their emotional world, their domestic and conjugal arrangements, their relations with employment and their techniques of sexual pleasure, to develop a 'style' of living that will maximize the worth of their existence to themselves" (N. Rose 1998, 157).

13. Others have challenged the premises and substance of role theory. Among these critics are Urry (1970), who points out how social position and behavior understood in terms of roles leads to the reification of social identities, and Coulson (1972). Wrong (1957) critiques socialization and role theory from a psychoanalytic perspective, observing that these paradigms overvalue normative commitments and neglect such psychodynamic factors as inner conflict. Also J. Rose (1986) employs psychoanalytic theory to challenge feminist sociological studies that update structural-functionalism to forge a theory of gender socialization and sex roles (e.g., Nancy Chodorow). For these feminist sociologists, Rose writes, "the internalization of norms is assumed roughly to work, [and] the basic premise and indeed starting-point of psychoanalysis is that it does not" (90).

14. The media provide innumerable examples of how statistics are understood by gay and lesbian political analysts as an accurate reflection of reality. For example, the statistic produced by the 1948 Kinsey report on male sexual behavior, which found that approximately ten percent of American men were exclusively homosexual for at least three years between the ages of 16 and 55, has been cited routinely by gay rights organizations to bolster claims for minority status. When much lower figures—as low as one percent—were produced by subsequent surveys these numbers were interpreted as a threat to the gay rights movement. The *New York Times* even featured one such story on its front page (Barringer 1993a), but ten days later, followed up with an interesting counterpoint (Barringer 1993b). However, the latter item did not seriously question the validity of statistics as a measure of social phenomena. The gay/lesbian media participates actively in the same devotion to statistical data, as evidenced in the monthly survey results published by the *Advocate*, the largest circulation gay or lesbian magazine in the U.S.

15. Perhaps the most sustained narrative of this kind in print is Duberman (1992). Shorter but similar tales of attempted cures for homosexuality can be found in such collections of lesbian coming out stories as Penelope and Wolfe (1989) and Cruikshank (1985). See also, the myriad autobiographical pieces in the gay and lesbian press. The first widely distributed film documentary inspired by gay and lesbian liberation, *Word Is Out* (1977), contains a searing account of a young lesbian's hospitalization and electroshock therapy.

16. See, for example, the sidebar that accompanied *Time*'s "Homosexuality in America" cover story, "Discussion: Are Homosexuals Sick?" (1969). A similar piece, "Is Homosexuality Normal or Not?" (1971), appeared in *Life*.

17. One can find evidence of these splits in the different gay liberation newspapers that appeared in New York City in 1969. *Come Out* was put out by a cell of GLF that belonged to the politically oriented faction and took a political line consistent with the group's radical left orientation. *Gay* and *Gay Power* were more culturally oriented and supported the liberal reformist politics of GAA when that organization was set up. Articles in *Come Out* railed against gay bar culture, because these spaces exploited patrons' marginalization and fears of exposure. *Gay* and *Gay Power* treated the bars as valid sites of gay cultural activity and explicitly distanced themselves from the GLF position.

18. Shelley, for instance, didn't make the transition to mainstream celebrity, and although Johnston continues to publish prolifically her writings consist mainly of personal autobiography or art criticism and commentary. Only a reprinting of some of her *Village Voice* columns in *Admission Accomplished* (1998) might indicate to younger readers the part she played in articulating the principles, as well as an analysis, of lesbian liberation.

19. The Rubyfruit Jungle Productions press release I located in the New York Public Library's International Gay Information Center Archives appears to have been designed to mobilize members of the gay rights movement to pressure recalcitrant film producers. The release explains that they were not interested in making a low-budget independent film based on the novel "because *we want this film to have the visibility that can be provided by a major studio. We are not interested in making a film that plays to the already sympathetic. The widest possible distribution is a perfect tool to help break down the barriers* of bigotry and reactionism" (emphasis added).

READING 15
QUEER EYE FOR THE STRAIGHT GUISE: CAMP, POSTFEMINISM, AND THE FAB FIVE'S MAKEOVERS OF MASCULINITY

By Steven Cohan

The big hit on American cable television in the summer of 2003 was the Bravo series *Queer Eye for the Straight Guy*, airing on Tuesday evenings. Every week five gay men, collectively referred to as the "Fab Five," take on a domestically and sartorially challenged straight man. He serves as their "trade" but not in the sense of the term suggested by the double entendre of the title; rather, they do a complete makeover of the straight guy. Each member of the queer team represents what is taken as a gay-identified specialty: Carson Kressley is in charge of fashion, Kyan Douglas grooming, Thom Filicia decorating, Ted Allen cooking, and Jai Rodriguez something vaguely called "culture" but more accurately a hybrid of dating or hosting etiquette and leisure entertainment skills. Typically, each episode focuses the straight guy's makeover around a particular "mission," with the Fab Five's renovation directed toward his achieving a personal or professional goal so that he can attain "confidence" and "grow up," as is frequently said on the show. Regardless of the particulars, the Fab Five's primary objective is to teach the straight guy how to satisfy the emotional and domestic needs of a present or potential female partner.

Queer Eye adheres to the makeover show format insofar as it defines a confident, mature masculinity through consumption and then normalizes it through a heterosexual couple, leaving the queer guys out of the loop except as spectators. Just as important, though, while decidedly aimed at restoring the straight guy's cultural capital in a postfeminist marketplace, *Queer Eye* also makes a concerted effort through camp to visualize queerness in its contiguous relation to straightness. How one weighs these concerns, I am going to argue, determines what one can find in the Fab Five's makeovers of the straight guys.[1] My discussion of the first season of *Queer Eye* will thus aim to situate its legibility as a queer show in light of this collection and the conference that inspired it. I have in mind (and am, to be candid, intentionally resisting) how some formulations of postfeminism have so readily absorbed the impact of queer theory but left out the queerness. Witness how, in addressing the woman now seemingly liberated by feminism, consumer culture and the mass media have transformed the visible gay male into what Baz Dreisinger aptly describes as "the trendy accessory for straight women," namely, the "postfeminist" female's best friend and confidante, and the inspiration for her ideal consort, that hip, het "metrosexual."[2] While recognizing the extent to which *Queer Eye* encourages a highly comforting view of homosexuality as a useful accessory of postfeminist femininity, I want to examine how the series simultaneously enables a queer viewer to see past that agenda.

GOOD FAIRIES TO THE RESCUE?

Queer Eye for the Straight Guy was Bravo's effort to exploit the popularity of makeover shows, twisting the format a bit with its five gay experts. Moreover, Bravo paired it with another gay version of a reality TV genre, the dating show *Boy Meets Boy*, to create a two-hour bloc of "alternative" programming on Tuesday nights. The intent was to establish a niche identity, thereby overcoming the blandness of this NBC-owned cable network, and possibly to find a signature show. Having gay or gay-coded hosts on a cable reality series was not new; nor did *Queer Eye* make any pretense of reinventing the makeover format. All the same, in the absence of a big, tabloid, TV event in the summer of 2003, *Queer Eye* immediately received a great deal of media coverage because, unlike *Boy Meets Boy*, it featured five gay men perfectly comfortable with their homosexuality and openly identified itself as a series respectful of queer tastes and attitudes.

Exploiting the buzz that resulted from so much attention, NBC subsequently reran episodes several times in its powerhouse Thursday night lineup during the summer months (a significant spot for advertising the opening of new movies each week), and the series' success prompted an appearance of the Fab Five on the network's *Tonight Show* in August to do a makeover of the host, Jay Leno. They performed the same job for preselected audience members on Oprah Winfrey's afternoon talk show in early autumn. In the fall as well, the Comedy Central satire *South Park* parodied *Queer Eye*, indicating how quickly this new series had entered popular culture awareness. Aside from the expected gay demographic, the series quickly attracted a strong female following, prompting a Yahoo! discussion group dedicated to this important segment of the viewing audience, "A Girl's View of *Queer Eye*." Yet the series also drew a cadre of straight men. One fan site, "Straight Eye for the Queer Shows" (now apparently defunct), featured four openly heterosexual men who rotated responsibility for writing detailed, tongue-in-cheek recaps of each week's episode. This is not to suggest that the male segment of the series' audience took its makeover lessons lightly. A December 2003 survey conducted by Jericho Communications revealed that whenever a new episode aired on Tuesday evenings it encouraged more males to go shopping with a buddy the day afterward than at any other time during the week.[3]

The currency of *Queer Eye* throughout its first season occurred at the same time that same-sex marriage became a controversial, publicly debated issue.[4] Two Canadian provinces legalized such unions in the summer of 2003, making it possible for gay and lesbian couples to travel there from the United States and marry, and in November of that year the Massachusetts Supreme Court upheld same-sex marriages, prompting local civil resistance to the federal Defense of Marriage Act in states on the East and West Coasts. This timeliness certainly contributed, if indirectly, to the attention *Queer Eye* and its five hosts received in the months following the premiere. In its year-end chronicle of events, the American Film Institute (AFI) listed *Queer Eye* as one of the two major cultural developments of 2003 (the other was the issue of film piracy). The AFI singled out *Queer Eye* because it brought "gay culture to the national fore by spoofing and celebrating stereotypes, and unlike other reality shows, it did so in a winning and genuine manner that developed a bond between the gay and straight man."[5] The AFI was not alone in applauding the series' liberal viewpoint. Oprah Winfrey expressed much the same sentiment, often tearfully, several times during the Fab Five's appearance on her show.

Alongside that liberal approval, *Queer Eye* received its fair share of negative criticism for perpetuating, not debunking, gender-sexual stereotypes. News stories on the suddenly hot new show balanced criticism and praise in their accounts of the response from gay viewers.[6] Skimming several gay-oriented discussion boards during the months following the series premiere, I found that the strongest charge against the Fab Five was directed at their "unmasculine" appearance and mannerisms, epitomized by their flamboyant personification of effeminate stereotypes, with Carson and Jai targeted in particular.

Inevitably, a comparison was made with the more attractive gay men to be found on Bravo's other new series, *Boy Meets Boy*. Its hook was that the gay bachelor did not know his dating pool included straight men. While this premise appeared to belie the distinction between gay and straight on the basis of appearance, *Boy Meets Boy* reinscribed the axiom that the most attractive gay men are those who can successfully pass as straight, and the series only proved that, when it comes to dating, gay men can be just as banal and superficial as their straight counterparts. But *Boy Meets Boy* capitalized on the thinking that motivates the many gay personal ads seeking straight-acting men, and it exploited the fantasy, a staple of gay erotica, that straight men are seducible. What stood out in the contrasting remarks about *Queer Eye*'s circulation of gay stereotypes was the discomfort felt by hostile viewers precisely because the Fab Five were not gym junkies; they did not conform to the "Abercrombie & Fitch" ethos inspiring (not to say inciting desire in) gay men of their generation, which, as Michael Joseph Gross observes, is to look like everyone else, to be "regular guys—[but] with better-than-average bodies."[7] In short, these viewers preferred the buff, twenty-something, heterosexual-looking guys on *Boy Meets Boy*. While the criticism declared that *Queer Eye* reconfirmed straight prejudices about nelly gay men, it could be reduced to the simpler question: why can't these five queers act and look more like straight guys?

When watching that first season of *Queer Eye*, my own answer at the time was: if they did, we wouldn't be able to tell the difference. True, *Queer Eye* defines the queerness of the Fab Five through their expertise as consumers, not through their sexual orientation. As Anna McCarthy points out, "The Fab Five are totally sexless. They may tease their subjects, but there is no chance that they will get to sleep with them."[8] Their queer eye is for the most part not focused through a gay gaze—it's not *that* kind of queer eye for a straight guy—but is meant to illuminate for heterosexual men what their girlfriends, wives, or mothers already know, namely, the value of "products," perhaps the most repeatedly used term on the show, as the cornerstone of heterosexual self-confidence and maturity. The five hosts function for each episode not as protagonists but in the capacity that narratology calls helper figures, serving the needs of a domesticated heteronormality; this subordinate role in the narrative of each episode enables a makeover to be focused through a decidedly straight eye for the queer guy, which is why the five hosts may encourage what is actually "the fantasy that [the series'] straight viewers gain entry into an otherwise inaccessible, unfamiliar gay culture."[9] With their homosexuality serving mainly as consumer culture's equivalent of professional counseling for the straight couple, and gay culture itself reduced to shopping, the Fab Five do end up seeming all too reminiscent of the three drag queens in *To Wong Foo, Thanks for Everything! Julie Newmar* (1995): the asexual good fairies who bring a hip Manhattanite's taste for style, flair, color, and cleanliness into a bland and dingy straight world and quickly depart as soon as they have spread their gay cheer.

As for its depiction of straights, *Queer Eye* follows the example of all the self-help relationship books that binarize the difference between men and women, depicting the genders as "different species entirely" and consequently promoting the expectation that heterosexual romance "is not a walk in the park but an arduous expedition."[10] I think it is safe to assume that the appeal of the series for many women lies in its mission of softening masculinity's rough edges for successful male-female cohabitation. Registering what Sasha Torres observes is "the incapacity of the heterosexual families that spawned the straight guys to sustain even a minimal quality of life," *Queer Eye* depicts not only the domestic rehabilitation but also the class elevation of straight men for the benefit of their women.[11] Like other makeover shows, the series teaches its viewers that this dual mission is most easily performed through one's appearance, and the urgency of such instruction is expressed every time the Fab Five obsess over men needing to shave in "the right way" and to remove all that gristly body hair, whether it's the straight guy's back hair, ear hair, or unibrow. As Torres notes, the show's preoccupation with shaving crystallizes, through the Fab Five's intervention, both the necessity of male-male tutelage in perpetuating the protocols of civil masculinity and the heterosexual family's failure to perform this crucial function for its unruly sons, much to the dismay of their future girlfriends and wives.

With successful straight coupling requiring endless negotiation between alien creatures polarized in their libidinal, emotional, and domestic needs, *Queer Eye* brings in the Fab Five to mediate heterosexual difference; their visible queerness then functions to speak for women in an unthreatening male voice. As a result, the series brings out the contradiction constructing the postfeminist female viewer being addressed from this vantage point. Straight masculinity is identified as problematic more than oppressive, and it can be remedied through a male's consumption of the same kind of products that enhance in order to regulate femininity. However, even though the makeovers serve the interests of women, *Queer Eye* concentrates on "the pleasures of companionship" between straight guys and their gay cohorts, relegating women to "a shadow presence on the show."[12] A female's main function is to nod approval at what the queer guys have achieved for her in her absence, which involves their pedagogical bonding with the straight guy as well as his makeover.

The cultural ideal of masculinity aimed for here—though it is a standard the straight guys on the series at best only approximate to provide the link between the makeovers and the advertising and product placement—is what the media has termed the metrosexual, the youngish, upscale, heterosexual male who spends so much time on his appearance (and so much money on hairstyling, fashionable clothing, and skin products) that he is readable as "gay" and too liberal to mind the mistake—but hands off, please! On the Fab Five's return visit (21 November 2003) several months after their makeover of the *Tonight Show*, Carson Kressley defined this suddenly ubiquitous yet sexually ambiguous figure for Jay Leno as the straight guy who moisturizes but doesn't have sex with other men. More accurately, the fashion guru quipped, he's "a moistrosexual."

A recent invention of marketing and the urban press, the metrosexual male gives every impression of revising how straight masculinity has traditionally been defined in opposition to feminine activities such as shopping, grooming, and cooking, as Martin Roberts points out elsewhere in this volume.[13] Such a refiguration of masculinity has a longer history, though, deriving from an earlier representation of what was termed the New Man in advertising, TV, and films of the 1980s, itself an outgrowth of the kind of marketing aimed directly at male consuming, which *Playboy* magazine perfected in the 1950s.[14] Somewhat like the metrosexual, the New Man of the 1980s was depicted as being "tough but tender, masculine but sensitive—he can cry, cuddle babies and best of all buy cosmetics."[15] This newly styled image of a straight masculinity geared toward consuming was perhaps first signaled by *American Gigolo* (1980), the neo-noir film starring Richard Gere that put the clothing designer Georgio Armani on the map, and it was featured in advertising campaigns for products such as Levi's 501 jeans and Grey Flannel cologne. By the end of the decade, when the Liz Claiborne company introduced its own brand of men's cologne, the marketing was specifically aimed at the New Man, "who attends Rob Reiner romances and tipples kir royales [and] might also want to take an introspective and vulnerable approach to the way he smells."[16]

According to Suzanne Moore, the 1980s New Man drew on the visual iconography of soft-core gay pornography, drawing attention to the male body "as a pleasurable object [but] on condition that his pleasure can be contained within a narcissistic/auto-erotic discourse."[17] Just as important, this image addressed women by offering "the possibility of an *active female gaze*."[18] Moore attributes this kind of radical shift in depicting the masculine, which blurs the distinction between the active male voyeur and the passive female exhibitionist, to popular culture's awareness of the "renegotiations over masculinity brought about by radical political discourses," feminism, and the gay and lesbian rights movement in particular.[19] Because of the homoeroticism informing the visual representation of the New Man, however, the heterosexuality of this image of masculinity was never fully secure. Hence paying attention to how one smelled could signal vulnerability as well as introspection, just as it still connoted suspicion about—and feminized as narcissistic—the type of man who was *too* concerned with how he looked.

The 1980s New Man, in short, could always turn out to be a closet case. By contrast, as the newer term suggests, the metrosexual willingly displays his toned but moisturized body as a means of performing his masculinity through his ability to consume, using his exhibitionism to assert his identity as an urban, middle-class male. While this newest incarnation of a male attuned to the same consumerist desires as his domestic partner is presumed to be heterosexual, he is still poised between assumptions about what makes a man readable as "straight" and what makes him readable as "queer," which is why he is more "metro" than "hetero." Appropriating the tropes formerly used to identify the gay male consumer, the metrosexual reimagines masculinity from a postfeminist perspective, but the price remains this new man's sexual ambiguity—the very anxiety that *Boy Meets Boy* appeared to celebrate but actually fostered by keeping its gay bachelor in the dark about the sexual orientation of the men he was scrutinizing, flirting with, and sharing his feelings with in one-on-one encounters. For single straight women, even if the metrosexual moisturizes but doesn't swing with the other team, his sexual ambiguity renews the motive for the much-quoted worry that all the best men are either already married or gay—for if they aren't gay they certainly look like they are, so how is a girl to tell?

This is where the Fab Five come in: to clarify who is and who isn't. *Queer Eye for the Straight Guy* outwardly deploys their queerness to facilitate the mating of a metrosexual wannabe with his postfeminist partner, but these makeovers of the sleeping woolly beast for his date with Princess Charming are primarily structured around the opposition of "queer" and "straight," not "masculine" and "feminine." The series' humor and its potential edginess reside in this opposition. The Fab Five's queer eye slyly acknowledges the regulation and deregulation of domestic and urban spaces through that dualism, which places gay men outside straight culture yet makes them central to its successful operation. At issue is the spatial differentiation pointed out by the series' title. *Queer Eye for the Straight Guy* does something akin to what Joshua Gamson argues about daytime talk shows, which perform "an ambivalence about just who is doing what and how in public—and, more fundamentally, just to whom public space belongs." "It's not so much the *gayness* that is bothersome," Gamson concludes, "it's the *publicness*."[20] *Queer Eye* does not represent that disturbance through violent confrontations in the manner of Jerry Springer or Ricki Lake. Rather, in order to stage the queer eye–straight guy encounter as a momentary deregulation of boundaries, *Queer Eye* foregrounds the public visibility of queerness in its adjacency to straightness through *camp*, although the Fab Five do not always maintain this viewpoint coherently or consistently in each episode.

CAMPING WITH THE FAB FIVE

Historically speaking, in the pre-Stonewall era of the closet (a crucial space for *Queer Eye* as it turns out), camp was a strategy of cultural differentiation for queers, one highly responsive to the imperative of passing—a "queer eye for the straight *guise*"—even more than it was a "sensibility" and "style" or a category of "taste," to refer to Susan Sontag's and Andrew Ross's early commentaries on camp.[21] As I have written elsewhere, "In response to that era's oppression and censorship of homosexuality, camp allowed for the ironic, self-reflective style of gay men passing as straight, who kept a 'straight face' so as not to let outsiders in on the joke, while simultaneously winking at the initiated in shared acknowledgment of it. *Camp* can be defined as the ensemble of strategies used to enact a queer recognition of the incongruities arising from the cultural regulation of gender and sexuality."[22] Despite its later appropriation by the mainstream during the 1960s and 1970s, which began to efface its history and politics, camp still works by exaggerating the homologous boundaries of the visible/straight/natural and invisible/queer/ unnatural in order to locate one side of the polarity in more direct tension with the other. This is why, as Esther Newton observes, "Camp is not a thing. Most broadly it signifies a *relationship between* things, people, and activities or qualities, and homosexuality."[23]

Today camp may seem politically incorrect because of its association with the oppressive politics of the closet, but its significance for gay culture, while reinflected according to the times, has not diminished. Camp still enables a queer perspective to be discerned through its *effect* (the ironic inflection of a witty putdown or pun, a coded allusion for those in the know, the exaggeration of artifice and theatricality) and, more profoundly, in its *affect* (the queer pleasure in perceiving, if not causing, the disruption of gender-sexual categories whether in representations of heterosexual normality, the values that reiterate it, or the commodities that derive from and reinscribe it). Although first feminism and then postfeminism have provocatively taken camp as a ground for theorizing the artifice of gender construction and regulation, and to serve as a strategy for reading against oppressive representations of women, I want to insist on what is still, to my mind, the intractable *queerness* of camp. It may illuminate the subordination of women alongside that of gay men, but because of its queer bias it is not reducible to either feminist political aims or postfeminist awareness of the interaction between feminine identities, gender performativity, and consumption.[24]

On *Queer Eye*, from Carson's double entendres to Jai's exaggeration of a drag queen in mufti to Ted's understated, straight-faced irony, the Fab Five engage in camp at the level of both effect (what they do and say to make viewers laugh at the straight people) and affect (how that laughter then yields pleasure in watching the makeovers, though a pleasure that exceeds the series' ideological purpose of recuperating heterosexual coupledom). Their camp enables them to be readily perceivable as "gay," in contrast to the straight men they remake for straight women, but it also allows them to cast a queer eye on their job of serving heterosexuality as its asexual helpers.

Rather effortlessly, yet somewhat violently, the team moves in and out of the regulatory boundaries that uphold the distinction, in private and public, between queer and straight spaces. Each episode begins with the Fab Five speeding across Manhattan in their sport-utility vehicle as they briefly describe their mission of the day. The opening credits then identify each member of the team individually according to his expertise; pictures them in a group as if they were the Mod Squad, the A-Team, and Charlie's Angels combined; and locates them at the imaginary intersection of Gay and Straight Streets. Following the credits, the first segment records them arriving at their destination like a gay brigade of terrorists or kidnappers invading the presumed sanctity of the straight guy's home and disrupting its heterosexual space. With pseudo-militaristic fervor, the five charge inside and register their offense at what they find there: disarray, dysfunctionality, and dirt. In this first segment, edited in a fast-paced montage that does not follow temporal chronology, they appropriate items from the kitchen, bathroom, or bedroom closet in order to mock the straight guy's ad hoc domesticity, indifference to sanitation, ineptitude with clothing, and, whenever the opportunity arises—for instance, if they find porn or condoms or even his underwear—his sexual prowess. The humiliated straight guy stands by watching helplessly, often laughing but rarely offering resistance to this demeaning ridicule except to avoid physical contact, while the five queer men proceed to trash the place literally as well as verbally, even going so far as to toss his furniture or clothing out a window or over a balcony.

The next set of sequences leads the straight guy through the physical makeover, which amounts to a take-over. He passively puts himself in Carson's hands for a shopping spree and in Kyan's for grooming at a salon or spa; usually there is a third outing with one of the others for furniture or cuisine. The ostensible point of these sequences is his instruction—on what clothes suit his body, what areas of his face, hair, or body need immediate attention, and how to select furniture or food. Visually and verbally, the camp humor in these sequences depends on the extent to which the team can expose how this consuming disturbs their subject's comfortable occupation of public space as a heterosexual male. These are indeed "outings." Not only is the straight guy undertaking an activity of specialized consuming presumed to be a gay man's preoccupation with his appearance for the appreciative gaze of another man, but this straight guy is doing it in public with an openly gay guy, so the act of consuming places the two together in a hybrid space that confounds a straight-queer dichotomy. Anyone who observes the straight guy in an upscale clothing store with Carson is not going to presume that these are two straight buddies—the pair identified by the Jericho Communications survey—picking up a new pair of jeans or polo shirt to replace a worn one. Flamboyantly rushing through the store with his straight guy in tow, Carson announces his queer presence at every turn by means of his camp manner. The straight guy, meanwhile, submits to a scrutinizing queer eye that is superior to his when Carson appraises his appearance; using a quick wit as well as a keen sense of style to exploit his discomfort and objectify him, Carson dresses down the straight guy while dressing him up.

Similarly, when Kyan supervises the straight guy's subjection to exfoliating, tweezing, plucking, and waxing—the work that goes into "femininity"—he also exposes him to the gaze of a queer eye. Although it does not occur in each episode, here the crossing of boundaries can most disturbingly question how *queer* and *straight* are still defined according to spatial regulation. This is most vividly apparent in episode 108, "Law and Disorder" (first shown on Bravo on 19 August 2003), which recounts the makeover of John Verdi, an Italian American cop living on Staten Island. A bald, pudgy, pasty, white man with gross toenails, John is taken to the Completely Bare spa for a spray-on tan. All he can mutter throughout is how embarrassed he is, not so much for appearing practically naked on national television as for doing so side-by-side with a gay guy. "See how he has a farmer's tan," Kyan remarks to the female attendant while pointing it out on John's chest and verifying that the process can contour and slendorize the body through the way the color is blended. John, in the meantime, has his eyes shut tight. "Dude," Kyan comments, "I have to say this is the most embarrassing thing ever done to help out a straight guy." But John seems more flummoxed: "Dude, this is so embarrassing, to be standing next to a gay guy in skivvies and … disposable skivvies, I might add."

Kyan: Well, you're no Prince Charming either, Big Boy.

John: I'm not—I'm not even looking at you. I don't want to look that way.

Kyan: Are you serious?

John: Dude, it's like … uh … you don't understand.

Kyan: What's gay about this situation?

John: Are you kidding me right now?

Kyan: I mean, over here it's gay. But (*pointing to John's space in the tanning booth*) what's gay about that?

John: Cause I'm in skivvies next to a gay—you don't understand.

But Kyan *does* understand. A short time later, he pressures the straight guy again, wondering to the attendant, "Can you make his penis look bigger?" "Guy," John asks defensively, "why are you looking at my penis?" Kyan laughs, and John begs, "Come on, please." Although Kyan demurs, his joke taken, the camera then focuses on crotch and butt shots of John as the tanning process is completed.

This segment questions what makes one space gay and another straight, and does so at the straight guy's expense, triggering his homophobic panic at being in such intimate proximity to a gay male body—the semi-nude Kyan, the member of the group whom fans and the media consider the "hottest." His gayness is for the moment defined in explicitly sexual terms as a queer eye not for products but for the straight guy's penis. This definition is then overlaid with the erotic display of Kyan's body for a gay and female viewer, as well as the camp deflation of John's endowment, which encourages one to infer that perhaps it is already looking a little "bigger." Joking about penis anxiety is an obvious sign of the discomfort that arises when heterosexual identity comes into contact with homosexual desire, harking back to the embarrassment, insecurity, curiosity, and/ or excitement that characterizes all those group showers straight boys have had to take after high school gym classes. However, the John Verdi episode is more complex than this for it also brings out how this straight guy's "Guido Mumbo" masculinity, as Jai calls it later in the hour, is not only a performance of heterosexual codes for the benefit of the queer guys but is also, shall we say, blended, contoured, and slenderized by homosexual codings as the condition of his being made over in order to be more compatible with his female partner.

As happens in each episode, following the physical makeover John Verdi returns home with his new queer buddies in order to see what Thom has accomplished in his absence ("You don't feel like you live in some gay guy's apartment?"), to perform a fashion show of the clothing Carson has selected for him ("Hip hop with a little more class," but remember to zhuzh up the sleeves), to learn from Kyan how to establish a grooming regimen (proper use of products, which happen to vary each week, for "long-term skin care"), and to receive final instructions on preparing and serving food for the evening from Ted (in this case, a torte or quiche, though Ted reassures John that this torte is "a manly quiche, a quiche with balls"—even though it is made with eggs). Then the Fab Five depart for an apartment in Manhattan where, in the final segment, cocktails in hand and getting visibly looped, they observe how successfully the straight guy follows their tutelage on closed-circuit television (fig. 2).

Once again this episode reveals how camp identifies a distinctly queer eye for the show. John's mission has been to rekindle his romance with his live-in girlfriend, Ayana, a "hot" African American model who is tired of mothering him. As soon as she enters, John abruptly readjusts his masculine persona: "Isn't this re-mahk-able?" he asks, further showing his excitement about the makeover of his body and their home by jumping up and down and talking baby talk, all the while appreciating how her "boobages" look in her new outfit, which was also selected by Carson. In the meantime, much as if they were watching *Sex and the City*, the Fab Five gather in front of the TV for some camp camaraderie. "He's bouncing around like a little girl, isn't he?" Kyan asks in disbelief. "He's acting gayer than I do," Carson agrees. "He was all tough guy around us, and now he's … " Ted cannot find the words, so he makes a flaming gesture. "He totally hopped out of the bedroom," Thom adds. Throughout this segment, the Fab Five note every potential disaster or faux pas, as well as every sign of slippage, between queer and straight in John's demeanor, as when he describes the dessert he has prepared as "divine." "Divine? He used the word *divine*," Ted exclaims, to which Carson replies, "He *is* gay." John confesses to Ayana how for a while he has been lacking confidence but now he has "a spark in his pants" again, and Thom mutters, "Don't look at me—I didn't put it there." "There's a lot of power in a pedicure and a spray-on tan," Kyan concludes, restoring the consumer orientation of the makeover. Mission complete, the Five toast their success in rescuing another straight guy from drabness.

Queer Eye may deserve the critiques it has received for its endorsement of class hierarchies based on consuming, but that does not mean the overt ideological agenda of the series warrants outright dismissal of the additional cultural work it performs as a queer show. The series remakes straight masculinity according to bourgeois norms, but it does so through the mediation of queerness, which foregrounds the instability of both masculinity and straightness. For all their disavowals, most of the straight guys appear to realize the fragility of their heteromasculinity at some point in the hour. For instance, while shopping, John Verdi tells Carson that he'd do anything for his female partner, "even start with five gay guys and get made over." His problem, however, is that he doesn't know "what sexy is." All he knows is that he wants it and the queer guys know how to gain access to it, so he submits to their tutelage.

John's confession makes explicit the gender instability on which the series' camp outlook spins. Straight masculinity is just another cultural product and a confused one at that. As John's makeover illustrates, the series just as explicitly recognizes how a so-called normative masculinity is a performance, frequently multiple in its signifying effects; that it achieves an impression of stability by maintaining the perceived boundaries strictly differentiating between and culturally locating hetero- and homosexual male identities; and that it occurs in a consumer-oriented society that, needing to exploit the male market, overlaps these two identities (as in the metrosexual advertising image), thereby requiring the performance in the first place. The series' understanding of how straightness is organized according to its disavowed proximity to queerness is best epitomized in the opening segment, which depicts the Fab Five's invasion of a heterosexual domicile, during which they ridicule the straight guy's veneer of manliness, exposing his dirty underwear literally and figuratively, and in the closing one, which records the Fab Five's withdrawal into their own camp camaraderie, where they laugh once more at the spectacle of a straight guy's performance of his newly acquired, upscale masculinity. This framing vantage point enables *Queer Eye for the Straight Guy* to pass, in effect, as "safe" entertainment and yet display an edgier outlook, as the John Verdi episode well illustrates. The series can be read as straight or nonstraight, as noncamp or camp, depending on which eye you look with.

The central joke driving the series, it bears repeating, is that men with no sexual interest of their own in women have to be brought in from outside a clearly delineated heterosexual space in order to teach a straight guy "what sexy is," which enables heartfelt appreciation by heterosexual men and women alike of this needed queer intervention. This joke defines what the queer eye can see in the makeover because it also highlights what the straight eye fails to see. Thus, the remarks posted by females on the "Girl's Eye View of Queer Eye" Web site, right after the John Verdi episode aired, confined themselves to appreciating how "adorable" the Fab Five looked or behaved at certain points and how striking John appeared in his new clothes, making him such an attractive date. A more interesting response appeared in the recap of this episode on the "Straight Eye for the Queer Shows" fan site. The writer, "Larry," goes into great detail; he describes all the bristly interactions between the cop and the Fab Five from their entrance through each stage of the makeover, including the trip to Completely Bare (although the point seems to be what NBC edited out when it reran this episode), and he quotes much of their dialogue. However, except for noting that the gay men dwell on the size of Ayana's breasts (their response to John's appreciation of her "boobages"), "Larry" ignores the final segment, in which the team watches the results of the makeover. Instead, as if the Fab Five's viewpoint were transparent, this straight fan disregards their camp commentary and only describes what they see—John and Ayana's night out. Expressing his appreciation of John's efforts to please Ayana, "Larry" concludes:

> Now a number of people have complained how John gets such a hot chick. In his defense, he's tall, pretty fit, and strong (though he's gained some weight) and a cop. He's apparently good at the kissing (full alignment with light tongue tizzle) and it seems like he had a good sized package while being spray tanned. Many women out there want a guy who can take care of them and really love them and this guy can do it. Any man willing to stretch himself to keep his relationship fresh, is a good catch, and most women should be so lucky.[25]

The difference between queer and straight viewpoints depends on the extent to which, as "Larry" typifies here, a viewer disregards the Fab Five's camp mediation and identifies primarily with the woman as the motivating force behind the straight guy's makeover—he's doing it solely for her, and she then serves as his private audience when he shows off the results of his makeover. However, in fulfilling that role for this type of viewer, Ayana is also participating in the performance, which the Fab Five simultaneously watch on their closed-circuit TV. Because they filter the straight couple through their camp spectatorship, it is difficult to extract a bona fide feminine viewpoint from the closure, however much "Larry" tries to do so. The couple themselves are rarely if ever shown recognizing any camp element in their performance of heterosexuality, even when they acknowledge the performative dimension of the makeover and its subsequent test run as the straight guy shows off what he has learned for his partner's inspection and approval.

Yet, by casting his closing response to this episode through an awareness of Ayana's needs and not the Fab Five's camp, "Larry" can display the post-feminist male sensibility that, one has to assume, allows him to take pleasure in the series and coauthor the "straight guy" Web site. No doubt influenced by all those self-help relationship books, which are supposedly written in the wake of feminism but present an option other than feminism when it comes to women's relations with men, "Larry" writes as a male seemingly liberated from sexist attitudes and, what is more, since he did notice John's "package," as a male not subject to insecurity about the stability of his own heteromasculinity. To sustain this viewpoint, he has to ignore both the Fab Five's camp eye and the subordinate role of women in the makeover. For her part, Ayana knows very well her limited contribution to the makeover process; on departing the premises so that the Fab Five can take charge of John's makeover, she loudly announces, "The vagina is leaving the nest." "Larry's" summary does indicate why a woman's presence, at least in the closure of each episode, is still a crucial element in the series' success. She facilitates the more sanguine, straight male response to the Fab Five's queer intervention in heterosexuality, which Larry typifies when he in effect rewrites the John Verdi episode to concentrate solely on the couple through Ayana's point of view.

A STRAIGHT EYE FOR THOSE QUEER GUYS

That a female figure cannot easily be removed from the series' formula stands out all the more when we look at the guest appearances of the Fab Five on the Oprah Winfrey and Jay Leno shows. Not surprisingly, given their target audience, each guest spot retains the series' premise but not its structure, more noticeably marginalizing the five gay men as outsiders for a predominantly straight female and male audience, respectively. The difference between the two spots is quite revealing. Winfrey's singling out of the female motivation for the makeovers considerably tames the Fab Five's impact, negating any jarring collision of straight and gay spaces, whereas a female's absence from the Leno makeover brings out more clearly the disturbance that the series itself manages more insightfully through camp.

On the Winfrey show (first shown in syndication on 22 September 2003), the queer makeovers of the various straight guys selected for a much-needed rescue, at least according to Oprah and the men's wives, cause members of the female audience to cry, with everyone who had a stake or hand in the renovations gathered together onstage for a big group hug at the end of the hour. One exemplary moment occurs in the final segment, when a formerly shaggy middle-aged man named Roland returns to display his new appearance, supervised by Kyan. Previously Roland had not shaved his beard or cut his hair in over twenty years, during which time his wife and two daughters had never seen what lay behind all the hair. Not only does the family break down in tears at the revelation that a well-groomed Roland is as handsome as "a movie star," but Oprah herself is open-mouthed when gazing at his dramatically different look. While Kyan, as befitting his role as product endorser, reflects that "shaving is all about preparation and products," Roland himself confesses, "I feel like I'm alive again." He grabs Oprah in a tight hug and begins to weep, and she gets caught up in the emotions too. "Let's all just have a cry," she sobs, inviting the predominantly female audience in the studio and at home to participate in the emotional outburst that confirms feminine gratitude for the queer intervention on behalf of what Oprah has earlier called "frustrated wives" who are unable to assist their "helpless husbands." The way the show is shot encourages such empathetic participation throughout the hour, and it does not involve the visual or verbal mediation of the Fab Five, despite the many times Oprah laughs heartily at Carson's camp barbs. The desperate wives who have "turned in" their husbands, as Oprah puts it, sit in the front rows as audience members, whereas the husbands stand uncomfortably onstage like wanted men; repeated close-ups of the wives' disgruntled then delighted faces equate their reactions with those of the audience members at large, fostering identification with this point of view by the home viewer as well.

By contrast, no tears are shed when Jay Leno receives his makeover. To publicize it, the Fab Five show up the night before the big reveal, appearing after Kevin Costner, who is promoting his new western, *Open Range* (2003), which was broadcast on NBC on 14 August 2003. As soon as the Fab Five make their entrance,

Leno begins to bait Costner, implying that the star's heteromasculinity, not Leno's own, is in doubt because of its proximity to queerness. After describing the *Queer Eye* slogan, "Five gay men out to make over the world—one straight guy at a time," Leno turns to Costner, warning, "and you're next, buddy." Leno goes on to joke that Costner intentionally lowered his voice when greeting the Fab Five, to tease Costner about getting his buttocks pierced, to propose that the Fab Five should plan Costner's upcoming wedding, and to suggest that, possibly because he had already spent too much time on the open range when making his movie, Costner is now rethinking the whole marriage thing. Although at moments Costner does seem uncomfortable, especially when the Fab Five first descend on him en masse, at other times he gets into the spirit of things (asking Jai, for instance, what he means by "working a room"), but Leno repeatedly attributes discomfort to him. Additionally, Leno turns every comment made by his guests into a joke about straight masculinity that actually endorses it as the impeachable norm—just in case any one is wondering. For instance, when Thom explains that the worst offense he finds in straight domiciles is bad lighting, typically supplied by a single torchiere halogen lamp, Leno again makes a joke at Costner's expense: "Straight guys like that porno lighting," Leno explains. "See, Kevin knows what I'm talking about." When Ted comments on straight guys' insecurity about ordering fine wines at restaurants, Leno similarly reasons, "it comes from going to strip shows."[26]

Without a straight male ally onto whom he can deflect his anxiety, the following night Leno resorts to homophobic jokes about the makeover process, playing up the gayness of the Fab Five in contrast to his own resistant straightness (broadcast on NBC on 15 August 2003). Distancing himself from the makeover even while going through it, Leno repeats his worry that the process effeminizes him by forcing him to think about fashion and skin conditioning. Not deterred, the Fab Five keep their banter going, chiding Leno for his appearance and his show's decor. They anticipate his stale straight-guy jokes, beating him to the punch line or turning the jokes awry, and four members of the team have an opportunity, with their customary chat and drinks, to view the remodeled set's disclosure and Ted's gourmet spot with Leno on a TV monitor from behind the scenes.

Somewhat like the tanning booth segment with John Verdi but with less good-natured candor, what seems disturbing to Leno, because it motivates so many of his jokes during the makeover, is how intimate contact with these gay guys makes his body vulnerable to anal penetration. Indeed, the makeover edition of the *Tonight Show* begins by explicitly identifying this fear and making it central to the whole enterprise of renovating Leno. On this night, the program forsakes its usual opening credits and begins instead with an imitation of the Fab Five's own series opening. As the team discusses its new mission, making over a famous talk show host, Kyan remarks that Leno is "a spa virgin" and Jai rejoins, "You're going to pop his spa cherry." Whether improvised or scripted, this exchange predetermines how the audience will subsequently view both Leno's discomfort during the shopping and spa montages and his many attempts to go for the easy, homophobic laughs. "I feel like the new guy on his first day in prison," Leno announces as the Fab Five inspect him, a sentiment also included in the teaser for the makeover shown the night before. Kyan's discovery of "a pubic hair" growing out of Leno's ear is just the proverbial tip of the iceberg. Carson insists on doing a "booty check" when Leno tries on pants. Displaying for a whining Leno a broad pinstripe suit (the one he will wear on the show), Carson compares the pattern to racing stripes, which Leno confirms he likes but does not want up his ass. During his hairstyling, Leno complains, "These guys are putting, like, KY Jelly in my hair."

On the two *Tonight Show* appearances by the Fab Five, women are excluded from all phases of the encounter. Without a woman to motivate the makeover and safeguard the straight guy's heterosexuality, the Fab Five's difference as gay men is more homosexualized and shown to be more potentially tempting to a straight guy, though not to Leno of course. On a shopping spree to buy new furniture for the show's set, Jai does a Christina Aguilera impersonation and Thom remarks to the young salesman, "It's kinda scary when he does that. He's so good acting like a woman." Sitting on the floor, the salesman replies, "The scary thing is, it doesn't bother me," so Jai mimes, "call me," drawing a big laugh from the studio audience. While this brief encounter seems daring for the *Tonight Show*, even as it reiterates the stereotype that gay men are at heart women (both are reasons for the laughter), it actually goes far beyond that (the reason I laughed). From the return of looks, we are encouraged to see the straight-looking salesman responding to Jai with homosexual interest, and, what is more, this not so straight guy is neither attracted to nor put off by Jai's effeminacy—rather, it just doesn't bother him. The Winfrey show, on the other hand, places the makeover's value for the straight guys' wives always in the foreground, which keeps queer and straight men at a much safer distance from each other while also sentimentalizing the beneficial results of their interaction, little of which is shown to viewers. The Fab Five serve as the wives' domesticating surrogates; unable to do the work of civilizing their mates themselves, for whatever reason, these wives, like the women on the series, have to rely on the kindness of queer strangers to clean up the mess.

In contrast to the Fab Five's appearances on the Winfrey and Leno shows, their own camp spectatorship of the straight guy's makeover in the closing segment of each *Queer Eye* episode parodies the hegemony of the straight guy and his mate in order to reverse the inside-outside dichotomy that marginalizes the queer. Even more than their expertise as specialists in fashion, grooming, cooking, decor, and "culture," their camp is the sign that these five men are the true insiders—the savvy cultural observers—as far as the series is concerned. When an episode can develop its edgy camp outlook, as in the John Verdi example, *Queer Eye* skillfully engages both queer and postfeminist viewpoints but also takes care not to make them identical. The series' camp target, after all, is straight masculinity, not femininity; while the Fab Five mockingly introduce straight guys to the domesticating regimes of grooming and housework long associated with femininity, the Fab Five never challenge the validity of such protocols, instead offering women the compensation of laughing at the ineptitude and insecurity of straight men when it comes to performing the social rituals that they have had to master in order to attract the guys in the first place. This camp perspective enables queerness to be visible amid straightness, just as it distinguishes the queer eye from a postfeminist one even though both are acutely aware of the construction of masculinity and femininity alike through consumption.

As telling of the culture industry's absorption of difference, though, *Queer Eye* has been unable to sustain its camp perspective week after week with any degree of rigor or consistency. The rigid formula of the makeover structure, the budgetary restriction to Manhattan and its outlying boroughs and suburbs, the sameness of the straight guys willing to expose themselves, the necessity for seemingly endless product endorsements on the series, and the Fab Five's own gleeful emersion in popular culture as the latest media darlings all work against the camp humor that made *Queer Eye* seem more queer than one could have expected when it first aired. The Fab Five have gone on to do a music video, star in commercials, and write self-help books; their celebrity keeps their queerness visible and in circulation but homogenizes it as a product—the gay accessory—for lifestyle consumption. As success begets repetition on television, it also breeds boredom, and even camp gets dull and predictable when prepackaged as a commodity in its own right.

NOTES

1. In a substantive analysis of *Queer Eye* that appeared after I wrote this essay, Beth Berila and Devika Dibya Choudhuri examine the multiple ways in which, by re-inscribing a white, middle-class bias through effacement or minimalization of racial, sexual, and class hierarchical differences, the series "contains gayness by reducing it to a commodity that services heteronormality" ("Metrosexuality the Middle Class Way," para. 4). I do not disagree with their careful and lengthy critique, which shares but develops much more fully the concerns of critics noted below; however, I think it is important to place alongside that kind of critique consideration of how the Fab Five's performance of the show's ideological agenda can at times also allow some viewers to see its transparency and laugh at it. Thus, while Berila and Choudhuri note that *Queer Eye* "troubles heteronormality on one level while reinscribing it through the commodification of gayness on the other" (para. 8), I am arguing that the series does not always manage this strategy so easily or readily and specifically that its cultural impact during its first season had much to do with the way episodes were not necessarily reducible to a single, recuperative, and heteronormative viewpoint in the makeover narratives.
2. Dreisinger, "The Queen in Shining Armor," 3.
3. "Survey Finds 'Queer Eye' Affects Shopping," Zap2it.com, 4 December 2003.
4. Gallagher, "*Queer Eye* for the Heterosexual Couple," 224.
5. "Piracy, 'Queer' on AFI Timeline," *Hollywood Reporter*, 16 December 2003.
6. During the summer of 2003, a Web search turned up articles reporting on both the positive and negative responses to the series and not only in the dailies of large urban areas. See, for example, Potts, "'Queer Eye' Makes over View of Homosexuals"; and Moon, "'Queer Eye' Opens Window to Gay Life."
7. Gross, "The Queen Is Dead," 64.
8. McCarthy, "Crab People from the Center of the Earth," 99.
9. Gallagher, "*Queer Eye* for the Heterosexual Couple."
10. Dreisinger, "The Queen in Shining Armor," 4.
11. Torres, "Why Can't Johnny Shave?" 96.
12. Gallagher, "*Queer Eye* for the Heterosexual Couple," 223.
13. See Roberts, "The Fashion Police," in this volume. Toby Miller chronicles the 1990s marketing invention of the metrosexual figure in "A Metrosexual Eye on *Queer Guy*."
14. See Cohan, *Masked Men*.
15. Moore, "Here's Looking at You, Kid!" 45.
16. Rothenberg, "Claiborne's Approach to Today's Man."
17. Moore, "Here's Looking at You, Kid!" 55.
18. Ibid., 45.
19. Ibid., 48.
20. Gamson, *Freaks Talk Back*, 201, 203.

21. Sontag, "Notes on Camp"; Ross, "Uses of Camp."

22. Cohan, *Incongruous Entertainment*, 1. The book's introduction elaborates more fully the historical understanding of camp that I am summarizing here (see pp. 1–19). For further discussion of the mainstream appropriation of camp, see pages 208–10.

23. Newton, *Mother Camp*, 105.

24. My point is that, while recognizing the affinities of camp and feminism, I do not want to erase the queer location of camp, which is crucial to understanding how it operates in practice, beginning with its ironic stance toward the regulation of heteronormality. To be sure, camp—in large part when it is solely equated with drag queens and their adoration of female stars—has a history of being read for its hostility to feminism. Camp was repudiated for its apparent misogyny in parodying "women's oppression," reflecting the tension between the feminist and gay rights movements of the 1970s, as Michael Bronski notes in *Culture Clash: The Making of Gay Sensibility* (205). Camp still bears this dubious status for many feminists. Yet, while certain instances of camp may be misogynistic, camp as a cultural strategy has another history of being quite valuable to feminism and of serving its transition into postfeminism. Although her source in camp is at best implicit, rendered through the extended example of drag, Judith Butler, in *Gender Trouble: Feminism and the Subversion of Identity*, has offered what is perhaps the most influential theorization of gender as a performance of identity through the convergence of camp and feminism. It is worth noting, however, that, even though *Gender Trouble* has become a landmark text for both queer theory and postfeminism, in her new preface to the 1999 edition Butler locates the agenda of her book in feminism, not queer theory, nor does she identify her project as a postfeminist one (rather, she cites its genealogy in poststructuralist French theory). For a different sort of example of how camp has been usefully linked with feminism as a cultural strategy taken up by women, see Robertson, *Guilty Pleasures*, though here, too, note the author's need to call what she is analyzing feminist camp in order to point out her paralleling of women's camp strategies and gay men's. From a different perspective, in *Female Masculinity*, Judith Halberstam examines the possibilities of a recent phenomenon, lesbian camp. According to her, masculinity stills tends to rely on tropes that efface its performativity, which resists the predication of camp "on exposing and exploiting the theatricality of gender," so she proposes, as an alternative to "the camp humor of femininity," a new term, *king-drag*, to designate "[lesbian] drag humor associated with masculinity" (237–38). While the enhanced theatricality of femininity has always been an easy target for camp humor and display—hence the long-standing but also somewhat limiting reduction of camp to drag—I think that camp can be sharply attuned to the performative dimensions of masculinity, as *Queer Eye for the Straight Guy* illustrates. But see also my chapter on Gene Kelly's camp masculinity in *Incongruous Entertainment* (149–99).

25. "Queer Eye #108—Law and Disorder: Special Picnic Unit," Posted by "Larry," www.straighteye.com, downloaded 21 March 2004.

26. During the Fab Five's return visit to the *Tonight Show* in November 2003, Leno baited the comedian Colin Quinn in the same way, causing the irritated guest to exclaim, "Jay, I thought it was going to be *me* and *you* against *them!*

CHAPTER 5
NEW AND EMERGING INTERACTIVITY: THE POLITICS OF SOCIAL MEDIA

EDITOR'S INTRODUCTION

NEW MODES OF PRODUCTION AND DELIVERY

Films tell stories in a relatively short two to three hours. At the end of a movie, audiences get up and relinquish their seats to new audiences. Radio and television offer an endless stream of programming that affords far more flexibility and opportunity for audiences. Sitcoms (situation comedies) present basic characters caught in similar half-hour scenarios week after week, while dramatic programming offers opportunity to develop story and character in season-long arcs. These forms of programming, if popular with audiences, can go on season after season, offering further opportunity for character development and new story directions.

These traditional forms of delivering media narratives are being challenged by new forms of media based on digitization of production and delivery. Video games offer the development of player interactivity with characters and direct control of the outcome of the story. Social media allows for audiences the self-publication of mediated messages over YouTube, Facebook, Instagram, and Twitter, to name a few.

Will new forms of media offer more complexity in the stories and representations of men and women, gay and straight, and trans? Will diversity of voices deliver more diverse representation? In her essay "Media in Our Image," Johanna Blakley describes the demographics of social media, which show that "women outnumber men in every age group on social networking sites around the world." Such representation is bound to have an impact. However, bell hooks reminds us in "The Oppositional Gaze: Black Female Spectatorship" that such opportunities demand vigilance and strategy as we move forward with new media. She reminds us "to know the present and invent the future."

In "An Old Enemy in a New Outfit: How Date Rape Became Gray Rape and Why It Matters" Lisa Jerris, and in "Looking the Other Way" Dianne Hayes, delve into the issues involved in acquaintance rape, and particularly rape on US college campuses. According to the Center for Disease Control and the 2015 documentary "The Hunting Ground" (Kirby Dick and Amy Ziering) as many as one in five women are sexually assaulted during their lifetime, the statistics are only slightly better for males. These rapes are often experienced during the victim's time in college, often perpetrated by people they know. Especially vulnerable are first year men and women unaware of the potential danger. These rape statistics are unacceptable by any standard, but campuses have a history of covering up or under reporting sexual assault, leaving their students unprepared and unprotected.

While "The Hunting Ground" may be considered "old media," women have turned to new media to take the message of the film to new audiences. The documentary screened on CNN and at film festivals and on college campuses, but YouTube and Twitter were the distributors of choice for Lena Dunham and Lady Gaga.

Gaga distributed a music video of her song "Til It Happens To You" and performed it at the Oscars. Dunham and her costars taped a short treatise called "She is Someone" (available on downvid.net) which Dunham premiered on Twitter.

In traditional media facts and information are the central focus, in the Lady Gaga's YouTube Video and Dunham's tweet, known faces and compelling voices approach the problem of rape in direct communication with the viewer. Advice is given, approaches to the problem offered. The formality of traditional media gives way to personal concern and healing messages. Gaga's well publicized sexual assault, and the female-centered voice of Dunham and the characters she creates, align with the pain and outrage of the receivers of their mediated messages, messages that are personal, strong and powerful.

Social media differs from the one directional, dominating voices of traditional media. The domination of media by males is being challenged by women. As access has expanded, new and multiple voices have evolved. The interactivity of the internet allows the receivers of a message to respond, to pass it on, to develop his or her own messages and post them for all to access. Contemporary media offers a powerful active voice to replace the passivity of the gaze. The ability to invent the future is in our grasp. How will we use it?

READING 16
MEDIA IN OUR IMAGE

By Johanna Blakley

Most people do not realize that women outnumber men in every age group on social networking sites around the world and they spend significantly more time on these sites than men do. Social media is having a transformative effect on traditional business models in every media industry, including publishing, TV, radio, film, music, and games. I am convinced that the growing influence of social media will help dismantle some of the silly and demeaning stereotypes that characterize media and advertising globally. In particular, I think that social media may help free us from the absurd assumptions we, as a society, have about gender.

Traditional media—which makes its living giving audiences what they seem to desire—has provided us with a surprisingly distorted mirror of our lives, and especially our gender. Most media businesses today use rigid segmentation methods in order to understand their audience. These methods are driven by classic demographics, which sum up human beings with a handful of restrictive labels based on how much money we make, the color of our skin, and our age and gender.

When marketers use demographics, they assume that certain demographics predict certain interests, which can predict a certain kind of purchasing behavior. Demographic-based marketing rose to dominance because it was too expensive to figure out people's *actual* interests, which is the marketer's holy grail because interests are much more closely aligned with purchasing behavior than any demographic model ever could be. But, because marketers, advertisers, and media companies could not reliably track the specific interests of individual members of very large audiences, these companies made a lot of assumptions about what people in certain demographic categories enjoy and want to buy.

The consequences of this business model are quite profound. Most of our popular culture is based upon assumptions about the interests of certain high-value demographic categories. The content that we hear on the radio, read in magazines, and see on screens large and small has been carefully crafted to deliver certain demographics to advertisers. The presumptions made about demographic preferences—what women want, what Hispanics like, what poor people prefer—comprise the underlying DNA of global popular culture.

I have studied the impact of demographics on advertising and media for several years. After focusing my attention on social media, I discovered the outsized role that women play in what many industry analysts acknowledge to be the most revolutionary technological development since the invention of the printing press.

Digital media, and especially social media, allows audience members to talk among themselves, to critique, remix, and redistribute content on an unprecedented scale. Of course participants in social networks belong to the same old demographic categories that media companies and advertisers have used to understand them, but now those categories mean even less than they did before. Geography and national boundaries are easily surmounted obstacles in our quest to network and converse with people who share our interests. And demographic categories often play no part in those conversations. In short, digital networks allow us to *opt out* of our demographic categories, which are often virtually invisible online ... and easily fudged as we go about constructing our own unique online identities.

Traditional media companies are desperate to understand these online communities because they realize that the future mass audience will be online and networked. That is the future. But one reason that the music, TV, and film industries are having a hard time understanding and monetizing these audiences is because they are still looking at them (that is, us) through the lens of demographics. Why? Because that is how ad rates are still determined.

But this will soon change. If you look at how people aggregate online, you do not find people clustering around age, gender, and income categories. What you find instead are "taste communities," heterogeneous groups of people who coalesce around the things they care about, which can range from serious political causes to pet toys. These audiences are ad hoc; they shift among sites, across link trails, they enter various walled gardens and then report back on their adventures on sites like Tumblr. Their meandering journeys across platforms and channels are driven by their effort to find compelling content that resonates with their taste, their beliefs, and their curiosity. I call them "transnational taste communities" (Blakley and Kaplan 2009, 37).

As media scholar Henry Jenkins observes, place and culture still matter, but fans who participate in these online communities are released from the constraints of geography to interact in real-time with fans around the world—many of whom have widely divergent understandings of the content that has brought them together, whether it's a Bollywood film, *Twilight*, *Harry Potter* books, or memes like Feminist Ryan Gosling (Jenkins 2006).

Shared values and interests are a far more powerful aggregator of people than age, gender, or income ever were. Those demographic categories are best understood as proxies, clues about what it is a potential customer *might* be interested in reading, watching, and buying. But any rational media company or advertiser would prefer to know what their potential customers have already indicated that they like, enjoy, and desire, which is one reason that online surveillance technologies such as cookies and web bugs are being used to capture the click streams and data trails of online audiences. While online citizens have every right to be alarmed by this new surveillance culture, they should also realize that there is something to be gained from being watched—from having their taste *respected* rather than *presumed*.

The fact that these transnational taste communities are being shaped primarily by women is nothing short of a game changer for global media industries. Although there are more adult men in the global Internet population, women not only outnumber men on social networking sites, they also spend significantly more time on these sites than men do. This is true in every region in the world, (Abraham, Mörn, and Vollman 2010) despite the digital divide between men and women in many traditional countries (Gill, Brooks, McDougall, Patel, and Kes 2010, 3).

Academic studies from a wide variety of disciplines have demonstrated that women do seem to have a much stronger drive to socialize than men. The fact that women, once online, gravitate toward social networks should not surprise us. But this dominance is not just in first world countries, but even in places where women have far less access to Internet-connected computers and smart phones. We do not tend to think about women as early adopters of new technology (Gill, Brooks, McDougall, Patel, and Kes 2010, 7), but all reports indicate that once women are online, they seek out social media sites far more passionately than men.

So what are the ramifications of women's demographic dominance of social media networks? We know that social media is transforming old media business models as companies try to figure out how to make money from online audiences. What might this mean for women, both inside the media industries and out? And what impact will it have on our media-saturated culture?

I believe that the content that makes up our current media environment is going to experience a profound shift. And one reason for this is that women are redefining what audiences are and what they actually want. But I do not believe we will simply trade demographic submission for demographic dominance. I think women will play a key role in planting a stake in the heart of the chick flick and all media content that is based on shallow demographic stereotypes about what men or Asians or young people really want. Instead, media and advertising will be a lot more data-driven and far less determined by demographic stereotypes and hunches about the appetites of eighteen to twenty-four year old men. They will be tailored to the taste of networked online communities where women happen to be the driving force.

But while women have taken over the online social media conversation, women are currently not in a position to dictate the development of those platforms nor the way they will be used by the media companies whose content is increasingly consumed there (Nielsen 2012). In Fortune 500 "technical" companies, women hold 10 percent of corporate officer positions and 11 percent of board of director positions (NCWIT 2010, 7). In the TV industry, only 16 percent of high-powered positions such as writing, directing and editing are held by women—down from a peak in 1998 (Lauzen 2011). Only four women have ever run a major film studio and on screen, the numbers are grim: the Screen Actors Guild reports that 62 percent of roles go to men (Masters, 2011) and a study found that less than 30 percent of all speaking characters in mainstream films were female (Smith 2010, 5).

Women have a tremendous opportunity, right here and now, to permanently adjust this picture. Social media has precipitated the emergence of audiences that were, as Xiaochang Li puts it, "unimaginable" in previous media distribution systems (2009, 77). Women's dominance of social media is a crucial development for feminist activists and scholars, who have doggedly documented the appalling way in which women have been represented in media, and the bizarre and destructive tactics that media industries have used to court (and exploit) female consumers. Global media companies and advertisers must learn to live without the primitive methods of audience segmentation that have produced debilitating stereotypes about women and every other demographic group that has been targeted with ad-supported content. Women now occupy the ground floor of the new media revolution: we need to make sure that we build the new media system in our own image, to our own specifications, customized for us.

THE PORTRAITS: MEDIA IN OUR IMAGE

These portraits meld together Renaissance conventions of portrait painting with contemporary visual-data mining. The goal was to create augmented portraits of ourselves that tell people more about our taste, values, and beliefs than about our demographic coordinates. We used word clouds, which reflect the relative frequency

Jasmine

Kate

of words within a data set, to summarize social media preferences and profile data from each of the portrait subjects. Inspired by the concept of lace veils that both reveal and obscure the subjects, we projected each sitter's own metadata on their physical bodies, creating a veil of revealing data.

The *Media In Our Image* portrait project was conceived by Johanna Blakley, Veronica Jauriqui, Sarah Ledesma, and photographer Jasmine Lord. Thanks to Kate Garner and Krystal Garber for revealing themselves to us. You can find more of these portraits, and more information about what inspired them, here:

http://mediainourimage.tumblr.com/

http://pinterest.com/sarahledesma/media-in-our-image/

WORKS CITED

Abraham, Linda Boland, Marie Pauline Mörn, and Andrea Vollman. 2010. *Women on the Web: How Women are Shaping the Internet*. comScore, Inc. June 30. http://www.comscore.com/Press_Events/ Presentations_Whitepapers/2010/Women_on_the_Web_How_Women_are_Shaping_the_Internet

Blakley, Johanna and Martin Kaplan. 2009. *The Business and Culture of Social Media: In search of the People Formerly Known as The Audience*. The Norman Lear Center. Presentation given at The Business and Culture of Social Media conference in Barcelona on June 26. http://www.learcenter. org/pdf/businessandcultureofsocialmedia.pdf

Gill, Kirrin, Kim Brooks, Janna McDougall, Payal Patel and Aslihan Kes. 2010. *Bridging the Gender Divide: How Technology Can Advance Women Economically*. International Center for Research on Women. http:// www.icrw.org/files/publications/Bridging-the-Gender-Divide-How-Technology-can-Advance-Women- Economically.pdf

Jenkins, Henry. 2006. *Fans, Bloggers and Gamers: Essays on Participatory Culture*. New York: New York University Press.

Lauzen, Martha M. 2011. *Boxed In: Employment of Behind-the-Scenes and On-Screen Women in the 2010–11 Prime-time Television Season*. Center for the Study of Women in Television. http://womenintvfilm.sdsu. edu/files/2010-2011_Boxed_In_Exec_Summ.pdf

Li, Xiaochang. *Dis/Locating Audience: Transnational Media Flows and the Online Circulation of East Asian Television Drama*. Master's thesis, Massachusetts Institute of Technology, 2009. http://cms.mit.edu/ research/theses/XiaochangLi2009.pdf

Masters, Kim. 2011. "State of the Industry: Are Things Better? You Might Not Like the Answer." *Hollywood Reporter*. December 13–16.

National Center for Women & Information Technology. 2010. *NCWIT Scorecard: A Report on the Status of Women in Information Technology*. http://ncwit.org/resources.scorecard.html

Nielsen. 2012. *State of the Media: The Cross-Platform Report: Quarter 3, 2011–US*. http://www.nielsen. com/content/dam/corporate/us/en/reports-downloads/2012%20Reports/Nielsen-Cross-Platform- Report-Q3-2011.pdf

Smith, Stacy L. and Marc Choueiti. 2010. *Gender Disparity On Screen and Behind the Camera in Family Films; The Executive Report*. Geena Davis Institute on Gender in Media. http://www.seejane.org/downloads/ FullStudy_GenderDisparityFamilyFilms.pdf

READING 17

AN OLD ENEMY IN A NEW OUTFIT: HOW DATE RAPE BECAME GRAY RAPE AND WHY IT MATTERS

By Lisa Jervis

It's very, very tempting to call gray rape a myth. As much as I want to (would that make it go away?), I can't. Because it's not a myth. No, no, my friends, gray rape—a term popularized by retro slut-shamer extraordinaire Laura Sessions Stepp, in September 2007's *Cosmopolitan* article "A New Kind of Date Rape," as "sex that falls somewhere between consent and denial" due to "casual hookups, missed signals, and alcohol"—is more like what one of the math teachers in my high school used to call an old friend in a new hat. More accurately, in this case it's an old enemy in a new short skirt. But hey, he was talking about a calculus variable and I'm talking about a disgusting, destructive, victim-blaming cultural construct that encourages women to hate ourselves, doubt ourselves, blame ourselves, take responsibility for other people's criminal behavior, fear our own desires, and distrust our own instincts.[1]

I'd love to dismiss this as the reactionary claptrap it is, but in the wake of Stepp's article and her casual-sex-will-damage-you-emotionally book *Unhooked: How Young Women Pursue Sex, Delay Love, and Fail at Both*, the concept has attracted the attention of criminal justice scholars, prosecutors, and sexual assault experts; news outlets from *The New York Times* to *Slate* to PBS's *To the Contrary*; college journalists; and countless bloggers, feminist and otherwise. And don't forget the other books that couch their disdain for sexual women in faux-concerned terms and urge us all to stifle our nasty urges in order to better society and/or preserve our chances of finding the love of a good man: Wendy Shalit's recent *Girls Gone Mild* (and its predecessor, the 1999 call to high collars *A Return to Modesty*), Dawn Eden's 2006 *The Thrill of the Chaste*, and Miriam Grossman's *Unprotected* in 2007. When mixed with the still-far-too-influential sentiments articulated by rape apologists like Camille "Woman's flirtatious arts of self-concealment mean man's approach must take the form of rape" Paglia and Katie "If 25 percent of my women friends were really being raped, wouldn't I know it?" Roiphe, it's a potent cocktail indeed.

Cosmo's sensationalistic headline declaration notwithstanding, everything about so-called gray rape seems awfully familiar: The experience is confusing, makes victims feel guilty and ashamed, and leaves them thinking they could and should have done something differently to prevent the attack. One of *Cosmo's* sources, Alicia, says she "ha[d] this dirty feeling of not knowing what to do or who to tell or whether it was my fault.... Maybe

I wasn't forceful enough in saying I didn't want it." Women also don't want to name their experience as rape because of the stigma of victimhood and the fear of not being believed: "While it felt like rape to her," writes Stepp of Alicia, "she was not sure if that's what anyone else would call it…. Even today, she is reluctant to call it rape because she thinks of herself as a strong and sexually independent woman, not a victim."

Having some déjà vu? That's because any therapist, sexual assault counselor, rape survivor, or close friend or family member of a rape survivor knows that feelings of guilt, shame, self-blame, and denial are common almost to the point of inevitability, no matter what the circumstances of the crime. People raped by strangers are going to torture themselves with thoughts of why they didn't know better and take a "safer" route home; people raped by dates, so-called friends, or the hot guy at the other end of the bar are going to torture themselves with thoughts of how they might have brought it on themselves by flirting, kissing, having that one last cocktail, fill in the blank with any detail a mind can seize upon in the wake of trauma. Rape survivors tend to echo one another in their comments, things like "I thought it was my fault. I felt humiliated and ashamed," and "I was too ashamed and confused to tell anyone what had happened. I tried to forget about it."[2]

Survivors of any attack that doesn't fit the most extreme stranger-in-the-bushes-with-a-knife paradigm are very often reluctant to name their experience as rape. When the culture teaches you that lack of consent is measured only in active, physical resistance, when *your* actions are questioned if your date refuses to respect "no," you're going to have a hard time calling rape by its real name. This is one of the reasons why feminists had to (and continue to) battle so hard for date rape to be taken seriously in the first place, and the reason why the title of the first major book examining the phenomenon, published in 1988, is *I Never Called It Rape*. It's a vicious cycle: Stigma and fear fuel guilt, shame, and denial, which our culture uses to shore up stigmas and fear. You can see the cycle at work in Alicia's experience above, in her desire to preserve her self-image as strong and sexually independent, as if someone else's actions were the key to those qualities in herself. You can see it in the way she worries that others might not agree that she was raped—and how she depends on their opinions to shape her own knowledge. You can see it in what Jezebel blogger Moe writes about her own assault, twisting herself like a verbal and emotional gymnast to cast her experience—with a "smarmy hair-product using type from [her] ex-boyfriend's frat" who, after being told repeatedly that she didn't want to have sex, waited until she slipped into a beery sleep before "sticking it in"—not as rape but as "one drunken regrettable night" and noting with something like approval that "*Cosmo* has come up with a new name for this kind of nonviolent collegiate date-rape sort of happening."

This is how the language of "gray rape" accelerates the victim-blaming cycle. The very concept the phrase relies on—that a supposed gray area of communication or intoxication means that you cannot trust your own memories, instincts, or experiences—is designed to exploit the stigma and fear that fuel the guilt, shame, and denial. But make no mistake—it is not a new concept, it's simply a new tactic. Gray rape and date rape are the same thing: a sexual assault in which the victim knows the attacker and may have consented to some kind of sexual activity with hir. Survivors of such attacks have always been reluctant to name their experience "rape." Despite gray rape proponents' eagerness to use this phenomenon to shift responsibility from rapists to victims, the fact remains that the reluctance in question is a symptom of the very social disease—sexism, misogyny, men's entitlement to women's bodies, and the idea that sexual interaction involves women's guarding the gates to the land of the sexy goodies as men try to cajole, manipulate, and force their way in—that enables rape in the first place.

And that social disease is evolving as fast as we can keep up. Weakness is no longer the prized quality of womanhood it once was, and despite the long, hard efforts of survivors and advocates to make clear that being a victim of rape says nothing about you and everything about your attacker (as Melissa McEwan of the blog Shakespeare's Sister puts it, "To be a survivor of rape does not have to mean shame and brokenness and guilt … it is brave, not weak, to say, plainly: 'I was raped'"), too many people still equate victimhood with frailty. Plus, though sexual expression for women has become destigmatized in some ways, culturally praised and accepted sexual expression (think *Girls Gone Wild*, pole-dancing classes, porn chic, and the Pussycat Dolls) tends to be more about display for a (presumably male) audience than about any kind of subjective pleasure. Women are now encouraged to look sexy for other people, but not to be sexual for ourselves. These messages about sexuality as culturally overdetermined sexiness have intensified over the last decade or so, keeping pace with supposed cultural acceptance of women's sexual activity in general—but they make it harder than ever for women to center our own authentic sexuality. When you're steeped in messages about looking hot at the expense of (or as a substitute for) feeling aroused or having sexual desire, it becomes all the easier for you to question your own judgment about what happened to you and believe the cultural forces telling you that your assault was just miscommunication and bad sex.

In the end, it's not all that surprising that someone would come up with an idea like "gray rape." Date rape and the cultural phenomena connected to it are something feminist anti-violence activists have been fighting to respond to and eradicate since there have been feminist anti-violence activists; anti-feminists, rape apologists, and proponents of a return to the days when women were roundly punished for doing anything but pinching a penny between their ankles have been trying to discredit our side all along the way. Over the two decades since the idea of date rape entered the public imagination, we've been pretty successful in getting cultural and institutional recognition that it's, um, wrong. Not that we've solved the problem or anything (if we had, this essay—and much of this book—wouldn't need to be written). But we've changed some cultural attitudes and taught many young people of all genders that consenting to some sexual activity with a person, or having consented to sex with a person in the past, doesn't mean you've consented to anything and everything with that person, or that you automatically consent to fuck that person again, and that a quiet "no," even if it's not accompanied by a knee to the groin or any other physical struggle, is still a valid "no." In other words, we've been at least moderately successful in demonstrating that date rape is, in fact, rape.

But backlash is a devious little douchebag, and there are still people who think that women are ruining everything with our slutty, sexually aggressive, entitled-to-our-own-pleasure (gasp!) attitude; these folks are always in need of ammunition, both legal and conceptual. The fact that feminism's battles are unfinished means that it's all too easy to enlist flat-out lies—that consent to kissing means consent to more, or that one person's drunkenness excuses another person's criminal acts—in service of beating back new sexual mores, ones with the potential to free women from being punished just for wanting the full human experience of sexuality and sexual exploration. So they've gone and rebranded their old friend, dressing her in a new outfit in the hope of keeping women feeling good 'n' guilty about our sexuality and our desires, scared to stand up for ourselves and demand accountability for violence against us, scared to insist on acceptance of our sexuality on equal terms with men's. *Cosmo* shows its ass quite clearly here, making obvious an investment in threats of violence to keep women in line: "So how do you avoid being a victim without giving up the right to be sexually independent and assertive? Many psychologists feel that the first step is to acknowledge the dangers inherent in the free-and-easy hookup approach to dating and sex. 'We all have vulnerabilities, and we all can be taken advantage of,' says [psychotherapist Robi] Ludwig. 'Though you're successful at school, sports, whatever, *you must see yourself—as a woman—as vulnerable*'" (emphasis added). In the context of the article, this is not an encouragement of commonsense caution; it's an attempt to enlist women in the project of our own subjugation. The message is clear: Your sexual desire is dangerous. You can stifle it or you can be a slut who lives in fear and gets what she deserves. These are the only two choices in the world of gray rape.

The cherry on top of this backlash sundae is that to the Laura Sessions Stepp/Wendy Shalit modesty-or-bust crowd, feminism is to blame for gray rape because feminism has promoted women's sexual freedom and power—and if women weren't feeling all empowered and happy about their sexuality, they wouldn't go hitting on guys, making out with them, or having consensual hookups. But here's the thing: Flirting and hookups do not cause rape. Rapists and the culture that creates them—with its mixed messages and double standards—cause rape. Feminism is working to dismantle that culture, but we've been only partly successful so far. Blaming feminism for the damage remaining when we've made insufficient change is just like exploiting a rape survivor's totally normal feelings of confusion and shame, far from a new strategy. Feminism has been blamed by right-wing commentators for everything from drinking among teen girls (because we've encouraged them to do anything boys can) to women's postdivorce poverty (because we've convinced women they can get along just fine without a man), when really those things have just as much to do with sexism as with anything else (in these cases, the need to relieve gendered social pressure toward perfectionism and a little thing called the wage gap, respectively). I'll happily admit that feminism has helped pave the way for more sexual autonomy (not, it's well worth noting, just for women but for people of both genders). The progress we've made toward integrating the virgin/whore split—that now women can want sex and still be good people (as long as their desire is bounded by love and commitment)—was driven by feminism. But the fucked-up attitude our culture has about consent, illustrated by the fact that too many people still think that "no" can be part of a coy seduction strategy, has nothing to do with feminism, except that it's still our goal to change it. The attitude itself is clearly the fault of our old friend misogyny, and we must continue to be vigilant about keeping the blame for sexual assault squarely where it belongs.

If you want to read more about Is CONSENT COMPLICATED?, try:
- Beyond Yes or No: Consent as Sexual Process by **Rachel Kramer Bussel**
- Reclaiming Touch: Rape Culture, Explicit Verbal Consent, and Body Sovereignty by **Hazel/Cedar Troost**
- An Immodest Proposal by **Heather Corinna**

If you want to read more about MEDIA MATTERS, try:
- Offensive Feminism: The Conservative Gender Norms That Perpetuate Rape Culture, and How Feminists Can Fight Back by **Jill Filipovic**
- The Fantasy of Acceptable "Non-Consent": Why the Female Sexual Submissive Scares Us (and Why She Shouldn't) by **Stacey May Fowles**
- In Defense of Going Wild or: How I Stopped Worrying and Learned to Love Pleasure (and How You Can, Too) by **Jaclyn Friedman**

READING 18

LOOKING THE OTHER WAY?

By Dianne Hayes

Calls for higher accountability intensify amid numerous recent sexual assault incidents on college campuses.

The reality of rape and sexual harassment on college campuses has long been a burden that many institutions have struggled to address. The image of fraternity parties gone bad, date rape and the incidents of stranger encounters on campus are all contrary to the idyllic image most universities want to portray.

However, in light of several high-profile cases, colleges are being called to a higher level of accountability when it comes to rape and the treatment of women on campus.

"Unfortunately, campus sexual assault is fairly common," said Holly Kearl, program manager, American Association of University Women (AAUW) Legal Advocacy Fund. "The Rape, Abuse and Incest National Network reports that college-aged women are four times more likely than any other group to face sexual assault. The reasons for this vary from students being new and in unfamiliar environments or maybe being in environments where they can drink for the first time. In many sports and [fraternity settings], there is a strong need to prove manhood."

Campuses are feeling the pressure to respond more quickly and publicly to sensitive issues of sexual assault.

At Yale University last March, a group of 16 students and alumni filed a 26-page Title IX complaint charging that the campus is a sexually hostile environment. The Department of Education's Office for Civil Rights has reportedly launched an investigation. One of the incidents described by the group involved men who were pledging a fraternity who gathered in a public spot on campus chanting: "No means yes, yes means anal." Federal authorities are investigating whether Yale has failed to effectively handle complaints of sexual harassment and assault.

The investigation, which began last year, came just after Washington spelled out higher education's new legal obligations to respond to sexual violence. Vice President Joe Biden announced the federal guidelines during an April 4 speech at the University of New Hampshire. "No means no, if you're drunk or you're sober," Biden said. "No means no if you're in bed, in a dorm or on the street. No means no even if you said yes at first and you changed your mind. No means no."

INCREASED TRANSPARENCY

Yale's administration has responded to concerns about transparency by issuing its first semi-annual report of 52 allegations in a period covering July 1 to Dec. 31, 2011. The allegations of misconduct by students or employees range from harassing remarks to rape. The new transparency is part of an overhaul adopted last year in the face of criticism about how it has handled some cases in the past.

The report was issued in January by Deputy Provost Stephanie Spangler, who was appointed last November to oversee Yale's Title IX compliance efforts and to lead the new educational and outreach initiatives.

"There is more that we must do as a community and as individuals to prevent sexual misconduct and to ensure that Yale's culture is optimally supportive and unfailingly respectful of all individuals," Spangler said.

In a statement to the community issued by the university, Yale President Richard C. Levin said, "The number of complaints of sexual misconduct brought forward and outlined in the report is a matter of deep concern. Even though only a very small fraction of our campus population is alleged to be violating our policies, our aspiration must be to raise the bar so that no one believes that sexual misconduct is acceptable—and all act accordingly."

Recently, the Department of Justice launched a civil investigation into more than 80 reported rapes in the past three years at the University of Montana at Missoula, where 11 student-related cases surfaced in recent months. The probe addresses complaints that authorities failed to aggressively investigate sexual assault reports in Missoula. The university has about 15,600 students.

The federal review follows a University of Montana investigation that began in December with allegations that two students were gang-raped, possibly after being drugged by several male students. According to reports, in February, the university notified a Saudi exchange student that he had been accused of rape but the student fled the country before his alleged victim filed a report with police.

A HOSTILE CLIMATE

The problem of rape and sexual harassment touches just about every campus in America. According to AAUW data, during the course of their college careers, between 20 and 25 percent of women will be sexually assaulted or experience attempted assault. Of those assaults, 95 percent go unreported—making sexual assault the most drastically underreported crime.

AAUW reports that 13 percent of women are stalked during the academic year, and 90 percent know the person who sexually assaulted or raped them. Seventy-five percent of the time, the offender, the victim, or both have been drinking. And most shocking is the fact that 42 percent of raped women tell no one about the assault and that same number expect to be raped again.

According to a 2009 investigation by the Center for Public Integrity, the primary reason that people don't report rape is because of institutional barriers from administrators who respond to students with disbelief or other inappropriate behavior and campus judiciary processes that are difficult to understand and follow. Frequently, students were discouraged and transferred or withdrew from their schools, while the attackers were rarely punished.

Last month, President Obama issued a proclamation acknowledging National Sexual Assault Awareness and Prevention Month. The proclamation stated, "Rape and sexual assault inflict profound suffering upon millions of Americans every year. Nearly one in five women has been raped, and still more have endured other forms of sexual violence or abuse. Tragically, these crimes take their greatest toll on young people; women between the ages of 16 and 24 are at greatest risk of rape and sexual assault, and many victims, male and female, first experience abuse during childhood. The trauma of sexual violence leaves scars that may never fully heal. Many survivors experience depression, fear, and suicidal feelings in the months and years following an assault, and some face health problems that last a lifetime."

A NEW GUARD

Biden joined Secretary of Education Arne Duncan in releasing new guidelines designed to help schools and universities protect students from the threat of sexual violence and urged young men and women to take a proactive stance on the issue.

Left: Joseph D. Vess, director of training for Men Can Stop Rape, addresses a group; Top: Men Can Stop Rape executive director Neil Irvin; Bottom: Georgetown University's Where Do You Stand program kicked off January 31 to combat sexual assault on campus.

The new guidelines are intended to clarify the legal obligations of schools receiving federal funding under Title IX—which prohibits discrimination in education programs and activities on the basis of gender—with regard to responding to incidents of sexual assault or violence.

Students are involved in efforts to change the culture on college campuses through programs like Men Can Stop Rape, headquartered in Washington, D.C. Men Can Stop Rape is a national organization that mobilizes boys and men to prevent all forms of physical and sexual violence, especially violence against women. The program has reached more than 2 million boys and men in the past 10 years with a message of "strength without violence."

Men Can Stop Rape offers student-led campus clubs where college men are taught to challenge traditional stereotypes of masculinity and also sponsors awareness events on campus. The organization also provides training on campuses and military bases and has launched several campaigns including the "Where Do You Stand?" campaign that empowers male bystanders to intervene in a variety of common and potentially dangerous scenarios that students face on campus.

"The laws have been on the books for some time including Title IX and the Cleary Act, which requires schools to report assaults, but whenever there are cases that make it into the media there is a lot more scrutiny," said Kearl of AAUW. "The Obama administration issued a letter urging people to do more. Certainly, having the administration recognize that this is a big problem helps."

Men Can Stop Rape programs include sexual assault prevention training, awareness events, partnering with women's groups like the American Association of University Women, and efforts to encourage classmates, fraternity brothers and friends to stand up against violence on campuses.

Joseph D. Vess, director of training and technical assistance for Men Can Stop Rape, said he gets mixed reactions when he first introduces the program to students.

"Some are excited and energized and a sizable minority really sees a need, while a vast majority is just confused. As a society, we don't tell men how they can play an active role in preventing violence against women. Many times the reaction is that they never thought of it that way. A lot of them come around and see how important it is."

READING 19
THE OPPOSITIONAL GAZE: BLACK FEMALE SPECTATORSHIP

By bell hooks

When thinking about black female spectators, I remember being punished as a child for staring, for those hard, intense, direct looks children would give grown-ups, looks that were seen as confrontational, as gestures of resistance, challenges to authority. The "gaze" has always been political in my life. Imagine the terror felt by the child who has come to understand through repeated punishments that one's gaze can be dangerous. The child who has learned so well to look the other way when necessary. Yet, when punished, the child is told by parents, "Look at me when I talk to you." Only, the child is afraid to look. Afraid to look, but fascinated by the gaze. There is power in looking.

Amazed the first time I read in history classes that white slave-owners (men, women, and children) punished enslaved black people for looking, I wondered how this traumatic relationship to the gaze had informed black parenting and black spectator-ship. The politics of slavery, of racialized power relations, were such that the slaves were denied their right to gaze. Connecting this strategy of domination to that used by grown folks in Southern black rural communities where I grew up, I was pained to think that there was no absolute difference between whites who had oppressed black people and ourselves. Years later, reading Michel Foucault, I thought again about these connections, about the ways power as domination reproduces itself in different locations employing similar apparatuses, strategies, and mechanisms of control. Since I knew as a child that the dominating power adults exercised over me and over my gaze was never so absolute that I did not dare to look, to sneak a peep, to stare dangerously, I knew that the slaves had looked. That all attempts to repress our/ black people's right to gaze had produced in us an overwhelming longing to look, a rebellious desire, an oppositional gaze. By courageously looking, we defiantly declared: "Not only will I stare. I want my look to change reality." Even in the worst circumstances of domination, the ability to manipulate one's gaze in the face of structures of domination that would contain it opens up the possibility of agency. In much of his work, Michel Foucault insists on describing domination in terms of "relations of power," as part of an effort to challenge the assumption that "power is a system of domination which controls everything and which leaves no room for freedom." Emphatically stating that in all relations of power "there is necessarily the possibility of resistance," he invites the critical thinker to search those margins, gaps, and locations on and through the body where agency can be found.

Stuart Hall calls for recognition of our agency as black spectators in his essay "Cultural Identity and Cinematic Representation." Speaking against the construction of white representations of blackness as totalizing, Hall says of white presence: "The error is not to conceptualize this 'presence' in terms of power, but to locate that power as wholly external to us—as extrinsic force, whose influence can be thrown off like the serpent sheds its skin. What Franz Fanon reminds us, in *Black Skin, White Masks*, is how power is inside as well as outside:

> The movements, the attitudes, the glances of the Other fixed me there, in the sense in which a chemical solution is fixed by a dye. I was indignant; I demanded an explanation. Nothing happened. I burst apart. Now the fragments have been put together again by another self. This "look," from—so to speak—the place of the Other, fixes us, not only in its violence, hostility and aggression, but in the ambivalence of its desire.

Spaces of agency exist for black people, wherein we can both interrogate the gaze of the Other but also look back, and at one another, naming what we see. The "gaze" has been and is a site of resistance for colonized black people globally. Subordinates in relations of power learn experientially that there is a critical gaze, one that "looks" to document, one that is oppositional. In resistance struggle the power of the dominated to assert agency by claiming and cultivating "awareness" politicizes "looking" relations—one learns to look a certain way in order to resist.

When most black people in the United States first had the opportunity to look at film and television, they did so fully aware that the mass media was a system of knowledge and power reproducing and maintaining white supremacy. To stare at the television, or mainstream movies, to engage its images was to engage its negation of black representation. It was the oppositional black gaze that responded to these looking relations by developing an independent black cinema. Black viewers of mainstream cinema and television could chart the progress of political movements for racial equality via the construction of images, and did so. Within my family's Southern black working-class home, located in a racially segregated neighborhood, watching television was one way to develop critical spectatorship. Unless you went to work in the white world, across the tracks, you learned to look at white people by staring at them on the screen. Black looks, as they were constituted in the context of social movements for racial uplift, were interrogating gazes. We laughed at television shows like *Our Gang* and *Amos 'n' Andy* at these white representations of blackness, but we also looked at them critically. Before racial integration, black reviewers of movies and television experienced visual pleasure in a context where looking was also about contestation and confrontation.

Writing about black looking relations in "Black British Cinema: Spectatorship and Identity Formation in Territories," Manthia Diawara identifies the power of the spectator: "Every narration places the spectator in a position of agency; and race, class and sexual relations influence the way in which this subjecthood is filled by the spectator." Of particular concern for him are moments of "rupture," when the spectator resists "complete identification with the film's discourse." These ruptures define the relation between black spectators and dominant cinema prior to racial integration. Then, one's enjoyment of a film wherein representations of blackness were stereotypically degrading and dehumanizing coexisted with a critical practice that restored presence where it was negated. Critical discussion of the film while it was in progress or at its conclusion maintained the distance between the spectator and the image. Black films were also subject to critical interrogation. Since they came into being in part as a response to the failure of white-dominated cinema to represent blackness in a manner that did not reinforce white supremacy, they too were critiqued to see if images were seen as complicit with dominant cinematic practices.

Critical, interrogating black looks were mainly concerned with issues of race and racism, the way racial domination of blacks by whites overdetermined representation. They were rarely concerned with gender. As spectators, black men could repudiate the reproduction of racism in cinema and television, the negation of black presence, even as they could feel as though they were rebelling against white supremacy by daring to look, by engaging phallocentric politics of spectatorship. Given the real-life public circumstances wherein black men were murdered/lynched for looking at white womanhood, where the black male gaze was always subject to control and/or punishment by the powerful white Other, the private realm of television screens or dark theaters could unleash the repressed gaze. There they could "look" at white womanhood without a structure of domination overseeing the gaze, interpreting and punishing. The white supremacist structure that had murdered Emmet Till after interpreting his look as violation, as "rape" of white womanhood, could not control black male responses to screen images. In their role as spectators, black men could enter an imaginative space of phallocentric power that mediated racial negation. This gendered relation to looking made the experience of the black male spectator radically different from that of the black female spectator. Major early black male independent filmmakers represented black women in their films as objects of a male gaze. Whether looking through the camera or as spectators watching films, whether mainstream cinema or "race" movies such as those made by Oscar Micheaux, the black male gaze had a different scope from that of the black female.

Black women have written little about black female spectator-ship, about our moviegoing practices. A growing body of film theory and criticism by black women has only begun to emerge. The prolonged silence of black women as spectators and critics was a response to absence, to cinematic negation. In "The Technology of Gender," Teresa de Lauretis, drawing on the work of Monique Wittig, calls attention to "the power of discourses to 'do violence' to people, a violence which is material and physical, although produced by abstract and scientific discourses as well as the discourses of the mass media." With the possible exception of early race movies, black female spectators have had to develop looking relations within a cinematic context that constructs our presence as absence that denies the "body" of the black female so as to perpetuate white supremacy and with it a phallocentric spectatorship where the woman to be looked at and desired is "white." (Recent movies do not conform to this paradigm, but I am turning to the past with the intent to chart the development of black male spectatorship.)

Talking with black women of all ages and classes, in different areas of the United States, about their filmic looking relations, I hear again and again ambivalent responses to cinema. Only a few of the black women I talked with remembered the pleasure of race movies, and even those who did felt that pleasure interrupted and usurped by Hollywood. Most of the black women I talked with were adamant that they never went to movies expecting to see compelling representations of black femaleness. They were all acutely aware of cinematic racism—its violent erasure of black womanhood. Anne Friedberg stresses in her essay "A Denial of Difference: Theories of Cinematic Identification" that "identification can only be made through recognition, and all recognition is itself an implicit confirmation of the ideology of the status quo." Even when representations of black women were present in film, our bodies and being were there to serve—to enhance and maintain white womanhood as object of the phallocentric gaze.

Commenting on Hollywood's characterization of black women in *Girls on Film*, Julie Burchill described this absent presence:

> Black women have been mothers without children (Mammies—who can ever forget the sickening spectacle of Hattie MacDaniels waiting on the simpering Vivien Leigh hand and foot and enquiring like a ninny, "What's ma lamb gonna wear?").... Lena Horne, the first black performer signed to a long term contract with a major (MGM), looked gutless but was actually quite spirited. She seethed when Tallulah Bankhead complimented her on the paleness of her skin and the non-Negroidness of her features.

When black women actresses like Lena Horne appeared in mainstream cinema, most white viewers were not aware that they were looking at black females unless the film was specifically coded as being about blacks. Burchill is one of the few white women film critics who has dared to examine the intersection of race and gender in relation to the construction of the category "woman" in film as object of the phallocentric gaze. With characteristic wit she asserts: "What does it say about racial purity that the best blondes have all been brunettes (Harlow, Monroe, Bardot?) I think it says that we are not as white as we think." Burchill could easily have said, "We are not as white as we want to be," for clearly the obsession to have white women film stars be ultra white was a cinematic practice that sought to maintain a distance, a separation between that image and the black female Other; it was a way to perpetuate white supremacy. Politics of race and gender were inscribed into mainstream cinematic narrative from *Birth of a Nation* on. As a seminal work, this film identified what the place and function of white womanhood would be in cinema. There was clearly no place for black women.

Remembering my past in relation to screen images of black womanhood, I wrote a short essay, "Do You Remember Sapphire?" that explored both the negation of black female representation in cinema and television and our rejection of these images. Identifying the character of Sapphire from *Amos 'n' Andy* as that screen representation of black femaleness I first saw in childhood, I write:

> She was even then backdrop, foil. She was bitch—nag. She was there to soften images of black men, to make them seem vulnerable, easygoing, funny, and unthreatening to a white audience. She was there as man in drag, as castrating bitch, as someone to be lied to, someone to be tricked, someone the white and black audience could hate. Scapegoated on all sides. *She was not us.* We laughed with the black men, with the white people. We laughed at this black woman who was not us. And we did not even long to be there on the screen. How could we long to be there when our image, visually constructed, was so ugly? We did not long to be there. We did not long for her. We did not

want our construction to be this hated black female thing—foil, backdrop. Her black female image was not the body of desire. There was nothing to see. She was not us.

Grown black women had a different response to Sapphire; they identified with her frustrations and her woes. They resented the way she was mocked. They resented the way these screen images could assault black womanhood, could name us bitches, nags. And in opposition they claimed Sapphire as their own, as the symbol of that angry part of themselves white folks and black men could not even begin to understand.

Conventional representations of black women have done violence to the image. Responding to this assault, many black women spectators shut out the image, looked the other way, accorded cinema no importance in their lives. Then there were those spectators whose gaze was that of desire and complicity. Assuming a posture of subordination, they submitted to cinema's capacity to seduce and betray. They were cinematically "gaslighted." Every black woman I spoke with who was/is an ardent moviegoer, a lover of the Hollywood film testified that to experience fully the pleasure of that cinema she had to close down critique, analysis; she had to forget racism. And mostly those women did not think about sexism. What was the nature, then, of this adoring black female gaze—this look that could bring pleasure in the midst of negation? In her first novel, *The Bluest Eye*, Toni Morrison constructs a portrait of the black female spectator; her gaze is the masochistic look of victimization. Describing her looking relations, Miss Pauline Breedlove, a poor working woman, maid in the house of a prosperous white family, asserts:

> The onliest time I be happy seem like was when I was in the picture show. Every time I got, I went, I'd go early, before the show started. They's cut off the lights, and everything be black. Then the screen would light up, and I's over right on in them picture. White men taking such good care of they women, and they all dressed up in big clean houses with the bath tubs right in the same room with the toilet. Them pictures gave me a lot of pleasure.

To experience pleasure, Miss Pauline sitting in the dark must imagine herself transformed, turned into the white woman portrayed on the screen. After watching movies, feeling the pleasure, she says, "But it made coming home hard."

We come home to ourselves. Not all black women spectators submitted to that spectacle of regression through identification. Most of the women I talked with felt that they consciously resisted identification with films—that this tension made movie-going less than pleasurable; at times it caused pain. As one black woman put, "I could always get pleasure from movies as long as I did not look too deep." For black female spectators who have "looked too deep" the encounter with the screen hurt. That some of us chose to stop looking was a gesture of resistance, turning away was one way to protest, to reject negation. My pleasure in the screen ended abruptly when I and my sisters first watched *Imitation of Life*. Writing about this experience in the "Sapphire" piece, I addressed the movie directly, confessing:

I had until now forgotten you, that screen image seen in adolescence, those images that made me stop looking. It was there in *Imitation of Life*, that comfortable mammy image. There was something familiar about this hardworking black woman who loved her daughter so much, loved her in a way that hurt. Indeed, as young southern black girls watching this film, Peola's mother reminded us of the hardworking, churchgoing, Big Mamas we knew and loved. Consequently, it was not this image that captured our gaze; we were fascinated by Peola.

Addressing her, I wrote:

> You were different. There was something scary in this image of young sexual sensual black beauty betrayed—that daughter who did not want to be confined by blackness, that "tragic mulatto" who did not want to be negated. "Just let me escape this image forever," she could have said. I will always remember that image. I remembered how we cried for her, for our unrealized desiring selves. She was tragic because there was no place in the cinema for her, no loving pictures. She too was absent image. It was better then, that we were absent, for when we were there it was humiliating, strange, sad. We cried all night for you, for the cinema that had no place for you. And like you, we stopped thinking it would one day be different.

When I returned to films as a young woman, after a long period of silence, I had developed an oppositional gaze. Not only would I not be hurt by the absence of black female presence, or the insertion of violating representation, I interrogated the work, cultivated a way to look past race and gender for aspects of content, form, language. Foreign films and U.S. independent cinema were the primary locations of my filmic looking relations, even though I also watched Hollywood films.

From "jump," black female spectators have gone to films with awareness of the way in which race and racism determined the visual construction of gender. Whether it was *Birth of a Nation* or Shirley Temple shows, we knew that white womanhood was the racialized sexual difference occupying the place of stardom in mainstream narrative film. We assumed white women knew it too. Reading Laura Mulvey's provocative essay, "Visual Pleasure and Narrative Cinema," from a standpoint that acknowledges race, one sees clearly why black women spectators not duped by mainstream cinema would develop an oppositional gaze. Placing ourselves outside that pleasure in looking, Mulvey argues, was determined by a "split between active/male and passive/female." Black female spectators actively chose not to identify with the film's imaginary subject because such identification was disenabling.

Looking at films with an oppositional gaze, black women were able to critically assess the cinema's construction of white womanhood as object of phallocentric gaze and choose not to identify with either the victim or the perpetrator. Black female spectators, who refused to identify with white womanhood, who would not take on the phallocentric gaze of desire and possession, created a critical space where the binary opposition Mulvey posits of "woman as image, man as bearer of the look" was continually deconstructed. As critical spectators, black women looked from a location that disrupted, one akin to that described by Annette Kuhn in *The Power of the Image*:

... the acts of analysis, of deconstruction and of reading "against the grain" offer an additional plea-sure—the pleasure of resistance, of saying "no": not to "unsophisticated" enjoyment, by ourselves and others, of culturally dominant images, but to the structures of power which ask us to consume them uncritically and in highly circumscribed ways.

Mainstream feminist film criticism in no way acknowledges black female spectatorship. It does not even consider the possibility that women can construct an oppositional gaze via an understanding and awareness of the politics of race and racism. Feminist film theory rooted in an ahistorical psychoanalytic framework that privileges sexual difference actively suppresses recognition of race, reenacting and mirroring the erasure of black womanhood that occurs in films, silencing any discussion of racial difference—of racialized sexual dif-ference. Despite feminist critical interventions aimed at deconstructing the category "woman" which highlight the significance of race, many feminist film critics continue to structure their discourse as though it speaks about "women" when in actually it speaks only about white women. It seems ironic that the cover of the recent anthology *Feminism and Film Theory* edited by Constance Penley has a graphic that is a reproduction of the photo of white actresses Rosalind Russell and Dorothy Arzner on the 1935 set of the film *Craig's Wife* yet there is no acknowledgement in any essay in this collection that the woman "subject" under discussion is always white. Even though there are photos of black women from films reproduced in the text, there is no acknowledgement of racial difference.

It would be too simplistic to interpret this failure of insight solely as a gesture of racism. Importantly, it also speaks to the problem of structuring feminist film theory around a totalizing narrative of women as object whose image functions solely to reaffirm and reinscribe patriarchy. Mary Ann Doane addresses this issue in the essay "Remembering Women: Psychical and Historical Construction in Film Theory":

> This attachment to the figure of a degeneralizible Woman as the product of the apparatus indicates why, for many, feminist film theory seems to have reached an impasse, a certain blockage in its theorization…. In focusing upon the task of delineating in great detail the attributes of woman as effect of the apparatus, feminist film theory participates in the abstraction of women.

The concept "woman" effaces the difference between women in specific sociohistorical contexts, between women defined precisely as historical subjects rather than as *a* psychic subject (or nonsubject). Though Doane does not focus on race, her comments speak directly to the problem of its erasure. For it is only as one imagines "woman" in the abstract, when woman becomes fiction or fantasy, that race cannot be seen as significant. Are we really to imagine that feminist theorists writing only about images of white women, who subsume this spe-cific historical subject under the totalizing category "woman," do not "see" the whiteness of the image? It may very well be that they engage in a process of denial that eliminates the necessity of revisioning conventional ways of thinking about psychoanalysis as a paradigm of analysis and the need to rethink a body of feminist film theory that is firmly rooted in a denial of the reality that sex/sexuality may not be the primary and/or exclusive signifier of difference. Doane's essay appears in the anthology, *Psychoanalysis and Cinema* edited by E. Ann Kaplan, where, once again, none of the theory presented acknowledges or discusses racial difference, with the exception of one essay, "Not Speaking with Language, Speaking with No Language," which problematizes notions of orientalism in its examination of Leslie Thornton's film *Adynata*. Yet in most of the essays, the theories espoused are rendered problematic if one includes race as a category of analysis.

Constructing feminist film theory along these lines enables the production of a discursive practice that need never theorize any aspect of black female representation or spectatorship. Yet the existence of black women within white supremacist culture problematizes, and makes complex, the overall issue of female identity, representation, and spectatorship. If, as Friedberg suggests, "identification is a process which commands the subject to be displaced by an other; it is a procedure which breaches the separation between self and other, and, in this way, replicates the very structure of patriarchy," if identification "demands sameness, necessitates similarity, disallows difference"—must we then surmise that many feminist film critics who are "over-identified" with the mainstream cinematic apparatus produce theories that replicate its totalizing agenda? Why is it that feminist film criticism, which has most claimed the terrain of woman's identity, representation, and subjectivity as its field of analysis, remains aggressively silent on the subject of blackness and specifically representations of black womanhood? Just as mainstream cinema has historically forced aware black female spectators not to look, much feminist film criticism disallows the possibility of a theoretical dialogue that might include black women's voices. It is difficult to talk when you feel no one is listening, when you feel as though a special jargon or narrative has been created that only the chosen can understand. No wonder then that black women have for the most part confined our critical commentary on film to conversations. And it must be reiterated that this gesture is a strategy that protects us from the violence perpetuated and advocated by discourses of mass media. A new focus on issues of race and representation in the field of film theory could critically intervene on the historical repression reproduced in some arenas of contemporary critical practice, making a discursive space for discussion of black female spectatorship possible.

When I asked a black woman in her twenties, an obsessive moviegoer, why she thought we had not written about black female spectatorship, she commented: "We are afraid to talk about ourselves as spectators because we have been so abused by 'the gaze.'" An aspect of that abuse was the imposition of the assumption that black female looking relations were not important enough to theorize. Film theory as a critical "turf" in the United States has been and continues to be influenced by and reflective of white racial domination. Since feminist film criticism was initially rooted in a women's liberation movement informed by racist practices, it did not open up the discursive terrain and make it more inclusive. Recently, even those white film theorists who include an analysis of race show no interest in black female spectatorship. In her introduction to the collection of essays *Visual and Other Pleasures*, Laura Mulvey describes her initial romantic absorption in Hollywood cinema, stating:

> Although this great, previously unquestioned and unanalyzed love was put in crisis by the impact of
> feminism on my thought in the early 1970s, it also had an enormous influence on the development
> of my critical work and ideas and the debate within film culture with which I became preoccupied
> over the next fifteen years or so. Watched through eyes that were affected by the changing climate of
> consciousness, the movies lost their magic.

Watching movies from a feminist perspective, Mulvey arrived at that location of disaffection that is the starting point for many black women approaching cinema within the lived harsh reality of racism. Yet her account of being a part of a film culture whose roots rest on a founding relationship of adoration and love indicate how difficult it would have been to enter that world from "jump" as a critical spectator whose gaze had been formed in opposition.

Given the context of class exploitation, and racist and sexist domination, it has only been through resistance, struggle, reading, and looking "against the grain" that black women have been able to value our process of looking enough to publicly name it. Centrally, those black female spectators who attest to the oppositionality of their gaze deconstruct theories of female spectatorship that have relied heavily on the assumption that, as Doane suggests in her essay "Woman's Stake: Filming the Female Body," "woman can only mimic man's relation to language, that is, assume a position defined by the penis-phallus as the supreme arbiter of lack." Identifying with neither the phallocentric gaze nor the construction of white womanhood as black, critical black female spectators construct a theory of looking relations where cinematic visual delight is the pleasure of interrogation. Every black woman spectator I talked to, with rare exception, spoke of being "on guard" at the movies. Talking about the way being a critical spectator of Hollywood films influenced her, black woman filmmaker Julie Dash exclaims, "I make films because I was such a spectator!" Looking at Hollywood cinema from a distance, from that critical politicized standpoint that did not want to be seduced by narratives reproducing her negation, Dash watched mainstream movies over and over again for the pleasure of deconstructing them. And of course there is that added delight if one happens, in the process of interrogation, to come across a narrative that invites the black female spectator to engage the text with no threat of violation.

Significantly, I began to write film criticism in response to the first Spike Lee movie, *She's Gotta Have It*, contesting Lee's replication of mainstream patriarchal cinematic practices that explicitly represent woman (in this instance black woman) as the object of a phallocentric gaze. Lee's investment in patriarchal filmic practices that mirror dominant patterns makes him the perfect black candidate for entrance to the Hollywood canon. His work mimics the cinematic construction of white womanhood as object, replacing her body as text on which to write male desire with the black female body. It is transference without transformation. Entering the discourse of film criticism from the politicized location of resistance, of not wanting, as a working-class black woman I interviewed stated, "to see black women in the position white women have occupied in film forever," I began to think critically about black female spectatorship.

For years I went to independent and/or foreign films where I was the only black female present in the theater. I often imagined that in every theater in the United States there was another black woman watching the same film wondering why she was the only visible black female spectator. I remember trying to share with one of my five sisters the cinema I liked so much. She was "enraged" that I brought her to a theater where she would have to read subtitles. To her it was a violation of Hollywood notions of spectatorship, of coming to the movies to be entertained. When I interviewed her to ask what had changed her mind over the years, led her to embrace this cinema, she connected it to coming to critical consciousness, saying, "I learned that there was more to looking than I had been exposed to in ordinary (Hollywood) movies." I shared that though most of the films I loved were all white, I could engage them because they did not have in their deep structure a subtext reproducing the narrative of white supremacy. Her response was to say that these films demystified "whiteness," since the lives they depicted seemed less rooted in fantasies of escape. They were, she suggested, more like "what we knew life to be, the deeper side of life as well." Always more seduced and enchanted with Hollywood cinema than me, she stressed that unaware black female spectators must "break out," no longer be imprisoned by images that enact a drama of our negation. Though she still sees Hollywood films, because "they are a major influence in the culture"—she no longer feels duped or victimized.

Talking with black female spectators, looking at written discussions either in fiction or academic essays about black women, I noted the connection made between the realm of representation in mass media and the capacity of black women to construct ourselves as subjects in daily life. The extent to which black women feel devalued, objectified, dehumanized in this society determines the scope and texture of their looking relations. Those black women whose identities were constructed in resistance, by practices that oppose the dominant order, were most inclined to develop an oppositional gaze. Now that there is a growing interest in films produced by black women and that those films have become more accessible to viewers, it is possible to talk about black female spectatorship in relation to that work. So far, most discussions of black spectatorship that I have come across focus on men. In "Black Spectatorship: Problems of Identification and Resistance" Manthia Diawara suggests that "the components of 'difference'" among elements of sex, gender, and sexuality give rise to different readings of the same material, adding that these conditions produce a "resisting" spectator. He focuses his critical discussion on black masculinity.

The recent publication of the anthology *The Female Gaze: Women as Viewers of Popular Culture* excited me, especially as it included an essay, "Black Looks," by Jacqui Roach and Petal Felix that attempts to address black female spectatorship. The essay posed provocative questions that were not answered: Is there a black female gaze? How do black women relate to the gender politics of representation? Concluding, the authors assert that black females have "our own reality, our own history, our own gaze—one which sees the world rather differently from 'anyone else.'" Yet, they do not name/describe this experience of seeing "rather differently." The absence of definition and explanation suggests they are assuming an essentialist stance wherein it is presumed that black women, as victims of race and gender oppression, have an inherently different field of vision. Many black women do not "see differently" precisely because their perceptions of reality are so profoundly colonized, shaped by dominant ways of knowing. As Trinh T. Minhaha points out in "Outside In, Inside Out": "Subjectivity does not merely consist of talking about oneself, … be this talking indulgent or critical."

Critical black female spectatorship emerges as a site of resistance only when individual black women actively resist the imposition of dominant ways of knowing and looking. While every black woman I talked to was aware of racism, that awareness did not automatically correspond with politicalization, the development of an oppositional gaze. When it did, individual black women consciously named the process. Manthia Diawara's "resisting spectatorship" is a term that does not adequately describe the terrain of black female spectatorship. We do more than resist. We create alternative texts that are not solely reactions. As critical spectators, black women participate in a broad range of looking relations, contest, resist, revision, interrogate, and invent on multiple levels. Certainly when I watch the work of black women filmmakers Camille Billops, Kathleen Collins, Julie Dash, Ayoka Chenzira, Zeinabu Davis, I do not need to "resist" the images even as I still choose to watch their work with a critical eye.

Black female critical thinkers concerned with creating space for the construction of radical black female subjectivity, and the way cultural production informs this possibility, fully acknowledge the importance of mass media, film in particular, as a powerful site for critical intervention. Certainly Julie Dash's film *Illusions* identifies the terrain of Hollywood cinema as a space of knowledge production that has enormous power. Yet, she also creates a filmic narrative wherein the black female protagonist subversively claims that space.

Inverting the "real-life" power structure, she offers the black female spectator representations that challenge stereotypical notions that place us outside the realm of filmic discursive practices. Within the film she uses the strategy of Hollywood suspense films to undermine those cinematic practices that deny black women a place in this structure. Problematizing the question of "racial" identity by depicting passing, suddenly it is the white male's capacity to gaze, define, and know that is called into question.

When Mary Ann Doane describes in "Woman's Stake: Filming the Female Body" the way in which feminist filmmaking practice can elaborate "a special syntax for a different articulation of the female body," she names a critical process that "Undoes the structure of the classical narrative through an insistence upon its repressions." An eloquent description, this precisely names Dash's strategy in *Illusions*, even though the film is not unproblematic and works within certain conventions that are not successfully challenged. For example, the film does not indicate whether the character Mignon will make Hollywood films that subvert and transform the genre or whether she will simply assimilate and perpetuate the norm. Still, subversively, *Illusions* problematizes the issue of race and spectatorship. White people in the film are unable to "see" that race informs their looking relations. Though she is passing to gain access to the machinery of cultural production represented by film, Mignon continually asserts her ties to black community. The bond between her and the young black woman singer Esther Jeeter is affirmed by caring gestures of affirmation, often expressed by eye-to-eye contact, the direct unmediated gaze of recognition. Ironically, it is the desiring objectifying sexualized white male gaze that threatens to penetrate her "secret" and disrupt her process. Metaphorically, Dash suggests the power of black women to make films will be threatened and undermined by that white male gaze, which seeks to reinscribe the black female body in a narrative of voyeuristic pleasure where the only relevant opposition is male/female and the only location for the female is as a victim. These tensions are not resolved by the narrative. It is not at all evident that Mignon will triumph over the white supremacist capitalist imperialist dominating "gaze."

Throughout *Illusions*, Mignon's power is affirmed by her contact with the younger black woman whom she nurtures and protects. It is this process of mirrored recognition that enables both black women to define their reality, apart from the reality imposed upon them by structures of domination. The shared gaze of the two women reinforces their solidarity. As the younger subject, Esther represents a potential audience for films that Mignon might produce, films wherein black females will be the narrative focus. Julie Dash's recent feature-length film *Daughters of the Dust* dares to place black females at the center of its narrative. This focus caused critics (especially white males) to critique the film negatively or to express many reservations. Clearly, racism and sexism so overdetermine spectatorship—not only what we look at but who we identify with—that viewers who are not black females find it hard to empathize with the central characters in the movie. They are adrift without a white presence in the film.

Another representation of black females nurturing one another via recognition of their common struggle for subjectivity is depicted in Sankofa's collective work *A Passion of Remembrance*. In the film, two black women friends, Louise and Maggie, are from the onset of the narrative struggling with the issue of subjectivity, of their place in progressive black liberation movements that have been sexist. They challenge old norms and want to replace them with new understandings of the complexity of black identity, and the need for liberation struggles that address that complexity. Dressing to go to a party, Louise and Maggie claim the "gaze." Looking at one another, staring into mirrors, they appear completely focused on their encounter with black femaleness. How they see themselves is most important, not how they will be stared at by others. Dancing to the tune "Let's

Get Loose," they display their bodies not for a voyeuristic colonizing gaze but for that look of recognition that affirms their subjectivity—that constitutes them as spectators. Mutually empowered they eagerly leave the privatized domain to confront the public. Disrupting conventional racist and sexist stereotypical representations of black female bodies, these scenes invite the audience to look differently. They act to critically intervene and transform conventional filmic practices, changing notions of spectatorship. *Illusions, Daughters of the Dust*, and A *Passion of Remembrance* employ a deconstructive filmic practice to undermine existing grand cinematic narratives, even as they retheorize subjectivity in the realm of the visual. Without providing "realistic" positive representations that emerge only as a response to the totalizing nature of existing narratives, they offer points of radical departure. Opening up a space for the assertion of a critical black female spectatorship, they do not simply offer diverse representations, they imagine new transgressive possibilities for the formulation of identity.

In this sense they make explicit a critical practice that provides us with different ways to think about black female subjectivity and black female spectatorship. Cinematically, they provide new points of recognition, embodying Stuart Hall's vision of a critical practice that acknowledges that identity is constituted "not outside but within representation" and invites us to see film "not as a second-order mirror held up to reflect what already exists, but as that form of representation which is able to constitute us as new kinds of subjects and thereby enable us to discover who we are." It is this critical practice that enables the production of a feminist film theory that theorizes black female spectatorship. Looking and looking back, black women involve ourselves in a process whereby we see our history as counter-memory, using it as a way to know the present and invent the future.

CPSIA information can be obtained
at www.ICGtesting.com
Printed in the USA
LVHW02s0506260118
563867LV00015B/133/P